THE INTERNATIONAL ASPECTS OF
THE SOUTH AFRICAN INDIAN QUESTION, 1860—1971

THE INTERNATIONAL ASPECTS OF THE SOUTH AFRICAN INDIAN QUESTION

1860 — 1971

B. PACHAI

PROFESSOR OF HISTORY, UNIVERSITY OF MALAWI,
CHANCELLOR COLLEGE

C. STRUIK (PTY) LTD.

CAPE TOWN

1971

C. Struik (Pty) Ltd.
Africana Specialist and Publisher

Copyright © 1971 by B. Pachai

ISBN 0 86977 008 X

PRINTED IN SOUTH AFRICA BY GOTHIC PRINTING COMPANY LIMITED,
FIR STREET, OBSERVATORY, CAPE

To my parents, and the humble
village of Umbulwana on the
outskirts of Ladysmith which is
my South African birthplace and home.

CONTENTS

Page

Preface ix

List of Abbreviations xi

CHAPTER ONE A domestic issue reaches national and international proportions, 1860–1900 1

CHAPTER TWO The genesis of an international issue, 1900–1914 21

CHAPTER THREE The beginning and the end of repatriation: the first phase, 1914–1927 73

CHAPTER FOUR The beginning and the end of repatriation: the second phase, 1927–1939 126

CHAPTER FIVE The significance of the war years, 1939–1945 151

CHAPTER SIX The road to United Nations, 1945–1946 184

CHAPTER SEVEN The United Nations, 1946–1950 197

CHAPTER EIGHT The United Nations, 1950–1961 236

CHAPTER NINE The South African Indian question as an international issue: Conclusion 272

CHAPTER TEN Epilogue: developments since 1961 275

APPENDIX A Definition Clause: Transvaal Immigrants Restrictions Act, 15/1907 . . 284
APPENDIX B Summary of the recommendations of the Indian Inquiry Commission, 1914 284
APPENDIX C Asiatic Population Censuses, 1904–1946 286
APPENDIX D The Smuts–Gandhi Agreement 287
APPENDIX E Imperial Conference Resolution: 1921 290
APPENDIX F Cape Town Agreement: 1927 290
APPENDIX G Joint Communique: 1932 294
APPENDIX H The Kunzru–Dönges Talks: 1950 295

Bibliography 296

Index 309

PREFACE

This book, which is based largely on material submitted for a Ph.D. degree of the University of Natal, concerns itself with the international aspects of the South African Indian question: the aspects which deal with inter-governmental matters as between states and countries (such as between the South African Republic and Natal, before the days of Union, and India and Great Britain) and international aspects involving international institutions such as the League of Nations and the United Nations. In short, the scope of this study embraces both inter-national as well as international aspects.

Though the aim is not to deal with local, national or domestic issues at length, it is necessary to point out that these issues cannot be ignored or overlooked. Any issue only reaches international proportions after it transcends its national limits. The external or international plane is nothing more than the lengthened shadow of the internal or national plane. Any understanding of the one is not possible, at least with any thoroughness, without a discussion, however brief, on the other. But pains have been taken to ensure that the international aspects do not take second place to the national aspects; local events have been dealt with as briefly as is necessary to elucidate the main points of this study.

Another facet of this study is that it cannot be dealt with in isolation. The Indian Question (which today represents the story of only 3 per cent of South Africa's population) cannot be entirely divorced from the rest of South Africa's racial problems and this study takes note of this situation.

An Epilogue has been included in the last chapter to bring the story of the South African Indian up to date. This has been necessary not only because the study from which this book has emerged itself stopped with the introduction of the Republic of South Africa in 1961 but more because the decade following it has been a significant one. Much of Africa has since become independent and in South Africa old policies have hardened and new ones have appeared. In these developments the international influences have had their say, with varying results.

When the thesis was originally written I was still in South Africa. Times were hard and financial support was hard to come by. In those difficult days local support was almost non-existent. It was not "fashionable" for a backwood man, the son of an ex-indentured labourer, to be engaged in such pursuits. No South African Indian had before this obtained a doctorate in History. To say the least, it was not the thing to do. The fact that the undertaking succeeded at all was due to my Supervisor, Professor Edgar H. Brookes, Head of the Department of History and Political Science of the University of Natal, who not only provided me with academic guidance but often found me sums of money to tide me through my many financial crises. He has remained a good friend.

Two of my colleagues in the service of the Natal Education Department must be remembered. They are Dallip H. Singh and Sarwanth L. Sewgolam.

For documentary material, I am grateful for the help I received from the United Nations headquarters; the Government of India, Ministry of External Affairs; the South African Institute of Race Relations; the Natal Society Library; the University of Natal Library; the Natal Archives and the Killie Campbell Library. Individuals who made available their private collections were Messrs. Muthray Pillay, S. R. Naidoo, P. R. Pather, S. B. Mungal, all of Natal, South Africa, and H. S. L. Polak of the United Kingdom. Mrs. D. Bramdaw of the *Leader* and Mrs. Manilal Gandhi of *Indian Opinion* also helped.

This publication is due partly to the encouragement given by the Indian Council for Africa, New Delhi. My wife and I were fortunate to make our first visit to India in 1969 when I participated in a Seminar on Indians Abroad mounted by the Indian Council for Africa and the Indian Council for Cultural Relations. I was struck by the deep and genuine interest in the history of Indians abroad. In particular where the history of the African continent was concerned the situation in South Africa was necessary to compare and contrast general and particular trends in the rest of the continent.

Publication economies have necessitated the inevitable excision of a considerable part of the original thesis. This has led to both losses and gains and whatever its present short-comings every effort has been made to put across the main points of the original work.

This Preface is being finished off, in revised form, in Malawi where I have been for the past six years. Here, as in my many peregrinations since we left South Africa, my wife has given me much of her time and patience in many kindly ways, not least in the preparation of typescripts for publication. To her, and to other members of the family in Malawi and South Africa, I say "thank you" for having helped to launch me on my way many years ago. Much has happened since those humble beginnings.

B. PACHAI

9th February, 1971.

LIST OF ABBREVIATIONS USED

U.G.	Union Government Publication.
N.P.P.	Natal Parliamentary Papers.
N. and I.B.B.	Natal and Imperial Blue Books.
C.S.O.	Natal Colonial Secretary's Office.
N.B.B.	Natal Blue Books.
U.N.	United Nations.
U.N.O.	United Nations Organisation.
S.A.I.C.	South African Indian Congress.
N.I.C.	Natal Indian Congress.
N.I.A.	Natal Indian Association.
S.A.I.O.	South African Indian Organisation.
T.I.C.	Transvaal Indian Congress.
G.H.	Natal Government House.
B.P.P.	British Parliamentary Papers.
Cd.	Imperial Blue-Book Correspondence.
I.I.	Indian Immigration Records, Natal.
G.N.	Government Notice, Natal.
N.I.O.	Natal Indian Organisation.
A.S.C.	Anti-Segregation Council.
U.K.	United Kingdom.
U.S.A.	United States of America.
U.S.S.R.	Union of the Soviet Socialist Republics.
U.D.F.	Union Defence Force.
S.A.I.R.R.	South African Institute of Race Relations.
I.C.S.	Indian Civil Service, India.

CHAPTER ONE

A DOMESTIC ISSUE REACHES NATIONAL AND INTERNATIONAL PROPORTIONS: 1860–1900

"The coming of the Indians to Natal was no spontaneous uncontrolled movement of adventurous individuals seeking a better livelihood than their home country gave them. It was part of an elaborate system organised and controlled by the Governments of Great Britain and India."

—DR. MABEL PALMER

It is inevitable that a study of the Indian question in South Africa should make mention of the fact, even at the risk of repetition, that Indians first came to South Africa as a result of a triangular pact between the governments of Natal, India and Great Britain – with Great Britain as the dominant partner because of its control over the governments of India and Natal.

This triangular pact serves to draw attention to the international aspects in the history of the South African Indian. The first objective is to show the extent of the involvement of the respective national governments in the South African Indian question: their hopes, fears, prejudices, failures and successes. Thereafter, it is necessary to evaluate the role and value of this inter-governmental intervention.

If this intervention was at first on the scale of separate governments acting on their own or in concert, it was not always so. At some stage, the separate actions of governments took second place to the force of the Commonwealth influence. It will be necessary to show this influence, particularly at the Commonwealth conferences and similar meetings of Commonwealth statesmen.

From this inter-governmental level the South African Indian question passed into the chambers of international organizations: the League of Nations and the United Nations.

In attempting all this, due regard is given to the internal situation in South Africa as this situation represents the hub around which the international machinery revolves. On the local scene, the attitudes and policies of the government of the day, of the parliamentary Opposition, of European politicians – and non-politicians alike – are defined, as are also the reactions of the Indians in South Africa and abroad to such attitudes and policies.

In the reactions of the South African Indians the power and the politics of local Indian political organizations can be discerned. These organizations have not always stood alone; they have received sympathy and support, as well as the displeasure, of political organizations both European and non-European. At some stage the Indian question merges with the larger question of race conflict in South Africa. The point of this merger – and its value – is traced.

When the first Europeans landed at the Cape, from the days of the Portuguese navigators, they encountered local inhabitants, the San (Bushmen) and the KhoiKhoi (Hottentots). They did not find a country uninhabited by indigenous peoples. Such was the position when Jan van Riebeeck and his men landed at the Cape to start their refreshment station at Table Bay and its environs on April 6, 1652. Racial heterogeneity existed from the

1

beginning. The pattern of South African life of that and later periods was born in the soil and circumstances of Table Bay on that April day, 1652.

Although the first Dutch government at the Cape had only three classes of persons to deal with: Company's servants, San and Khoikhoi, the picture was greatly confused in later years with the advent of imported slaves, Dutch and German settlers and Huguenot refugees from France.

The composition of the European population at the Cape was further complicated by the first British occupation of the Cape in 1795, the second British occupation in 1806 and the coming of the 1820 settlers but racial heterogeneity received its most powerful and numerous addition with the arrival of the Bantu-speaking cattle farmers at the banks of the Fish River around 1775 after a long south-westerly trek. It was this migration of the Bantu, more than any other movement or settlement of people, that added explosive force to the picture of South Africa's racial heterogeneity. What happened in other parts of South Africa in later years did little to alter materially the picture of South Africa's racial heterogeneity as first drawn in the Cape Colony. In 1891, for example, out of a total population in that Colony in whole numbers of approximately one and a half million, only a little over one-quarter of a million were whites.

In Natal, which later became the first home for Indians in South Africa, the first Europeans came after the arrival of the Albany settlers of 1820. They were a handful of traders who set up a small unofficial British settlement at Port Natal in 1824 for the purpose of trading in ivory with Zululand but "not to make homes for their wives and children".[1] But the Voortrekkers who followed in 1837 had come to settle in Natal. During the next few years this infant settlement saw a rapid succession of changes: the victory of the Boers over the Zulus at Blood River in 1838 and the British annexation of Natal in 1843.

In their negotiations with the Republic of Natalia at the conclusion of hostilities in 1842, the British Government took great pains to postulate certain conditions under which this government was prepared to come to terms with the Republic of Natalia: the first of these conditions read that "there shall not be in the eye of the law any distinction of colour, origin, race or creed; but that the protection of the law, in letter and in substance, shall be extended impartially to all alike".[2]

These negotiations were followed by the British annexation of Natal, by which Natal became a district of the Cape Colony. With the extension of British rule into Natal, the bulk of the Voortrekkers left during the years 1843 to 1848 while the trickle of English settlers into Natal during the same period soon increased to sizeable proportions with the arrival into this colony of some 5 000-odd European settlers from 1849 to 1851.[3]

The Natal Charter of 1856, in keeping with the declared policy of the British Government that "there shall not be in the eye of the law any distinction of colour, origin, race or creed . . ." provided that every man over the age of 21, who owned immovable property to the value of £50, or who rented property to the value of £10 per annum was entitled to a parliamentary vote.[4]

The infant colony of Natal had great mineral and agricultural possibilities. There was coal to be had in the northern districts but this had to wait for railway transport to be made available. Agriculture offered the greatest possibilities. In the uplands maize showed promise of developing into an important crop; on the coast the important crops were arrow root, indigo, cotton, coffee and sugar cane. It was sugar which finally led the way. The year 1850 marked the beginning of much of Natal's later history and prosperity when Edward Morewood planted the first cane on the Umhlali, about 35 miles north of Durban. Eight years later the sugar industry of Natal was said to be producing 500 tons of sugar.[5]

For all the progress that was taking place land was plentiful; experience was not lacking; money was available — the first bank in Natal had opened in 1854. But it was the question of labour that presented the greatest obstacle to the continuance and the expansion of the sugar industry. The labour potential was present and in abundance, too. In 1850, for instance, the white population of Natal was in the region of 5 000 while the African population was between 90 000 and 100 000. The Zulus proved to be good domestic servants but the chief difficulty was their unwillingness to be subjected to the disciplines of regular attendance at work. With them it was an established habit to be satisfied with the work that was done for a few months at a time; between these months there were frequent periods of unauthorized absence from duty, caused by a combination of factors which included different concepts of labour discipline and the demands of a largely subsistence economy which meant the tilling of their own lands when their labour was most in demand on the European plantations. Their attitude towards labour had a serious effect on the employers of labour and caused great financial losses to the industries and concerns served by this labour force.[6] To offer an explanation for this phenomenon of labour shortage four points need to be considered: the innate habits of the Zulus; the official attitude of the British Government; the policy of the man on the spot – Theophilus Shepstone – who virtually ruled the African population for over thirty years, first as Diplomatic Agent and then as Secretary for Native Affairs; and, finally, the psychological attitude of the European to manual labour.

In a brief consideration of these points, we start with the official attitude of the British Government (the habits of the Zulus being already disposed of above), which is abundantly clear in the following remarks made by Thompson: "Natal was annexed as a wedge between the Zulu nation and the Cape Colony, and between the Boer republics and the sea. In it beginnings were to be made in 'the civilization and improvement of the inhabitants of this part of Africa'. It was to be a Native country. That it was, too, a struggling European colony was of secondary importance."[7]

In order to see how this attitude contributed to the question of labour shortage, we have to consider the policy of Theophilus Shepstone who, though left more or less to formulate his own policy was, nevertheless, tied down to a set of principles which governed his administration. Shepstone's system was the restoration of tribal authority by the method of segregation and retribalisation. The Africans were apportioned to reserves where they were able to maintain their traditional economy. "In Shepstone's eyes Natal consisted of two watertight compartments, Native and European. To coerce the Native to become dependent on the European by economic pressure was not compatible with this outlook."[8] With such a policy in operation it was not to be wondered at that whereas 300 000 labourers were required in the colony in 1857 only 6 000 Africans were available.[9]

Three points have been attempted thus far to explain the labour shortage. The fourth point remains – that of the psychological attitude of the European to manual labour (an attitude of mind which is certainly traceable to the evil effects of the introduction of slavery at the Cape in the mid-seventeenth century): that all hard manual work was to be done by the non-white peoples. Though Dr. Mabel Palmer writes that it was unreasonable to expect the European to undertake manual work in the climatic conditions of Natal, both for geographical and psychological reasons, it is clear that the latter factor was the weightier of the two. The very fact that a contemporary journal exhorted immigrants from England to put their "shoulders boldly to the wheel" instead of venting their "indignation in various ways", is proof enough that the "fields (of Natal) are as fair, and its climate as wholesome, as they have been represented to be".[10]

These factors, then, which contributed to the shortage of labour in Natal were weighty enough in their separate effects to call for assistance from outside the colonial borders; but in their cumulative effects they constituted a colonial problem of such dimensions that in order to avert a tragedy the apparently inexhaustible reservoirs of the East had to be tapped, after all efforts to import labour from the West had failed.[11]

Although it was as early as October, 1851 that a public meeting of interested persons in Durban debated the possibility of importing labour from the East, it was only in 1855 that the first effective steps were taken towards this importation when the Durban Corporation decided in July of that year to take full advantage of the proposed visit of the newly-appointed Governor of the Cape Colony, and High Commissioner for Natal, Sir George Grey, in November of that year and to get him "to sanction the introduction" of labour from the East.[12]

When the High Commissioner visited Natal in November, 1855 he visited some of the sugar estates and expressed a preference for Indian labour to that of Chinese labour. Sir George Grey had seen personally the reliability and usefulness of Indian labour. This experience had much to do with the eagerness with which Grey undertook to obtain this labour.[13] He instructed his Colonial Secretary to inform the Government of India that Natal had an excellent climate, with rich lands suitable for the cultivation of sub-tropical crops; that opportunities were present for constant employment for Indian labourers and for their becoming petty proprietors of land when they chose to retire.[14] At the same time he made representations to the British Government to sanction his proposals.

The British Government acted on Grey's despatch by referring it to the Land and Emigration Commission, the government agency set up in 1840 to supervise all schemes of mass emigration in the British Empire. Though the Commission did not actually object to Grey's proposals, it remarked on obvious shortcomings in his report which it would like to see remedied. And, in India, the Court of Directors of the East Indian Company – the ruling power there till 1858 – agreed with the attitude of the Land and Emigration Commission. In effect, Great Britain and India, through their appropriate agencies, had now sanctioned the labour Grey had requested but each asked for safeguards to be introduced which would protect the interests of labourers.

But before immigrant labourers could be brought to Natal, general opposition in India to the scheme approved of by the government agencies temporarily halted its implementation. The reasons advanced in India against it were that in Mauritius and the West Indian colonies there were greater advantages; there was abundant demand for labour in India, particularly in Bombay; the wages offered in Natal were very low and there was an absence of satisfactory information on the point of wages in Natal; it was difficult enough to satisfy the labour needs of Mauritius and the West Indian colonies.[15]

Though these first efforts proved to be abortive, they show, nonetheless, the part played by the respective governments in trying to make indentured Indian immigrant labour available to Natal. They indicate, too, the absence of an effective alternative available to the Natal planters and lend strength to the conclusion that it had to be Indian labour at any cost if the Natal economy were to be saved from ruin. These early negotiations also show the self-interest of the British Government in this issue. Grey's letter to Lord John Russell made reference to the benefits that would accrue (through this labour) to the "commerce, prosperity and security, of the rest of Her Majesty's possessions in South Africa".[16] There were all-round gains envisaged. The issue was not looked at solely from the narrow viewpoint of how imported Indian labour would serve Natal alone. In it was seen something of a genesis of a more prosperous South Africa. That it could also lead to serious complications does not seem to have worried many people at the time.

The year 1858 introduced many changes in the negotiations for labour. In India itself the authorities were now prepared to allow indentured immigrant labour to Natal provided that the necessary protective laws were drawn up and that labourers were prevailed upon by legitimate offers to emigrate. Natal was informed of this decision by the Indian and British governments. When this happened, the constitutional position in India had changed. The rule of the English East India Company had ceased in 1858 and the country came under the direct control of the British Government. In her famous proclamation of 1858, Queen Victoria, announcing the commencement of her rule in India, said: "We hold ourselves bound to the natives of our Indian territories by the same obligations of duty which bind us to our other subjects, and these obligations, by the blessing of Almighty God, we shall faithfully and conscientiously fulfil."[17] By this declaration the British Government pledged itself to safeguard the interests of its subjects everywhere on the basis of a single standard.

By its willingness to permit the emigration of Indian labourers to Natal, the British Government had incurred the responsibility of keeping a benevolent watch on the future welfare of its wards in South Africa. And the Natal Government, in having persistently appealed to India and to Britain for permission to import this labour, completed the triple entente that gave birth to Indian immigration to Natal. Though some detractors of this immigration have tended to ridicule the "persons who introduced Indian Coolie labour into Natal" the words of L. M. Thompson on Indian immigration seem to approximate most closely to the true position obtaining at this time: "In short, so far as things can be said to be inevitable, the importation of foreign labourers into Natal was the inevitable sequel to the adoption of a dual policy. Since Natal was treated both as a Native state and as a European colony, the Natives were self-sufficient and the colonists had to look elsewhere for labour."[18]

If the coming of Indians to Natal can be said to have been inevitable, this inevitability stems from local and not external sources. It has been necessary to trace these local events and conditions in some detail, though, admittedly, the main points are matters of accepted historical fact today. The importation was the result of a series of protracted negotiations which took some five years to finalize. In looking back at the events today, in distant retrospect, and especially as the background to the international aspects of the South African Indian question, the events of these five years have a more than ordinary significance. They do show that the Indian labourers did not come uninvited. They show, too, that the approving stamp of the British Government was all too easily given.

The three measures which started off Indian immigration to Natal were the Natal Laws 13, 14 and 15 of 1859. Law 13 dealt with the introduction of immigrants from territories east of the Cape of Good Hope but not from India; Law 14 dealt with the introduction by the government of Natal of labourers from India; and Law 15 enabled persons to introduce, at their own expense, immigrants from India.

Of these Laws the most important was Law 14 which was based on the Mauritian Act 15/1842. In terms of Section 6 of Law 14, the Government of Natal advanced all initial monies required to start this importation but the employers of labour were required to repay three-fifths of the whole cost involved during the time of the first assignment which was valid for three years and a further fifth per year for two years on re-assignment. In terms of Section 9 of the Law every Indian immigrant labourer was at liberty to hire or dispose of his services or to change his residence after the expiry of his five-year indenture in the colony of Natal. He was deemed to be as free and unfettered as any other non-indentured labourer in the Colony after five years of "industrial service". Section 24 of the Law entitled a labourer to a free return passage to India after ten years' residence in the Colony. Section 28 made provision for the commutation of this right of return passage for a grant of land equal in value to the cost of the return passage. For such commutation to be effective the approval of the Lieutenant-Governor had to be obtained. Laws 13 and 15 were only independent of the main Law 14 insofar as the government did not apportion funds for their administration. In all other respects labourers brought out in terms of these two laws were subject to the same conditions as applicable in the case of Law 14.

Even though matters had reached this stage, Natal still found it necessary to send an agent to India to ensure that no further delays would be met in sending the labour force that the colony was so badly in need of. It was well that such a step was taken as the Agent from Natal, W. M. Collins, found, on arrival in India, that the Indian Government had not completed the legal machinery to begin the emigration of labourers to Natal. There was a hitch over the proposed salary scheme. Finally, matters were straightened out and the Indian Act XXXIII of 1860 became the counterpart of Natal's Laws 13, 14 and 15, and the first ship, the *Truro*, sailed from Madras to Natal on 12th October, 1860.

The first shipload of immigrant labourers from India arrived in Natal on 16th November, 1860. Immigrants continued to arrive until 1866 when a general depression in Natal caused by the world-wide collapse of markets after the end of the American Civil War temporarily put a stop to it. Between 1866 and 1874 no indentured Indian labourers were introduced into Natal. This temporary cessation of immigration had two significant results. With the return to normal prosperity in Natal in 1872 the need for imported labour once again became imperative and in India the intervening returning immigrants carried home complaints of unfavourable conditions of work in Natal. In view of these complaints,[19] the Indian Government and the Commission for Land and Emigration in London refused to authorise any further emigration until better arrangements had been made for the treatment of indentured labourers in Natal. The Government of India wrote to Lieutenant-Governor Musgrave of Natal on 10th May, 1872 that they regretted that unless proper measures were taken for the protection of emigrants resident there, the Indian Government would be obliged not to send out any more labourers. The complaints of the Indian Government were endorsed by the British Government.

In these ways the concern felt by the British and Indian Governments for the welfare of indentured labourers was officially communicated to the Natal Government only twelve years after they had sanctioned the emigration of Indian labourers to Natal. The upshot was that the Natal Government appointed a Commission in 1872 and on the recommendation of the commissioners, Michael Gallwey, Attorney-General of Natal, and Lieutenant-Colonel Price-Lloyd, an ex-officer in the Indian army, the Natal Government passed Law 12 of 1872. Its main provisions were that a Protector of Indian Immigrants was to be appointed; medical attendants were to be appointed in each district, and free Indians were to be exempt from the sentence of flogging for minor offences. This new law was the forerunner to many others in the 'seventies. It was at this time that the Secretary of State for India, Lord Salisbury, speaking on behalf of the British Government – which had then the ultimate responsibility for the administration of the colony of Natal, stated on 24th March, 1875, in a long despatch to the Government of India upon the subject of the Revision of the System of Emigration from India to the Colonies:

"Above all things we must confidently expect, as an indispensable condition of the proposed arrangement, that the colonial laws and their administration will be such that Indian settlers, who have completed the terms of service to which they agreed, as the return for the expense of bringing them to the Colonies, will be free men in all respects, with privileges no whit inferior to those of any other class of Her Majesty's subjects resident in the Colonies."[20]

Her Majesty's Indian subjects in Natal were at this time divided into three classes: (a) indentured, (b) "free" and (c) "free passenger". The first two have already been dealt with. It is the third group – the natural concomitant to the first two – that now became prominent in the 'seventies of the nineteenth century. "Free passenger" Indians were those who came to Natal under the ordinary immigration law, paying their own passages and enjoying the same citizenship rights as the Europeans until this was changed.

"Free passenger" Indians were also called "Arabs". They belonged primarily to the Muslim trading community. They had come mostly from the Bombay Presidency in India, though some had been in Mauritius for a few years. It was quite natural that Indian traders should follow the indentured immigrants in order to supply them with Indian spices and other goods. Prominent amongst these traders was Aboobaker Amod, who reached Natal towards the end of the 'seventies.

Though it is difficult to single out these Muslim traders as their numbers were always included in the "free" Indian population figures, it is safe to say that they constituted a small minority of the Indian population.[21] Though a very small number in the over-all composition of Natal's population, the business acumen and the success and prosperity of these traders soon startled the local European population.[22] The Indian Immigrants' Commission, presided over by Mr. Justice Wragg, reported thus: "We are convinced that much of the irritation existing in the minds of European Colonists against the whole

Indian population of the Colony has been excited by the undoubted ability of these Arab traders to compete with European merchants . . .".[23]

This "irritation" was, no doubt, accentuated by the rapid growth in the Indian population from 6 000 in 1870 to over 30 000 in 1885, an average annual increase of 1 600, which added fear and uncertainty in the European mind, especially because there was already a large local African population. Various steps were taken by the Natal Government from the last quarter of the 19th century to make Natal safe from the prospects of – what they feared – an Asiatic invasion or intrusion into what was deemed to be essentially a European colony. These steps affected both the indentured and the "free" Indian population but as these groups were economically apart, the first-named will be treated first.

Eleven years after the resumption of Indian immigration from India in 1874 the Wragg Commission was appointed by the Natal Government to go into the social and economic aspects of the Indian question in Natal. The Commission reported in 1887 that the general European opinion in Natal was that Indians should remain in the colony as indentured labourers only; if this could not be done, some Europeans demanded, African labour should replace that of the Indian – even if this meant a form of forced labour. Those Europeans who did not object to the presence of Indians in Natal demanded that the status of the free Indian be reduced to a lower level than it was at that time.[24]

Two points emerge clearly from this report: the Indian was welcome in the colony as an indentured labourer. Though not welcome as a free Indian, this latter position might be rendered tolerable with a diminution in status. The first point was one of urgency: indentured labourers were needed on certain terms and it was this that the Natal Government treated as a priority.

Four years after the Wragg Commission Report a beginning was made to introduce various changes in the laws relating to indentured immigrants. The feelings of the colonists in Natal were revealed in 1891 in the passage of the immigration law, Act 25/1891. This Act, *inter alia*, revoked the grant of Crown Lands to time-expired labourers granted in terms of Section 28 of Law 14/1859 and Section 51 of Law 2/1870.[25] Thus the possibility of residence in Natal after the completion of indentures, first suggested in Grey's despatch of 1855 and later incorporated in the immigration laws, was now abrogated and the British Government raised no demur. This was the first serious breach in the original undertaking and promise.

The next step was to send the Protector of Indian Immigrants, L. H. Mason, and Henry Binns, M.L.A., to India to work out an arrangement with the Indian Government for the time-expired labourers to return to India. The memorandum of the Binns-Mason delegation contained in one of its paragraphs the following statement: "In a country where the Native population is in number so far in excess of the European, the unlimited settlement of Indians is not considered desirable, and there is a general wish that when they have completed their last period of indenture, they should return to India. There are already about 25 000 Indians settled in the Colony, many of whom have allowed their right to a return passage to lapse; this is exclusive of a very considerable Banyan trading population."[26] Estimating the African population in 1893 to be approximately 470 000 as compared with the European population of 45 000 and the Indian population at 46 000, the report went on to say that if there had been no African population there would not have existed any reasonable ground for opposition to the presence of the Indians. This was an unusual statement at this time: there had always been a formidable African population in Natal; the British and Natal Governments had always been aware of this position, if not before, then, after 1843. This statement could probably be accounted for by the fact that Natal in the 1890's was not struggling as much for labour as it had done in the 1850's – the presence of 46 000 Indians was hope enough in this field. The trading propensities of the free Indians on the other hand presented a serious threat to the English traders in Natal. And, above all, should the difficult days of the 1850's and the 1860's re-appear, immigration could be resumed by inter-governmental negotiations for Great Britain was at the head of affairs in Natal and in India.

The Binns-Mason delegation was in India to pave the way for the Natal Government to introduce a Bill which would cause the time-expired labourers to return to India after the completion of their indentures. A similar plan of the Natal Government, attempted four years earlier, had met with opposition from the Secretary of State for Colonies – Lord Knutsford – who had on that occasion written to the Governor of Natal on 24th September, 1891 stating that such a move would be construed as an interference with the ordinary rights of British subjects.[27]

What the British Government had opposed four years earlier was now possible of reversal for Natal had in the meantime, in 1893, received Responsible Government. The Indian Government verbally informed the Binns-Mason commission that it would raise no objection to an arrangement for time-expired labourers to return to India, "provided that failure to fulfil the condition shall not constitute a criminal offence".[28]

The Binns-Mason Report culminated in the Immigration Law Amendment Act of 1895. In moving the second reading of the Bill, the Attorney-General, Harry Escombe, summed up the colonial European point of view by saying that the Indians were appreciated as labourers only and were not welcomed as settlers and competitors.[29]

The Act imposed a residential tax of £3. It offered three options to Indian immigrant labourers: to return to India on the expiry of the contract of service, to re-indenture for a further period; and, finally, to pay an annual licence of £3 for the right to remain in the colony. At first the tax was payable by adults only but in 1903 it was extended to apply to girls aged thirteen and boys aged sixteen years.

By legislative enactment free Indians were now made unwelcome. Their equal status as defined in the Natal Charter of 1856 and in the despatch of the Lieutenant-Governor of Natal, Sir Henry Bulwer, of 7th September, 1878, to the Secretary of State for the Colonies was revoked. Sir Henry had said:

"Time-expired Indians are, as regards the general law of the Colony, in all respects free men, with rights and privileges not inferior to those of any class of the Queen's subjects in the Colony. There are many who have acquired the right of voting and are registered as voters."[30] In 1883 the provisions in the Charter of 1856 were amended but the changes did not unduly affect the position of the free Indians, though the indentured Indians were affected by the changes made (not that any would have qualified for the franchise in any case). This was the position which obtained in regard to the status of the "free" Indian when on the 29th July, 1884, the Natal Legislative Council debated a motion introduced by Arbuckle for the appointment of a Commission to report upon the Indian Immigration Laws and Regulations. During the debate a vigorous and forthright speech was made by Harry Escombe who was, nine years later, to become Attorney-General of Natal, and twelve years later, to become Prime Minister. In view of his own later stand on this issue and because of its sound view, this speech is of great importance to an understanding of the feelings of that day. Adverting to the commercial pursuits of the "free" Indians, Harry Escombe said: "Another objection is that they compete in trade. I wish with all my heart that they would compete more, because competition is for the benefit of the country. What does it mean? It may mean an injury to the trader, but it means a profit to the consumer, and it is an extraordinary thing the Colony is so misled that it cannot see that the competition of the Indian trader is for the benefit of the whole Colony." Escombe took cognisance of the position of the British Government in this issue and the many earlier assurances of protection and justice made by it, and he said, ". . . you may have Commission after Commission, you may make what Laws you please, but while we are under the English constitution and this place suits the Arabs, they will come into this Colony just as naturally as the waters from the Drakensberg flow into the sea. No legislation will keep them out".[31]

Later events proved Harry Escombe to be both right and wrong. Right in so far as the future continuance of Arab trade was concerned; not so right when he asserted that "no legislation will keep them out".

To keep them and their lesser wealthy ex-indentured "free" Indians out and restricted, Natal took various steps in spite of what the Wragg Commission finally reported in respect of the "free" Indians: "In fairness to the free Indians we must observe that the competition is legitimate in its nature and it certainly has been welcomed by the general community." The report went on to say that Natal was admirably suited as a home for Indian immigrants and if any steps were taken to keep the Indians out the investors of capital in industries dependent on Indian labour would be seriously affected, as would the whole colony. The same report vindicated the Indian traders: "We are content to place on record our strong opinion based on much observation that the presence of these traders has been beneficial to the whole Colony and that it would be unwise, if not unjust, to legislate against them."[32]

But in spite of the above statements, made with such clarity and force, important restrictive legislation followed. In 1894 the newly-elected Responsible Government of Natal introduced Act 25 which sought to deprive Asiatics of the parliamentary franchise. Royal assent to this measure was refused. The Colonial Secretary, Mr. Joseph Chamberlain, informed the Natal Government of the attitude of the British Government to the proposals to disenfranchise Indians. On this occasion the British Government took a firm stand against the proposals. It is doubtful whether the British Government took this firm stand purely as a matter of principle and not as a matter of political expediency. These were the uncertain days of the vigorous attempts made to establish British supremacy in South Africa: the days of the Uitlander problem in the Transvaal, when the British Government could not with justice and consistency support in Natal what it opposed in the Transvaal. For an understanding of the position Chamberlain's reply is given at some length:

"We ask you", he wrote, "to bear in mind the tradition of the Empire, which makes no distinction in favour of or against race or colour, and to exclude, by reason of their colour or by reason of their race, all Her Majesty's Indian subjects should be most painful, I am quite certain, to Her Majesty to have to sanction it. The United Kingdom own, as its brightest and greatest dependent, the enormous empire of India with 300 millions of subjects, who are as loyal to the Crown as you are yourselves, and among them are hundreds and thousands of men who are every whit as civilised as ourselves: who are, if that is anything, better born in the sense that they have older traditions and older families, who are men of wealth, men of culture, men of distinguished valour, men who have brought whole armies and placed them at the service of the Queen, and have in time of great difficulty, saved the Empire by their loyalty. I say you who have seen all this cannot be willing to put upon them a slight, which I think is absolutely unnecessary for your purpose, and which will be calculated to provoke ill-feeling, discontent and irritation, and would be most unpalatable to the feelings, not only of Her Majesty but of all her people."[33]

This homily might have proved to be a deterrent in ordinary circumstances. But Natal, in the early days of her Responsible Government rule, was in no mood to be dictated to as a recalcitrant schoolboy. In 1896 a new Bill was introduced and passed into law as Act 8 of 1896. This excluded from the voters' roll all persons who, not being of European origin, were natives or descendants in the main line of natives of countries which had not hitherto possessed elective representative institutions founded on the parliamentary franchise. Two reasons were advanced for the disenfranchisement of Indians in 1896: the high privileges of citizenship should not be available to persons who did not have the educational qualification to enable them to exercise such a right usefully; and the fear of the Indian voter swamping the European voter.[34]

Though the fear of the Indian voter swamping the European voter did not exist in reality at that time – the proportion being 1 to 38, the colonists must no doubt have been thinking of the future in terms of the developing pattern of the past. In 1874 Natal's Indian population was a paltry 6 000 but in 1893 it was almost 50 000. These fears seemed justified, if only from the point of view of population figures. The fears were further exacerbated in the tense atmosphere of suspicion of the time when on the 18th December, 1896 about 800 "free passenger" Indians arrived in Durban in the *Courland* and the *Naderi*, among them being Mohandas Karamchand Gandhi, returning from a brief visit to India. In the colonial mind Gandhi was held responsible for this "invasion" – which was not the case – and steps were taken to tighten up the immigration laws. The result was the passing of the Immigration Restriction Act, 1 of 1897.

Though the political disabilities hurt the susceptibilities of the "free passenger" Indians they did not affect the purses of those who were already engaged in commercial pursuits in the Colony and the trading activities of these Indians became the next target of the Natal Government. On the 25th March, 1897, Harry Escombe, Prime Minister of Natal, moving the second reading of the Dealer's Licences Amendment Bill, said: "The Bill originated at the instance of the three principal boroughs of the Colony on the petitions of the Mayors of Durban, Pietermaritzburg, and Newcastle, who asked that powers might be given to the Municipalities in excess of the present powers to control the issuing of licences. There is no hesitation on their part in saying what their object is, and there is no objection on the part of the Government in admitting their proposal to prevent certain persons coming to this country to compete with Europeans on unequal terms and getting the licences to trade which are required by the Europeans." On a very important point, viz., that law courts were to be precluded from interfering with the licensing authorities – a point of controversy and conflict for many years to come – Harry Escombe said: "An objection has been taken to the Bill, especially by an hon. friend of mine, to whose opinion I attach great weight, that this Bill out-Herods Herod in that you will not allow the courts of law to interfere. If you want the courts of law to say whether the licences shall be granted, the Bill should go out altogether, because the intention is that the courts of law are not to have the discretion, but the licensing authorities."[35] The Bill became Law as Act 18/1897 and set the pace for similar restrictive legislation in subsequent years.

"Free" Indians had now been in Natal, either as ex-indentured Indians or as "passenger" Indians for 37 years during which time some had become small gardeners carrying on a lucrative trade in the sale of vegetables and tobacco. In the 'seventies of the 19th century they had secured the monopoly of supplying the Durban and the Pietermaritzburg markets with vegetables and all along the coast from Verulam in the north to Ifafa in the south they had set themselves up as small farmers. In 1885, of the 3 711 Indians resident within the borough of Durban, about 2 000 had bought or rented land. By this time the "free" Indians had begun to compete with European coastal farmers in the production of maize and garden produce. But this competition was welcome as it provided the markets with vegetables which must otherwise have been a scarce commodity. C. P. Reynolds, a prominent sugar planter of Umzinto, giving evidence before the Lands Commission (1900–2) stated that the Indians improved waste lands which Europeans would not use. He had himself given out lands on lease to Indians "which suffer terribly from drought and are not suitable for care". Another farmer said: "You will see the Indian and his wife, weeding his fields, even by moonlight." This industry and perseverance caused the value of land to increase and what had previously stood at twenty shillings and thirty shillings an acre now rose to eighty shillings and a hundred shillings.

But in this contribution and advancement also lay the genesis of another problem and another fear in the minds of the European colonists: that the Indians being exemplary cultivators would soon buy up all the coastal lands.

This latest fear, in spite of the positive contribution made by Indians to the general prosperity of the colony, spotlighted an important aspect of Indian immigration into South Africa: that the Indian, of whatever class and engaged in whatever occupation, was at the beginning of his stay a most welcome addition to the local population. But with the passage of time his presence was deemed to be both unnecessary and a threat. This pattern transferred itself to the Transvaal where many Indians moved to after living in Natal or where they went to directly from India.

In the Transvaal (which was a fully independent Afrikaner republic from 1852 to 1877 and partly independent since 1881) the relationship between whites and non-whites had been defined in the Rustenburg Grondwet of 1858 which prescribed that no equality would be tolerated in either church or state. This provision was a clear indication of the attitude of the Republic on the colour question. Indians emigrating into this state would have to accept the defined position, though there were safeguards for them in the London Convention signed by the British and Transvaal Governments in 1884.

The London Convention of 1884 took the place of the Pretoria Convention of 1881 which had put an end to the hostilities consequent on the British annexation of the South African Republic in 1877. At the time of the Pretoria Convention Indians had already been in Natal for twenty-one years. From here some of them had filtered into the Transvaal and some had come directly from India through the port of Lourenço Marques. There is some uncertainty about the exact date of the arrival of Indians in the Transvaal. According to the statement made by E. F. Bourke, an old resident of Pretoria, to the "National Convention" concerning Indians in 1904 there were no Asiatics in the Transvaal in 1881.[36] And according to a publication by Indian traders in the Transvaal the "presence of Indians in Pretoria can be traced as early as the year 1876".[37] The Transvaal Indian Congress, on the other hand, states that "enquiries reveal that the Indians first entered the Transvaal in the year 1882".[38]

It is safe to say that Indians first entered the Republic during the last quarter of the nineteenth century and even if they were in the Transvaal before the Pretoria Convention of 1881 their numbers were so negligible as to make it unnecessary for the Convention to make any reference to them. But by 1884 there was a fairly large population of Indians settled within the Republic, engaged in commerce and in the catering industry, with the Indian traders firmly established in towns such as Pretoria and Pietersburg.

The result of this development was that a Memorial was presented to the Volksraad on the 26th May, 1884, requesting it to legislate against Asiatics and suggesting that a licence fee of £100 be levied on Asiatic traders. This petition did not originate from the burghers of the Republic or from members of the general public. It was inspired by the Chamber of Commerce and signed by Englishmen, viz., T. W. Beckett and E. F. Bourke. Though another petition complained of the Indian's "neglect of sanitary measures and loathsome mode of living", it was clear that the agitation was primarily engineered "by European commercial and trade rivals of the Indians and was solely due to trade jealousy".

Three months after the first anti-Asiatic petition was submitted to the Volksraad, a counter-petition by Indian traders themselves was submitted to the Volksraad on the 25th August, 1884 in which they urged the Volksraad not to introduce discriminatory legislation against the Indians and pointed out that they were men of substantial standing who were engaged in flourishing businesses in the Transvaal at that time.[39] The Indian merchants were quick to draw attention to the difference between them and the labouring class of Indians and the Chinese.[40]

The case for and against the Indians in the Transvaal was now before the Volksraad. Before the Volksraad could act in the matter it had to consider the position created by the London Convention of 1884 and in particular Article 14 of the Convention which read:

"All persons, other than natives, conforming themselves to the laws of the South African Republic:

(a) will have full liberty, with their families, to enter, travel or reside in any part of the South African Republic;

(b) will be entitled to hire or possess houses, manufactories, warehouses, shops and premises;

(c) may carry on their commerce either in person, or by any agents whom they may think fit to employ;

(d) will not be subject in respect of their persons or property, or in respect of their commerce or industry, to any taxes whether general or local, other than those which are or may be imposed upon citizens of the said Republic."[41]

The Volksraad did not act in defiance of this Article but sent the petitions against the Indians submitted to it, as well as the counter-petition sent in by the Indian merchants, to the British Government, requesting at the same time in a covering letter dated 6 January, 1885, the views of the British Government on the complaints received and on the matter of proposed legislation to meet complaints received. The important point of query was whether the proposed legislation would be interpreted as a contravention of Article 14 of the London Convention.

From the considerable correspondence that ensued the Republican Government concluded that the British Government had waived their right to insist upon the strict interpretation of the London Convention, and proceeded to draw up Law 3 of 1885, which, in view of its importance, deserves full mention. The law as originally framed and passed by the Volksraad, enacted that:

"Persons belonging to any of the aboriginal races of Asia, including thereunder the so-called Coolies, Arabs, Malays, and Mohammedan subjects of the Turkish Empire

(a) shall not acquire the rights of citizenship in the South African Republic;

(b) shall not be owners of landed property in the Republic (this provision has no retroactive effect);

(c) shall, as far as those who settled in the Republic with the object of trading, etc., are concerned, have to be inscribed in a register, to be specially kept for that purpose by the Landdrosts of the respective districts, according to a model to be prescribed by the Government."

Paragraph (c) provided for the payment of a registration fee of £25 for each person and paragraph (d) stated that "The Government shall have the right to assign to them special streets, wards and locations for habitation". This latter provision was not to apply to those who resided with the masters in whose services they were.

Muslim traders and other Indian merchants protested immediately to the British High Commissioner who, in turn, took up the cudgels on their behalf, pointing out to the Republican Government that the British Government looked upon Law 3 as a breach of the understanding upon which the British Government had originally waived their right to insist upon the strict interpretation of the London Convention. He added that it was expressly understood by the Secretary of State that the proposed legislation was not to apply to Muslim traders or merchants, but to Indian or Chinese Coolie immigrants.

In a letter dated 6th September, 1886 the State Secretary of the South African Republic pointed out that there had been an apparent misconception in respect of the object for which the law was made. He explained that it was necessary for sanitary reasons and in the interest of the public health and that the Republic proposed to make certain amendments to Law 3. In view of this explanation the High Commissioner, Sir Hercules Robinson, replied on the 24th September, 1886, that:

"Although the amended law is still a contravention of the 14th Article of the Convention of London, I shall not advise Her Majesty's Government to offer further opposition to it in view of your Honour's opinion that it is necessary for the protection of the public health."[42]

The law as amended was promulgated on 26th January, 1887, and the significant amendment read that those persons for whom the original Law 3 was intended "cannot be owners of fixed property in the Republic, except only in such streets, wards and locations as the Government for purposes of sanitation shall assign to them to live in".[43]

The amendment to Law 3/1885 of January, 1887 made one point clear: restrictive legislation had been introduced on sanitary and not economic grounds. Whilst restrictions were placed on the acquisition of fixed property, the right of the Indian trader to remain and trade in the Transvaal was recognised.

That the people in the Transvaal benefited by the presence of the Indian trader is clear from a statement recorded in the Proceedings of the Volksraad, in 1896, that "the European storekeepers charged poor people very high prices for the staff of life, while the coolies charged much less". On another occasion President Kruger himself refused to do away with the Indian hawkers when requested to do so by a deputation of European storekeepers on the ground that they were "useful" to his people.[44]

However, many extremists in the Transvaal were dissatisfied with the Law as it stood. The Volksraad passed a resolution on the 17th June, 1887, requesting that negotiations be resumed with the British Government to restrict the entry of Indians into the Transvaal. But Article 14 hung like the Sword of Damocles, and the State Attorney, W. J. Leyds, advised that any such prohibitive legislation would be contrary to the existing arrangement with the British Government.

Nothing further was done by the South African Republic to amend the law. In fact the law as it stood was not strictly enforced, possibly because of the difficulties encountered in fixing locations or because of the fear of opposition from the British Government. It is possible that the South African Republic did not wish to estrange feelings between the late belligerents at a time which was only six years removed from the first Anglo-Boer War. Indians in the Transvaal were permitted, consequently, not only to trade but to reside outside locations. They were even allowed to own fixed property outside locations through a nominal European trustee. This practice received official approval and assistance as was shown in the case of Mahomed Ismail and Company.[45]

When we consider that Law 3/1885 as amended in 1887 was not strictly enforced to the detriment of the Indians resident in the Transvaal, due regard must be given to the fact that the Indians were British subjects and that in the Transvaal in the years following the discovery of gold on the Rand in 1886 the politics of that state was largely influenced by the presence of another group of British subjects, the Uitlanders, whose claims were championed with such vigour and consistency that all other issues concerning British subjects in the Transvaal were relegated to the background (and where kept in the foreground were used as levers to promote the cause of the Uitlanders). The promotion of the Uitlander case was itself tied to the larger issue of British supremacy in South Africa. The following remarks reveal the true picture – and motives:

"Milner and Chamberlain handled all non-white questions in the light of their primary aim, viz., the extension and consolidation of British supremacy in South Africa. In order to achieve this aim they considered it most important to have the support of a large section of the white colonists. To take too strong a line in defence of non-white interests might easily lose them that support."[46]

The non-white policy of the British Government in the Transvaal, therefore, fell within concentric circles of three parts: the smallest part represented its interest in the welfare of the non-white peoples – including its subjects of Indian origin; the next part, its interest in its white subjects – the Uitlanders; the largest part, its concern at consolidating British supremacy in South Africa.

It is in this context that we have to see the rest of the developments in the Transvaal in the years after 1886. The amendment made to Law 3/1885 in 1887 was not, as has been noted, strictly enforced though the position was not so lax in some of the towns where locations were actually assigned to Indians where they were bidden to trade as well as to reside. Trading outside the locations was forbidden. This led to various litigations, the first of which was heard in the High Court of the Transvaal in August 1888 when an Indian firm, Ismail Sulieman and Company, applied for an order compelling the landdrost to issue to them a licence for trading purposes in the town of Middelburg on an erf formerly occupied by them. The landdrost had earlier refused to do so on the ground that the erf was not situated within the location pointed out to the Indians for occupation. The Court refused the application, holding that it would be inconsistent with the spirit of Law 3 of 1885 to draw a distinction between "living" and "trading".[47]

The judgment in the Ismail Sulieman case sparked off a serious dispute between the British and the Transvaal Governments. The British Government maintained that it was never intended that Asiatics should be relegated to locations, except for residential purposes and for sanitary reasons; that Law 3/1885 referred to residence and not trade which was to be permitted anywhere. The Republican Government resisted these claims and insisted upon adherence to the judgment.

For years the dispute went on in the form of protests and correspondence, with the Transvaal Government taking no active steps to carry out the law as they interpreted it. But when, in September, 1893, the Volksraad passed a resolution to the effect that Law 3 of 1885 would be strictly applied to restrict Asiatic trade and residence to locations, the old dispute was revived with greater intensity. As no settlement could be arrived at between the British and the Transvaal Governments, it was agreed to submit the matter to arbitration, the Chief Justice of the Orange Free State Republic, Justice Melius de Villiers, being appointed arbitrator.

The claims put forward before the Arbitrator on behalf of the British Government were that residence could be restricted to certain areas but that trade could not. The South African Republic claimed that it had full liberty to legislate for both residence and trade and to restrict these to whatever areas it deemed fit for particular people.

The Arbitrator's award, dated 2nd April, 1895, was that he rejected both claims as made by the respective parties. He held the view that the South African Republic was bound to give full force and effect to the provisions of Law 3/1885 as amended in 1886. Where objections were raised against the operation of these provisions, the ruling of the Transvaal law courts was binding.

The Arbitrator, referring presumably to the case of Sulieman and Co., said that in regard to the question whether the words "for habitation" and for "sanitary purposes" had reference only to dwelling places, and not to business premises, he would feel bound by any decision of the High Court of the Republic; but as no such decision had yet been given it was left to the courts of the Republic to decide on this point at a later date.

Referring to the resolution of the Volksraad of the 8th September, 1893 (that Law 3/1885 would be strictly enforced) the Arbitrator said that the British Government was justified in objecting to it as the resolution had the effect of establishing a legislative interpretation of Law 3/1885.

The important thing was that the Arbitrator's award was made in favour of the Transvaal Government, which meant that it could give "full force and effect" to Law 3/1885 as amended. The award was accepted by the British Government.[48]

The dispute (or points of disagreement) between the British Government and the South African Republic was by no means over. In August 1895 the Volksraad of the South African Republic appointed a commission to investigate the administration of Law 3/1885. In its report the Commission stated that as time was required to survey and beacon off locations in all towns the operation of the law should be suspended in the meantime. The Volksraad accepted the recommendation and no immediate steps were taken to enforce the law. Indians continued to reside and trade outside locations generally, though a few towns continued to enforce the law. In the course of this enforcement an Indian merchant, Tayob Hadji Mohomed Khan, sued the government for a declaration of rights in August, 1898 in a case similar to that of Ismail Sulieman's (of 1888). The Court, by a majority of two to one, upheld the judgment given in the Ismail Sulieman case (that Indians had to reside and trade in locations set aside for them). This was not the last to be heard of this matter.[49]

At this time, viz., the end of 1898, the South African League (which championed the rights of the Uitlanders in the Transvaal) protested to the British Government against "certain alleged outrages perpetrated by the police on Cape Coloured people in Johannesburg during the night of 29 October, 1898". Chamberlain, the Secretary of State for the Colonies, authorised Fraser, the Secretary to the British Agent in Pretoria, to invoke Article 14 of the London Convention in order to protect the interests of the Coloured people. Fraser used this instruction to begin negotiations with the Transvaal Government, by which he succeeded in obtaining a postponement of the intentions of that government as foreshadowed in the Tayob Khan case of 1898. At the same time Fraser tried to use the Coloured question in the Transvaal "as a lever to extract concessions for Asiatics". A draft agreement entered into by Fraser and Smuts (representing the Transvaal Government) proposed that Coloured persons as well as Asiatics then living or trading in towns might remain where they were provided that no transfers of these businesses could be effected to persons of the same race group upon the death of the persons concerned or when the businesses closed down for any other reason. These businesses could only be transferred to Europeans. Asiatics and Coloureds were to take out passes every half-year; newcomers had to reside in locations; hawking in towns and counties would be permitted as before. But before these proposals could receive further official attention, the outbreak of bubonic plague in Madagascar in February, 1899, and the detection of two cases in the Transvaal resulted in a temporary ban on the entry of Asiatics and

Coloured peoples into the Transvaal through the eastern frontier of this state. At the same time Asiatics were forbidden from travelling within the Transvaal without a permit from the State Secretary.[50]

The events resulting from the outbreak of bubonic plague had the effect of postponing a final decision in regard to the Fraser–Smuts draft agreement mentioned above. Milner finally caused a break-up in the negotiations by insisting upon separating the Indian and Coloured questions – which separate treatment was contrary to the Fraser–Smuts draft agreement. The negotiations broke down early in April, 1899. On the 25th April, 1899, a proclamation was issued in the name of the President of the Republic announcing streets, wards, and locations for Asiatic residence and trade in the Transvaal.

Though this last proclamation was not enforced, the British Government, through its High Commissioner, Milner, now opposed the anti-Asiatic legislation and regulations of the Transvaal Government with more vigour than before, not so much for the sake of the Asiatics themselves but largely to capitalize on the gains resulting from the solid British opinion in South Africa against the Kruger regime after the breakdown of the Bloemfontein Conference in May–June, 1899. One occasion which revealed this new attitude was the latest proposal of the Transvaal Government to remove the Indians of Johannesburg to a location nearly five miles from the centre of the town. Chamberlain agreed that Milner should inform the Transvaal Government that "we . . . claim strict compliance with the sanitary reasons for applying the (segregation) law of 1885, so as to exempt Indians who can produce a medical certificate that their premises are not insanitary". This stand amounted to a repudiation of the Melius de Villiers arbitration award of 1895. On another occasion, when the Transvaal Government refused to issue more licences to British Indians, the British Agent advised them to tender the licence fees, and, if the licences were still not issued, to trade without licences. A little later, when the Government threatened to prosecute the traders, and about forty of them were actually arrested, the British Agent approved of their intention not to pay fines or apply for bail but to court imprisonment.[51]

The position had now been reached when the grievances of the Transvaal Indians became a cause for war against the South African Republic. In the seven-clause British ultimatum to the Transvaal Government agreed upon by the British cabinet on 29th September, 1899, one of the demands read: "The concession of most-favoured-nation rights to Great Britain . . . in all matters affecting British interests or the position of British subjects, whether white or coloured."[52]

And, in Sheffield, Lord Lansdowne said: "Among the many misdeeds of the South African Republic, I do not know that any fills me with more indignation than its treatment of these Indians."[53]

Within forty years the South African Indian question had ceased to be a mere domestic issue. It was no longer a simple economic issue of importation of labour or of control of trade. It was now brought into the imperial arena to suit British interests in the conflict between Briton and Boer.

FOOTNOTES

1. A. F. Hattersley, *The Natal Settlers*, 1849–1851, p. 1.
2. Despatch from Lord Stanley to Sir G. T. Napier, Governor of the Cape Colony, 13th December, 1842. J. Bird, *Annals of Natal*, vol. II, p. 146.
3. Hattersley, *The Natal Settlers*, pp. 1–11.
4. Natal Indian Congress, *Memorandum on Civic Status*, submitted to the Natal Indian Judicial Commission, p. 4. *Vide* also Interim Report of Commission of Enquiry into matters affecting the Indian population of the Province of Natal, U.G. 22/1945, p. 14.
5. L. M. Thompson, *Indian Immigration*, p. 4 and B. Pachai, *The History of the "Indian Opinion"*, p. 1.
6. Mabel Palmer, *The History of Indians in Natal*, p. 10, for the population figures and Ferguson-Davie, *The Early History of Indians in Natal*, pp. 1–2 for some contemporary views on African labour.
7. Thompson, *Indian Immigration*, p. 5.
8. Thompson, *Indian Immigration*, p. 7. For a detailed study of Shepstone's Native Policy *vide* Brookes, *History of Native Policy in South Africa*, pp. 41–65 and J. R. Sullivan, *The Native Policy of Sir Theophilus Shepstone*, especially p. 34 for certain guiding principles laid down by the government.
9. Aiyar, *Conflict of Races in South Africa*, p. 16, quoting Johnstone's statement in the Natal Legislative Council.
10. *Natal Witness*, 21 June, 1850, in an editorial under the heading "Hints to Emigrants". For Dr. Palmer's views see *History of Indians*, p. 10.
11. *Vide* Ferguson-Davie, *The Early History of Indians in Natal*, pp. 3–4 for efforts to get labour from the West.
12. *Natal Mercury*, 25th July, 1855. *Vide* also Thompson, *Indian Immigration*, pp. 9–10.
13. *Natal Mercury*, 9 November, 1855. Chinese and Malay labourers were first brought out to Natal from Java by the Umzinto Sugar Company in 1858. These labourers proved to be unsatisfactory for the Chinaman's idea of emigration was to make money quickly and retire. This was not possible with a meagre sum of 10/– a month. *Vide* B. Pachai, *The History of the "Indian Opinion"*, p. 3.
14. *Leader*, 9th November, 1946, containing a reproduction of these early negotiations from documents presented to the United Nations.
15. Thompson, *Indian Immigration*, p. 11.
16. *Leader*, 9th November, 1946.
17. Polak, *The Indians of South Africa*, p. 5.
18. Thompson, *Indian Immigration*, p. 8.
19. *Vide* Thompson, *Indian Immigration*, Chapter VI, pp. 45–54.
20. *Principal Documents*, p. 10.
21. The Binns-Mason Report of 1894 gives interesting population figures.

Population of Natal – 1893 (*approximately*)

European: 45 000   *Indian:* 46 000   *African:* 470 000

The number of Indians is inclusive of an estimated population of 5 500 Arabs. *Vide* C.S.O. 5549/1893, with Government Notice No. 144/1894.
22. The following table illustrates the population changes and the commercial effect of "Indians" and "Arabs", 1870–1885.

	Population of Natal			*Retail stores in Durban Borough*
Year	European	Asiatic	Free Indians	Kept by Passenger Indians or Arabs
1870	14 445	6 000	2	0
1875	16 261	9 914	10	1
1880	25 271	20 536	30	7
1885	36 701	30 159	26	40

Wragg Commission Report, 1885–7. N. and I.B.B., Vol. 66, Chap. 40, cited in Thompson, *Indian Immigration*, p. 69.
23. Wragg Commission Report, p. 74.
24. Asiatic Inquiry Commission Report, U.G. 4/1921, p. 41.

25. For a full and critical account of Act 25/1891 *vide* Pachai, *History of "Indian Opinion"*, pp. 12–13.
26. C.S.O. 5549/1893. Binns-Mason Report.
27. C.S.O. 994/1895.
28. C.S.O. 5549/93. Binns-Mason Report, 20th January, 1894.
29. Henderson, *Speeches of Harry Escombe*, pp. 292–3.
30. Ferguson-Davie, *The Early History*, p. 20. In 1880, 181 Indian voters were registered, 124 of these were in Victoria County—*vide* Sirkari Naidoo, *Indian Imbroglio*, p. 3.
31. Henderson, *Speeches of Harry Escombe*, p. 109.
32. South African Indian Congress, *Treatment of Indians in South Africa:* A Memorandum of Facts compiled by A. I. Kajee, P. R. Pather, and Advocate A. Christopher—S.A.I.C. delegates to the U.N. debates in 1946, p. 8.
33. Natal Indian Congress, *Memorandum on Civic Status*, submitted to the Natal Indian Judicial Commission, September, 1944, pp. 5–6.
34. Natal Indian Congress, *Memorandum on Civic Status*, p. 6. M. K. Gandhi, *The Indian Franchise*, pp. 8–9. According to Sirkari Naidoo, *Indian Imbroglio*, p. 3, there were 181 Indian voters registered in 1880. Gandhi gives the figure as 251 in 1895 which was about 1/38 of the European voters. In his pamphlet, *The Indian Franchise*, pp. 1–9, Gandhi tabulates the six commonly-held objections to the granting of the franchise to Indians. He then refutes these objections point-by-point.
35. Henderson, *Speeches of Harry Escombe*, pp. 342–3.
36. Report of the Asiatic Inquiry Commission, 1921, p. 9.
37. H. E. Joosub, *Bitterness Towards Indians*, p. 10.
38. Transvaal Indian Congress, Memorandum submitted to the Asiatic Land Laws Commission, 1938, p. 8.
39. *Ibid.*, pp. 2–3.
40. Report of the Asiatic Inquiry Commission, 1921, p. 4. In the context of anti-Indianism that was now developing in the Transvaal the following remarks by Muriel Horrell in an address delivered at Pretoria on the 21 August, 1958, are full of meaning:

    "It is possible that the root of anti-Indian sentiment in South Africa is economic. There were other reasons too. White South Africans had developed a feeling of racial superiority, which, so far as the Indians are concerned, was re-inforced by the fact that, as the indentured workers were drawn from the lower castes in India, they were originally illiterate and unaccustomed to Western standards of hygiene. Later, the fear arose that Indians would in time outnumber the Whites because their birthrate is higher. This is largely a misconception. . . .

    Another important reason was that the religious, dress and food-habits of the Indian were alien— and South Africans do like uniformity . . .". M. Horrell, *Indians in Pretoria*, pp. 1–2.
41. Eybers: *Select Constitutional Documents Illustrating South African History*, p. 473.
42. *Ibid.*, pp. 4–5.
43. Asiatic Inquiry Commission, 1921, p. 5.
44. Polak, *Indians of South Africa*, p. 73.
45. Asiatic Inquiry Commission, 1921, p. 6.
46. J. S. Marais, *The Fall of Kruger's Republic*, p. 182.
47. Asiatic Inquiry Commission, 1921, p. 6.
48. J. S. Marais, *The Fall of Kruger's Republic*, p. 182.
49. Asiatic Inquiry Commission Report, 1921, p. 8.
50. Marais, *The Fall of Kruger's Republic*, pp. 235 and 258–61.
51. Polak, *Indians of South Africa*, pp. 74–5.
52. Marais, *The Fall of Kruger's Republic*, p. 262 and p. 382.
53. Polak, *Indians of South Africa*, p. 74. Lord Lansdowne went on to show how damaging this position was to Anglo-Indian relations.

CHAPTER TWO

THE GENESIS OF AN INTERNATIONAL ISSUE
1900–1914

The War which was foreshadowed since the dark days following the Jameson Raid had at last come. It put a stop temporarily to Indian claims for redress of existing grievances as well as to anti-Indian pressures calling for the imposition of fresh disabilities. With the effective British occupation of the former Boer republics, the Government of India sent a despatch dated 12th July, 1900, urging that "while the recollection of the loyalty and valuable exertions of the Indian population of Natal and of the valuable services rendered to Natal by India in the war was still fresh in the minds of the colonists", a just settlement of the outstanding differences should be attempted.[1] It must be noted that, largely through the instrumentality of M. K. Gandhi, local Indians played an important part in the war. Gandhi saw that the war offered a golden opportunity to the Indians to serve as non-combatants in an Indian Ambulance Corps as stretcher-bearers and to dispel the opinion held against the Indians that "they went to South Africa only for money-grabbing and were merely a dead-weight upon the British. Like worms which settle inside wood and eat it up hollow, the Indians were in South Africa to fatten themselves upon them".[2] The Indian Ambulance Corps, when organised, had about 1 100 strong, of whom about 300 were free Indians and the rest indentured Indians. Though the Corps was disbanded after six weeks' service when the British Commander decided to abandon the attempt to relieve Ladysmith and to await reinforcements from England and India, the work of the unit was highly commended by General Buller in despatches and the thirty-seven leaders were awarded the War Medal.

Though Gandhi's personal sympathies were with the Boers, "a small nation . . . fighting for its very existence", the deciding factor for him was the following train of reasoning: "I felt that, if I demanded rights as a British citizen, it was also my duty, as such, to participate in the defence of the British Empire", although he knew as clearly as any thinking man did that the "British oppress us equally with the Boers. If we are subjected to hardships in the Transvaal, we are not very much better off in Natal or the Cape Colony. The difference, if any, is only one of degree".[3]

But the War made no difference to the position in which Indians had found themselves in Natal. In reply to the despatch from the Government of India asking that all outstanding differences be settled, the Natal Government, independently, asked that emigration to Natal should be freed from certain legal restrictions, and asked to be placed on the same footing as Ceylon for the purposes of emigration. This request was promptly turned down by the Government of India mainly on the grounds that in Natal "the settlement of labourers whose terms of indenture had expired was discouraged and subjected to penalties", that "all free immigrants were treated as being more or less on the level of aboriginees" and "subjected to special treatment which was degrading and injurious to their self-respect", and, finally, because the recent legislation was "inequitable in its effect on those who had been permitted to settle and acquire property in the country".[4]

The anomaly in the situation at this time was that though Natal was not prepared to settle the outstanding differences it still required labourers from India. In 1902 a Select Committee of the Natal Legislative Assembly was appointed to consider Petition No. 1 of 1902 of the Indian Immigration Trust Board of Natal for labourers from India. Evidence showed that applications for Indian labourers for various purposes had increased from 2 000 to 4 000 and 6 000 and more recently to 15 000 owing to the increased scarcity of African labour. The shipping contracts of the Indian Immigration Trust Board had arranged for 8 000 adults whereas applications had been received for 15 000 adults.[5]

The Natal Government agreed to the appointment of a deputation to visit India to discuss matters affecting Indian immigration. C. B. De Gersigny and H. C. Shepstone were appointed commissioners to go to India in 1903. The exact points which the commissioners were required to discuss were:

    (i) relaxation of recruiting restrictions in India;
    (ii) possibility of obtaining greater facilities to recruit labour for the mines of Natal; and
    (iii) modification of terms of indenture so as to secure termination of engagement in India.[6]

The Indian Government informed Natal that they were not unwilling to meet the wishes of the Natal Government in the matter so long as the labourer was not compelled to be indefinitely in a state of indenture and so long as the agreement for the labourer's return to India was enforced without any undue harshness. In return for this the Government of India wanted the free Indian to be better treated in the following respects: the £3 tax should be waived after ten years; the law governing trading licences should be amended to provide a right of appeal to a court of law against decisions of licensing boards.

Failing favourable consideration of these requests, the Government of India warned the Natal Government that they reserved the "fullest liberty to take at any time such measures in regard to emigration to Natal as they may think necessary in order to secure to their subjects proper treatment in that colony". The Government of Natal declined to accept these conditions.[7]

Many years later, in 1946, the Union Government observed that the negotiations of 1903 had failed because the Natal Government had been careful not to press the matter in order not to embarrass the British Government because that government was being attacked by Indian politicians, who were members of the Indian Congress, for not protecting the rights and interests of its Indian subjects in Natal.[8]

To say that the Natal Government's failure to effect any enforcement was due to political agitation and protest in India is to credit the Government with more finesse than the records reveal. It is nearer the point to say that the Natal Government went to the limits permitted in its legislative programme concerning Indians on Natal soil in spite of agitation and protests from whatever source. In short, Natal did little to avoid embarrassment to either the British or the Indian Governments.

This does not, however, suggest that Indian politicians and Indian political organisations did not protest whenever just grounds existed for protest. The very first political organisation for Indians in Natal, the Natal Indian Congress, was founded because of the action of the Natal Government in attempting to disfranchise the Indians in 1894.

This led M. K. Gandhi to organise a committee of protest against the measure. He sent a telegram to the Natal Government requesting that the Disfranchising Bill be delayed. He sent a petition bearing 400 signatures to the Natal Government and another containing about 10 000 signatures to Lord Ripon, Secretary of State for the Colonies. Natal, as we have seen, passed the measure but the British Government disallowed it.

The significant result of this protest was that the disallowance by the British Government of the Disfranchising Act stimulated the Committee of Protest which had been set up by Gandhi to organise itself into a political organisation. Thus the Natal Indian Congress was inaugurated on 22nd May, 1894. The first Hon. Secretary of the N.I.C. was Gandhi himself.[9]

The Natal Indian Congress was further strengthened by the establishment of the first Indian newspaper in South Africa, also by M. K. Gandhi, on 4th June, 1903, the *Indian Opinion*, whose headquarters was the Phoenix Settlement which was established in 1904, also by Gandhi. Thus Gandhi had been responsible for the establishment of the Natal Indian Congress, the *Indian Opinion*, and the Phoenix Settlement – all dedicated to the service of Indians in South Africa and to the furtherance of greater harmony in Indo-European relations in South Africa.[10]

The Natal Indian Congress was not officially recognised at first as representing the interests of the indentured labourers. When, in 1903, the Natal Government decided, after the failure of the De Gersigny–Shepstone mission to India, to extend the £3 tax to the children of indentured labourers, Congress sent a memorial to the Natal Government for transmission to the Secretary of State for Colonies in London in which a protest against the extension was lodged. The Natal Colonial Secretary, in his remarks, said that the "Memorialists claim to represent the Indian community of Natal but from enquiries made by the Protector of Immigrants, it is apparent that this is a misrepresentation".[11] However, the Natal Indian Congress was soon to receive official recognition.

Though the Natal Government failed to settle the outstanding differences and showed its disapproval of the Indians by extending the 1895 law to include children in 1903, its labour shortage compelled it to appeal once again to the Indian Government in September, 1904. In this request it again asked for certain facilities to promote the flow of labour from India. These were the opening of the port of Karachi and the reduction of the statutory proportion of women who must emigrate from 40 per cent to $33\frac{1}{3}$ per cent of emigrant males. The Government of India declined to meet the wishes of the Natal Government until the treatment of Indian immigrants in Natal was "substantially modified". An important solution to the impasse was suggested by Joseph Baynes, M.L.A., of Natal, who visited India in 1905 and suggested, on his return, to the Natal Government that they should invite a deputation from India to visit the colony. He was impressed by the strength of Indian feeling on the treatment of Indians in Natal, though he thought that the reports on which this was based were exaggerated. Nothing came of the suggestion.[12]

The Natal Government made very little attempt to settle the outstanding differences between itself and the Indian Government up till 1905. It was apparent that settlement after this date would become increasingly difficult for the year 1905 heralds the beginning of National India, a beginning which saw a greater measure of self-government and self-expression. The appointment of the Liberal, John Morley, as Secretary of State for India and of Lord Minto as Viceroy was in keeping with the new development. The Morley–

Minto reforms were aimed at securing better representation of important Indian interests, the enlargement of the powers of the legislative councils, and the introduction of Indians as members of the Executive. In spite of these reforms the British Government still retained a controlling influence in India through checks and balances which gave it an official majority; another reason for this influence was the small number of Indian members in the civil service. Though it was only after 1907 that Indians were given seats in the higher councils, the flood-gates to greater constitutional changes in India were opened in 1905, the date which marks the beginning of more turbulent political relations between the states of South Africa and India. The effects of these changes on the South African situation were seen first in the Transvaal for, though the concentration of Indians was in Natal, the events in the Transvaal concerning Indians grew out of all proportion to their numbers and it is to these developments that we must now turn.[13] As from September, 1900 the former Boer republic of the Transvaal came under effective British administration and the sign of the new times became clear when some of the local officials under the new administration adopted a policy of strict enforcement of the segregation law of 1885 as amended in 1887.

On the 3rd April, 1902, the High Commissioner, Lord Milner, telegraphed the following proposals for the approval of the British Government:

"1. That all Asiatics, whether then resident in the Transvaal or subsequently entering it unless specially exempted, should take out a certificate of registration to be annually renewed at a charge of £3 (Law 3/1885 had prescribed a registration fee of £25 but this was reduced to £3 by a Volksraad Resolution of 1886).

2. That registered Asiatics, unless living with a European employer, should be obliged to reside and carry on their business in special quarters of the towns set apart for them, the sites for these locations to be selected by the Governor, and their control for sanitary purposes to be exercised by the municipal authorities.

3. That certificates of registration should be refused to undesirable persons.

4. That exemption from registration should be granted to educated and civilised Asiatics.

5. That the prohibition against holding real property should be repealed, but that the right of Asiatics to acquire such property should be restricted to town areas for five years."

The Secretary of State for the Colonies, Joseph Chamberlain, replied on 6th August, 1902 that it would be impossible to defend what would practically be a continuance of the policy of the South African Republic against which the British Government had so strongly and repeatedly protested.

The Government of India studied the position very carefully and saw that in their unwillingness to offend "colonial prejudice", the authorities would cause the Indians much hardship. On 14th May, 1903 the Government of India addressed a strong despatch to the Secretary of State for India in which they urged:

"(i) that no restrictions should be imposed on the entry of Indians into the Transvaal. If any were considered necessary they should take the form of a literary test which should recognise non-European languages equally with European;

(ii) that the policy of confining Indians to locations for residence should preferably be abandoned, but if its application was found necessary for sanitary reasons, such application should be confined only to the lower classes; and

(iii) that Indians should be free to trade anywhere they liked."[14]

The intervention of the Government of India did not succeed in improving the position. There was a faint hope yet that Lord Milner's need for Indian labourers to construct railways in the Transvaal and the Orange River Colonies would strengthen the case of the Indian Government to get the desired improvements for the Transvaal Indians. In a telegram dated 2nd January, 1904 the Government of India repeated their request of the 14th May, 1903. But Lord Milner was unwilling to admit Indian languages into the literary test for admission which he proposed should be made the basis of the immigration restrictions. Lord Milner said that the violent anti-Indian prejudice which was said to exist in every town of the Transvaal stood in the way of the other points being satisfactorily met. Indian labour was not agreed upon for the Transvaal and an opportunity to ameliorate existing conditions was thereby lost.

Events were fast turning in the direction of the Transvaal becoming the battleground for the Indian struggle in South Africa. Already in May, 1901, the Asiatic Immigration Office was set up in Johannesburg where Indians were required to change their passes for new ones. To regulate the entry into the Transvaal of Asiatics who had been resident there before the war, the Transvaal Government passed the Peace Preservation Ordinance of 1902 as amended by the Peace Preservation Ordinance No. 5 of 1903. Permits were granted to *bona-fide* refugees returning to the Transvaal as a matter of course but owing to the absence of records it was very difficult to verify or disprove claims to prior residence in the Transvaal; consequently some Asiatics who were not *bona-fide* residents entered the Transvaal with the returning refugees. "Partly to blame for this illegal entry was the lax and improper behaviour on the part of Government officials at the Immigration Office. The Transvaal British Indian Association (which had been founded by M. K. Gandhi in 1903) brought to the notice of the Government the existence of bribery and corruption among Government officials. In addition to entry with the connivance of Government officials, many Indians entered by fraudulent means."[15]

It was to check this situation that Milner appealed to the Indian leaders in 1903 to agree to a voluntary re-registration of the entire Indian community whereby the Peace Preservation permits – which contained a name with no means of identifying it with any particular person – would be exchanged for new registration certificates, containing particulars of the holder's name, family, caste, father's name, height, occupation, age, and the impression of the holder's right thumb where signatures could not be affixed. Lord Milner told the Indians at this time that registration gave them a right to free movement; it would benefit them as it would help the government keep a check on illegal entry into the Transvaal. He said that no further registration would be required nor would other documents be called for. Indians answered this call in good faith. Their action finds support in the words of H. S. L. Polak who wrote in 1909 on the matter of registration: "Registration today has proved successful only because of the bona-fides of the Asiatics shown in 1903 and since, and re-identification would be impossible even today but for their voluntary act performed six years ago."[16]

The willingness on the part of Indians to register in 1903 did not serve to do their cause much good. More was yet to come. In a lengthy despatch to Chamberlain, the Secretary of State for the Colonies, Lord Milner wrote on the 11th May, 1903 on the position of British Indians in the Transvaal. He stated that he was reluctant to embark on fresh legislation in view of the many difficulties; that the best way seemed to be to carry out the existing law in accordance with the principle adopted till then, viz., that the laws of the late Republic, imperfect as they were in many respects and even contrary to British ideas, had, nevertheless, to be enforced until they could be replaced by more satisfactory legislation. He said that the principle of segregation had been adopted mainly for sanitary reasons, though he agreed that on this score the lower-class Indians were the greatest offenders. He maintained that the Government was satisfied that the European population was entitled to protection on that point and that such a measure was in the interests of the Asiatics themselves. Not only would it be advantageous to their health but it would mitigate the intense hostility felt towards them by the European element, a hostility which, in view of the possible grant of self-government to Transvaal Whites, was a serious difficulty which the Indians would be called upon to face.

Milner then went on to show that in three respects the policy of the new British administration towards Indians was an improvement on that of the former Boer regime: special quarters, with healthy sites for residence and suitable sites for trading, were being provided in every town; Asiatics who had established themselves in business before the war would not be disturbed; Asiatics of a superior class would be exempt from special legislation.

The despatch conveyed the policy of the new Government: "The policy of the present Government is not directed against colour or against any special race. It is dictated by the necessity of preventing people of a higher degree of civilisation, whatever their race or colour may be, from being degraded by enforced contact with people of lower grade."

The policy of the new Government as expressed in Lord Milner's letter to Chamberlain was put into operation on 8th April, 1903. The provisions stated that those Asiatics whose "intellectual attainments, or social qualities and habits of life appear to entitle them to it" would be exempt from the terms restricting trade and residence to certain defined areas.[17]

The new British administration was, by this step, perpetuating the policy of the Kruger Republic which it had so stoutly opposed a few years back; it was capitulating to the insistent demands of the British in the Transvaal that it take firm steps to carry out the existing anti-Asiatic laws. With the Boer–Briton clash now resolved the Asiatic issue became the centre of European agitation in the Transvaal. One good example of this increasing feeling against Indians can be found in the deliberations of the "National Convention" (not to be confused with the National Convention of 1908–9). The "Convention" convened in Pretoria in 1904 and adopted resolutions which stated that the delay in dealing with the question of the status of Asiatics had been prejudicial to the best interests of the Transvaal; that Asiatic immigration should be prohibited except under the provisions of the Labour Importation Ordinance (that is, under contract of labour terminable outside the borders of the Colony); that all Asiatic traders should be confined to bazaars – compensation to be paid to those who acquired vested interests legally; that further issue of trading licences to Asiatics should be discontinued; that all Asiatics should be required to reside in bazaars (which is another word for locations).[18]

The last resolution proposed that cultured persons of a good standard of education should be exempt from the restrictions. This was rejected. This rejection prompted L. E. Neame to write that the " 'Convention' bound itself down to the principle that an educated British Indian, even if he happened to be a Member of the House of Commons, or a Prince deemed socially worthy of entertaining the future King and Queen of England, should be forced to reside in a location with the Madrassi waiters from a Railway Restaurant, or the Bombay hawker from the gateway of a mine compound".[19]

Meanwhile Indians in the Transvaal were taking note of the storm clouds that were gathering. Hopes of any better things from the new British administration were dashed with the appearance of Milner's regulations on trade and residence in 1903. The Indian community regarded this as an infringement of their trading rights. An Indian trader, Habib Motan, brought up a test case against the restrictions in the Transvaal Supreme Court early in 1904. This case was instituted because of the refusal of a licence to trade on a stand in Pretoria, outside an Asiatic bazaar. The refusal was based on the construction placed by the authorities on Law 3/1885. The decision of the Court was that the Law of 1885 as amended in 1886 prescribed special areas for residence but not for trade and the appeal was upheld.

By this judgment the two previous decisions given by the High Court of the South African Republic in the Ismail Sulieman case of 1888 and the Tayob Hadji Mohomed Khan case of 1898 were disapproved and overruled. In the course of his judgment the Chief Justice said that "it was remarkable that without fresh legislation the officials of the Crown in the Transvaal should put forward a claim which the British Government had always contended was illegal and which in the past it had strenuously resisted". The strange contradictions in British policy were emphasised in the Chief Justice's observations and were of special significance in view of the correspondence that was passing at this very time between the Transvaal authorities and the Imperial Government on the subject of proposed legislation regarding Asiatics.

On 13th April, 1904, just four weeks before the judgment in Motan's case was delivered, Sir Arthur Lawley, Lieutenant-Governor of the Transvaal, addressed a despatch to Lord Milner, British High Commissioner, for transmission to the Secretary of State for the Colonies, asking for the consent of the Imperial Government to the introduction of restrictive legislation in the Transvaal Legislative Council. In advocating the necessity for legislation in the direction indicated by the Government Notice 356 of 8th April, 1903, Sir Arthur Lawley emphasised the strong public feeling upon the subject. He said: "Trade jealousy undoubtedly exists, but it is really prompted by the instinct of self-preservation in the minds of the European trading community. The problem is far reaching and does not begin and end with a shopkeeper's quarrel. . . . I do not seek to justify the prejudices which exist; I merely wish to set them forth. They cannot be ignored. They have got to be reckoned with."[20]

The Lieutenant-Governor went on to advise that the sentiments of the European people could only be ignored with disastrous consequences for the country. He drew a picture of the colour line very vividly when he said: "Under the old Grondwet the line was distinctly drawn between coloured and white. It is there stated, there shall be no equality between coloured and white; and, though in the eye of the law they are equal, there is not in this country one man in a hundred who would agree to recognise the coloured man as capable of admission to the same social standard as the white. I do not urge that these sentiments are reasonable, but they imbue the mind of every South African, and find expression in the universal cry of 'a white man's country'. Any attempt to ignore them would be attended, I feel sure, with most deplorable results."

Lord Milner, in his covering letter to the Secretary of State, endorsed the statement of Sir Arthur Lawley on the extent of the strong anti-Asiatic feeling among the European population. He indicated, however, a desire that Asiatics of a superior class should, if possible, be liberally treated by giving them a special status. On this point he remarked that he did not see any immediate prospect of the Asiatics receiving any recognition in the Transvaal for "the Asiatics are strangers forcing themselves upon a community reluctant to receive them".[21]

The Secretary of State, Lyttelton, in replying to the despatches of Sir Arthur Lawley and Lord Milner on 20th July, 1904, drew a distinction between British Indians who might in future enter the country and those who were then resident there. With regard to the former class he recognised the strong opposition among the European population to a continued and unrestricted influx of Asiatic traders, and intimated that his Government would give their sanction, though reluctantly, to the immediate introduction of a measure in the Transvaal Legislative Council restricting immigration on the lines of the Cape and Natal Acts.[22]

With regard to the settled community of Indians already resident in the Transvaal, Lyttelton said that "an apprehended trade competition from the British Indians now in this country, whose number is now comparatively small and will under proposed restrictions on emigrants be in a diminishing proportion, cannot be accepted as sufficient reason for the legislation proposed. His Majesty's Government have steadily declined to allow this fear to influence their views in the past. On the contrary, for many years they protested before the Empire and the civilised world against the policy and Laws of the late South African Republic in relation to this subject". On the important question of the holding of land, he said that British Indians who were entitled to reside outside locations must at least have the right to acquire property in the premises which they occupied for business purposes.

The despatches which passed between the Transvaal and the British Governments clearly indicated the different angles from which the Indian question in the Transvaal was being viewed. After the reply from the Secretary of State for Colonies was received no further steps were taken by the Crown Colony Government in the direction of the proposed legislation and Law 3/1885 was allowed to remain unaltered.

But the policy of the Crown Colony Government of the Transvaal disappointed Indians in the Transvaal and in India where the Indian National Congress, among other institutions, followed the developments closely. In his Presidential Address to the Congress at the end of 1904, Sir Henry Cotton recalled that the treatment by the late Boer Government of their Indian subjects was mentioned as one of the causes of the Second Anglo-Boer War. Sir Henry said: "It was on these grounds that the war was justified to the British public. In this way hope was afforded that at the close of the war the anti-Indian policy of the Boer would be reversed. But has it been reversed? Far from it. Peace having been secured, the British rulers of the Transvaal have applied themselves with British vigour and precision to the task of enforcing Boer law. In dealing with Indian Colonists their little finger has been thicker than Mr. Kruger's loins, and where he had chastised with whips, they have chastised with scorpions."[23]

The Transvaal was particularly singled out for special attention at the Congress conference for, as one of the speakers, the Editor of the *Indian Opinion*, Madanjit, who was in India at this time, said: "The Transvaal is the real theatre of war. It is there that the situation is most critical. In fact Transvaal Indian policy will be the policy of all the South African States, and once the Indian question is settled there, other States will cast themselves in the same mould."

Resolutions were passed at the conference appealing to the British Government to accord just treatment to Indian settlers in the Crown Colony of the Transvaal and thanking the Government of India and the Secretary of State for India "for their firm stand in the interests of Indian emigrants".

The deliberations of the Indian National Congress – the strongest Indian political body in India – indicate the welter of feeling against the British administration in the Transvaal. A notable authority on the position in the Transvaal blames Milner for the contradictions and weaknesses in the new administration in the Transvaal.

For the ineptitude of the new British regime during the Milner administration, to accord more rights to the Indians, A. B. Keith takes Lord Milner to task for his partiality towards segregation. Lord Milner, as a die-hard imperialist, had fixed ideas on the colour question and these ideas did nothing to ease the position for the Transvaal Indians following the cessation of hostilities in 1902.

Keith's comparison of the Milner policy of that day with that of a later day makes interesting reading: "Lord Milner's love of segregation reappeared in his scheme in 1920 to impose segregation in residence and business in Kenya, a device fortunately rejected by the final settlement. Similarly, his approval of exploitation of native labour in Kenya is shown in his despatch of 22nd July, 1920. His attitude, as shown in his conception of Imperial relations, was true to the doctrine of race superiority to the last, and, undoubtedly, now as in his lifetime, his view has many followers. But it is not a possible basis for retaining India in the Empire. Nor does a naturalized South African Jew appear more British than an Indian."[24]

But if Milner's attitude was uncompromising, there was hope when he left in 1905 that his successor, Lord Selborne, would be more accommodating. Almost immediately after the arrival of the new High Commissioner early in 1905, complaints began to pour in that there was continued illicit influx of Indians into the Transvaal. Because of the persistent nature of the complaints, Lord Selborne instituted an inquiry into the alleged complaints. In September, 1905, he expressed his satisfaction that the complaints were unfounded. Until the end of that year everything went well. But during December, however, the Chief Secretary for Permits committed an error, which might well have developed into an international incident, when he refused a permit to a Japanese merchant who was armed with credentials from his Government. Consequent upon this the administration of Asiatic affairs was transferred to an official known as the Protector of Asiatics.

The title of the official was afterwards altered to that of Registrar of Asiatics.[25]

The first months of Selborne's stay in the country found the Asiatic question particularly quiet especially in comparison with the ominous developments during the Milner administration. In a despatch to the Secretary of State for the Colonies dated 21st August, 1905, Lord Selborne made the observation that the Asiatic question had not been as prominent as the Native question. He thought that if the people of the Orange River Colony and the Transvaal were quite assured that there would be no further immigration of Asiatics, it would be possible, gradually, to settle the status of those who were then residing in the country. He was firm on the point that there should be no further Asiatic immigration into the country but that British subjects of European origin should be encouraged to settle in the country, "for in these colonies a white man must always be a fighter, whereas this is the one thing the Asiatic can never be, both owing to the peculiar circumstances of the country and to the fact that the Asiatics who come here are not of any martial race. It is the fact that the Asiatic does displace the white fighting man".[26]

Lord Selborne suggested a compromise solution that in return for a measure which would have the practical effect of preventing future Asiatic immigration in the Transvaal a satisfactory assurance should be given that those Asiatics already resident in the country would receive proper treatment. His policy was the forerunner of the Gokhale–Gandhi plan of 1912.

Lord Selborne's compromise solution was conveyed to the Government of India for its consideration. On the 31st January, 1906, almost six months after the compromise solution was first suggested, the Government of India replied regretting the necessity for the first part of Selborne's proposals whilst giving its assent to the proposed solution contained in the steps outlined.[27]

But there were more difficulties in the way before Lord Selborne's suggestions could be put into operation. In the Transvaal Supreme Court the case of Lucas Trustees versus Ismail and Amod (the heirs of Aboobaker Amod) in 1905 threw the whole Indian question there into more confusion. The British Government asked for details and enquired whether the existing law should be amended.

Lord Selborne used the opportunity to give a detailed review of the position in the Transvaal. He saw two distinct claims, that of the Europeans who wished to preserve it as a white man's country and that of the Asiatics who wished to acquire the right of entry. Eventually, said Selborne, one of these two claims would have to give way. Both could not be granted. The alternatives, it seemed to him, rested between the preservation of a white man's country or a country peopled by brown and black people in which the controlling influence would be vested in a small white minority.[28]

Referring to the specific case of Lucas Trustees versus Ismail and Amod, which set off the correspondence between Elgin and himself, Selborne pointed out that the heirs of Aboobaker, an Indian, who was entitled to hold property in his name as a right which had accrued prior to the passing of Law 3/1885, claimed that they, too, were entitled to have this property passed on to them as heirs of the holder. The effect of the Court's decision in the case was that the legal "dominium" in the stands in question was at the time of Aboobaker's insolvency in Lucas, who was a friend of the Indians, and who, at their request, held the stand licences for them as they were prevented by the terms of the Gold Law No. 15/1898 and Law 3/1885 from so doing. Secondly, the Court decided that Lucas must be regarded in law as holding the stands not as trustee for the Indians but in his individual capacity. Thirdly, that the Indians, though not registered owners of the stands and, therefore, not holders of the dominium, having been in continuous occupation for a considerable time and being able to show that they effected considerable improvements on the stands during their occupation were entitled to a compensation of £650 for the improvements made.[29]

Though Lord Selborne was sympathetic with the plight of the heirs of Aboobaker Amod, he was unable to advise that Article 2 of Law 3/1885, which imposed on Asiatics restrictions in regard to the ownership of property, be repealed. He said that the Government was in honour bound to mitigate the undoubted hardships Asiatics, who were in the country legitimately, were experiencing. Where it appeared, said Selborne, that laws passed by the late Republic or laws passed by the Crown Colony Government operated harshly on the Asiatics in ways which were not foreseen, and which were not intended, then it was the duty of the Government to modify those laws. At the same time the Government had to assure the Legislature that it was doing everything possible to check a general influx of Asiatics into the country.

In bringing his argument and opinion to bear more specifically in the case of the heirs of Aboobaker Amod, Lord Selborne said that he agreed that the heirs of Aboobaker Amod were prevented by the technical wording of Law 3/1885 from inheriting the estate due to them. He agreed also that the Legislature should redress their grievances.[30]

Though Lord Selborne advised administrative concessions in the case of laws operating harshly against Asiatics, he was unable to go as far as advocating the repeal of such laws for the "feeling, in fact, on this subject is so strong that the Government could only carry an amending Ordinance by a vigorous use of the official majority".

At the same time he was desirous of closing the loopholes that allowed illegal immigrants to enter the country and obtain registration certificates by fraudulent means and sometimes with the connivance of Government officials. He informed Lord Elgin that he proposed to pass legislation which would enable Asiatics, within a specified date, to place their names on a new register and to receive new certificates of registration. This proposal was a violation of the assurances given to the Indians by Milner in 1903 when he appealed for voluntary registration of all Indians in the Transvaal.

The result was the appearance of the Asiatic Law Amendment Ordinance on the 22nd August, 1906. The decision of the Transvaal Government to introduce the Ordinance was precipitated by the case of Lucas Trustees versus Ismail and Amod in which the Supreme Court ruled, inter alia, that under Law 3/1885 "children were not subject to registration". This ruling threw doubt upon whether Asiatics not trading on their own behalf were subject to Law 3. The Government then decided to clear up the matter with a new Bill, subjecting every Indian to registration.

In terms of the Ordinance every Indian man, woman, or child of eight years of age, who were entitled to reside in the Transvaal, had to register their names with the Registrar of Asiatics and take out certificates of registration; old permits had to be surrendered and applicants had to give their names, residence, age, and caste. Important marks of identification as well as finger and thumb impressions were to be taken. Failure to register was an offence punishable by fine, imprisonment or deportation.

Asiatics who were deemed for the purpose of the Ordinance to be lawfully resident in the Transvaal were those who were duly authorised to enter and reside in the colony by a permit issued under the Peace Preservation Ordinance; those who had been in the Transvaal or the Orange River Colony on 31st May, 1902; those born in these colonies since the 31st May, 1902, but not the descendants of labourers imported into the Transvaal under the Labour Importation Ordinance of 1904. Trading licences would not be granted to Asiatics except upon production of a registration certificate.

M. K. Gandhi – one of the Indian leaders – reacted immediately to the proposed Ordinance and commented that there was "nothing in it except hatred of Indians".[31]

Gandhi had hitherto spoken out against discriminatory legislation. But he also rendered support to any deserving cause. He had organised the Indian Ambulance Corps in the War of 1899–1902. In 1901 he had returned to India where he set up a legal practice the following year. He had promised to return should the Indian community in South Africa require his services again. This call was not long in coming. When Joseph Chamberlain, Secretary of State for the Colonies, visited South Africa in 1902, Indians in the country wanted Gandhi to lead their deputations to Chamberlain and to assist in the preparation of their case.

Though Gandhi was permitted to make representations to Chamberlain in Natal, he was denied permission by the Asiatic Immigration Department to lead a deputation of Indians in the Transvaal. This denial was of the utmost importance in many respects for it impelled Gandhi to remain in the Transvaal and resist the difficulties posed by the Asiatic Immigration Department. He said of this experience:

"I must no longer think of returning to India within a year, but must get enrolled in the Transvaal Supreme Court. I have confidence enough to deal with this new department. If we do not do this, the community will be hounded out of the country, besides being thoroughly robbed. Every day it will have fresh insults heaped upon it."[32]

Thus Gandhi stayed on. When the Zulu Rebellion broke out in Natal in 1906, he saw in the event an opportunity to serve once again with an Indian Ambulance Corps. The Zulu Rebellion had an important bearing on his life and through this on the lives of other Indians in the country. It revealed to him the stark horrors of war and awakened a realisation that that form of violence was "no war, but a man-hunt".[33] Two important results emerged from the "heart searchings" that Gandhi experienced during the Rebellion. One of these was the consolidation of his feelings about non-violent methods of protest; the other was the need to renounce worldly life and to become an ascetic. Since 1900 he had been troubled by this thought and no decision had yet been taken, though he had observed the life of chastity "willy-nilly since 1900". During the Rebellion he moved relentlessly towards a decision "that I should have more and more occasions for service of the kind I was rendering, and that I should find myself unequal to my task if I were engaged in the pleasures of family life and in the propagation and rearing of children". Towards the end of 1906 he took the vow of "brahmacharya" (chastity) for life.

The transformation that took place in Gandhi's psycho-physical attitudes is significant because it shows that Gandhi was a changed man and that the change was to be clearly manifest in his leadership of the Indian cause in the country from 1906 to 1914.

It was when this transformation had already taken place that the Draft Asiatic Law Amendment Ordinance appeared in 1906. Gandhi objected to its terms on many grounds. It stipulated that registration was compulsory. Gandhi saw serious implications in this compulsory registration. Any police officer could demand to see the registration certificate at any time and place and from any Asiatic; defaulters could be deported; the compulsory requirement of finger-prints presupposed that the Asiatics were looked upon as criminals; he objected to the registration of women and of children under sixteen. The Ordinance appeared to him as the thin end of the wedge which was directed at driving the Indians out of the Transvaal. To resist it was therefore a question of honour, not only to the Indians in the Transvaal but throughout South Africa as well as India.

The position created by the Draft Ordinance of 1906 was different in various details from that of the Peace Preservation Ordinance of 1903. On the latter occasion registration was voluntary; it did not embrace women and children under sixteen; thumb-prints were required only of those who could not sign their names. There was no demand for finger-prints as well as thumb-prints.

The Draft Ordinance of 1906 did not stop with local implications. There were other implications as Gandhi saw them and the worst of these was the insult to India implied in its provisions. Gandhi reasoned that an "insult offered to a single innocent member of a nation is tantamount to insulting the nation as a whole."[34] In this interpretation can be seen the rapidity with which the Indian question in the Transvaal was beginning to loom large in the international sphere.

The Transvaal Indians moved into action against the Ordinance. The Transvaal British Indian Association, which was founded by Gandhi in 1903, organised a public protest meeting of some 3 000 British Indians at the Empire Theatre, Johannesburg on 11th September, 1906. At this meeting several important resolutions were passed, the most important of which was the Fourth Resolution which read:

> "In the event of the Legislative Council, the Local Government, and the Imperial Authorities rejecting the humble prayer of the British Indian community of the Transvaal in connection with the Draft Asiatic Law Amendment Ordinance, this mass meeting of British Indians here assembled solemnly and regretfully resolves that, rather than submit to the galling, tyrannous, and un-British requirements laid down in the above Draft Ordinance, every British Indian in the Transvaal shall submit to imprisonment, and shall continue so to do until it shall please His Most Gracious Majesty the King-Emperor to grant relief."[35]

It was also resolved to send a deputation to England to present the case of British Indians in the Transvaal before the public there and to the Imperial Ministry, and to endeavour to persuade the British Government to withhold Royal assent.

Meanwhile, the Draft Ordinance was passed by the Transvaal Legislature in the form of the Asiatic Law Amendment Ordinance, No. 29/1906. The Transvaal British Indian Association informed the Secretary of State for Colonies through the Governor of the Transvaal that it was sending an Indian deputation to England. On 21st September, 1906, the Secretary of State, Lord Elgin, instructed the Governor of the Transvaal, Lord Selborne, to inform the British Indian Association that the Ordinance in question had received the approval of the Secretary of State and that no useful purpose would therefore be served by sending a deputation to England.[36]

The Transvaal British Indian Association, however, persisted in their resolve to send a deputation to England. They sent a telegram to Lord Elgin expressing regret that he had approved of the Ordinance and informing him that M. K. Gandhi and H. O. Ally would be proceeding to England forthwith. This determination paid dividends and the Secretary of State gave way and informed the Transvaal Governor that the Ordinance would not receive Royal assent until the deputation had arrived and had received a hearing.[37]

The deputation reached England towards the end of October, 1906. Gandhi and Ally met influential sympathisers such as the first two Indian members of the House of Commons, Dadabhai Naoraji and Sir M. M. Bhownaggre, as well as Sir Lepel Griffin. The British Committee of the Indian National Congress gave the deputation much assistance and guidance. The deputation also put forward its case at a meeting of the Committee of the House of Commons for Indian Affairs. To enable all sympathisers and institutions desirous of helping the deputation to meet on a common platform the South Africa British Indian Committee was founded. The President of this Committee was Lord Ampthill and the Secretary, L. W. Ritch, a South African White who had been articled to Gandhi in the Transvaal at an earlier date and who was then a student for the bar in London.[38]

When the deputation met the Secretary of State for the Colonies on the 8th November, 1906 its leader, M. K. Gandhi, pointed out that the Peace Preservation Ordinance of 1902–3 had the situation concerning Indians under control and was severe enough in its application to them; that the proposed Ordinance was in fact no progressive amendment but a repressive one, giving no relief whatsoever to the Indians; that there was no considerable unauthorised influx of Indians in the Transvaal; that the best solution to the problem of British Indians in the Transvaal would be the appointment of a Commission before any drastic measures were taken. The British Government could not see its way clear to appoint a Commission at this stage because of the impending grant of Responsible Government to the Transvaal.

But the deputation's representations were not wholly unrewarding. In one very important respect there was victory for the deputation, even though it turned out to be a Pyrrhic victory in the final analysis. On the 29th November, 1906, Lord Elgin informed Lord Selborne as follows:

". . . At the present time the position is by no means so simple as it was when I approved your original proposals. . . . Messrs. Gandhi and Ally have come to this country as the representatives of the British Indian Association, and though I have been informed that the British Indian community in the Transvaal does not accept them with complete unanimity as its spokesmen, I must, in the absence of stronger evidence to the contrary, regard them as really representative of the majority of their compatriots. They have protested against the Ordinance, not on the ground that it affords inadequate relief, but on the ground that it actually aggravates the disabilities from which they at present suffer; and they have urged that the retention unamended of the provisions of Law No. 3 of 1885 would be preferable to the allowance of the new Ordinance."

Lord Elgin's decision was in effect a rejection of the Ordinance and did not meet with Selborne's approval. Selborne informed Elgin that he did not think that the Ordinance was unnecessarily harassing to the Asiatics already lawfully resident in the Transvaal and that he regretted the British Government's decision not to proceed with it.[39]

The stand taken by Lord Selborne clearly indicates that the Transvaal Government was convinced of the necessity to assure the European population of that colony that there was not only sympathy for its cry to prevent Asiatics from gaining easy entry into the colony but that the sympathy would be backed by legislative action. The British Government, however, with an eye on the possible implications this held for the Commonwealth, could not be expected to see the position in the same way. Rather than be assailed in the Commonwealth family for a decision which was calculated to offend one of its members, the British Government left it to the Responsible Government of the Transvaal to take the important decision. In doing so, the British Government merely transferred the responsibility for the act to the coming Transvaal Government when it could have given the lead itself with a firm decision, especially since such a decision would be concerned with the merits and demerits of the proposed legislation and not with the side issue of who should make the decision. This postponement of the decision was an admission of weakness on the part of the British Government and was a signal to the Transvaal to proceed without fear of opposition from that quarter.

On 1st January, 1907, the Transvaal received the Responsible Government which had been promised by the Peace Treaty of Vereeniging in 1902. In March of the same year the new Parliament met and with its enhanced status it was determined to rule out the success which Gandhi and Ally had gained in England when Elgin had disallowed the Asiatic Law Amendment Ordinance, 29/1906. The Colonial Secretary, General Smuts, introduced the Asiatic Law Amendment Bill to amend Law 3 of 1885. Polak, who was one of Gandhi's closest assistants in the Transvaal and Natal, wrote as follows on the introduction of the Bill: "Within 24 hours, and practically without discussion, the old Ordinance, re-enacted, passed both Houses of Parliament, not a single member venturing to voice his protest. The memorials of the Indian community were completely ignored – in fact, in the Legislative Council, an attempt was made to prevent their being read."[40]

The new Bill was identical to the disallowed 1906 Ordinance. The objections of the Indians to the measure were therefore the same as expressed by Gandhi and Ally in England in 1906. Though the British Government was not prepared to allow the measure to pass into law in 1906, it was prepared to throw overboard its objections to it in 1907. Lord Elgin informed the Governor of the Transvaal that though the new measure was identical to the Ordinance of 1906 the fact that it was introduced by a state which enjoyed Responsible Government gave it a different weight of authority. Royal assent was recommended for this measure as was expected and it raises the issue whether an unjust and one-sided legislation which fails to receive approval under a lower type of parliamentary government is rendered equitable by the mere fact of its being passed by a responsible government representing minority interests. For those who constituted this minority rule the occasion offered much to rejoice over; for those who depended upon an overriding and benevolent or just authority to protect their interests the action of the British Government was deeply regretted.

The attainment of Responsible government seemed to invest the Transvaal legislature with the power to conduct all its affairs without fear of intervention by an overriding authority. The *Transvaal Leader*, commenting upon the action of the Transvaal Parliament in passing the measure of 1907, wrote: "It is a cause of intense satisfaction to us, and, we doubt not, to men of all parties, that the first Legislative enactment of the new Parliament should be one which asserts the right of the colony to manage its own affairs."

Members of all parties in the Transvaal Parliament gave the measure their fullest support. The election speeches made earlier in 1907 were a clear indication of this tendency. General Botha, in an election speech at Standerton, was reported to have said that if his party, the Het Volk Party, were returned to power, it would undertake to turn the "coolies" out of the country within four years. Abe Bailey, afterwards appointed Chief Whip of the Progressive Party, said at Volksrust that he was one of those who believed that it was the right thing to have the Asiatics leave the Transvaal. And General J. C. Smuts, then legal adviser to Het Volk, wrote in October, 1906 to Ralph Tatham, then leader of the Natal Labour Party: "The Asiatic cancer, which has already eaten so deeply into the vitals of South Africa, ought to be resolutely eradicated." Finally, Sir Richard Solomon, who had been the Transvaal Agent-General in England and who was himself in the running for the Premiership of the Transvaal, returned to the Transvaal from England where he had repeated conferences with Lord Elgin. He said in his first election address in Pretoria that it would be found in practice that the reservation clause in the constitution would be a dead-letter, that is the Transvaal legislature could assume unrestricted internal authority.[41]

The reservation clause was a safeguard of the utmost importance to the Asiatics in the Transvaal. The Letters Patent of the Transvaal Responsible Government Constitution provided for the reservation of any bill which subjected persons not of European birth or descent to any disability or restriction to which persons of European birth were not also subjected.

Urged on by the united efforts of Lord Selborne, General Botha, who was in England to attend the Imperial Conference of 1907, and Sir Richard Solomon, the Transvaal Agent-General in London, Lord Elgin side-stepped the reservation clause and Royal assent was advised. Thus the Asiatic Law Amendment Act, 2/1907 found its way into the statute book and a severe challenge was thrown out to those persons who were adversely affected by it. The Act was to become operative from 1st July, 1907 when all Asiatics in the Transvaal had to be registered.[42] The main grounds of opposition to the measure were that compulsory registration was repugnant to Indians as it placed them on the same footing as criminals; the requirement that registered Indians should give their finger impressions as marks of identification was galling to their self respect.[43]

Act 2 of 1907 was now an accomplished fact. What remains – before intensified Indian opposition to it is discussed – is to pin-point who was most responsible for its existence. On this point the views of A. B. Keith appear to be authoritative and penetrating. Keith observes that the British Government made no effort to secure the elementary rights of the Indians in the Transvaal before granting that colony responsible government; that the British Government should have made it a condition with that colony that in return for responsible government the Indians living there would receive just treatment. Keith takes both the Conservative and Liberal governments in England to task for their failure to protect the interests of the Indians in the Transvaal. As for the attitude of the Boers on this issue, Keith states that theirs was a consistent attitude. As it had been before the war so it was after the war – an attitude based on racial superiority; though wrong in itself this attitude had nevertheless the virtue of consistency. Above all, states Keith, the Boers owed no moral obligations to India as did the British.[44]

Keith summed up the position very aptly and in his commentary he shows up the weaknesses in British policy towards Indians in the Transvaal. With this protection gone, there was no hope that they could depend upon the remedy available through exercising the franchise. When the Constitution Committee had been sitting in the Transvaal early in 1906 preparing for the grant of Responsible Government to the Colony, the Transvaal British Indian Association pointed out that the most natural means of protecting their interests was the franchise but were informed that the Treaty of Vereeniging had specifically excluded this possibility. Winston Churchill went so far as to say in the House of Commons that the meaning given to the word "native" in South Africa included "Asiatic". Lord Milner, who had been a party to the Treaty of Vereeniging, declared that he himself had never intended to include in the term even half-castes of mixed African and European descent. H. S. L. Polak, who was on the spot at the time, writes: "At this time, too, the Imperial Government could have insisted upon the remedy of the Indian grievances prior to the grant of Responsible Government, but no bargain was attempted . . .".[45]

Any hope that the Transvaal Indians had of protection from the British Government was dispelled with Act 2 on the Statute Book. For the immediate present, self-help seemed to offer the best hopes. This remedy appeared possible in the direction of passive resistance which had been foreshadowed in the Fourth Resolution of 11th September, 1906.

As passive resistance has played such a big part in the struggle of the South African Indians and later of other non-European peoples in South Africa for improved conditions in that country, its origins deserve mention. Its theory can best be described in the words of its architect in South Africa, M. K. Gandhi: "Its equivalent in the vernacular, rendered into English, means Truth-Force. I think Tolstoy called it also Soul-Force or Love-Force, and so it is. Carried out to its utmost limit, this force is independent of pecuniary or other material assistance; certainly, even in its elementary form, of physical force or violence. Indeed, violence is the negation of this great spiritual force, which can only be cultivated or wielded by those who will entirely eschew violence. It is a force that may be used by individuals as well as by communities. It may be used as well in political as in domestic affairs. Its universal applicability is a demonstration of its permanence and invincibility."[46]

The doctrine of passive resistance was not Gandhi's original idea; neither was he the first man to use it in practice. He admitted that it was "the New Testament which really awakened me to the rightness and value of Passive Resistance"; he was particularly influenced by the Sermon on the Mount. *The Bhagavad Gita* deepened the impression created by the New Testament and Tolstoy's *The Kingdom of God is Within You* gave the impression permanent form. He was also influenced by Ruskin and Thoreau, particularly the former's *Crown of Wild Olives*. It was to passive resistance, then, that the Indians in the Transvaal now transferred their hopes.

Before the Transvaal Indians could organise their campaign against the one objectionable Act, another one was introduced imposing restrictions on entry into the Transvaal. The result was the passing of the Immigrants Restriction Act, 15/1907 which prescribed a dictation test in a European language for would-be immigrants. This Act was of general application but read together with Act 2/1907, the law treated as prohibited immigrants those who could pass its education test but were not eligible for registration.[47] Amongst the various classes of persons defined as prohibited immigrants was included any person who fell foul of any law in operation in the Transvaal at the time of his entry, by which default he could be ordered to leave the Colony. In terms of this immigration law any person who did not comply with the requirements of any other existing law would be deemed to be a prohibited immigrant.[48]

The Government of India informed the Secretary of State that it was opposed to the principle of the Bill but it recognised that the Transvaal Government had to decide the question on other considerations than the interests of the Indians in that colony. The Government of India would be satisfied if Act 2/1907 preserved the rights possessed by Indians under the Peace Preservation Ordinance of 1903.[49] The Indian Government did not go into the details of the Immigration Bill and thereby allowed this seemingly innocuous measure to go through without its opposition.

With the Indian Government adopting this placid attitude, the only real opposition centre was that organised by local Indians. Even so, it was not against the Immigrants Restriction Act that the first steps were taken. Separated from the registration law, the immigration law was a comparatively innocuous measure. It was, consequently, at the former that the first blows were aimed. Transvaal Indians formed themselves into the Passive Resistance Association. On 31st July, 1907 an open-air meeting was held in Pretoria and the momentous Fourth Resolution of 11th September, 1906 was re-affirmed, in spite of the presence at the meeting, at General Botha's request, of William Hosken, M.L.A. who brought a message from the Premier stating that Act 2 was passed in deference to the wishes of the Europeans in the Transvaal and had the force of having been endorsed by the British Government. If the In dians would co-operate the Premier said, General Smuts would look carefully at any representations made suggesting minor changes in the regulations framed under the Act. On his own behalf, Hosken advised the meeting that " the Transvaal Government is firm regarding this law. To resist it will be to dash your head against a wall".[50]

The Transvaal Indians were determined to resist the measure. To do so they resorted to passive resistance which took the form of failing to take out registration certificates and, later, hawking without licences. Between 1st July, 1907 and December, 1907 some 500 Indians only took out permits under Act 2. The former Colonial Secretary of the Transvaal Crown Colony Government, Patrick Duncan, wrote: "The Asiatic leaders had been so successful in their agitation against the Registration Act that practically the whole Asiatic population in the Transvaal had refused to comply with its provisions."[51]

Gandhi had, however, offered a compromise solution as early as April, 1907, when he undertook to get the Transvaal Indians to re-register voluntarily provided Act 2 was repealed. His offer was rejected. Again in September, 1907, a petition bearing nearly 5 000 signatures of members of the Indian community was addressed to the Transvaal Government, making the offer of voluntary re-registration conditional upon the suspension of the operation of Act 2, and its subsequent repeal if voluntary re-registration were successful. Again the offer was rejected.[52]

With the rejection of the compromise suggestions put forward by the Indian leaders, the struggle in the Transvaal was now actively on. The first arrest for failure to comply with the Act requiring Asiatics to take out permits of registration was effected on 8th November, 1907, when Pandit Ram Sunder of Germiston was arrested. He was sentenced to a month's imprisonment. His example set the pattern for hundreds to follow.

The arrest of Pandit Ram Sunder marks the beginning of the great passive resistance struggle in the Transvaal. The details in connection with this struggle are described in detail in an earlier publication by the writer.[53] Only those local features which have a bearing on the international aspects of this study and international events resulting from the local developments will be traced here.

The principal parties in this stirring epoch were, for the Indians in the country, M. K. Gandhi, assisted by his journal, *Indian Opinion*; for the Transvaal Government, the Colonial Secretary, General J. C. Smuts, with the colony's legislature and European population solidly behind him; abroad, the Indian and British Governments, with the Indian Government prepared to help in many ways, though its Executive and Legislature were still controlled by British personnel, and the British Government with its sympathy and little else. In both India and Great Britain there was a formidable force of public opinion on the side of the Indians and no small number of active sympathisers of both races.

The struggle which Gandhi preferred to call "Satyagraha",[54] with the passive resisters called "Satyagrahis", was recorded in the columns of *Indian Opinion*. The journal explained, in a nutshell, why Indians were opposing the Act: "The answer is, because the Act, read in conjunction with events that preceded it, is one that takes away the very manhood from British Indians who claim to be just as civilised as the law-givers themselves in all the essentials of life."[55]

On the other hand, the stand taken by General Smuts was an emphatic commentary on Government policy and it left little room for compromise. In a speech delivered at Melville, Smuts said that he would not repeal the Act. He said that the Indians objected to the Act because it was class legislation and because they should not be differentiated against as they were British subjects. Smuts agreed that it was class legislation, as it had always been since 1885 and if the Indians objected to having their finger-prints taken he pointed out that they had submitted to having that done since 1903 and that there had always been social or sectional distinction between them and the Europeans.

The viewpoints of the opposing parties being irreconcilable, a compromise solution, which was the only solution possible, was difficult to arrive at. However, in the new year of 1908, the editor of the *Transvaal Leader*, Albert Cartwright, made a move in the direction of a compromise. Gandhi who, with 25 other leaders, had been summoned to appear before the court in Johannesburg on 28th December, 1907, was sentenced to two months' imprisonment on 11th January, 1908 for failing to be in possession of the new registration permit. He had not been in jail for a fortnight when Cartwright began his mediation between Smuts and Gandhi.

The substance of the proposed settlement was that the Indians should register voluntarily and not under any law; that the details to be entered in the new certificates of registration should be settled in consultation with the Indian community; that once the majority of Indians underwent voluntary registration, the Government should repeal Act 2/1907 and then legalise the voluntary registration.

The draft scheme submitted to Gandhi by Cartwright did not make quite clear the conditions under which the Government would repeal Act 2. When Gandhi sought a change to place this beyond all doubt, Cartwright informed him that Smuts considered the draft to be final and that Act 2 would be repealed once voluntary re-registration was completed.

On 28th January, 1908, a letter signed by Gandhi and his two colleagues, Leuing Quinn and Thambi Naidoo, was sent to General Smuts informing him that they agreed to the terms of the compromise put forward by Cartwright. They did not recapitulate the fears they had expressed to Cartwright that repeal of the Act under certain conditions should be unequivocally spelt out in the agreement. Theirs was an assumption that that was what Cartwright's mediation was aimed at.

On 30th January, Gandhi was taken from prison in Johannesburg to Pretoria for an interview with Smuts. At this interview Gandhi reported that Smuts told him that he was only doing his duty towards the Europeans in the Transvaal who wanted the Act in question; these Europeans, he said, were mostly Englishmen. Smuts informed Gandhi that once the Indians had undergone voluntary re-registration he would repeal Act 2 and legalise the registration under another Act.[56]

There remained some uncertainty about the steps the Government would take once the Indians had carried out their part of the bargain. This uncertainty was further magnified when Gandhi interviewed the Registrar of Asiatics, Chamney. Following immediately on this interview Gandhi wrote to Smuts on 1st February, 1908 pointing out that he understood from Chamney that the voluntary registration agreed upon would be legalised under Act 2 and that if this was so the question was being re-opened at the sorest point, the retention of Act 2.[57]

Whatever the Government's intentions in the matter, one fact remained incontrovertible. The Indian leaders had clearly expressed their wishes and their expectations, leaving no room for doubt or uncertainty. They desired that once voluntary re-registration was accomplished, the Asiatic Law Amendment Act, 2/1907, should be repealed and that the voluntary re-registration should be legalised under another Act.

There is sufficient documentary proof to show that Smuts knew exactly what was desired by the Indians and what was expected of him. A few days after receiving Gandhi's letter expressing concern at Chamney's statements, General Smuts spoke at Richmond on 5th February, 1908. In the speech which was reported in the *Star* on 6th February, Smuts said that the Act would not be repealed as long as a single Asiatic had not complied with its requirements.[58] The logical inference was that once all Asiatics had re-registered the Act would be repealed.

Acting on this assumption Gandhi advised that voluntary re-registration should be undertaken speedily. Educated persons, merchants, and property holders could give their signatures instead of the ten finger-prints required in terms of the Act. Some Indians, especially a section of the Muslim population called the Pathans, disagreed with Gandhi on the matter of voluntary re-registration. They suggested that the obnoxious Act 2/1907 should be repealed first, and that registration should follow – not precede – its repeal. Basing his arguments on grounds of trust, Gandhi proceeded with his plans. The immediate result of this was that Gandhi was brutally assaulted by a Pathan, Mir Alam, when he was on his way to re-register on 10th February, 1908. After this assault the Government gave way to the objections of Muslims to the giving of ten finger-prints and it became optional for those who desired on religious grounds to give thumb-prints instead of finger-prints.

Voluntary re-registration went on. In the three months which ended in May, 1908, Indians re-registered in terms of the compromise of January, 1908. But instead of repealing Act 2/1907, Smuts announced that he would pilot through Parliament the Asiatics Registration Amendment Bill which would validate voluntary re-registration by way of amending Act 2 but not repealing it. Thus a new position was created which was unacceptable to the Indians.

On 13th June, 1908, Gandhi wrote to Smuts pointing out that the Asiatics who had not yet entered the country but who were entitled to do so should be treated in the same way as those who had voluntarily taken out certificates of registration; refugees who were not in possession of Peace Preservation Ordinance permits but who had been resident in the Transvaal before the outbreak of war (i.e. before 1899) should be protected and should be allowed to prove their claims before a court of law; Asiatics who were in possession of other documents issued in the Transvaal should be protected; those whose educational qualifications merited it should be treated as the European immigrants were treated; and, finally, Asiatics whose applications for citizenship were being considered by Chamney, or had already been refused by him, should be permitted to have their applications decided by a court of law.[59]

No favourable reply was received and the Passive Resistance Association sent a letter to the Transvaal Government asking that Act 2/1907 be repealed and stating that if a favourable reply were not received by 16th August, 1908, all registration certificates would be burnt in a cauldron. About 3 000 Indians from all parts of the Transvaal collected outside the Hamidia Mosque at Fordsburg, Johannesburg, on the appointed day, 16th August. A number of Chinese were also present. A significant fact concerning the meeting was that representatives from political bodies in Natal and the Cape were also present. The internal developments in the Transvaal were fast attracting the attention and sympathy of the other colonies in the country. The Natal Indian Congress and the Capetown British Indian League were represented by their respective Presidents.[60]

As the meeting was about to commence a telegram was received from the Transvaal Government regretting the determination of the Indian community and announcing that Government would not change its line of action. It remained for the Indians to strengthen theirs. United action was one way of achieving this. Commenting on the presence at the meeting of representatives from the Cape and Natal, the Chairman of the Transvaal British Indian Association, Essop Ismail Mia, said that they had come to assist the Transvaal Indians and to show that they were as ready to suffer as those in the Transvaal; their presence demonstrated that the question in the Transvaal was a South African question; indeed, an Imperial question. Mia repeated the demands made on 13 June, 1908 in the letter sent by Gandhi to Smuts. These demands constituted the claims of the Transvaal Indians for a just settlement of their grievances on questions of registration and immigration in that colony. He said that the Transvaal Indians went about honouring the compromise arrangement of February, 1908, in the sincere belief that it would lead to an improvement in their position. Smuts' failure to carry out his part of the bargain had now compelled the Indians to destroy the certificates which they had taken out in terms of the compromise. The Secretary of the Association, M. K. Gandhi, addressed the gathering and exhorted all those who were present never to submit to unjust legislation.

After Mia and Gandhi had addressed the gathering, a large three-legged pot was filled with the registration certificates, about 1 300 in all, and about 500 trading licences. Paraffin was then poured in and the certificates set on fire.

The meeting ended with the adoption of three resolutions protesting against the Asiatic Voluntary Registration Validation Bill; re-affirming the resolution of the Indian community not to submit to the Asiatic Act and affirming that the Asiatic Voluntary Registration Validation Bill was a breach of the compromise entered into by the Government with the Asiatic communities and hoping that the colonists would demand an honourable fulfilment of the terms entered into by General Smuts on behalf of the Transvaal Government and in their name.[61]

The burning of the registration certificates was an indication that the compromise of February, 1908 was at an end and that the Indians were ready to prosecute their campaign of passive resistance in keeping with the six-point programme outlined in Gandhi's letter to General Smuts of 13th June, 1908.

The Transvaal Government took early cognizance of the determination of the Indians to carry on with the struggle. Two days after the burning of the certificates, a meeting took place between representatives of the Asiatics, the Prime Minister, General Botha, the Colonial Secretary, General Smuts, and representatives of the Parliamentary Opposition. Nine points were put forward by the Asiatics as representing their final demands. On eight of these, including the much disputed Act 2/1907, the Transvaal Government granted concessions. But with regard to Act 2 the concession offered was that while the Act was to remain on the Statute Book the Government promised to exempt from its provisions all Asiatics holding certificates under the new Act, the Asiatic Voluntary Registration Validation Act. The ninth – and last point – led to a break up of the meeting. This point was the demand that educated Asiatics should be allowed to come into the colony subject to the same tests as Europeans.

On the issue of educated Asiatics and their admission into the Transvaal, General Smuts accused Gandhi of making capital in a matter which was never the focal point at dispute. The argument of the Indians, on the other hand, was that complete stoppage of fresh immigration would "eventually result in communal deterioration, corruption and final effacement".[62]

The question of the entry of educated Indians into the Transvaal led to the failure of the meeting of 18th August, 1908. With this failure, all hopes of a solution at the conference table were dashed for the moment. The Transvaal Government went its way and the Asiatics went their way.

On 21st August, 1908, the Colonial Secretary, General Smuts, moved the Second

Reading of the Asiatic Voluntary Registration Validation Bill. He said, *inter alia*: "They say that a promise was made to repeal Act 2 of 1907; but from the Correspondence that has been laid on the Table of the House it will be seen that there never was the slightest intention of repealing the Act."[63] This was how Smuts always saw it.

The Act finally became law as Act 36/1908. Writing many years later on the part played by General Smuts in bringing Act 36 about, Gandhi said that "the General's action did not perhaps amount to an intentional breach of faith. . . . It could not be described as breach of faith if the intention was absent. My experience of General Smuts in 1913–14 did not then seem bitter and does not seem so to me today, when I can think of the past events with a greater sense of detachment. It is quite possible that in behaving to the Indians as he did in 1908 General Smuts was not guilty of a deliberate breach of faith".[64] This was a charitable view not quite borne out by the General's conduct. It left the Indians with no choice but to test the operation of the registration and immigration laws by all non-violent methods available.

The Passive Resistance Association which was in charge of the passive resistance campaign and which was called the Satyagraha Committee by Gandhi chose an educated Indian from Natal, Sorabji Shapurji, who had not been to the Transvaal before, for purposes of testing whether an Indian with sufficient education could demand entry into the Transvaal under the Immigrants Restriction Act. Hitherto all Indians who courted imprisonment in protest against Act 2/1907 were Transvaal residents. The participation of Sorabji Shapurji meant that Indians from Natal were ready to take an active part in the struggle in the Transvaal.

On 27th June, 1908, it was decided that in view of General Smuts' contention that his interpretation of the Immigrants Restriction Act excluded Indians with educational attainments, Shapurji, a well-educated Parsee Indian of Charlestown, would bring in a test case. On 8th July, it was learnt that Shapurji who had entered the colony was now a prisoner in the Transvaal and was being prosecuted under the Asiatic Law Amendment Act and not the Immigrants Restriction Act, that is under the registration law and not the immigration law. He was sentenced to one month's imprisonment. The arrest and imprisonment of Sorabji Shapurji fired the Indians with greater enthusiasm in the Transvaal and in Natal. The prevention by law of the entry of educated Indians into the Transvaal meant that the Colony was to be deprived of the services of professional men who were the only people to ensure that standards of civilization among the Indian people in the Transvaal would not be lowered.

The significance of the Shapurji case was that the passive resistance campaign was intensified by the entry of other Indians from Natal into the Transvaal. Both traders and educated men from Natal now crossed into the Transvaal. The following sequence of events generally followed: they were arrested, ordered to leave the Transvaal within 7 days, re-arrested on failing to carry this out, deported without trial, and, finally, when they re-entered the Transvaal after deportation, they were sentenced to a fine of £50 or three months' imprisonment with hard labour. All elected to go to prison.

Almost simultaneously with the Shapurji case came the notice from the Registrar of Asiatics on 7th July, 1908, instructing Licensing Officers in the Transvaal that it had been decided to retain the Asiatic Law Amendment Act on the Statute Book and that Asiatics, whether voluntary registrants or otherwise, had to comply with the requirements of the said Act in order to receive their licences. The result was that Asiatic traders now began trading without licences in order to court arrest in line with the passive resistance campaign. A contemporary estimate of the number of Indians who courted arrest and imprisonment at this time was 120.

While Asiatic traders thus resorted to trading without licences, Gandhi, in a letter to Chaplin, the Registrar of Asiatics, pointed out that the "Indians did not ask for anything new at all under the Immigrants Restriction Act. Indians with educational attainments can enter not as a matter of form, but as a matter of right. It is General Smuts who now asks Indians to consent to an alteration of that law so as to make such Indians prohibited immigrants".[65] The position was that whereas educated Indians could gain entry into the Transvaal by passing the dictation test in the immigration law, they could not remain in the colony in terms of the registration law. The Immigrants Restriction Act and its bearing on Asiatics were further aired in the case of Laloo v. Rex in which Laloo appealed against judgment given against him when he was charged with contravening Section 25 of the Immigrants Restriction Act, in that "being unable to write in European characters, having insufficient means to support himself, and being the son of a prohibited immigrant", he was himself a prohibited immigrant. Sir William Solomon in giving judgment said that Laloo could not write any document in a European language. The appellant failed because it was proved that he was unable to fulfil the requirements of the educational test, i.e. to write out from dictation a sentence in a European language.

Commenting upon the judgment in the case of Laloo v. Rex, Gandhi said: "It will, therefore, be seen that according to the learned Judge, the Immigrants Restriction Act does not debar Asiatics possessing educational qualifications from entering the country."[66]

What, then, was the point at dispute between Smuts and Gandhi over the Immigrants Restriction Act? The following seems to be the answer. During the negotiations between Smuts and Gandhi in regard to voluntary re-registration, the question arose as to how such voluntary registration should be legalised, seeing that the time prescribed by the Registration Act (Asiatic Law Amendment Act, 2/1907) had expired and Gandhi still expected that the Act itself would be repealed. Gandhi suggested a slight amendment of the Immigration Law (Immigrants Restriction Act, 15/1907), which, while it retained the definition of prohibited immigrant, excluded from that term those who had taken out voluntary certificates, as well as domiciled absentees who should, within a certain period, voluntarily apply for them. General Smuts appeared to have had no objection to this course provided that Gandhi consented to a further amendment completely shutting out Indian strangers, irrespective of their educational qualifications as required by the Act as it then stood. Smuts was willing to repeal the registration law if Gandhi would consent to such an amendment. Gandhi declined, arguing that he had bargained for the repeal of the registration law upon one condition, namely, voluntary registration, which condition the Indians had practically fulfilled, and that if there had been any misunderstanding and the repeal of the registration law was not to take place, he must revert to the *status quo ante*. Gandhi argued that Smuts was at liberty to construe the immigration law as already shutting out all Indians as such, by reading it in conjunction with the registration law. Smuts, however, declined to do this, preferring to read the immigration law by itself, and the construction that Smuts therefore placed on it was that Indians were by its term under no other disabilities than any other class of would-be immigrant. That, of course, could not be the position as the immigration law (Act 15/1907) had to be read together with the registration law (Act 2/1907).

These, then, were the points of friction between the Indians in the Transvaal and the Government, which were to lead to serious international complications in New Delhi and London, though the Indian and British Governments did not seem to be able to influence any appreciable changes in the existing conditions. Both these Governments, however, saw the need and felt the urgency for intervention on behalf of the Transvaal Indians.

The Secretary of State for India, Lord Morley, in a despatch to the Colonial Office, London, on 30th September, 1908, pointed out that the Transvaal Government was entirely responsible for the troubles caused by the passing of the Immigration Restriction Act which, on the surface, required an education test to be passed but which, deep down, rendered this stipulation nugatory by other provisions not easily understood except by trained minds. The Indians in the Transvaal were, consequently, disappointed to learn that the immigration law was not the same as in force in Natal and the Cape.[67]

For the difficulties that had now arisen the Government of India were also to blame for not having given the details of the Immigration Bill their serious attention when it had been submitted for the attention and comment of that Government.

The Government of India viewed the position in the Transvaal with great concern. On 30th January, 1908 it sent a lengthy despatch to Lord Morley, Secretary of State for India, in which it was stated that while it realised that it was too late to protest against the immigration law itself it was not late to ask that in the administration of the law respectable and educated Indians would not be subjected to harassing restrictions imposed on the inferior class of Indians. The despatch went on to state that though the demands made recently in the Transvaal by the Indians went farther than any made by the Government of India itself it had to be admitted that at the bottom of the agitation there were real grievances which might be removed by friendly intervention. The Government of India viewed with the greatest concern the possibility of a feeling being established that the British Government had failed to protect its Indian subjects from worse treatment than they had to endure in the Transvaal under foreign rulers.[68]

In the same vein, Transvaal Indians sent a petition in September, 1908 to the British Government asking for its intervention to end the struggle in the Transvaal. In this petition sworn affidavits were attached to the effect that the Registrar of Asiatics had assured Indians that the Asiatic Law Amendment Act would be repealed after the voluntary re-registration had been effected. This appeal was in vain.

The only remedy seemed to be to court arrest. On the 24th October, 1908, Gandhi was arrested at Volksrust. Before being imprisoned, he anticipated the struggle ahead when he sent the following historic message to the Indians: "Keep absolutely firm to the end. Suffering is our only remedy. Victory is certain." Victory at the end was what the Transvaal Government hoped for as well. The struggle was unequal. There were just about 13 000 Indians in the Transvaal at the time.

According to Polak, who was editor of *Indian Opinion* from 1906 to 1916 and who was also Assistant Secretary of the Transvaal British Indian Association, it was estimated that from the beginning of January, 1908 until the end of June, 1909, no less than 2 500 sentences of imprisonment, varying from three days to six months, had been imposed by the Transvaal Courts on Indians. Some Indians had been to prison over six times and their ages ranged from 16 to 60.[69]

Polak states that in order to break the resistance of the Transvaal Indians, the Transvaal Government entered into a secret compact with the Natal Government whereby the latter refused to allow Indians returning to the Transvaal from India, via Natal, to land unless they agreed to apply for registration under the new Act, 36/1908; the alternative was their compulsory return to India. With this same object in view the Transvaal Government made a secret compact with the Portuguese Administration of the province of Mozambique, whereby British Indians who were arbitrarily deported from the Transvaal would be taken to the Portuguese port of Lourenço Marques and thence deported to India. The Transvaal Government realised that it would be legally impossible for the Government of Natal or the Cape Colony to do this friendly act for them as the deportee could apply to the Supreme Courts of these colonies for his release on the ground that, "having been forcibly removed from the Transvaal, and not being therefore a willing entrant into those territories, he was not a prohibited immigrant, and could not therefore be deported by sea".

The Imperial Government did not oppose this manner of deportation on the ground that only non-domiciled British Indians were being deported in this manner, and that therefore they had no legal right of residence. This, however, was not always the case, as legally domiciled Indians were also among the deported.

Fine, imprisonment and deportation were the prescribed punishment for offenders under the Asiatic Law Amendment Act. The first two had not deterred the Indians from continuing their opposition to the Act. The Transvaal Government now resorted to deportation. It is not possible to arrive at the total number of Indians deported though, on the testimony of a high authority, no less than a thousand deportations to India from the Transvaal had taken place through the port of Lourenço Marques. It is safe to estimate the number at several hundreds. On one occasion alone, 92 Indians were deported to India. On another, 54 Indians were deported. When this latter group was deported it re-entered the Transvaal and filed an appeal to the High Court.

The sub-section under which this party of 54 was convicted gave the definition of a prohibited immigrant. In his judgment, Chief Justice Innes commented on this subsection in the following words: "That is a definition clause. Now one's general idea of a definition is that it is intended to explain what might otherwise be obscure. . . . I have seldom seen a definition which needed so much defining and so difficult of application to the statute to which it related. Nobody can be positive about the meaning of this subsection."[70]

The framers of the Act must have known quite clearly what the Act and all its subsections were aimed at even if the judiciary now experienced difficulty in interpreting them. The deportations which started in 1908 raised a storm of protest in India and in England. But they had the effect the Government desired. Gandhi himself confessed: "Not all could overcome the fear of being deported to India. Many more fell away and only the real fighters remained." One might easily say that for the real fighters the real fight remained.

The resentment of Indians in the Transvaal was increased by further anti-Asiatic legislation. Two measures were passed in 1908 which materially affected the trading rights of Asiatics. These were the Townships Amendment Act, 34/1908 and the Precious and Base Metals Act, 35/1908. The latter Act and certain provisions of the former Act applied to "proclaimed land", i.e., to land proclaimed as a public digging. On lands so proclaimed non-whites were debarred from trading or from mining. These restrictions led to litigation and to increasing uncertainty but for the moment the main focus rested on the immigration and registration laws.

Indians in the Transvaal were, in the important year of 1908, preoccupied with, what was for them, a titanic struggle, the passive resistance campaign to gain the repeal of Act 2/1907 and to ensure that highly-educated Indians would not be prevented from entering the Transvaal. To this end, they had received the sympathy and the active support of Indians from Natal, traders and professional men alike. But Natal had its own internal upheavals and external difficulties with the resident Indian population in that colony. The struggle of the Indians in the Transvaal and in Natal was gradually assuming the same colour and was soon to develop into a concerted struggle.

The complaints and objections raised against the Indian community by the Europeans in Natal were on much the same lines as in the Transvaal, so far as the social and economic aspects were concerned. The general picture in Natal was that whereas the Government of Natal was urged by suger and other industrial interests to ensure the continuance of the system of labour immigration from India, it was at the same time prevailed upon by European interests to oppose the untramelled trading activities of Indians.

The continuance of the indentured labour system placed a responsibility on the authorities in Natal to ensure fair standards of treatment of labourers employed in the colony. It also meant that the natural consequence would be the increase of the free Indian population of Natal. This increase was certain to affect the trading activities of Indians. The result seemed to be the creation of a vicious circle, with the fault at the beginning, not along the line or anywhere at the end.

In Natal, after a time, the question of Indians became a single one with the old distinction of indentured and free Indians giving way to Indians as a people for it was obvious that ultimately all Indians would become free Indians with a stake in the South African sun.

The indenture system was one of the thorny aspects of Indian life in Natal. Many contemporary statements found fault with this system. Some likened it to a form of slavery where the employee was nothing more than a commercial asset. The system gave rise to grave complaints of ill-treatment on the part of the employers of this labour; the Protector of Indian Immigrants could not afford the complete protection expected of him where thousands of workers were scattered over hundreds of miles. This was one aspect of Indian life in Natal which drew forth bitter denunciations not only in Natal but in Britain and in India.

An important though reprehensible link between indentured and free Indians was the £3 tax imposed by Act 17/1895 on those ex-indentured Indians who elected to remain in Natal after the expiry of their indentures.

According to the report of the Indian Immigration Commission (the Clayton Commission) of 1909 the collection of the £3 tax was not strictly enforced from 1901 to 1903 (it must be remembered, however, that the Government of India had insisted at the time of the Binns–Mason mission to India in 1893–4 that failure to pay the residential tax was not to be deemed to be a criminal offence) but after this date the enforcement of the tax was effective to a very large extent. According to information supplied to the Commission by the Protector of Indian Immigrants, out of a total number of 7 735 Indians who came out of their first or subsequent indentures in 1908, 3 989 returned to India and 3 304 re-indentured; only 342 Indians, representing 4 per cent of the total, were therefore liable to pay the tax. The rest of the immigrants, either being unable to pay the tax or for other reasons, chose the other option available.

The Protector himself admitted that the £3 tax was onerous. In his report for 1908 he stated: "Another sign of the growing difficulty of living experienced by the free Indians subject to the yearly licence of £3, is the fact that men and women re-indenture themselves and often with arrears of licences to pay. This remark applies to 1 104 men and 426 women. A good proportion may be expected, after completing their further service of two years, to avail themselves of their regained right to a free return passage to India; but so far I incline to think that most of them re-indenture from sheer necessity, and not from choice or any notion of prospective rights . . .".

The imposition of the £3 tax led to considerable hardship, especially since it was payable by a girl aged 13, a boy aged 16 and by men and women when the average monthly wage of a free labourer was between twenty and twenty-five shillings. Those who were unable to pay were charged and imprisoned.

In August, 1908, a petition was addressed by some 400 free Indians, men and women, liable to pay the £3 tax annually, to the Legislative Assembly of Natal. The petitioners recounted their difficulties and pleaded for relief. None was forthcoming.

The question of the £3 tax, in the years following 1908, was to be raised again and again in Parliamentary debates in India and in England and was to form the subject of much negotiation and communication at inter-governmental level until it finally reached explosive force in the disturbances of 1913 in South Africa. The £3 tax – though not the only unfavourable aspect in the indenture laws and system and a burden which did not overshadow the other evil aspects such as treatment of indentured labourers and the extremely high suicide rates among Indians on the Estates – was seen as the culminating point in an evil system and strenuous efforts were therefore made both internally and externally to seek its repeal. The other aspect of Indian life in Natal which received much attention because of its detrimental effect on those whom it concerned dealt with Indian traders and their trading activities.

The Indian trader in Natal was the least welcome constituent of Natal's population as far as the European traders were concerned. His rapid progress, undoubted business sense, and desire to set himself out to please his customers, were traits not easily acceptable to the European traders who found their customers gradually going the other way.

The Dealers Licences Law was introduced in 1897 to curb the trading activities of Indian traders. Its operation gave rise to many and bitter disputes in the colony and to innumerable court cases. In most cases the Indian traders were on the losing end for in terms of Sections 5 and 6 the decision of a Licensing Officer was not liable to review, reversal or alteration by any court of law, though a right of appeal to the Town Council or the Town Board and to a special board of three persons in the case of an area outside a Borough or Township, was permitted. An appeal to a court of law could only be made on grounds of procedure not fact.

The Dealers Licences Act received the attention of the Governments of India and Great Britain. On 20th May, 1899, the Secretary of State for the Colonies advised the Natal Government that great injustice was being done in the administration of the law and if provision was not made for appeal to the Natal Supreme Court emigration from India would probably be stopped. In July, 1900, the Government of India wrote to the Government of Natal in similar terms. But no heed was taken of these desptaches,[71] and the difficulty for the Indian trader remained, only to become progressively worse.

One of these particularly bad patches was struck in 1907 when a violent wave of anti-Asiatic prejudice swept over Natal, which Polak described as follows: "The colony is subject to these periodical phrenetic outbursts of race-mania; they have almost become endemic – and an attempt was made to crush a number of the most important traders."[72]

The difficulties which followed can best be imagined when regard is had to the following two statements. The *Times of Natal* wrote: "The real coolie curse is the trader, and if the local authorities took advantage of the licensing law, as it stands, the Asiatic trader would almost disappear in the course of time." And in the *Ladysmith Gazette* the following news item appeared: "The Licensing Officer for the borough of Ladysmith has notified the local Arab Storekeepers that renewal of their licences will not be granted after the termination of the current year, and that no transfer of licences will be granted during the same period. The announcement has been met with great favour, except by the Arab storekeepers."

Indians, who had been deprived of their licences in 1907 or who were threatened by this deprivation, despairing of any relief from the Natal Parliament, convened a mass meeting at which it was resolved to appeal to the Imperial Government for intervention.[73]

Though the British Government did not intervene at that time, the next step taken by the Natal Government brought forth this intervention in resounding terms and with unequivocal force. On 21st April, 1908, the Principal Under Secretary, Natal, wrote to the Secretary of the Law Department, Natal, informing him that the Colonial Secretary required the following Bills for consideration:

(1) To provide that from and after the date of coming into operation of the Act no more Indians shall be introduced into the Colony under the provisions of the Indian Immigration Acts of the Colony.

(2) A Bill to provide that:
   (a) from and after the 31st December, 1908, no new licences shall be granted to Indians;
   (b) all existing licences (including hawkers' licences) now held by Indians shall cease on and after the 31st December, 1918;
   (c) compensation to be paid up to a sum for the loss of such licences;
   (d) an appointment be made of valuators to assess the amount of compensation to be paid to the Indians.[74]

The Bill to stop the flow of indentured labour from India was not proceeded with, as was expected, and the Government decided to appoint a Commission to go into the question of labour immigration. Though an experiment with African labour was carried out in 1908, it failed and the comments of the Protector in this regard are interesting: "For the first time for many years native men have turned out and not only cut the standing cane, but helped to load the same into trucks. Employers, however, never feel safe when depending on them, and it sometimes occurs that 100 men have to be engaged to ensure an average attendance at work of about 25. An instance of this unreliability occurred during one of my visits of inspection. The employer had 100 natives working for him, and during the night there was a slight rainfall of about $\frac{1}{4}$ inch, and as the morning broke damp only 16 men out of 100 turned up to work. The employer had to requisition Indians from the adjoining Estate."[75] Situations such as the above appear time out of number and though they provide conclusive proof of the self-interest of the colonists of Natal in the matter of the presence of Indians there they are quite conveniently shelved when the Indian question as a whole is considered. Thus we see that in the year 1908 a Bill to terminate indentured Indian labour for Natal was set aside; not so the Bills dealing with Indian trading.

The Government proceeded with its Bills on trading and submitted the draft Bills to the Imperial Government in May, 1908, prior to their introduction in the Natal Parliament. On 22nd July, 1908, the Secretary of State communicated the views of the Imperial Government in the following strong terms, which, because of their bearing on the international aspects of the Indian question, are given in some detail:

"Your Ministers will recognise that, even if for the moment account is not taken of the question of the relations between His Majesty's Government and the Indian Empire, the position of His Majesty's Government with regard to the Indians in Natal is one of peculiar responsibility. The grant of self-government to the colony was not made until 1893, and many of the Indians now within its borders were introduced before that date, while the Colony was still administered under the direct authority of the Crown. The principle followed by His Majesty's Government in dealing with recent Asiatic legislation in the Transvaal has been to defer with reluctance to the feeling in favour of excluding further Asiatic immigrants, but at the same time to aim at securing fair and proper treatment for Asiatics already in the country. His Majesty's Government are under an especial obligation to ensure that this principle should be upheld in Natal."[76]

After tracing population figures in the next paragraph, the despatch went on, in the third paragraph, to state that it was a difficult matter to justify the steps envisaged in the Bills; it reminded the Natal Government that Indians were brought to that colony to satisfy the necessities of that colony and that their numbers were augmented by the voluntary action and policy of the successive colonial governments. The despatch ended with the decision that His Majesty would not be advised to assent to the Bills in the event of their being passed by the Colonial Legislature.

It is difficult to account for the firm stand taken by the British Government with regard to the Bills to deprive Indians in Natal of their trading rights, when one remembers that in 1906 and in 1907 it was quite prepared to sanction the deprivation of rights already enjoyed by its Indian subjects in the Transvaal. It was prepared to allow the newly-appointed Responsible Government in the Transvaal in 1907 to proceed with the Asiatic Law Amendment Act, 2/1907 and the Immigrants Restriction Act, 15/1907. And now, in 1908, it was not prepared to approve of a measure which, in principle, ranks on a par with the Transvaal laws of 1907 in their effect on the lives of the Indians. Was it because of the greater British influence and interests in Natal? Or was it because of the greater number of Indians in Natal? These possibilities can hardly be depended upon for the complete answer, for both Natal and the Transvaal had Responsible Governments, with the power of veto vested in the British Government; both had Indian subjects of the same origin and history – their numbers did not matter. In the Transvaal Indians were not depended upon for the functioning of the mines and other industries; they were predominantly traders. In Natal only a small percentage of Indians were engaged in trade; the rest worked in the agricultural plantations and in the important industries – the survival of which depended almost exclusively on Indian labour. It seems that the attitude of the British Government in Natal at this time can only be explained by its desire not to antagonize Indian opinion in India, which might result in reduction or termination of Indian labour for Natal. This development would adversely affect British interests in Natal. Whatever the final explanation, one point emerges clearly. British policy in South Africa at this time towards the Indians in the country was not based on a defined and consistent programme. It was as dilatory as it had been before and since the Anglo-Boer War. This dilatoriness must, no doubt, have influenced the Natal Government to ignore its advice regarding the trading Bills of 1908.

The Natal legislature persisted with the Bills and passed them on 27th August, 1908. The *Natal Mercury* commented on this occasion: "It is the rankest hypocrisy on the part of the Colonial Secretary to say that the Bills are conceived in the interest of the native population. . . . Could there be anything more ludicrous than the practical shelving of a Bill to stop Asiatic immigration and the passing of the two Bills to prevent Asiatics, and even Natal-born Indians, from trading in any shape or form?"[77]

When the Imperial Government disallowed the Bills and the earlier correspondence was released, the same journal tried to account for the strange behaviour of the Natal Government: "In proceeding with the fore-doomed Licensing Bills, it would rather appear as if the Government wanted to tide over the session by making Parliament believe that they were in earnest about anti-Asiatic legislation. All the time they were keeping to themselves the fact that the Imperial Government had disallowed the Bills in advance."[78]

With the situation in Natal having reached this serious stage it was most unlikely that the other two Governments most closely concerned with the developments there would remain detached and unconcerned. Indeed, they were greatly troubled by the turn of the latest events in Natal, while the position in the Transvaal was giving rise to equal apprehension. On 4th September, 1908, the Secretary of State for India suggested that the Government of India consider whether any changes were necessary in the system permitting the recruitment of indentured labour to Natal.[79]

The Government of India responded to this suggestion by issuing a despatch to the local governments of Bombay, Madras, and the United Provinces, asking these local governments what views they had on the decision which the Government of India had arrived at to discontinue emigration of indentured labourers to Natal as from 30th June, 1909. Paragraph 4 of this despatch contains in a nutshell the reasons which had prompted the decision to discontinue emigration to Natal: The first point which prompted this decision was the failure of the government to secure necessary amendments to the Dealers

Licences Act, 1897 of Natal; the government anticipated that if the Natal Government persisted in its present attitude the lot of the free Indians in Natal in later years would grow worse and as their numbers were certain to increase so would the points of friction become more marked. With the passing of time feeling in India would become intensified against the continuance of the indentured labour system in Natal. Finally, with the growing industrialization in India there was no longer the prospects (and the necessity) for a surplus labour force to be sent to Natal.

The Indian Government did not anticipate any opposition from the local governments to whom the despatch was addressed and taking agreement for granted informed the Secretary of State for India of their decision to discontinue emigration to Natal as from 30th June, 1909.

This extreme step taken by the Government of India was forced upon them particularly because of the position of Indians in Natal. Though sanction to the proposal to discontinue emigration to Natal was only given by the Secretary of State for India in September, 1909, the Natal Government was brought round to see the serious consequences for the colony in the event of this materializing. One way in which the Natal Government came to see the catastrophe that threatened was by way of the Report of the Indian Immigration Commission of 1909. It was appointed to go into the question of Indian immigration to Natal as a result of the Natal Government's decision to abolish indentured labour from India in 1908.

The Commission reported that ". . . evidence shows that demand is made in many quarters *that another adequate supply of labour shall be guaranteed before Indian immigration is stopped, as essential to the maintenance of the interests of the Colony*".[80]

The Commission went on to say that there existed a general impression throughout the Colony that Indians were being used to supply labour to one or two particular industries to the disadvantage of the Colony in general but the figures obtained by the Commission showed that the employment of Indians was widespread, there being 2 429 employers of Indian indentured labourers.[81] The report stated that the abolition of indentured Indian labour would cause the local industries to decline and that it would accentuate African labour difficulties for "it would require at least two natives to perform the work done by one Indian".

The Report of the Clayton Commission had the effect of sharply reminding the Natal Government that unless it took immediate steps to improve the lot of the free Indians complained of in various despatches from the Government of India, there was the possibility that it would no longer get immigrant labour from India. The Natal Government acted in November, 1909, two months after sanction had been given by the Secretary of State for India to the Indian Government to introduce enabling legislation to abolish Indian immigrant labour to Natal. It introduced the Wholesale and Retail Dealers Licences Law Amendment Bill, which became law in December, 1909 in the form of Act 22/1909. Section 2 of the Act provided for an appeal to the Supreme Court against the refusal of an application for the renewal of a trading licence. The right of appeal did not embrace new licences or transfers of existing licences.

Such was the position in South Africa when developments were afoot to set up a political union. There was new hope in the coming Union for many South Africans but for the Indian population of the country there was little hope of improvements. In Natal the amendment to the Dealers Licences Act was little more than a sop to Cerberus to keep the flow of Indian immigrant labour uninterrupted and did nothing to appease Indian resentment and increasing hostility here and abroad. In the Transvaal the passive resistance campaign was at its height, though local resources were gradually decreasing. In June, 1909 the situation had become so desperate that the Transvaal Indians decided to make one last appeal to the justice of the British people and to the sense of patriotism of the people of India. Two delegations were elected in June, 1909 – the one to proceed to England and the other to India. Though each delegation was to consist of four members, the well-timed arrest of five of the members reduced the delegation which left the country. The delegation to England consisted of two, namely, M. K. Gandhi and Hajee Habib and that to India of one man, H. S. L. Polak.[82]

Gandhi and Habib, in addition to their brief for the Transvaal Indians, had to present to the Imperial Government a petition from the Natal Indian Congress regarding the position of Indians under Closer Union. In this petition the grievances of the Indians in Natal were recounted and the petitioners asked that the Draft South Africa Act be amended so as to give the British Indians in the country equal civil rights and that a Royal Commission should be appointed to investigate the grievances of British Indians in South Africa.[83]

The position of Indians under Closer Union had been receiving the attention of the Imperial Government even before the petition of the Natal Indian Congress was drafted. On 18th February, 1909, the Secretary of State wrote to Lord Selborne, asking how far the passing of the Union Act would affect the position of Indians. The High Commissioner replied that the Indian question as a whole had not been considered by the National Convention and had been left to be dealt with by the first Union parliament.[84]

The Indian question, like other non-white questions in South Africa, was considered to be a thorny question which might well cause serious dissensions in the National Convention. Rather than jeopardise the success of the Convention on contentious issues, they were deferred for later attention. If the past was any index to go by there was not much to be hoped for.

Gandhi and Habib left for England aboard the s.s. *Kenilworth* from Cape Town on 23rd June, 1909. Merriman, elder statesman of the Cape Colony, was also on board. Smuts and Botha were already in England in connection with the South Africa Act. The delegation arrived in London on 10th July, 1909 and met Lord Crewe, Secretary of State for the Colonies, Lord Morley, the Secretary of State for India, and Generals Botha and Smuts. Smuts offered to repeal the Asiatic Law Amendment Act but not the Immigrants Restriction Act. He was prepared to concede to a limited number of British Indians, other than former residents of the Transvaal, certificates of permanent residence.[85]

This concession was unacceptable to the Indian delegation who demanded equality before the law with Europeans in regard to immigration regulations. It was prepared, however, to see the number of Asiatic entrants limited by "administrative action", their argument being that educated Indians were required to maintain the civilization standard of the Indians in the Transvaal. Whichever way the Indians argued their case, according to Patrick Duncan, the Transvaal Colonial Secretary, the main point was that they were not prepared to accept legal restrictions on their immigration, which were not also imposed on the Europeans.[86] The demands made by Gandhi and Habib were rejected. They blamed the British Government for failing to support them. Though a number of individuals offered moral and financial support the delegation did not gain anything besides arousing sympathy for the passive resisters in some quarters.

Gandhi returned to South Africa to plan afresh. With the aid of his German friend, Kallenbach, who bought a farm about 1 100 acres in extent at Lawley, 21 miles from Johannesburg, Gandhi established the headquarters of the passive resistance movement in the Transvaal at this farm called Tolstoy Farm, in 1910. He received two donations of 25 000 rupees each from Mr. (afterwards Sir) Ratanji Tata which meant that he had enough funds for the present – in the region of £5 000, to carry on with the campaign.

In the meantime the one-man delegation to India was actively canvassing support. Polak's main business in India was to gain both moral and financial support for the struggle in the Transvaal. In this regard his mission was a great success. To begin with, he published a book entitled *The Indians of South Africa*, Part II of which was devoted to the Transvaal under the title: *A Tragedy of Empire*. Polak explained the purpose of his publication as well as of his mission by stating that he would speak out boldly in defence of the Indians, for the greater suffering borne by the Indians in South Africa was due to the ignorance and the carelessness of their European fellow-colonists. Polak believed that in spite of all the ignorance and the carelessness that existed there were elements in the South African nation who were concerned with truth and fair play and that in time these elements would realise that the Indian community constituted an important and useful part of the South African nation. As a European, Polak set himself the task in India at this time to put across his views and his claims for the South African Indians.[87]

Polak addressed many meetings in India. At one of these meetings held at Calcutta on 3rd December, 1909, a committee called the Indian South Africa League was formed on the same lines as the South Africa British Indian Committee formed in England in 1907. At this meeting resolutions were adopted condemning the injustice which the Transvaal Indians were being subjected to and calling upon the Government of India to take steps to stop all further recruitment of Indian labour for South Africa.

While in India, Polak placed himself in the hands of Professor G. K. Gokhale whose Servants of India Society convened meetings in every part of the country. One of the most important meetings addressed by Polak was the twenty-fourth session of the Indian National Congress conference. After Polak had addressed this meeting, Gokhale moved a resolution in three parts: firstly, appealing to the people of India for funds. Gokhale said that a million rupees had to be found by April, 1910 (a rupee then was the equivalent of 1s. 6d. i.e. £75 000 in all); secondly, that the Government of India should take retaliatory steps against the Natal Government by abolishing indentured labour to that Colony; and, finally, appealing to the Imperial Government to revise its policy of creating white colonies for white people only.[88]

Professor Gokhale was destined to play an important role in the Indian question in South Africa in later years. The Morley–Minto reforms which were embodied in the Indian Councils Act of 1909 permitted, *inter alia*, the Indian members of the Imperial Legislative Council asking supplementary questions and tabling resolutions. Though these members could not move any unofficial Bills nor introduce any vote of censure on the government the new opportunities meant that information could be got on awkward subjects by means of questions; furthermore, non-official views could be conveyed by means of resolutions. Gokhale, in particular, made use of this latter facility. His political star was in the ascendancy and he and his Society, the Servants of India Society, rendered great assistance to Polak at this time.

The most important result of Polak's mission to India was the ultimate abolition of indentured immigrant labour to Natal. The Natal Government came in with an effort late in the day to introduce a Bill to repeal the £3 tax upon women and girls under Act 17/1895 as amended in 1903.[89] But the Natal Government wavered in this progressive and necessary step and thereby lost the chance of re-gaining ground. The Bill was not passed in its original form, to the great disappointment of the Indians. The result was the passing of Act 19/1910 which gave magistrates of the Colony power to relieve deserving Indian women of the annual licence of £3. The onus to prove inability to pay rested with the women and girls concerned. *Indian Opinion* saw that this was a distressing and degrading feature and said that it hoped that not a single Indian woman would do anything of the kind. The British Government considered the amendment to be a good measure.[90]

The changes made in the amending Act hardly brought any appreciable benefits to the labourers. The remarkable anomaly that never ceased to exist till the very end was that the demand for Indian labourers never decreased. Yet their peculiar hardships generally remained unassuaged till the end. Whatever the merits of the amendment it came too late in the day to save labour migration to Natal. Already on 25th February, 1910, the Honourable G. K. Gokhale successfully moved the following resolution in the Imperial Legislative Council: "That the Council recommends that the Governor-General-in-Council should be empowered to prohibit the recruitment of indentured labour in British India for the Colony of Natal."

Speaking on the resolution, Gokhale said that though the indenture system was not a system of slavery, it was not far removed from slavery. He said that it was improper to remove helpless men and women from India to a strange country where their language, customs and habits were not understood and where any attempt by them to improve their lot was branded as a criminal offence. But it was not because of the evils inherent in the indenture system that Gokhale asked for the abolition of this labour. It was on the issue of the welfare of the free Indian population in South Africa that Gokhale desired this abolition. In the normal course all indentured labourers would ultimately become free and would then swell the free Indian population. In the absence of any guarantee that the interests of this part of the Indian population would be protected in the future, Gokhale called for a stoppage to the indenture system in Natal.

Gokhale's resolution received a mixed reception in the Natal Press. The *Natal Mercury* supported the resolution and called many of the things done in Natal "a travesty of justice". It said that the Indian Government was not expected to give approval to the many disabilities Indians laboured under in Natal and that it had to give heed to the growing opposition in India against the indenture system and the condition of free Indians in the Colony.[91] The *Natal Advertiser* took the other view and criticized the British Government for using the threat that if the Natal Government did not accord full civic and political rights to its free Indian population, indentured Indian labour for Natal would be stopped.[92] The *Indian Opinion* was disappointed that Gokhale's resolution sought to stop indenture by way of penalty for non-redress of the grievances of the free Indian population of South Africa. It wrote: "We must make it clear that we ask for the stoppage of indentured labour for its own sake and because we consider that it is detrimental to the moral well-being of those who re-indenture."[93]

The comments in the Press are a fair indication of the general feeling in the country in the matter of the treatment of Indians. It was clear that indentured labour would soon come to an end; but what was not yet clear was the position of the free Indians in the country. It was not as simple a matter to resolve this issue as it was to stop the emigration of indentured labourers to Natal. In the Transvaal the difficulties that existed there in regard to this issue far overshadowed the lesser issue of the abolition of indentured labour to Natal.

The position in the Transvaal had certainly grown worse in 1910. The relation between the Transvaal and Natal had an important bearing on the acceptance by the Indian Government of Gokhale's resolution of 25th February, 1910.

The passive resistance in the Transvaal was at its peak, with support from Natal being an important part. On 11th March, 1910 nearly three hundred Indians gathered on the Durban platform to see off a big batch of passive resistance recruits to the Transvaal.[94]

The Transvaal Indians were themselves thick in the fight, particularly the Tamil-speaking section of the Indian community, nearly a hundred of whom were in custody at this time in Diepkloof prison, with a number awaiting deportation, the worst form of punishment for the resisters.

Since the commencement of the struggle in the Transvaal in 1907 up till about the middle of June, 1910, over 3 000 individuals were imprisoned, of which number many hundreds were deported. The picture for the Indians was a gloomy one; the sufferings of individuals and families aroused great pity everywhere. Gandhi explained in a letter to Gokhale that deportations had a serious effect on the resisters; that many Indians who were domiciled in the Transvaal and in Natal were among the deportees; that among the deportees were people who were born in South Africa. In spite of all the misery and poverty brought about by these deportations the wives, sisters or mothers of the deported men refused to accompany their men-folk to India which they called a foreign land. Gandhi went on to say that the men who participated in the struggle earned as employees wages ranging from £6 to £15 and those with independent calling from £20 to £30 per month. "All of those are now reduced to poverty, and their families receive from the passive resistance fund the barest sustenance money." It was impossible (even for him), wrote Gandhi, to write "about these deportations with sufficient restraint".[95]

The deportations caused a storm of protest in India as well as in Britain. In the House of Lords, Lord Ampthill, who was also the President of the South Africa British Indian Committee, raised the question of the deportations. Replying on behalf of the Government, Lord Beauchamp said that "every opportunity would be afforded British Indians to prove domicile in South Africa". *Indian Opinion* in a comment pointed out that many deportees had been able to enter Natal on their return and had served further periods of imprisonment at Diepkloof. They were not illegal immigrants and should never have been deported and "that the Imperial Government has been hoodwinked by the Transvaal Government". And on 3rd August, 1910, a public meeting was held in London to protest against the treatment of Indians domiciled in the Transvaal, especially against the deportation via Mozambique. The meeting passed a series of resolutions appealing to Earl Crewe, Secretary of State for Colonies, for protection and reminding him of his and Colonel Seeley's statement that Indians domiciled in the Transvaal should be fairly and honourably treated. A resolution was also passed urging Lord Morley, Secretary of State for India, to prevent further emigration of indentured labourers to South Africa until redress had been secured. Sir M. M. Bhownaggree, M.P., who was also chairman of the South Africa British Indian Committee, pointed out that the pledges of the Imperial Government had been violated by the action of the Transvaal.[96] These pledges were that in return for the strict measures contained in the Transvaal Immigrants Restriction Act, 15/1907, free Indians in that Colony would receive just treatment. As these were mere pledges without any firm safeguards they could very easily number among the many broken pledges for which the Imperial Government were responsible. Their effects were now being felt in a magnified form as a result of the deportations not only of Indians who were domiciled in the Transvaal but of those who were also born in that Colony.

With the political scene complicated by the deportations it was not likely that the Indian Government would delay their actions following on the acceptance of Gokhale's resolution to abolish indentured labour to Natal on 25th February, 1910. A notice appeared in the *Gazette of India* on 1st April, 1911, to the effect that emigration to Natal would be prohibited as from the 1st July, 1911 because of "the position created by the divergence between the Indian and Colonial standpoints, and also owing to the absence of a guarantee that Indians will be accepted as permanent citizens of the South African Union after the expiration of their indentures".[97]

The divergence between the Indian and the Colonial standpoints was seen in particular in the opposition in India to the system of indenture in general and public resentment at the position of Indians in Natal and the Transvaal. It was also seen in the sustained and prolonged efforts of the Government of India to induce the colonial governments to redress legitimate Indian grievances, which efforts evoked little response and finally exhausted the patience of the Indian Government.

There remained the faint ray of hope that what the colonial governments were either unable or unwilling to do to redress the grievances of Indians in Natal and the Transvaal, the newly-established Government of the Union of South Africa would do. Thus after the establishment of Union, which came into being on 31st May, 1910, the Imperial Government addressed to the Union Government the memorable despatch of 7th October, 1910 in which they recommended the repeal of the Asiatic Law Amendment Act, 2/1907 of the Transvaal; the removal of the racial bar and the substitution for the latter of the Indian suggestion of non-racial legislation, modified by administrative differentiation, limiting future Indian immigration to a minimum number annually of highly educated men. In the despatch, Lord Crewe, the Secretary of State for Colonies, observed as follows: "In the opinion of His Majesty's Government, it may be anticipated that the new Government and Parliament would view the whole position in a broader and more generous spirit.

I trust, that in dealing with the position in Natal, your Ministers will recognise the great services of the Indian population in developing that Province, not only by remedying specific grievances as far as possible, but also by exerting the whole power and influence of the Union Government to secure considerate treatment of them."[98] The Union Government responded by way of a minute, dated 20th December, 1910, from the Prime Minister, General Botha, laying down the policy of the Union in which it was stated that amending legislation would be introduced in the first Union Parliament to remove "as far as possible" the grievances of the Indians. Once this was done, the despatch went on to state, it was hoped that that would put an end to the "vexed Indian question". In this despatch the Union Government was certainly non-committal: it admitted that the question was a difficult and troublesome one; it promised to remove the grievances not fully but only "as far as possible". How far this would be was not difficult to visualize if the attitude of mind of the policy-makers remained what it was prior to Union. The real test was yet to come.

The first post-Union legislation of special significance to the Indians, which also carried with it the extent to which General Botha's assurances given on 20th December, 1910, were being implemented, was the Immigrants' Restriction Bill of 1911.

The Bill foreshadowed the repeal of Act 2/1907; prescribed a dictation test as a condition of entry – the education test to be differentially applied so as "effectually to check the entry of coloured persons"; provincial barriers were to be retained. The Secretary of State for the Colonies, at the instance of the Secretary of State for India, drew attention to the fact that the Bill seemed to jeopardise the rights of entry, after temporary absence, of Indians lawfully resident in the Union and unduly limited the number of educated entrants. The measure was not, therefore, in line with the expectations of the British or Indian Governments.

The Bill was introduced in the House of Assembly and passed its second reading, but after much criticism from both Indians and Europeans, it was withdrawn. The O.F.S. members of Parliament objected to the clause that permitted educated Indians to enter that province. Gandhi insisted on this right and protested that the Bill did not exempt educated Indians from the obligation to register in the Transvaal.[99]

Gandhi informed Smuts that failure on the part of the Government to grant the concessions desired by the Indians meant that passive resistance would continue. But the Private Secretary to the Minister of the Interior wrote to Gandhi informing him that the Government were keenly desirous of arriving at a solution and that in the recess they would go into the matter; that in the meantime "General Smuts feels that the passive resistance movement, which has caused and still continues to cause considerable suffering, might now well be brought to a close". In his reply Gandhi sought from General Smuts an assurance that at the next session of parliament, Act 2/1907 would be repealed; that equality before the law concerning the immigration of Asiatics in the Transvaal would be restored; that existing rights would be safeguarded; that the Immigration Bill for the whole country would be free of a racial bar; that passive resisters should be allowed to take out certificates of registration in the Transvaal; that educated passive resisters should be allowed to remain in the Transvaal although they were not eligible for registration under Act 2/1907; their number was not to exceed six.[100]

General Smuts agreed to the terms contained in Gandhi's letter. The settlement was accepted by a mass meeting of Indians in Johannesburg as a provisional settlement pending the fulfilment of the assurance given by General Smuts.

The Union Immigration Bill was introduced in the 1912 session of Parliament. It contained an entirely new section which exempted educated Indians from the provisions of the Transvaal Asiatic Registration Amendment Act; educated Indians who passed the language test prescribed in the Bill could enter the Orange Free State provided they did not trade or own fixed property there. But there were other features which were unacceptable to the Indians. These were the transfer from the law courts to the Immigration Officer of the right to determine the domicile rights of Asiatics, including those of the wives and children of Asiatics; stricter conditions governing inter-provincial movements were included. Natal and the Cape had a special grievance in that educated Indians of the status of clerks and assistants would be practically deemed prohibited immigrants under the arbitrary education test of the 1912 Bill. The Secretary of State for India raised the question whether wives of those Indians who could lawfully contract polygamous marriages would be admitted. The Union Government gave a reply in the negative.

The Bill was opposed by members of the Opposition who feared that it would keep out white immigrants while the Nationalists wanted Asiatic immigrants to be explicitly excluded.[101] The Bill was therefore withdrawn as it had met with all-round opposition.

The two Immigration Bills of 1911 and 1912 had appeared and disappeared for various reasons, the most important being that the Asiatics felt they did not go far enough to remove their grievances while many Europeans felt that they did not protect European interests sufficiently enough by not only retaining the former disabilities of the Asiatics but by actually accentuating these. The old paradoxes in the Indian question were coming into prominence once again: what the Indians complained of as being not enough, the Europeans complained of as being too much. It was announced at the time of the withdrawal of the 1912 Bill that the Hon. Gopal Krishna Gokhale, a member of the Viceroy's Council in India, would visit South Africa to take a personal part in the settlement of the Indian question in South Africa. Passive resistance was suspended during this period of negotiation and the provisional settlement of 1911 was extended for another year.

Professor Gokhale was formerly a member of the Imperial Legislative Council in terms of the Morley–Minto reforms aimed at giving Indians more say in the legislature. He had used this opportunity with great distinction and was elevated to the Executive as a member of the Viceroy's Council. By virtue of his rank, he was the most important Indian Government official to visit South Africa. It was a visit of great significance for it marked a tacit acceptance of India's interest in the welfare of South African Indians.

Professor Gokhale arrived in Cape Town on 22nd October, 1912, for a six weeks' visit. He addressed meetings at all the important centres in the Union after which he had an interview with the Union Ministers, including Smuts and Botha, for about two hours. After the interview, Gandhi, who acted as Secretary to Gokhale in South Africa, reported that Gokhale told him: "You must return to India in a year. Everything has been settled. The Black Act (Act 2/1907) will be repealed. The racial bar will be removed from the Immigration Law. The £3 tax will be abolished."

In addition to the promises already given by the Union Government to the Indian leaders in South Africa, the new promise given to Gokhale was that the £3 tax would be repealed. There is a measure of uncertainty about this promise. Gokhale always maintained that the promise was given. Smuts and the other Union Ministers denied that an unconditional promise had ever been given. Eric Walker seems to support both views when he states that though Gokhale was given to understand that the £3 tax would be repealed, no actual pledge was given. The misunderstanding resulting from either an error of omission or commission was to have serious consequences a year later.

In his dealings with the Union Government, Gokhale advocated the "closed-door" policy – that fresh immigration be discontinued in favour of improvements in the living conditions of the resident Indian population in the country until full civic rights were attained. His was a moderate policy which received Gandhi's approval and support, though it was not popular in many quarters in South Africa and in India. It did, however, form a reasonable basis for all future negotiations between the Union and Indian Governments.

Gokhale was a man of immense political and intellectual stature.[102] Though he was severely criticized for his moderation and had the humiliation of finding that the All-India National Congress refused to ratify his work in South Africa, from the point of view of practical politics and realism, the farewell speech he gave at the Pretoria Town Hall on 15th November, 1912, deserves attention. Gokhale said that in the search for a way to secure a just and equitable treatment for the 150 000 Indians in South Africa the solution by repatriation should be ruled out as an impractical one. He said that for a practical solution to be secured it had to be recognized that the European community was dominant in South Africa and that this dominant power had to be assured that there was no desire on the part of the Indians to flood out the country by immigration. Once this assurance was given and the fears of the Europeans on this score allayed a just and permanent solution was possible. Once that assurance was given, Gokhale said, "the aim of the Government should be to make the Indians feel that they were living under equal laws, and that these laws are administered towards them with no undue harshness, but the same as towards the other people of the country".[103]

Gokhale's critics among the Indian community in South Africa based their opposition to his policy of "closed-door" on a less optimistic picture of the future. Some argued: "Assuming that we accept the 'closed-door' policy . . . what guarantee is there . . . that our lot will be improved? And is there any positive assurance that we can look forward to the day when they will attain full civic rights?"[104] The opposition to Gokhale's "closed-door" policy came more particularly from colonial-born Indians who looked upon South Africa as their only home and who were, therefore, deeply concerned that a settlement of their grievances should be based on more solid grounds than on the mere assurances of the moment. What Gokhale had achieved in South Africa was, nevertheless, a good starting point which could be used to good purpose for the ultimate solution, with goodwill and sincerity on all sides. Gokhale left for India in a blaze of glory as a statesman who had achieved much with his brilliant oratory and sharp wit, having given the Europeans of South Africa the opportunity of seeing a man of great erudition and renown (which was really a different side of the picture they had become accustomed to, the picture which depicted Indians as illiterate labourers with insanitary habits and strange Oriental customs). But in regard to his achievements as a mediator in the Indian question in South Africa, his "closed-door" policy did little to enhance his prestige either among the Indians in general in South Africa or in his own country.

With his departure from South Africa the stage was set for the appearance of the Immigrants' Regulation Bill in 1913. It became law in the form of the Immigrants' Regulation Act, 22/1913. The five points in it to which objections were raised by Indians were the following:

(1) The definition of the term "domicile" appeared to place Indians who were introduced into Natal under Act 17/1895 in the class of prohibited immigrants.

(2) Educated Indians were required to make a declaration in terms of Sections 7 and 8 of Chapter XXXIII of the Orange Free State Law Book and this, to them, appeared derogatory.

(3) The proviso to Section 5 deprived Indians born in South Africa of the free right to enter the Cape Province which they had hitherto enjoyed under the Cape Immigration Act, 30/1906.

(4) The admission and status of Indian women married in accordance with the rites of their respective religions were left in a state of uncertainty; especially Muslims regarded this as an injury and insult.

(5) The non-repeal of the £3 tax.[105]

The admission and status of Indian women – one of the points in the new Bill to which objection was taken – was complicated by the Searle judgment in the Cape Supreme Court on 14th March, 1913, two weeks before the appearance of the Bill. In his judgment in the case Essop v. Rex, Justice Searle declared that non-Christian marriages, whether solemnized in India or in the Union, which were not performed by a civil marriage officer were invalid in the eyes of the law and jeopardised the right of entry of the wives of the majority of domiciled Indians.[106]

Following on this case, came the Kulsum Bibi case, heard in the Natal Supreme Court. Kulsum Bibi was declared to be a prohibited immigrant when she applied to be allowed to join her husband, who was already domiciled in Natal. Her reputed husband already had a wife living with him in Natal. Section 5(g) of the Immigrants' Regulation Act exempted from the definition of prohibited immigrant the wife or child of a lawful or monogamous marriage celebrated according to the rites of any religious faith outside the Union. The Court held, in the Kulsum Bibi case, that under the words "lawful and monogamous marriage" were included only such marriages as were recognized as valid in South Africa and in England, i.e. "the voluntary union of one man with one woman, to the exclusion, while it lasts, of all others".[107]

The Searle judgment nullified all Indian marriages celebrated according to non-Christian rites and affected the whole Indian community whereas the Kulsum Bibi case restricted the entry of plural wives of a polygamous marriage. On these two judgments Gandhi wrote to the Secretary for the Interior, E. M. Gorges, asking that legislation should be introduced during the next session of parliament to legalise monogamous marriages, already solemnised or to be entered into thereafter, which were solemnised by Indian priests. With regard to those Indians (Muslims) who had plural wives, Gandhi said that he did not ask that polygamy be recognised legally but that such plural wives of Indians already domiciled in the country be permitted to enter the country without having any legal status.

Gorges replied that the Minister of the Interior could not give any assurance that legislation on the lines indicated by Gandhi would be introduced in the next session of Parliament. Gandhi replied that passive resistance had started once again and that this time women had joined the struggle in protest against the Searle judgment.

Five days after a party of 16 from the Phoenix Settlement, including women, had been sentenced to three months' imprisonment with hard labour for entering the Transvaal without permits, the £3 tax question loomed large again. Its non-repeal in the Immigrants' Regulation Act, 22/1913 had been a sore point because Indians had been led to believe, after Gokhale's visit, that it would be repealed. Even the *Natal Mercury* wrote that the non-repeal of the tax "will stand as one of the most conspicuous instances of the cynical disregard of promises of which General Botha's cabinet has yet been guilty".[108]

The £3 tax question came to the forefront when Gandhi informed Smuts that the step which he now proposed to take would consist "in actively, persistently and continually asking those who are liable to pay the £3 tax to decline to do so and to suffer the penalties for non-payment, and, what is more important, in asking those who are now serving under indenture, and who will, therefore, be liable to pay the £3 tax on completion of the indentures, to strike work until the tax is withdrawn".[109] This was a most serious step and it was calculated to bring the passive resistance struggle to a climax. It meant that, whereas in the past this struggle was carried on by small numbers, with the inclusion of indentured labourers the movement would be accelerated by the addition of thousands more to the resistance group. All that was now to take place must be attributed to the unfortunate misunderstanding that was allowed to develop when Gokhale visited the country in 1912.

On the same day as Gandhi wrote to Smuts informing the latter of his decision to bring the indentured labourers into the struggle, Smuts said in a speech to the South African Party at Pretoria that what Gokhale had been told in 1912 was that if the Natal members of Parliament did not object to the repeal of the tax it would be repealed but as these members had objected the tax had not been repealed. Smuts said that the Indians were being misled by their leaders and that if their opposition was not stamped out, revolutions might break out in the country.[110]

A revolution was in the offing. Women from the Transvaal, mostly Tamilians, crossed into Natal and under the guidance of G. K. T. Naidoo, they made their way from mine to mine in Northern Natal, eloquently appealing to the Indian labourers and their families to cease work. The women were arrested and this stirred the hearts of Indians in South Africa and abroad, as it did also in the case of many non-Indian sympathisers. Hundreds of labourers on the coal mines struck work. On 28th October, 1913, Gandhi, accompanied by strikers and their families, numbering over 2 000 in all, began a march into the Transvaal with the deliberate object of contravening the Immigrants' Regulation Act, 22/1913.

This Great March of 1913 is one of the most stirring chapters in South Africa's turbulent history. The credit for its organisation and success is due largely to M. K. Gandhi who was himself arrested at Volksrust but released on bail, re-arrested at Standerton and again released on bail, arrested a third time at Greylingstad and removed to Dundee for trial.

On the 11th November, 1913, he was sentenced to nine months' imprisonment with hard labour, after which he was tried at Volksrust on a charge of aiding and abetting prohibited persons to enter the Transvaal, the principal charge at Dundee being one of inducing indentured labourers to leave Natal. He was finally sent to jail in Bloemfontein – far from the scene of activity.

The labourers and their families were stopped at Balfour on 11th November and returned to Natal by rail. The next day, i.e., 12th November, 1913, the movement spread to the North Coast when some four hundred labourers struck work at La Mercy Estate near Verulam. The number soon increased to 1 200. On 23rd November about 200 labourers on the Beneva Estate, near Esperanza, on the Natal South Coast, struck work. And on the 27th November there was a serious clash between the police and a number of labourers on the Natal Estates near Mt. Edgecombe. These strikes were organised to support the strike on the coal mines of Northern Natal. Domestic labourers and municipal employees in some towns of Natal also struck work in sympathy.

At Mt. Edgecombe and in Esperanza violence broke out with both the police, who used firearms, and the labourers, who used sticks, being involved in the clashes which resulted in 9 Indians being killed and 25 being wounded. Serious charges of brutality were levelled at the police and India was aroused to action on behalf of the Indians in South Africa. In one of the most remarkable speeches ever made by a head of state against a friendly government in the Commonwealth, the Viceroy of India, Lord Hardinge, echoed the widespread resentment in India when he spoke at Madras on the 24th November, 1913. Lord Hardinge had succeeded Lord Minto as Viceroy in October, 1910. It was left to him to carry out the Morley–Minto constitutional reforms embodied in the Indian Councils Act of 1909. The Congress leaders, though not wholly satisfied with the reforms – especially in the matter of communal representation – accepted them as being progressive. Hardinge made good use of this favourable feeling in his public measures and by his private contacts with Indian leaders; during his term of office "the government and nationalist opposition were more nearly in accord than at any time between 1888 and 1937".[111] As an indication of this accord and because of its great significance in the context of inter-governmental negotiations, Hardinge's speech is quoted in detail:

> "... it is unfortunately not easy to find means by which India can make her indignation seriously felt by those who hold the reins of Government in that country (South Africa). Recently your compatriots in South Africa have taken matters into their own hands by organizing what is called passive resistance to laws which they consider invidious and unjust, an opinion which we, who watch their struggles from afar, cannot but share. They have violated, as they intended to violate, those laws with full knowledge of the penalties involved, and ready with all courage and patience to endure those penalties. In all this they have the sympathy of India – deep and burning – and not only of India, but of all those who like myself, without being Indians themselves, have feelings of sympathy for the people of this country.
>
> But the most recent developments have taken a very serious turn, and we have seen the widest publicity given to allegations that this movement of passive resistance has been dealt with by measures which would not for a moment be tolerated in any country that claims to call itself civilized.

These allegations have been met by a categorical denial from the responsible Government of South Africa, though even their denial contains admissions which do not seem to me to indicate that the Union Government have exercised a very wise discretion in some of the steps which they have adopted. That is the position at this moment, and I do feel that if the South African Government desire to justify themselves in the eyes of India and the world, only one course is open to them and that is to appoint a strong and impartial committee, upon which Indian interests shall be fully represented, to conduct a thorough and searching enquiry into the truth of these allegations."[112]

This statement was a severe indictment of the Union Government and shows that the Government of India were deeply troubled by the turn of events and that the Viceroy had followed the events very closely. Almost immediately after the strikes and disturbances had spread to the coastal regions of Natal, he made representation to the Secretary of State for India. In a telegram he asked the Secretary of State for India what steps were being taken to bring pressure to bear on the Union Government to negotiate with the Indian leaders and he said that the rioting and possible bloodshed in Natal "would in itself be calamitous and disastrous in its effect upon public opinion in India".

When the Secretary of State for India replied that the Union Government had denied the various allegations of ill-treatment during the disturbances, the Viceroy stated that "a bare denial . . . will not satisfy Indian public opinion" and that an impartial and thorough enquiry should be instituted.[113]

This was followed up by the Viceroy's dramatic declaration at Madras on 24th November. Nor did he rest at that. Two days later another telegram was sent to the Secretary of State for India stating that "the fact that it is now admitted that three hundred Indians were flogged by Mr. Hult, a mine manager who was charged with their custody as prisoners, renders the necessity for an impartial and full enquiry into the whole question of the recent treatment of Indians in South Africa, as the only means of allaying the feelings of indignation and strong resentment in India, and of convincing India of the sincerity of General Botha's professions that he courts inquiry and of the truth of the the denials of the South African Government".

Lord Hardinge's perseverance was rewarded when on 13th December, 1913, he received a telegram from the Secretary of State for India conveying the notification received from the Governor-General of the Union, Lord Gladstone, that the Government had appointed a Commission, "(1) to hold forthwith a public judicial enquiry and to report as soon as possible as to the disturbances in connection with the recent strike of Indians in Natal, the causes and circumstances which led to that strike and to those disturbances, the amount of force used for suppression of disturbances, and the necessity for the use of such force, and as to any acts of violence alleged to have been committed upon persons sentenced to imprisonment in connection with the strike, and (2) to make recommendations in respect of any of the above".[114]

The members of the Commission were Sir William Solomon, K.C.M.G. (Chairman), Edward Esselen, K.C., and Lieutenant-Colonel J. S. Wylie, K.C.M.V.O. The appointment of Esselen and Wylie met with much opposition from local Indians who considered them to be avowed anti-Asiatics. Another point of grievance against the membership of the Commission was that it did not have any Indian member. Gandhi, Polak and Kallenbach, who were released on 18th December at the request of the Commission, wrote to Smuts asking for the names of Sir James Rose-Innes and W. P. Schreiner to be added as Commissioners. When this suggestion was rejected, Gandhi informed Smuts that a passive resistance march would commence from Durban on 1st January, 1914, and that he would not give evidence before the Commission.

The Government of India, too, was advised to make the request that an Indian be included on the Commission. When all these representations failed, the Government of India arranged that it would be represented by Sir Benjamin Robertson at the Commission sittings. Two other Europeans, viz., the Rev. C. F. Andrews and Mr. Pearson, came out to South Africa from India at the behest of G. K. Gokhale to use their influence to end the deadlock in the country.

Though the passive resistance march which Gandhi had planned for the 1st January, 1914 was suspended by him at the request of Vere Stent, editor of the *Pretoria News*, who asked that it be held over while the railway strikes were taking place on the Rand, he refused to appear before the Commission. This decision was regretted by the Commission and criticized by Indians in South Africa as well as in India. However, in a letter dated 21st January, 1914, Gandhi wrote to the Secretary for the Interior explaining that the Indians desired relief on the following points: the repeal of the £3 tax in such a manner that the Indians relieved would occupy the same status as the indentured Indians discharged under the Natal Act, 25/1891; the marriage question; the Cape entry question; the O.F.S. question; and, finally, "an assurance that the existing laws, especially affecting Indians, will be administered justly with due regard to vested rights".

Meanwhile the work of the Indian Inquiry Commission went on in spite of the handicap of a general boycott of its sittings by local Indians. Its report was completed on 7th March, 1914. Its main recommendations were the following: that Section 5(*g*) of the Immigrant's Regulation Act of 1913 be amended so as to admit one wife and the minor children by her of an Indian who was entitled to reside in any Province or who might in future be permitted to enter the Union, irrespective of the fact that his marriage to such wife might have been solemnised according to tenets that recognised polygamy, or that she was one of several wives married abroad, so long as she was his only wife in South Africa; a register of all plural wives already in South Africa and their minor children to be kept by Immigration Officers so as to enable these persons to travel to and from India for as long as the husband continued to live in this country; marriage officers from amongst Indian priests of different denominations to be permitted to solemnise marriages in accordance with the rites of the contracting parties; *de facto* monogamous marriages to be validated by registration; the £3 tax to be repealed; the taking of finger-prints in Immigration Departments to be discontinued.[115]

The Government of India welcomed the Commission's Report, particularly in regard to the recommendation to repeal the £3 tax. It expressed an awareness of the fact that the Mohommedans were dissatisfied with the solution to the marriage question but stated that it could not press for the full recognition of polygamous marriages contracted by them; the Government of India was quite satisfied with the recommendations of the Commission in respect of polygamous marriages.[116]

In regard to the liability for the rioting and violence, it regretted that Indian non-co-operation with the Commission resulted in there being no conclusion on this point. The letter went on to criticize the decision of the majority of Indians in South Africa to boycott the proceedings of the Commission as the Government of India had hoped that through the co-operation of local Indians evidence might have been led on the issue of violence and ill-treatment during the period of the strikes in November, 1913.

However, though the Government of India had failed to obtain satisfaction on the point of the responsibility for the violence and ill-treatment during the strikes, it was a great gain for India to have succeeded not only in having the Commission appointed but in having gained, through the participation of Sir Benjamin Robertson, satisfaction on so many points which represented the grievances of British Indians in South Africa. It was now left to the Union Government to give expression to the recommendations of the Commission.

Acting on the recommendations of the Commission of Enquiry the Government of the Union of South Africa introduced the Indian Relief Bill in May, 1914. It finally became law in the form of the Indian Relief Act, 22/1914. The Act embodied the following main points: the appointment of marriage officers to solemnize marriages according to the rites of Indian religions; the validation of monogamous marriages by magistrates or marriage officers; the inadmissibility into the country of the legal wife of an exempted Indian if such a person had any offspring in South Africa by any other woman who was still living; the granting of free passages to India to any Indian who abandoned his right to domicile in South Africa, as well as the right of his wife and his minor children; the acceptance of thumb-prints on a certificate of domicile as conclusive proof of the holder's former residence or domicile in Natal; the abolition of the £3 tax with the provision that no proceedings would be taken for the recovery of arrears.

The Indian Relief Act conceded half the number of points which Gandhi had mentioned in a letter to Smuts on 21st January, 1914 as representing the points on which the Indians desired a settlement. The administrative matters which did not come under the Indian Relief Bill were settled in a series of correspondence, between Gandhi and Smuts, in what is known as the Smuts–Gandhi Agreement, in confirmation of the interviews held between them. These letters were exchanged on the 30th June, 1914.

The recommendations of the Solomon Commission, the passing of the Indian Relief Act, and the Smuts-Gandhi Agreement of 30th June, 1914 can justly be deemed to be stages leading to the grand finale of the drama of the first Indian Passive Resistance campaign in South Africa. Of this drama, it can be said that the curtains fell when Mohandas Karamchand Gandhi took his bow on 20th July, 1914, when he left South Africa for England and then India – never to return again. But the curtains did not fall on the question of Indians in South Africa. It was merely the end of an era, a most chequered one.

In this era, though the passive resistance struggle overshadowed the other developments, they were nonetheless of great import, both in this country and abroad. In the Transvaal the British administration headed by Milner carried out a programme of legislation against the Asiatics resident there or entitled by the old laws to reside there quite in violation of the promises given before the outbreak of hostilities. Questions which were raised by British statesmen before the Anglo-Boer War were answered to the discredit of the British Government after the War by the actions of this very government in the Transvaal. One of these questions had been raised by Lord Selborne in the House of Lords in 1899 when he asked: "Was it or was it not our duty to see that our dusky fellow-subjects in the Transvaal, where they had a perfect right to go, should be treated as the Queen in our name had promised they should be treated?" With the grant of Responsible Government to the Transvaal in 1907 what had before then been uncertain as far as the future of the Indians in that country was concerned was cleared up in the Transvaal policy of restrictive legislation in 1907. This was done without any demur on the part of the British Government. The same happened when the Union of South Africa came about in 1910. All that the British Government did was to ask for assurances of just treatment, which assurances were given in equivocal terms and accepted as given. In India, the Morley–Minto reforms heralded the greater Indianization of the Government of India, though this was, for the present, to be seen in a handful of Indians holding executive positions while most of the other members had to be content with asking questions and moving resolutions. This era represented certain definite developments: the withdrawal of the British Government from the position of authority and restraint in South Africa; the transference of the Transvaal attitude against Indians to the first Union Government; the increased power of Indians in the Government of India.

From the international standpoint certain factors emerge from the events in the period up to 1914. The Indian question in South Africa was finally confirmed to be not a purely domestic issue and not even a narrow national issue but an important international issue in that it affected the relations between more than one national government. No one could any longer claim with any justice that it was a domestic issue. The deputations of Gandhi and Habib to England and of Polak to India and, what is of greater significance, the visit of Professor Gokhale to South Africa in 1912 and the participation by the Government of India through its official, Sir Benjamin Robertson, in the Solomon Commission of 1913, finally served to disprove this contention. It shows, too, that since the British Government did not use its power of veto it finally capitulated to the force of the anti-Asiatic programme in South Africa. This programme was a perpetuation of the existing position in the Transvaal and in Natal, particularly that of the Transvaal which also gave to the first Union cabinet its majority. As England receded into the background in the affairs of the South African Indians so India drew more into the forefront, especially after 1909 and took the few steps of any importance and abolished indentured immigrant labour to Natal, sent Gokhale to South Africa in 1912 and called for the Commission of Inquiry in 1913. This government did everything possible to allay the fears of the Europeans in South Africa that Indians would soon swamp the European population in South Africa. There were now sufficient guarantees against this fear in Gokhale's "closed-door" policy; in Section 4(1)(a) of the Immigrants' Regulation Act; and in the Relief Act which made provision for the repatriation of Indians who desired to leave the country on their own free will.

With the Indian Councils Act of 1909 introducing a measure of Indianization of the Government of India and with this slight measure already rewarding in many ways already shown, the international aspects of the Indian question in South Africa after 1914 would have to take note of this development. This issue, in so far as it was in need of a lasting and equitable solution, had only reached the crossroads, though General Smuts considered that 1914 marked the parting of the ways.

Smuts considered the drama over. In the letter of 30th June, 1914, Gorges concluded thus: ". . . he (General Smuts) wishes no doubt on the subject to remain, that the placing of the Indian Relief Bill on the Statute Book of the Union, coupled with the fulfilment of the assurances he is giving in this letter . . . will constitute a complete and final settlement of the controversy which has unfortunately existed for so long. . . .".

In his reply, Gandhi referred to the many points his compatriots required him to draw into the negotiations and stated: ". . . Whilst, therefore, they have not been included in the programme of passive resistance, it will not be denied that some day or other these matters will require further and sympathetic consideration by the Government. Complete satisfaction cannot be expected until full civic rights have been conceded to the resident Indian population."

Gandhi was equally explicit when, just before his departure for England on 20th July, 1914, he gave a letter to Reuter, which stated that he had assured the Indians in South Africa that the present settlement did not preclude them from agitating for the removal of other disabilities contained in the Transvaal Gold Law, the Townships Act and Law 3 of 1885 and the trade laws of Natal and the Cape. He said that the promises made by Smuts to administer existing laws with due regard to vested rights gave to the Indian community a "breathing time" within which to consider their next steps.[117]

It was clear that Gandhi considered the settlement of 1914 to be a temporary one; a settlement which left the doors open for future negotiations. The next chapter concerns itself with these negotiations and how they affected the international aspects of the South African Indian question after 1914.

FOOTNOTES

1. Government of India, *Papers Relating to the Round Table Conference Between the Representatives of the Govt. of India and the Govt. of the Union of South Africa on the Indian Question in the Union—* 1926–27, pp. 6–7. This is cited hereafter as *Govt. of India Papers*, 1926–7. Since the beginning of the Boer War more than 13 000 British officers and men had been sent from India and about 9 000 native Indians came as followers or attendants. At least 9 000 British Indians served during the War. Vide *Indian Opinion*, 30th July, 1903.
2. Gandhi, *My Experiments with Truth*, p. 214.
3. Gandhi, *Satyagraha, in South Africa*, p. 71.
4. Govt. of India, *Papers*, 1926–7, p. 7. The legislation complained of were the following: Immigration Law Amendment Act, 17/1895; Immigration Restriction Act, 1/1897; Dealers Licences Act, 18/1897.
5. G.H. 1265/1902.
6. Govt. of India, *Papers*, 1926–7, p. 7. *Natal Mercury*, 6th March, 1903 stated that the labour shortage in Natal was something like 18 000. To improve recruiting in India it suggested that a white man be sent to the villages and that the "moral force of such a white man" would assist.
7. Govt. of India, *Papers*, 1926–7, pp. 7–8.
8. Memo by the Govt. of the Union of S.A., on the subject of Indian legislation to UNO, Document A/167, 31st October, 1946, par. 10.
9. Gandhi, *My Experiment with Truth*, Chapter XIX, pp. 148–152. The All-India National Congress was formed in India in 1885.

10. B. Pachai, *The History of the "Indian Opinion"*, Chap. II, pp. 30–44.
11. C.S.O. 5924/1902, N.I.C. Memorial for transmission to the Secretary of State for Colonies, 11/9/02.
12. Govt. of India, *Papers*, 1926–7, p. 8. The feeling of the Natal Government was revealed in the introduction of the Natal Municipal Corporations Bill in 1905, which sought to take away the Municipal franchise from the Indians.
13. *Asiatic Population of Provinces: 1904.*
    Total: 122 734   *Cape:* 10 242   *Natal:* 100 918   *Transvaal:* 11 321   *O.F.S.:* 253
    Vide Official Year Book of the Union of South Africa, No. 3, p. 184. For the Morley-Minto reforms, *vide* Smith, *The Oxford History of India*, pp. 773–5.
14. Govt. of India, *Papers*, 1926–7, pp. 16–17.
15. B. Pachai, *The History of the "Indian Opinion"*, p. 46.
16. "The Asiatic Question in the Transvaal", *The State*, Vol. I, 1909, p. 681.
17. B.P.P. No. 79. Despatch from the Governor of Transvaal Respecting the Position of the British Indians, Milner to Chamberlain, 11 May, 1903.
18. H. S. L. Polak, *The Indians of South Africa*, p. 76.
19. L. E. Neame, *The Asiatic Danger in the Colonies*, p. 65, quoted in Polak, *Indians of South Africa*, p. 77.
20. Report of the Asiatic Inquiry Commission, 1921, pp. 11–12.
21. *Ibid.*, p. 12.
22. *Ibid.*, p. 13. In Natal immigration was controlled by Act 1/1897 as amended by Act 30/1903, which prescribed an education test in any European language for would-be immigrants. Distinguished Indians who spoke the vernacular only could be granted visiting passes, extendable for considerable periods. Indians, other than indentured, could obtain certificates of domicile which enabled them to leave and return at any time without molestation. Those who could pass the education test did not require domicile certificates. In the Cape the Immigration Restriction Act of 1903 as amended by Act 30/1906 was also based on the Natal law. The Act, however, did not define "domicile". An Indian desirous of leaving the Colony on a visit had to provide himself with a permit to return or he would be treated on return as a prohibited immigrant. B. Pachai, *The History of the "Indian Opinion"*, pp. 84–5.
23. *Indian Opinion*, Special Congress Supplement, 18th February, 1905.
24. A. B. Keith, *Responsible Government in the Dominions*, p. 827, footnote 1.
25. Polak, *The Indians of South Africa: Part II, A Tragedy of Empire*, pp. 8–9.
26. Government of India, *Important Correspondence relating to the Two Passive Resistance Movements in South Africa* (1905–1914), p. 1. This is cited hereafter as *Important Correspondence, 1905–1914.*
27. *Important Correspondence, 1905–1914*, p. 3.
28. Cd. 3308: Correspondence relating to Legislation Affecting Asiatics in Transvaal, 1906, Lord Elgin to Governor of the Transvaal, May 11, 1906.
29. Cd. 3308: Governor to Secretary of State for Colonies, 18th July, 1906.
30. Govt. of India, *Important Correspondence, 1905–1914.*
31. Gandhi, *Satyagraha in South Africa*, p. 99.
32. Gandhi, *My Experiments with Truth*, p. 261.
33. *Ibid.*, p. 315.
34. Gandhi, *Satyagraha in South Africa*, p. 101.
35. H. S. L. Polak, *The Indians of South Africa: Part II, A Tragedy of Empire*, p. 11.
36. Cd. 3308: Secretary of State to Governor, 21st September, 1906.
37. *Ibid.*, Secretary of State to Governor, 11 October, 1906.
38. Gandhi, *Satyagraha in South Africa*, pp. 118–9.
39. Cd. 3308: Governor to Secretary of State, January 14, 1907.
40. H. S. L. Polak, *The Indians of South Africa: Part II, A Tragedy of Empire*, p. 13.
41. *Ibid.*, pp. 12–13.
42. With regard to registration in the Transvaal it must be noted that in his Report for 1906 the Registrar of Asiatics stated that between May 1903, when re-registration had commenced, and December

1906, 12 543 registrations had been effected; of this number only 4 144 were accepted as valid; that 8 000 Asiatics had managed to enter the Transvaal illegally; that there was a flourishing market for registration certificates; permits were bought, sold or stolen; that 154 Asiatics had died during 1906 but only 4 permits were recovered; that during 1906, 876 male Indians entered or were found in the colony without legal authority.

Vide *Natal Mercury*, April 9th 1907. In its editorial comment the same paper stated that it was futile for Gandhi or others to contend that the present registration system was effective. In a letter dated 9th April, 1907, Gandhi write to the *Natal Mercury*, pointing out that the message transmitted by Reuter was incorrect; that 4 144 had made good their claims by paying the £3 registration fees; that the rest were in possession of permits; to state that 8 000 had entered illegally was to be far off the mark; that those who had died and whose permits had not been returned had died in India.

Vide *Natal Mercury*, April 13th, 1907.

43. Govt. of India, *Papers*, p. 21.
44. Keith, *Responsible Government in the Dominions*, pp. 827–8.
45. Polak, *The Indians of South Africa: Part II, The Tragedy of Empire*, p. 77.
46. C. F. Andrews, *Documents Relating to the Indian Question*, pp. 13–14.
47. *Vide* Transvaal Government Gazette, C.S.O. Vol. 54, July–December 1907.
48. Patrick Duncan, *State*, 1909, Vol. 1, p. 165.
49. Telegram No. 9499–108, 5th November, 1907, Govt. of India, *Important Correspondence*, 1905–1914, p. 11.
50. Gandhi, *Satyagraha in South Africa*, p. 131. B. Pachai, *The History of the "Indian Opinion"*, p. 59.
51. Patrick Duncan, *State*, Vol. 1, 1909, p. 165.
52. Polak, *The Indians of South Africa: Part II, A Tragedy of Empire*, p. 14.
53. B. Pachai, *The History of the "Indian Opinion"*, Chap. III, The Passive Resistance movement in the Transvaal, pp. 45–80 and Chap. IV, The Passive Resistance Movement in Natal and the end of the struggle in the Transvaal, pp. 81–118.
54. "Sat" means truth and "agraha" firmness—hence "firmness in a true or just cause".
55. *Indian Opinion*, 30th November, 1907.
56. Gandhi, *Satyagraha in South Africa*, p. 156.
57. Cd. 4327: M. K. Gandhi to Colonial Secretary, Smuts, 1st February, 1908.
58. Cd. 4327: Chairman of the Transvaal British Indian Association to the Transvaal Colonial Secretary, 27th July, 1908.
59. Cd. 4327: Gandhi to Smuts, June 13, 1908.
60. *Transvaal Leader*, August 17th, 1908, reproduced in the Govt. of India, *Important Correspondence*, 1905–1914, p. 12.
61. *Transvaal Leader*, 17th August, 1908, reproduced in *Important Correspondence*, 1903–1914, pp. 12–15.
62. Govt. of India, *Papers*, 1926–7, p. 22.
63. Transvaal Legislative Council Debates, Second Session of 1st Parliament, p. 513.
64. Gandhi, *Satyagraha in South Africa*, p. 190.
65. Govt. of India, *Important Correspondence*, 1905–1914, pp. 21–25.
66. *Ibid.*, p. 21.
67. Govt. of India, *Important Correspondence*, 1905–14, p. 24–26.
68. Govt. of India, *Important Correspondence*, 1905–14, pp. 32–3.
69. Polak, *The Indians of South Africa: Part II, A Tragedy of Empire*, p. 20. Polak was also an attorney of the Transvaal Supreme Court.
70. H. S. L. Polak, *State*, Vol. 1, 1909, p. 683–4. See Appendix A, p. 284, *infra*.
71. B. Pachai, *The History of the "Indian Opinion"*, p. 120. Chap. V of this study deals with Indian Trading in Natal, pp. 119–140.
72. Polak, *Indians of South Africa*, p. 11. In 1907 there were 1 260 Indian storekeepers in Natal and 648 European storekeepers. Vide *Natal Advertiser*, 15th March, 1907.
73. The *Natal Mercury*, 13th March, 1907 and *Indian Opinion*, 16th March, 1907.

74. C.S.O. 2479/1908, 21st April, 1908. In 1907 various resolutions had been moved asking that no new licences be granted to Asiatics and that Asiatic immigration to Natal be abolished but these came to nothing, though they are important indications of the temperament of the day. *Vide* Votes and Proceedings of the Legislative Assembly of Natal, 30th July, 1907, 4th July, 1907.
75. Report of the Protector of Indian Immigrants, 1908, pp. 7–8.
76. Report of the Asiatic Inquiry Commission, U.G. 4/1921, p. 45.
77. *Natal Mercury*, 5th August, 1908.
78. *Ibid.*, 17th November, 1908.
79. Govt. of India, *Important Correspondence*, 1905–1914, p. 29.
80. Report of the Indian Immigration Commission, 1909, p. 4. Words underlined in the original.
81. *Ibid.* The distribution of indentured Indian labour was as follows: General Farming: 6 149. Sugar Estates: 7 006. Coal Mines: 3 239. Tea Estates: 1 722. Natal Government Railways: 2 371. Domestic Servants: 1 949. Corporations: 1 062. Brick Yards, etc.: 740. Wattle Plantations: 606. Landing & Shipping Agents: 422. Miscellaneous: 313. Total: 25 569.
82. B. Pachai, *The History of the "Indian Opinion"*, p. 77. As the name of Henry S. L. Polak features quite prominently in this chapter, it is well to recall that he came to South Africa for health reasons in 1903 and became engaged in journalistic work for *The Transvaal Critic* in Johannesburg. He became one of the original settlers when Gandhi founded the Phoenix Settlement in 1904. He became editor of the *Indian Opinion* in 1906 and held this position till 1916. Since 1906 he acted as Assistant Hon. Secretary to the Transvaal British Indian Association, the Secretary of which body was M. K. Gandhi. In 1906 he took articles with Gandhi and in 1908 he was admitted as an attorney of the Supreme Court of the Transvaal. Polak was the delegate of the South African Indians to India in 1909–1911. He left South Africa for England in 1916 and set up practice there. He died in 1959. A matter of personal gratification to the writer was correspondence he had with Mr. Polak from 1957 onwards in connection with the thesis on the *Indian Opinion*. Mr. Polak was so kind as to send to the writer his only spare copy of *The Indians of South Africa*, from London.
83. C.S.O. 5595/1909. Natal Indian Congress to Colonial Secretary for transmission to the Imperial Government. The petition was dated at Durban on 10th July, 1909 and was signed by 1 135 persons.
84. Govt. of India, *Important Correspondence*, 1905–1914, p. 35. Section 147 of the South Africa Act read as follows: "The control and administration of native affairs and of matters specially or differentially affecting Asiatics throughout the Union shall vest in the Governor-General-in-Council. . . ." *Vide* Sir Edgar H. Walton, *The Inner History of the National Convention of South Africa*, Appendix p. 1.
85. Natesan, *Speeches and Writings of M. K. Gandhi*, p. 57.
86. P. Duncan, *The State*, Vol. 1, 1909, pp. 171–2.
87. H. S. L. Polak, *The Indians of South Africa*, Foreword, pp. iii–iv.
88. Natesan, *Speeches of Gopal Krishna Gokhale*, pp. 730–733.
89. C.S.O. 300/1910, 16th January, 1910.
90. C.S.O. 1921/1910, Secretary of State to Lord Gladstone, 12th July, 1910, for transmission to the Natal Indian Congress. The new Act suspended the payment of arrears in the case of men and women who reindentured and in the event of these persons electing to return to India the arrears so suspended were *ipso facto* cancelled.
91. *Natal Mercury*, 26th February, 1910.
92. *The Natal Advertiser*, 26th February, 1910.
93. *Indian Opinion*, 5th March, 1910.
94. *Indian Opinion*, 19th March, 1910.
95. *Ibid.*, 7th May, 1910.
96. *Indian Opinion*, 6th August, 1910 for letters by deportees to the Indian Press, particularly one from David Ernest, which starts thus: "I am an Indian Christian, born in Natal, and this is the first time I have ever set foot upon Indian soil. I was married in South Africa and all my children were born there. Our future and that of Colonial-born Indians lies in South Africa. . . .".
97. *Indian Opinion*, 7th January, 1911.

98. South African Indian Congress, Emergency Conference, 1926, *Compendium of Anti-Asiatic Legislation*, p. 4.
99. Govt. of India, *Papers*, 1926–7, p. 28.
100. Govt. of India, *Papers*, pp. 23–25.
101. Govt. of India, *Papers*, 1926–7, pp. 29–30.
102. In 1914 during the debates on the Indian Relief Act, Mr. H. M. Meyler, M.P., said: "He (Gokhale) could make speeches which would be an ornament to this House". During his six weeks' tour his speeches created a sensation in the country.
103. Natesan, *Speeches of Gopal Krishna Gokhale*, pp. 736–7.
104. Aiyar, *Conflict of Races in South Africa*, p. 141.
105. Govt. of India, *Papers*, 1926–7, p. 31. The declaration referred to in (2) deals with the undertaking not to own fixed property or to trade. The first two objections were resolved between Gandhi and Smuts as follows: (1) Smuts gave an assurance that such immigrants, if they had resided in Natal for three years after completing their indentures, would be treated as lawfully domiciled; (2) An agreement was reached to print at the back of the permit the declaration required under Section 14 of the Act, the disabilities set forth in Section 7 of Chapter XXXIII of the O.F.S. Law Book.
106. B. Pachai, *The History of the "Indian Opinion"*, pp. 97–98.
107. Indian Inquiry Commission, 1914, pp. 16–17.
108. *Natal Mercury*, 3rd June, 1913.
109. Govt. of India, *Papers*, 1926–7, p. 31.
110. *Indian Opinion*, 5th November, 1913.
111. Smith, *The Oxford History of India*, p. 777.
112. Govt. of India, *Papers*, 1926–7, pp. 32–3. *Round Table*, No. 15, June, 1914, pp. 474–476.
113. Govt. of India, *Important Correspondence*, 1905–1914, p. 46.
114. *Ibid.*, p. 51.
115. Report of the Indian Inquiry Commission, U.G. 16/1914, *Summary of the Recommendations*.
116. Govt. of India, *Important Correspondence*, 1905–1914, p. 53.
117. Govt. of India, *Papers*, 1926–7, p. 40.

CHAPTER THREE

THE BEGINNING AND THE END OF REPATRIATION:
THE FIRST PHASE, 1914–1927

"Standing now at the cross-roads of South African History and surveying, in retrospect, the changes of varying fortune and vicissitudes of the Indian in this country, one might say with Tennyson: 'Perhaps evil is even sometimes the way to good . . .', for in the continuous struggle has come strength . . ."
– Dhanee Bramdaw, Editor of the *Leader*, in *Out of the Stable*.

The Smuts–Gandhi Agreement of 1914 was more than a simple understanding between two gentlemen: each expected the full acceptance of his viewpoint. For Smuts, the Agreement, read together with the Indian Relief Act, meant that a lasting solution had been arrived at. For Gandhi, the Agreement offered a hope that the beginning to a lasting solution had been made. These two irreconcilable views represented the anomaly in the situation. For the Europeans in the country there was no longer any problem presented by the Indians – if they could always be kept in check; for the Indians their difficulties (except for the respite granted by the Agreement) were there all the time. Some of the more urgent difficulties which lay before the Indians were those created by the Transvaal Law, 3/1885, the Gold Law of 1908 and the Townships Act of the same year. These laws seriously affected the position of the Indians in connection with their trading rights and their rights to acquire and occupy property. Indeed, the ownership of land, its occupation, and the right to trade outside Asiatic bazaars were the urgent matters for the moment.

If friendly negotiations and consultations between the Indians and the government were maintained in order to resolve these difficulties the future did not offer great hardships. Gandhi had himself dubbed his agreement with Smuts "the Magna Charta of our liberty in the land" for it established the right of the Indians not only to be consulted in matters which affected them but also to have their reasonable wishes respected.[1]

In any settlement in the future the Colonial-born Indians would feature prominently as they would be the affected people. It was obvious that in the coming years the entire character of the Indian population in South Africa would be South African. In 1936, 21 per cent of the total Indian population in South Africa were born outside the Union; in 1946 the figure dropped to 11 per cent. With Gandhi now no more in the country the Colonial-born Indians would have to play a greater role in the coming events. One of them was Advocate Albert Christopher.

Commenting on the Smuts–Gandhi Agreement, Advocate Albert Christopher, who was a close lieutenant of M. K. Gandhi, wrote thus in 1914: "To the South African-born Indian, then, must they, who would solve the Indian Question, turn, and in him they will find material worthy of a part in the structure of South Africa. He is in a state of transition from the East to the West, and, if it were possible that the virtues of the Occident and the Orient could be blended in him, then the prediction of Kipling, that the East and the West will never meet, will have been falsified. And there is hope for the Colonial-born

73

Indian, given the opportunities of trade, calling, occupation and freedom of locomotion, with facilities for academic, technical, agricultural, and industrial education, that he will hold his own; but his condition will be cribbed, cabined and confined, so long as the proverbial barriers remain in the country with a Union which cannot for ever keep the Indians born in South Africa from realising their oneness of interests and aspirations in life; and this must happen sooner than most people would expect . . .".[2] Christopher's statement could be likened to a manifesto of demands by the resident Indian population.

As a Colonial-born Indian with an interest in the stake, Advocate Christopher saw, in 1914, that the realisation of the interests and aspirations of the Indian community in South Africa would come "sooner than most people would expect". Disinterested people, too, were apt to think the same way, at least in some instances. In this respect, the views of a European journalist, Vere Stent, one time Editor of the *Pretoria News*, are worthy of note. Looking into the future he wrote in 1914 that he foresaw the day when the colour-bar would be removed from the Franchise Act and when this happened the Asiatics would be the first to come in for voting rights. But, after the recent agitation, he counselled that the Asiatics should wait and not engage themselves in any political agitation.[3]

Viewed in the light of the optimism that prevailed in some quarters, the settlement of 1914 offered hopes of a better future. But the day of realization and hope was postponed when the World War broke out. The South African Indian question and, indeed, all major international issues were ignored while efforts were directed to win the war.

M. K. Gandhi left South Africa for England, his work done, on the 20th July, 1914, ten days before the "Sarajevo affair" culminated in the declaration of war by Austria on Serbia. Gandhi was still on the high seas when Germany declared war first on Russia on August 1st and then on France, on August 3rd. Britain was drawn into the conflagration on August 4th. Six days later, the Union Government, under Louis Botha, entered the struggle on the side of the British Government and dispatched a force to destroy the German wireless stations in South West Africa.[4]

The Indian question in South Africa took a back step as the world stage was occupied by Armageddon. As in 1899 and in 1906, the patriotism of the Indian community in South Africa was not found wanting. Nor was Indian patriotism and duty found wanting in India. In South Africa the Indian community gave its support by active enlistment in and service with the two Indian Bearer Companies in East Africa and by financial contributions, an example of which was the Indian War Fair held in Durban when a cheque for £931 6s. 6d. was handed to the Mayor of Durban on 5th January, 1917. This effort brought forth a letter from the Governor-General thanking the Indian community, in particular the Indian gardeners in the neighbourhood of Durban who each gave a day's produce to the Fair.[5]

India's war effort was even greater. Financially alone, the Indian Government made available to the British Government £100 000 000 as a special war contribution, over and above the additional charges which the war entailed on India's own military budget. The strength of the Army in India at the outbreak of the war was 239 561. And 1 161 789 men, of whom 757 747 were combatants, were recruited during the war, till September 30th, 1918. Of this number, 953 374 were sent overseas for service. The casualties numbered 33 051 killed, died, or missing; 59 296 wounded; 9 092 taken prisoner.[6]

India's role in the war brought forth favourable comments from various sources. The British Prime Minister, Asquith, said in September, 1914: "We welcome with appreciation and affection India's proferred aid in the Empire which knows no distinction of race or class, where all alike are subjects of the King–Emperor and are joint and equal custodians of her common interest and fortunes. We hail with profound and heart-felt gratitude their association side by side and shoulder to shoulder with the Home and Dominion troops under a flag which is a symbol to all of the unity that the world in arms cannot dissever or dissolve."[7] Lloyd George re-echoed these sentiments in the House of Commons in 1917.

India's part in the war was given practical recognition when the country was invited to participate in the Imperial War Conference in 1917. About a month before the Conference met in London, the Indian National Congress adopted a resolution moved by H. S. L. Polak, former Editor of the *Indian Opinion* at the Phoenix Settlement, Durban, expressing dissatisfaction at the continued ill-treatment of Indians in the Dominions and Colonies and asking that advantage be taken of the brotherhood engendered by the war struggle to put an end to the existing disabilities. The appeal to do so was addressed to the British Government.[8]

Though the World War was now being waged in full force, the fact that India and South Africa ranked among the allies of Great Britain thrust upon the head of the British Empire the responsibility for resolving any outstanding differences among the allies. Foremost among these differences was the question of the Indians resident in the Dominions. This question was now to be raised at the level of Imperial conferences.

The Imperial War Conference of 1917 was to take a step in the direction envisaged in the resolution of the Indian National Congress. The Imperial Conferences were at first known as Colonial Conferences. The first Colonial conference was held in 1887 and the last one was held in 1907 when it was decided to change the name to Imperial Conference. The first Imperial Conference took place in 1909 and the last one in 1937. After that year Prime Ministers' Conferences or Commonwealth Conferences took place in 1946, 1948, 1949, 1951, 1952, 1953 and almost every year since then. The Conference of 1917 was also known as the Imperial War Conference because of the war.[9]

The Imperial Conference of 1917 was not the first Conference to discuss the position of Indians in the Dominions. The honour goes to the Imperial Conference of 1911 which discussed the position of British Indians resulting from the efforts of Australia and New Zealand to exclude them from ships visiting their coasts. This move elicited from Lord Crewe, Secretary of State for India, an effective statement. Lord Crewe conceded the right to exclude Indians from the Dominions because of the prevalence of race prejudices; he agreed that economically the Indians were very powerful competitors but, he added, it was incorrect and unjust to say that they had a lower standard of living. He could not see any reason for preventing Indians from visiting the Dominions on a temporary basis or for imposing disabilities on those lawfully resident in the Dominions on the grounds of race or colour. He reminded the conference of the religious and intellectual greatness of India and of her unswerving loyalty to the British Crown.[10]

None of the Dominion Premiers sought to answer the arguments though they insisted on the economic impossibility of competing with Indian labour. For South Africa, Malan, one of the Union delegates, pointed out that the racial question was made complex by the presence of Indians. No solution was attempted or achieved at this Conference with regard to the position of Indians in the Dominions.

The Imperial Conference of 1911 was the first conference of this nature to be attended by a Prime Minister of the Union of South Africa. It is significant, therefore, to recall what General Botha, the Union's first Premier, had to say about the place of such conferences in Commonwealth affairs. General Botha said that these conferences must not be looked upon as affording the opportunity to the members of the British Empire to adopt resolutions which would be put into effect throughout the Empire.[11] In this statement General Botha made it quite clear how his country saw the position and this stand is particularly important when it is remembered that the statement was made when the position of Indians was being discussed at the Imperial Conference of 1911.

Though General Louis Botha did not look upon the conference as meetings convened primarily for the purpose of passing a number of resolutions which were to be carried into effect throughout the Empire, the Imperial War Conference of 1917 not only discussed the position of Indians in the Dominions but adopted a resolution thereon for the consideration of the Dominions.

In his speech at the Imperial Conference of 1917, one of the Indian delegates, Sir Satyendra P. Sinha, recalled one of the passages from the Memorandum presented by the Marquis of Crewe, Secretary of State for India, to the Imperial Conference of 1911, which read: "It does not appear to have been thoroughly considered that each Dominion owes responsibility to the rest of the Empire for ensuring that its domestic policy shall not unnecessarily create embarrassment in the administration of India."[12]

He said that it was difficult for statesmen who had seen Indians represented only by manual labourers and petty traders to realise the importance to the Empire of a country with some three hundred million inhabitants, possessing an ancient civilisation of a very high order. It was difficult to convey to those who did not know India the intense and natural resentment felt by veterans of the Indian army, who had been treated by their British officers with consideration and courtesy, finding themselves described as "coolies" and "treated with contemptuous severity in parts of the British Empire". The main burden of Sinha's resolution was directed at Canada which banned the entry of wives and children of British Indians domiciled there.

The Memorandum presented by the Indian delegates touched upon the position of British Indians in all parts of the British Empire and was not confined to South Africa alone. It recalled that while Australia and New Zealand imposed an educational test upon immigrants, Canada and South Africa had taken power to exclude immigrants belonging to any race deemed to be unsuitable as residents. The Memorandum stated that South Africa, which had a large permanent Indian population, differed from the other Dominions in allowing, subject to strict precautions, any Indian who had acquired the right of residence to bring his wife and his young children from India, to take up permanent residence.

On the question of political grievances, such as the absence of political equality with full citizens, the Memorandum stated that though such matters were entirely within the discretion of the several governments, it was of importance to note that the biased administration of municipal regulations regarding trading licences might in practice inflict more injury on individual resident Indians than did some statutes against which Indians had protested. The Memorandum offered the following points as the basis of an Agreement on the question of British Indians in the Empire:

"(1) As regards Indians already permanently settled in the Dominions, they should be allowed to bring in wives (subject to the rule of monogamy) and minor children, and in other respects should not be less privileged than Japanese settled immigrants.

(2) Future admission of Indians for labour or settlement should, if possible, be regulated on lines similar to, and not less favourable than, those governing the admission of any other Asiatic race.

(3) If this is not possible, there might be reciprocal treatment in India and each Dominion of immigration for purposes of labour or permanent settlement. If a Dominion is determined to exclude these two classes of immigration from India, India should be free to do the same as regards the Dominion. It would be clearly recognised that the exclusion in either case was not motivated by prejudices of race, but as the outcome of different economic conditions.

(4) Along with such exclusion reciprocal arrangements would be made for granting full facilities for the admission of tourists, students, and the like and for business visits entailing temporary residence."

On 27th April, 1917 the Conference unanimously accepted the principle of reciprocity of treatment between India and the Dominions and recommended the Memorandum submitted by the Indian delegates for the favourable consideration of the governments concerned.[13]

The Memorandum submitted by the Indian delegates was deemed to be too mild in some circles. The *Indian Opinion* criticised it by stating that it had an Anglo-Indian flavour about it which could possibly be accounted for by the fact that the Indian representatives at the conference were appointed by the Government of India (which in turn was controlled by the British Government) and did not represent the views of the masses. The chief complaint against the case presented by the Indian delegates was that it did not make any firm suggestions for the removal of existing grievances.

That there were legitimate grievances was admitted by South Africa's chief delegate to the conference, General Smuts, who recalled the trouble caused in the past on the question of the treatment of Indians in South Africa. Smuts said that in South Africa the fundamental trouble was the fear of the European community to admit Indians freely into the country because such a practice would aggravate the position of the white man there for, as things stood, the Europeans made up a small "white population on a black continent". There was no reason other than that of protecting European interests in the country that prompted his country to keep out Asiatic immigrants from South Africa. But with the present restrictions on Indian immigration to South Africa, the former fears, said Smuts, no longer existed and the way was cleared for the peaceful solution of all minor administrative troubles of the present and future. He recognised the great changes that were taking place by the admission of India to the conferences of the Empire. This, he felt, would assist in solving the problems confronting India and South Africa on the position of the Indians in South Africa.[14]

Two important factors emerge from Smuts' speech at the conference. One was his admission of the increasing importance of India in the Empire. India's war effort had much to do with the growth of India's status in the Empire. And this war effort, in turn, was made possible by the popularity of Hardinge's administration. If India had now gained greater recognition at Empire level it followed that constitutional reforms at home would not be long in coming. And these reforms would naturally influence the relations between India and South Africa with regard to the Indian question in South Africa. Indeed, on 20th August, 1917, the Secretary of State announced in the House of Commons that the new policy towards India was one of "the increasing association of Indians in every branch of the administration, and the gradual development of self-governing institutions, with a view to the progressive realisation of responsible government in India as an integral part of the Empire".[15] The reforms proposed, known as the Montagu–Chelmsford reforms, became law in December, 1919 and committed the British Government to the development of Indian self-government along parliamentary lines. This development was one of the significant aspects of the Indian question which Smuts had taken note of in his speech at the Imperial Conference of 1917. The other pointed to the fact that the fear of an Asiatic influx into South Africa no longer existed.

General Smuts had made a frank admission that the Immigrants Regulation Act, 22/1913 had the effect of allaying European fears of an Asiatic influx into South Africa. Gokhale had said in 1912 that this assurance had to be given to the Europeans in South Africa. Hence his championship of the "closed-door" policy. Five years after Gokhale's memorable visit to South Africa, General Smuts was admitting at an Imperial Conference that the question of immigration having been solved, "the question of India will (not) trouble us much in the future". Statistics show that the percentage of Asiatics to Europeans in the Union, in the period covered in this chapter, dropped progressively, no longer leaving any justifiable grounds for fears that the Asiatics would in time swamp the Europeans in the Union of South Africa.[16]

Statistics also show clearly that in the one Province, Natal – where reasonable apprehension might have existed of the Indian population swamping the European – the latter had, by 1932, rapidly overhauled the former, with the result that whereas the percentage of Asiatics to the total European–Asiatic population in Natal was 57,49 per cent in 1911, it had dropped to 47,34 per cent in 1932, the percentage being equal in 1922.

The position in the Dominions was further reviewed at the second session of the Conference which was held in 1918. Two notable representatives from India were Sir Satyendra P. Sinha and the Maharaja of Patiala. The former moved a resolution which called for practical effect to be given to the principle of reciprocity adopted in 1917. The conference agreed that the different governments of the British Commonwealth should control the composition of their populations by imposing whatever immigration restrictions they wished on the basis of reciprocity of treatment. This gave India the right to treat British Europeans residing in India in the same way as British Indians were treated in the Dominions and Colonies. India gained little in actual practice from this arrangement. It was further agreed that Indians domiciled in other parts of the Empire should be permitted to bring in their monogamous wives, and children.

In the Memorandum which Sir Satyendra P. Sinha presented to the conference, he included the main grievances of South African Indians in connection with trading licences, the franchise, ownership of land and railway regulations.

On the subject of trading licences, the Memorandum stated that it was generally conceded that the municipalities arbitrarily refused to grant licences to Indians "with the improper and indirect object of destroying Indian trade". If this continued the Indian community would be impoverished and would be reduced to "industrial helotry". The remedy, the Memorandum went on to state, was to give the fullest right of appeal in all cases of refusal of licences to the Provincial Division of the Supreme Court, on questions of fact as well as of procedure.

On the matter of the franchise, the Memorandum stated that there were stronger and more obvious grounds for extending the municipal franchise to the Indians resident in South Africa than the parliamentary franchise, especially in view of the trading difficulties.

In regard to the question of the ownership of land, the Memorandum stated that Law 3/1885 of the Republican Government of the Transvaal imposed difficulties upon the Transvaal Indians which were not encountered by Indians in Natal or in the Cape. The system of indirect ownership, through nominal European ownership, originally suggested by the Republican Government themselves, prevailed until quite recently and was still occasionally adopted. "The process is roundabout, cumbrous, and expensive, but the facts are notorious, and the circumstances are legally recognised by the Courts", the Memorandum stated.

It said that since the year 1914 the practice had grown up of forming and registering, under the Transvaal Companies Act, 1909, small private companies, with limited liability, whose members were all Indians, and possessing legal persona for the purpose, among other things, of acquiring fixed property. "It is said that attempts are now being made by interested parties to deprive Indians of this right of indirect ownership of fixed property."[17]

On the subject of land ownership the Memorandum suggested that the prohibition against Indian ownership of fixed or landed property should be repealed by Parliament, on the grounds that it tended to foster insincerity on all sides and it deprived Indians of elementary citizenship rights which were not denied to other non-whites in the Transvaal nor to the Indians living in Natal. It called for the repeal of Law 3/1885 of the Transvaal, which law it dubbed an "anachronism".

In the Memorandum, the fourth principal grievance mentioned by Sir Satyendra P. Sinha dealt with the railway regulations in the Union of South Africa and the segregation policy employed. Sir Satyendra Sinha quoted an excerpt from a speech made by Gokhale in November, 1912, when he addressed a European audience in South Africa. On that occasion Gokhale had said to the Europeans: "You have all the power, and yours, therefore, is the responsibility for the manner in which the affairs of this land are administered. You owe it to your good name, you owe it to your civilization, you owe it to the Empire of which you are a part and whose flag stands for opportunities for progress for all who live under its protection, that your administration should be such that you can justify it in the eyes of the civilized world."[18]

It was as if Sinha was appealing to the European delegates present at the Imperial Conference as Gokhale had appealed to the Europeans in South Africa. He suggested the provision of a convenient agency by which Indian grievances could be brought to the notice of the local government authorities. He said: "The appointment of a local agent of the Indian Government at Pretoria should be an advantage both to the Indians in South Africa and the South African Government which has to deal with them." And, in conclusion, he said: "It is also obvious that these important questions should be settled not in any petty huckstering spirit of reciprocity only, far less of militant animosity and retaliation, but on those broad principles of justice and equality which are now more than ever the guiding principles of the British Empire . . .".[19]

In his eloquent appeal Sinha made it quite clear that there was no doubt about the reality and the burden of the disabilities under which Indians laboured in South Africa, more especially in the Transvaal. He suggested, too, that as the Europeans held all power theirs was the responsibility to remove the existing grievances. All these facts though clearly known for many years were now recounted for the first time at an Imperial Conference.

For South Africa, the Minister of Railways and Harbours, Burton, admitted that there were difficulties and that it would be idle to disguise the fact that many of those difficulties were of substantial importance. He did not despair of a satisfactory solution being arrived at. "As far as we are concerned, it is only fair to say – and it is the truth – that we have found that the Indians in our midst in South Africa, who form in some parts a very substantial portion of the population, are good, law-abiding, quiet citizens; and it is our duty to see . . . that they are treated as human beings, with feelings like our own, and in a proper manner."

But, Burton said, he felt that the complaints made in the Indian Memorandum were exaggerated and that South Africa would welcome a visit by the Indian delegate, Sir Satyendra Sinha, to South Africa to investigate the position himself. South Africa, said Burton, welcomed the proposal referring the Memorandum for the sympathetic consideration of his government.[20]

The Union delegates not only allowed the question of Indians in South Africa to be discussed at the Imperial War Conference of 1917–1918 but promised to give the Memorandum submitted by the delegates from India "their most sympathetic consideration". How, in any case, was the Reciprocity Resolution to affect the position? Let the editorial of the *Indian Opinion* pose the same question and answer it:

"How is that arrangement going to work? An educational test in any of the Indian languages would effectively bar intending immigrants from South Africa or elsewhere. But that test is out of the question because the official language of India is English. How would the economic test apply? The standard of life, and habits and customs of Europeans, are certainly different to those of the majority of Indians. They are expensive – we might say extravagant – and therefore the standard is termed 'high'. But would it be possible to exclude a person because of his high standard of life? . . . We are therefore puzzled to know how India could reciprocate to protect herself from invasion by residents of the Dominions on any ground whatsoever. . . .

. . . Until India is granted self-government on similar terms to the Dominions, the resolution of the Imperial War Conference is a 'scrap of paper' and nothing more."[21]

Neither did Mahatma Gandhi see anything in the Reciprocity Resolution of 1918 to be enthusiastic about. He said: "We need not consider it as a great achievement that we can pass the same law against the colonies that they may pass against us. It is like a giant telling a dwarf that the latter is free to give blow for blow . . .".[22]

That the Reciprocity Resolution did not affect the position of the Union of South Africa was quite evident in the remarks made by Burton in a speech at Cape Town on his return from London. He pointed out that he did not know of a single step which had been taken that would be construed by even the wildest misinterpretation as having been injurious to South Africa.

The Imperial War Conference of 1917–1918 was in essence a war-time conference aimed at strengthening the solidarity of the Commonwealth against the common enemy. There was no room in it for any serious cleavage. Neither did it reflect the unequivocal consensus of Commonwealth feeling and attitudes. These were best discerned in the peace-time atmosphere without the motivation of the defence of the Commonwealth influencing such feelings and attitudes.

The true position was revealed in 1919 after the cessation of hostilities. Before this is considered the main developments in the Transvaal after the Smuts–Gandhi Agreement must be reviewed. The position in the Transvaal after 1914 was fraught with great hardships for the Indians there. The basic difficulty was one of acquisition and occupation of land either for residence only or for trade. As the years passed by the situation grew worse and it can be said that the era of South African politics concerning the Indians in the country, spanned by the end of one world war and the outbreak of the next – 1919 and 1939 – revolved on the land question – the question of land holding not for agricultural purposes or for speculation but for trading purposes for the most part. It was on trade that the economy of the Indians in the Transvaal was dependent. The land question in the Transvaal, then (until it was extended to Natal years later), constituted the main issue after the Smuts–Gandhi Agreement. These land developments, to be seen in correct perspective, need to be traced from 1908 by way of recapitulation. Up to 1908 an Asiatic had the right to hire a stand on proclaimed land from the European licensed holder of it, and to carry on business upon it. There was nothing in the Gold Law of 1898 or any other law to prevent his doing so. By Section 130 of the Gold Law of 1908, Asiatics were prohibited from acquiring a lease in respect of a stand granted after the promulgation of that Law. Though no mention was made of trading rights, the effect of that section and of Section 131 was to preclude Asiatics, amongst other coloured persons, from exercising such rights by reason of their being prohibited from hiring such stands and occupying them and residing on them.[23]

In a letter to the Secretary for the Interior, dated 7th July, 1914, M. K. Gandhi defined "vested rights" in connection with the Gold Law and Townships Amendment Act as follows: "By vested rights I understand the right of an Indian and his successors to live and trade in the township in which he was living and trading, no matter how often he shifts his residence or business from place to place in the same township."[24]

The provisions of the Gold Law and Townships Act of 1908 were not strictly enforced with the result that between 1908 and 1914 a considerable number of new businesses had been established by Indian traders in several places, in spite of the law. After the Smuts–Gandhi Agreement, the Indian question was left in abeyance because of the war. Indian traders continued to apply for, and obtained, new licences to trade and they formed private companies with limited liability for the purpose of acquiring land and fixed property which individual Asiatics could not own because of Law 3/1885. Under the Transvaal Companies Act of 1909 only two shareholders were necessary to form a private limited liability company. A company could be formed by a single trader who held most of the shares himself and registered a few in the name of a friend or relative. After this, land could be purchased from a European owner and registered in the Deeds Office in the name of the company thus formed. For all intents and purposes the land now belonged to the Indian trader who had formed the company.

Though an evasion of Law 3/1885, this practice was declared to be legal in the case of Reynolds v. Oosthuizen, which was heard before Mr. Justice Ward, in September, 1916, in the Witwatersrand Local Division of the Supreme Court at Johannesburg. Three years later, in the case of Krugersdorp Municipal Council v. Dadoo Limited and Others, which was heard before the Provincial Division of the Supreme Court at Pretoria, it was held that such a transaction was *in fraudem legis* and therefore invalid. This decision was reversed by the Appellate Division of the Supreme Court in June, 1920, and the position as laid down by Mr. Justice Ward in 1916 remained, that there was nothing in the law to prevent such private companies, consisting entirely of Asiatic shareholders, from owning land in the Transvaal.

The war held the position in check. With its conclusion the question of Indians in the Transvaal once again came under the spotlight. The scene of the revival of agitation was now centred in Krugersdorp where the Municipal Council, despairing of the Government acting against Asiatic traders, decided to "step into the breach" themselves. The Municipal Council obtained an interdict in January, 1919, restraining a European firm, Messrs. T. W. Beckett and Company, from permitting the residence of certain Indians in a stand in Krugersdorp which had been leased by that firm to an Indian tailor and was at the time occupied by him and several other Indians.

The Indians were shocked by the latest developments. They held a conference and a deputation waited upon Sir Thomas Watt, the Minister of the Interior, and placed their various grievances before him. They also sent a petition signed by members of the Committee of the Transvaal British Indian Association, and by the Chairman of the Krugersdorp branch of the Association. In the petition they complained, *inter alia*, of certain disabilities which had been imposed on the British Indian community in the Transvaal in respect of the application of Sections 130 and 131 of the Gold Law of 1908. The petition was referred to a Select Committee of the House of Assembly, with instructions to take evidence and report on the alleged evasions by Asiatics of Law 3 of 1885 by means of forming themselves into limited liability companies.

In his evidence before the Select Committee on Disabilities of Indians in the Transvaal, L. W. Ritch, former Secretary of the South Africa British Indian Committee which was formed in London in 1906 on the occasion of Gandhi's visit to London in that year, said that the basic issue was the status of the Indians in the Transvaal; it was so in 1885 and in 1903; it was the same again in 1907 and 1908. Then in 1913, with the introduction of the Immigrants' Regulation Act, it was the issue of the status of the Indians in the Union. It was always a matter of relegating the Indians to the status of undesirables whenever their lot was considered.[25]

The Select Committee reported that the vested rights of Indians trading in proclaimed mining areas in June, 1914 should be respected; the same treatment should be accorded those Indians who acquired the same rights after that date; that Indians should have the right to transfer their existing businesses to other Indians legally resident in the Transvaal; that steps should be taken to make it impossible in future for Indians or other Asiatics to obtain trading licences in respect of new businesses.[26]

Before the steps taken by the Union Government to implement the report are considered, it is important to review the position of Indian political opposition in the country. In Natal there was the Natal Indian Congress founded on 22nd May, 1894. This body became defunct in 1915 shortly after the departure of M. K. Gandhi. Natal Indians remained without a political organisation for a number of years. It was revived and reorganised on 6th March, 1921.[27] In the Transvaal, there was the Transvaal British Indian Association and in the Cape, the Cape British Indian Council. There was not, as yet, a national body. The events of 1919 were to bring this about.

It was the Cape British Indian Council that took the initiative to convene a South African Indian Conference in Cape Town on 20th January, 1919. In a letter to the Editor of the *Dharma Vir*, the Chairman and the Secretary of the Council, Messrs. Sheikh Ismail and A. Ismail, respectively, wrote: "A common interest, a common danger, and a common purpose has welded us all into a strong body of brotherhood to demand our rights with no uncertain voice."[28] In opening the session of the South African Indian Conference, John X. Merriman, elder statesman of the Cape, said: "I hope one result of this conference will not be to carry us further apart and sow angry feeling, but to bring us closer together, that we may recollect that here in South Africa we who live under the British Flag and the right which the flag is supposed to cover, should all be in the words of your prophet, 'one brother'."[29] A Committee was appointed consisting of twelve representatives to frame the Constitution of an organisation to unite all Indians in the Union.

Meanwhile, when the report of the Select Committee on Indian Disabilities became known, a mass meeting of the Transvaal Indians was held in Johannesburg on 12th May, 1919 under the auspices of the Transvaal British Indian Association to organise their opposition to the Bill recommended in the report of the Select Committee.

The recommendations of the Select Committee were embodied in the Asiatics (Land and Trading) Amendment Act (Transvaal), 1919, in the form of Act 37/1919. The Act consisted of two parts. Part I of the Act protected Indians from the restrictions imposed by Sections 130 and 131 of the Gold Law of 1908: those who were lawfully engaged in trade on proclaimed land on 1st May, 1919, could continue to hold this right on the same ground, stand or lot, in the same township. Part II of the Act prohibited the ownership of fixed property by companies in which one or more Asiatics had a controlling influence. The ownership of land by Asiatics through nominees was not prohibited and Asiatics were still able to acquire an interest in fixed property by means of companies wherein the controlling interest was not Asiatic.[30]

The Act had a mixed reception and gave little satisfaction to any side. The European opponents of the Indian community felt that the Act did not go far enough. The Potchefstroom Chamber of Commerce sent a telegram to the Minister of Justice informing him that a Conference of the Western Transvaal towns would be convened to discuss the seriousness of the Asiatic question which was "becoming a matter of life and death for a large number of the European population".[31]

On 4th and 5th September, 1919, a Congress was held at Pretoria under the auspices of the Anti-Asiatic League. It was attended by delegates from a large number of towns and districts of the Transvaal, including representatives of 26 Municipalities, 30 Chambers of Commerce, 9 Agricultural Societies, 12 Churches and 40 Unions and other bodies. The Chairman of the Congress was L. J. Phillips, an attorney practising at Krugersdorp.

In his opening speech, Phillips said that the Asiatic menace threatened the Union in its very foundation. Unless the Union realised the danger, South Africa would not remain a country for white men and women. He asked for the question to be lifted above party politics. Phillips maintained that certain commercial and other bodies were not given an opportunity of being heard by the Select Committee, the result of whose work was that Act 37 was a Magna Charta for the Indians on the Rand. But the Indians, he said, were not satisfied. They wanted full civic and political rights. If the claim of the Indians was equality before the law, it was not a question of trading – the real underlying question went much further than that. The question was: could South Africa remain a white man's country if the Indians were allowed to progress on their own lines, unrestrainedly? If that question were answered in the negative, their duty was plain. It was a duty not to a few traders, but to every white woman and man in the country – not to this generation alone, but to posterity.[32] Turning to the position in Natal, Phillips said that in that Province, Europeans had been ousted by Indians. He suggested that a deputation of four or six members of the trade unions should go to Natal and see for themselves, and if they found there was no danger from Indian penetration, he would resign from the League. In conclusion, he said the evidence was against the contention that the Imperial Government was answerable for the position as it existed. It was not under pressure that Royal assent had been given to restrictive legislation. Every true Briton would acclaim the services of the fighting forces of India to Great Britain, but when the Indians in South Africa fell back on the services of the troops of India they challenged comparison. The Indians of South Africa had produced 660 stretcher-bearers and 42 other members of medical units, 702 in all, as against 199 298 who had remained behind and waxed fat.

The Congress adopted various resolutions calling upon the Government to deal firmly with Asiatic encroachments in trade, their evasions of the law. It opposed the grant of civic rights to Asiatics. A resolution was also passed urging public bodies to collect all available information regarding Asiatics and to lay it before the Commission which the Government proposed setting up to enquire into the Indian question. The Conference decided upon the formation of the South African League, the objects of which, *inter alia*, were to aim at the expropriation of all immovable property held by Asiatics and the general elimination, "by all statesmanlike means" of Asiatics resident and trading in the Transvaal. Sir Abe Bailey was elected first President of the South African League.

If the Europeans in the Transvaal were greatly agitated over the position created by Act 37/1919, the Indians were not less so. In the Transvaal an emergency committee was formed for the purpose of calling a South African National Indian Emergency Conference in August, 1919 to consider the new situation that had arisen, especially in view of the announcement that a commission would be appointed to enquire into the Indian question.

The Indians were satisfied that the agitation (if allowed to go unchecked) would spell their ruin.

The conference was to be held from 3rd to 6th August, 1919, in Johannesburg. In a circular exhorting the Indian community in South Africa to give its full support to the conference, the Emergency Conference Committee, whose chairman was E. I. Patel, and whose joint-secretaries were N. A. Camay and P. K. Naidoo, made a strong appeal to the Indians in South Africa to display their national strength by supporting the conference and in so doing to stand united against the steps being taken to deprive them of their legitimate rights promised so often in the Imperial proclamations of the past and recently repeated at the Imperial Conference of 1917–1918.

The steps that were now being taken by the Indians to show their national solidarity were the most important ones since the days of the passive resistance struggle of 1907–1913. But the high hopes cherished by the conveners of the conference failed to materialise. The main purpose behind the conference was defeated by internal dissensions which resulted in division and disunity. No national body was formed and the position remained as before with the Indians in the different provinces belonging to their own provincial political organisations.

If some parts in the proceedings of the conference left much to be desired, especially in the direction of the unity of the Indian community, the resolutions passed by the conference summed up in an adequate manner the demands of the Indians. The resolutions included a request for a just and sympathetic administration of the existing laws in regard to vested rights and the rights of entry, the franchise, the regulations of the South African Railways, the right of appeal to the Supreme Court against the refusal of a new licence, free and compulsory education, and technical and industrial training. There was no hope of any of the resolutions being accepted by the Government. The *Natal Mercury* said that though, for the present, absolute equality was not possible, once the Indians acquired the same levels in every respect with the Europeans, there would certainly be some justification for equality between them. This was an enlightened view which did not have much support in the country, especially in the Transvaal, but it represented a reasonable yardstick for the future: that all things being equal there should be no room for inequality; that there need be no room for discrimination between white and non-white but only between good and bad.

As for the conference itself, the important fact emerging from it from the Indian angle was that no national body was formed at that point, though it was a milestone towards the establishment of such a body. In February, 1919 the first Indian Conference convened by the Cape British Indian Council was held with a view to forming one central body for the whole Union but the lack of any definite mandate from the different Provinces did not lead to the formation of such a body. The second conference was called by the Transvaal British Indian Association in August, 1919, for a similar purpose. A provincial constitution for the creation of a South African Indian Congress was framed "but for some inexplicable reason it did not see the light of day". In 1923, the Natal Indian Congress, in accordance with an understanding given by the Natal delegates at the second conference in Johannesburg in August, 1919, convened – what was to be recognised as – the Third Session of the South African Indian Conference. The conference opened in

Durban on 31st May, 1923, under the chairmanship of the Mayor, Councillor Walter Gilbert, J.P. The Cape British Indian Council, the Transvaal British Indian Association and the Natal Indian Congress affiliated to the newly formed South African Indian Congress. The first officials of the South African Indian Congress were: President, Omar Hajee Amod Jhaveri; Hon. Treasurer, S. Emmamally; Hon. General Secretary, V. S. C. Pather. The councillors were Joseph Royeppen, N. A. Camay, P. K. Naidoo, representing the Transvaal British Indian Association, A. Ismail, V. A. Pillay, and S. S. Cassoojee, representing the Cape British Indian Council and A. Christopher, Sorabjee Rustomjee and S. R. Naidoo, representing the Natal Indian Congress.[33]

The Indian community had at last, in 1923, thrown in their resources into a national body which was to speak in the name of the whole community. Though internal dissensions prevented unanimity at all times and even led to the formation of another national body, the South African Indian Organisation, on 11th September, 1948, the significance of the formation of the S.A.I.C. in this study is that as far as the international field was concerned the Indian community of South Africa spoke as one, were united, and, consequently, more respected and more powerful.

In the final estimate the formation of the S.A.I.C. is traceable to the events of 1919. In addition to what transpired earlier, the Indian question on the local and international plane was kept in the limelight in 1919 as a result of General Smuts' historic address to the Indians in Durban and by the hopes vested in the Treaty of Versailles and the League of Nations. It is to these developments that we must now turn.

It was suggested in some circles that South African Indians should be represented at the Peace Conference in 1919. One supporter of such a move was the *Dharma Vir*. The *Natal Advertiser*, among others, opposed this suggestion, maintaining that the Indian Government was to be represented and this representation was sufficient. A South African Indian journal, the *Dharma Vir*, pointed out that the rank and file in India had refused to recognise the Indian delegates selected by the Indian Government. Those who were fighting for Indian Home Rule wanted more militant men to represent them. However, as the South African Indians could not be represented at Versailles in any other way they appealed to the Indian delegates to press for the removal of existing disabilities.

The hopes of the world were centred on the Peace Conference, which, in addition to the peace settlement, was to give effect to the formation of the League of Nations. Naturally, all oppressed and depressed peoples looked to the new compact for succour. When President Woodrow Wilson, one of the founders of the League of Nations, addressed the Peace Conference on the new expectations, he stirred the hopes of many. There were problems at the Conference itself. One of these was the question of representation.

The British Empire delegation to the Peace Conference comprised five delegates with the addition of two each for India, Canada, South Africa, Australia and one for New Zealand. The membership of the delegation tied the hands of the Indian delegates who could not stand up for certain rights. One such occasion arose when the Chinese and Japanese delegates presented a Memorandum to President Wilson and the Allied Premiers on the matter of removing the colour-bar from every European and American State. As the Dominion Governments had not themselves removed the colour-bar from their own territories, they could not support the demands of China and Japan. And as the British

Empire delegation constituted one unit, the Indian delegates could not very well vote against their colleagues in the delegation.[34]

Another occasion was described by the Rev. C. F. Andrews, in the *Bombay Chronicle*. This concerned the attempt by the Chinese delegates to have inserted in the preamble of the League of Nations a principle asserting racial equality. South Africa and Canada raised strong objections and yet they were members of the same delegation of which India was a part. The Indian delegates could not speak against their co-delegates. It was a strangely anomalous position.

The case for the South African Indians was presented by the delegates from India. It was a repetition of old grievances and a renewal of old demands. What was new in the South African situation in 1919 was the intensification of problems concerning land occupation and ownership. In India the special problems introduced in 1919 were associated with the Rowlatt Acts which gave the Government emergency powers to deal with national insurrections. It was against the Rowlatt Acts that Gandhi launched his passive resistance campaign in India just as he had done against the Transvaal Act, 2/1907, years before in South Africa. The year of Versailles brought both glimmer and gloom.

General Smuts of South Africa, one of the heroes of the late war as well as of the Peace Conference, was one of those who saw a glimmer and felt optimistic.

When Smuts returned to South Africa in 1919 he expressed the hope that the new broader and kinder spirit which had been generated by the war would help to resolve many of South Africa's problems.

The Indian community in Durban joined with the rest of South Africa to honour Smuts on his return in 1919. Smuts was not a stranger to South African Indians or to their politics and aspirations. He saw that South Africa's domestic problems could not be localised and as India continued to grow in stature so would she increasingly champion the cause of South African Indians. He was prepared to involve India more in the attempts anticipated to resolve the outstanding differences between South Africa and India. As a scholar he recognised India's greatness; as a politician he recognised India's threat. He said:

"Some of you think I look down upon Indians, but this is not so. I look up to them. They come from a very old civilization – much older than ours. They are able to hold their own. We have our difficulties in South Africa, and we as a small white community cannot withstand a great influx of Indians. We would be crushed and overwhelmed if we had an open door. . . . But now that the Indians are here, I hold that they should have fair treatment in all parts of the Union. We have to live side by side in conciliation, and we must endeavour to understand each other's standpoint, so that we may live together and grow together. We are members of the one family and belong to the same Empire."[35]

What Smuts had said would soon carry the stamp of a Prime Minister. A day after the address General Louis Botha, South Africa's first Prime Minister, died. His mantle fell on Smuts, that shrewd politician with whom Gandhi had matched his wits before. Smuts had spoken of India and South Africa as belonging to one family.

The Great War struggle had knit the Empire together. No one understood this better than did General Smuts. But the forces at home were too determined to allow their steadfastness to crumble before the Empire strain. The British Empire, whatever South Africa's own views and attitudes, was seriously affected by the dissensions within its fold between the people of India and the other Dominion countries, especially South Africa. Lord Sinha, Under-Secretary of State for India, made his views known on the Empire question in the following terms when addressing the annual meeting of the National Indian Association in London on 10th June, 1919: ". . . The position of Indians there (South Africa), which I hoped was, as a result of the War Conference, going to be con-siderably improved, is now far worse than it was before the war. That is the kind of thing which, if permitted, will estrange Indians. I will not suggest to you for a moment that the fault is that of England or of any Englishman; but if South Africa is to be part of the Empire, and if India is to be part of the Empire the same as South Africa is, then I look to other parts of the Empire to see that South Africa does not impose such humiliating restrictions upon us . . .".[36]

The point was carried further by the Rt. Hon. E. S. Montagu, Secretary of State for India, when speaking in London to a deputation from India, which had called on him in connection with the Asiatics (Land and Trading) Amendment Act (Transvaal), Act 37/1919, with the following proposals: that Royal assent be withheld from the Asiatic Act; that responsible Indians be associated with the impending Commission of Enquiry; that the reciprocity resolutions be given effect to; and that the power of retaliation be utilised.

Tracing the assurances given by Burton, delegate of the Union of South Africa to the Imperial War Conference of 1918, Montagu said that the demeanour of the Dominion colleagues both in conference and in Committee was such that the representatives of India felt confident that the future was going to be brighter than the past. But the first legislative action taken by the Union Government after the conference aroused a great depth of feeling and emotion. He said that both he and Lord Sinha continually discussed the matter with General Smuts and General Botha in Paris during the Peace Conference, "and I would beg you to remember in discussing this matter that it may well be that the forces arrayed against you are not the Colonial Office . . . or the High Commissioner, . . . the Governor-General, or even the Government itself, but certain powerful people who live in that country. . . . We have suggested what appears to all of us in this room too obvious, that this is not a domestic enquiry. It is an Imperial Enquiry. An Enquiry upon which I would go so far as to say not only the good relations of the members of the Empire depend, but upon which the sincerity of the welcome which the Dominions gave to the representatives of India at the Imperial Conference would be decided by the world and, therefore, I have asked that the Government of India should be directly represented upon the Commission, and in case anybody might think, which I know is not the case, that there is any difference of opinion between officials and non-officials, we have suggested that the Government of India should be represented by one official and one non-official on the Commission."[37]

The reactions to Montagu's reply to the deputation showed that his handling and assessment of the position were both too mild and too optimistic. As one journal put it: "Mr. Montagu harbours a conviction that Union Ministers will act broad-mindedly. We do not share his optimism. The Union Ministers have the habit of saying one thing and doing something else."[38] Many people recalled the unkept promises that Smuts had made to Gokhale and Gandhi and could not share Montagu's expectations. An "Imperial Enquiry" should have originated in Great Britain. Even so, no such enquiry would be meaningful since the Empire was not a Federation.

What the Indian people hoped for, and what the deputation from India asked for, was that the Imperial Government should veto the recent Transvaal Act, 37/1919. But the Secretary of State for India informed the deputation that as South Africa was a self-governing dominion the veto could not be used against her. The editorial of the *Indian Opinion* commented on the position in the following terms: "We do not agree with Mr. Montagu that the Imperial veto will be politically unfeasible. . . . So long as this legislation stands in the Statute Book, so long as the Imperial Government will haggle on without protecting the rights of Indians in the Dominions where the British flag flies, the term 'British citizenship' is but a farce and a delusion."[39]

The British Government had, in an earlier period in the Transvaal, failed to veto legislation which the Indians had protested against very strongly, such as Act 2/1907 and, consequently, those people who had hopes that Act 37/1919 would be vetoed had based their hopes in defiance of the examples of the past.

The Government of India had always watched over the interest of Indians in South Africa, though their watching brief was little more than expressions of concern. However, in the matter of the impending Commission of Enquiry, the Government of India was invited to play more than a passive role. The Viceroy of India announced in the Imperial Legislative Council that the Indian Government would be represented on the Commission by Sir Benjamin Robertson, K.C.S.I., K.C.M.O., late Chief Commissioner of the Central Provinces of India. Making this announcement, the Viceroy said:

". . . the Government of India have not failed to press the Indian point of view upon his Majesty's Government, and we can claim that we have the full support of the Secretary of State. We have urged that the recent legislation in South Africa is unjustified and is not consonant with the understanding given by the South African representatives at the Imperial War Conference . . .". The Viceroy admitted that there was strong feeling in India on the South African Indian question but advised that there was need for calmness and moderation in dealing with this subject so as not to make the position any worse.[40]

There was no denying the "strength of feeling" displayed by the European against the Indian in South Africa. There was ample testimony to this in the activities of the South African League which sent a deputation to see the Prime Minister on this question on 16th October, 1919. The expressions of goodwill and fellowship which Smuts had so frequently included in his pronouncements after, and even before, the Imperial Conference of 1917 and 1918, and after the termination of hostilities, did not, according to the South African League, reflect the real attitude of the white South Africans towards the Indians; the League programme was directed towards producing a clear national expression of this attitude.[41]

The South African League saw in Great Britain a potential protector and in the Indian Government a threat to South Africa. Its president, Sir Abe Bailey, said of the former that Great Britain would not sacrifice the interests of the million and a half white people in South Africa for the sake of the two hundred thousand Indians in South Africa. Of India he said that unless checked by the united opposition of the Europeans in South Africa there was the grave threat of an Indian invasion of the country; that South Africa would become the country for the extension of the Indian Empire.

The Rev. C. F. Andrews, among others, did not accept the contention that Asiatics were ready to swamp the Union, as Sir Abe Bailey claimed. Andrews had had a lifetime of experience in Indian affairs in India and in other parts of the British Empire. The argument which the Rev. Andrews used to show that the population figures of Indians in this country would have been very low had it not been for the introduction of Indian indentured labour – something in the region of 10 000 or even less, was based on the statistics which he advanced for the rest of the African coast where no settlement had a population of Indians very much in excess of 10 000.[42]

The Rev. Andrews' conclusions were that there was no truth in the claims that hordes of "hungry Asiatics" were waiting to enter Africa. On the other hand, he said, Indians would prefer to remain in India rather than migrate to foreign lands.[32] The observations of the Rev. C. F. Andrews are worthy of the most serious consideration especially in view of the fears of the South African League and the average European that India desired to make the Union of South Africa an appendage for her surplus population. The extravagant claims in this respect by the South African League and other anti-Asiatic bodies in South Africa were used to stir up the European masses to action and in that process they hoped to carry the Union Legislature with them in a common programme of keeping the Asiatic in his place, preferably outside South Africa; and, if within, then in clearly defined areas. The Rev. Andrews was no stranger to the real position.

He and Mr. Pearson had first come out to South Africa at the behest of Professor G. K. Gokhale in 1913 to assist in solving the turbulent events concerning the Indians in their passive resistance struggle. He came again to South Africa on various occasions after that, in 1919, 1925–1927 and 1930–1932. Most of these visits were sponsored by the Imperial Citizenship Association. He was, therefore, as a European, able to ascertain from the Europeans in this country what their fears in regard to the Indians were. What he learnt was that many people were shockingly ignorant of India. It was this discovery that prompted the Rev. Andrews to write: "Intellectually, it is ardently to be desired that the greatest change of all will come about. I have found nothing more desperately disappointing and disheartening in South Africa than the ignorance of the average man about India and Indian affairs. And this ignorance appears to me to have gone beyond the average man to the higher centres of South African culture."[44]

The Rev. C. F. Andrews said that the Indians who were born in India had close ties with India and that quite a number had been brought out to Natal as labourers through the adoption of questionable means; that of their own accord the Indians would not have come to South Africa in such large numbers as to total in the vicinity of 150 000 when indentured Indian immigrant labour to Natal was abolished as from 1st July, 1911. But the composition of the Union's Indian population in 1921 revealed that only 35 per cent of the total of 165 731 were born in India and would, consequently, have close ties with India; of the rest, 63 per cent were born in the Union and therefore knew no other home. The large percentage of Indians now born in the Union was an important fact: a fact which showed that for this number South Africa was home and all that a home meant.

There was no hope that this percentage of South African-born Indians (or any fraction) would forsake the land of their birth for the land of their forebears.

The first post-Union attempt to either repatriate Indians, that is, send those born in India back to their motherland, or expatriate them, that is, in the strict sense of the word, to uproot any number of the 63 per cent born in the Union and settle them in the land of their forefathers, but not their own, was started off by Section 6 of the Indian Relief Act, 22/1914. This scheme, which was officially called the repatriation scheme, was publicised amongst the Indians by means of pamphlets. In 1924 a European official was appointed to recruit Indians for repatriation. Repatriates, on arrival in India, were given bonuses of £5 per head, with a maximum payment of £20 per family. In 1924 the bonus was increased to £10 per head, with a maximum of £50 per family. By the end of 1926, 21 710 Indians had voluntarily repatriated from the Union under Section 6 of Act 22/1914 at a total expenditure of £186 059. But of the total number of repatriates only about 33 percent were South African born.[45]

Indians had accepted the repatriation scheme of 1914 because it was purely voluntary but, to their disappointment, a decade later, some form of recruiting was adopted by the Government to urge their return. Indians were not anxious to return. The Report of the Asiatic Inquiry Commission of 1921 made mention of the increasing difficulty to get Indians to leave South Africa.[46] Subsequently, as a result of the recommendations of this Commission, the bonus of £5 per head was initiated.

But these measures were, at the most, weak palliatives. What was needed at this stage was a spirited attempt to take the Indian bull by the horns and to lead him to the commons, or make short-shrift of him at the price that would have to be paid; but not to toy with him in the arena of doubt and fear. The Indians themselves were quite clear about what they wanted or expected: they had fought in the late war, had won a place in the Imperial Conference, had taken part in the League of Nations; in all these they had shown their qualities. Surely then, they argued, they were ready for "the rights and duties of citizenship".[47] Indians in South Africa had never ceased to press for these rights since the departure of Gandhi in 1914. Now, in 1920, some heed was being paid to their claims (even though this was being done in an atmosphere of fierce agitation against them) when the announcement was made that a Commission of Enquiry was appointed to enquire into and report on the land and trading rights of Asiatics in the country.[48]

The Government of India was represented at the public sittings of the Commission by Sir Benjamin Robertson. As in the case of the Indian Enquiry Commission of 1914, on which India was represented by the same official, the Governments of India and the Union of South Africa were in close co-operation in matters concerning Indians in South Africa.

Sir Benjamin Robertson emphasised that India had always felt a peculiar responsibility for the welfare of Indians in South Africa and acknowledged special obligations to a community which originated from an organised system of recruitment to which the Government of India had assented. Nor could the Government of India distinguish between the labourer and the trader. Sir Benjamin pointed out that the Government of India felt their responsibility to be especially heavy in those Provinces where Indians had not been granted political rights.[49] He recalled the assurances given by General Smuts and Burton, Ministers representing the Union of South Africa at the Imperial Conferences of 1917 and 1918. Similarly, in 1918, the Memorandum submitted by Lord Sinha and the Reciprocity Resolution of the same year had received favourable response from Burton. It was urged by Sir Benjamin Robertson that the repressive legislation recommended by so many witnesses was no solution of the problem and that fresh restrictions would be regarded not only by the Indian community in South Africa, but also by the Government and the people of India, as a breach of the settlement of 1914, which had been universally accepted as a guarantee that the status which the Indian community had acquired in 1914 would at least be maintained.

The Report of the Commission of Enquiry was completed on 3rd March, 1921. It reported, *inter alia*, that the restrictive measures in existence in the Transvaal be retained; that there should be no compulsory but voluntary repatriation; likewise, it reported that there should be no compulsory segregation but that a system of voluntary separation should be worked out. In Natal, the Commission reported, the right of Asiatics to acquire and own land for farming or agricultural purposes should be confined to the coastal belt extending to about 20 to 30 miles inland.[50]

From the international angle, one of the Commission's main findings dealt with the question of an Asiatic influx into South Africa. The Commission exploded the myth of an Asiatic "invasion" of South Africa – a fear which had haunted the minds of Europeans for many generations. On this point, the Commission said: "We are . . . satisfied that there are no substantial grounds for those apprehensions, and that, if there is any leakage at all at the present time into the Transvaal, it is entirely negligible. We deem it most important that the public mind should be disabused of that obsession, for it undoubtedly lies at the root of a great deal of the alarm about the 'Asiatic menace'."

The Report came in for much criticism and comment, not only from Indians and Europeans in South Africa, but from responsible opinions in India and in Great Britain. The *Natal Mercury* in its editorial comment said that the Asiatic question in South Africa was made more complex by exaggerations and by impossible demands such as for the expulsion of Indians from the country. If the Europeans could not match the Indians fairly in economic competition there was no point in resorting to unfair methods; and that if one generation had made the mistake of bringing Indians to South Africa another generation could not correct this "by an act of injustice".[51]

The *Natal Mercury* editorial called for justice and for promises to be kept. Coming from Durban, the chief centre of Indian settlement in the country, the views of this journal deserve the greatest respect and attention. In India, the *Bombay Chronicle* protested against the imposition of fresh restrictions, saying that the Commission had entirely ignored the Indian view and Indian representations.[52]

The Government of India cabled the Secretary of State for India on 29th March, asking him to make an immediate protest against the recommendation to impose fresh restrictions on the acquisition of land by Indians in Natal, because it was not merely a breach of the agreement concluded with General Smuts, but in the case of ex-indentured Indians it was a breach of the conditions of recruitment. The Government of India also asked that the South African Government be requested not to take action on the Report until the whole question of the position of Indians in the Empire had been discussed at the Imperial Conference in June, 1921.

The President of the Anti-Asiatic South African League, Sir Abe Bailey, M.P. for Krugersdorp, took the first opportunity to criticise the Report. In the debate on the Additional Estimates in the House of Assembly, he said that the Report was one of the weakest he had ever seen. He said that those who were opposed to the Asiatic danger would continue their opposition, and he trusted that the Government would use its endeavours to induce the Indians "to depart for more congenial climes".

Local Indians, too, protested against the Report. A mass meeting of Indians was held in Durban on 3rd April, 1921 to protest against the Asiatic Enquiry Commission Report and the Townships Franchise Amendment Ordinance. A similar meeting was held in Johannesburg on 17th April.

There seemed little doubt now that the South African Government would not hesitate to take the steps necessary to implement those sections of the Report which suggested the introduction of restrictive measures against Indians. Two months after the appearance of the Report, J. S. Marwick, South African Party, Illovo, moved in the House of Assembly that when drafting the legislation to implement the Report of the Commission, the Minister of the Interior should be mindful of the present and future interests of the European and African population of South Africa.

The Minister of the Interior, Patrick Duncan, admitted that there were difficulties in the matter of the proposed legislation and that they were of an external nature. Speaking in the House of Assembly, he said that "in view of the seriousness and far-reaching effect of this question, the Government was not able to bring in legislation this season. This was a question in which they must look outside South Africa, and even had they the Nationalists' panacea of an independent South African republic, that would not help them. . . . This matter was not merely one of a conflict of races, it was a conflict of civilisation. He pointed out how other Eastern countries were waking up, and so was India gradually achieving a state of development and self-government. (Nationalist jeers.) Yes, he knew they would get jeers from the Nationalists, but he would tell them that if India was not a member of the British Empire she would be a far greater menace to us."[53]

The Union Government had, no doubt, recognised the international implications of any anti-Indian measures in the Union, especially in view of the Imperial Conference of 1921 which was scheduled to begin on 20th June. The Indian delegates from India were already in England. The Natal Indian Congress sent a cable to the Hon. Srinivasa Sastri, of the Indian delegation, asking him to advocate the cause of the Indians in the Colonies by demanding their full rights. The Natal Indian Congress recounted some of the more pressing difficulties experienced by Indians in South Africa and asked that the members of the Indian delegation at the Imperial Conference get further details from H. S. L. Polak, the representative of the Congress in England.[54]

The question of Indians in the British Empire had been discussed in the war-torn atmosphere of 1917 and 1918 and great hopes were vested in the Imperial War Conference of 1917–1918 of an early solution to the differences that existed, especially because of the solidarity of the British Empire in the war struggle. The Conference of 1918 had accepted the Reciprocity Resolution submitted by Sir Satyendra P. Sinha, of India. Three years had passed since and the position of Indians in the Union of South Africa had worsened as a result of the recommendations of the Asiatic Inquiry Commission of 1921. The question of racial differences in the Empire could not be overlooked by the Imperial Conference of 1921 and, in his opening remarks to the delegates at the Conference, the Prime Minister of Great Britain, the Hon. Lloyd George, said on June 20th, 1921:

"No greater calamity could overtake the world than a further accentuation of the world's divisions upon racial lines. The British Empire has done signal service to humanity in bridging these divisions in the past. The loyalty of the King-Emperor's Asiatic peoples is proof that to depart from the policy and fail in that duty will not merely greatly increase the dangers of international war, but will divide the British Empire against itself. . . . Our foreign policy can never range itself upon differences of race and civilisation between East and West. It would be fatal to the Empire . . .".[55]

Even if the foreign policy of the British Empire was not based on differences of race and civilisation, the status of the Indian delegates at the Imperial War Conference was not equal to that of the other Dominions. Sastri made mention of this when he said that the Indian delegates were the nominees of their Government whereas the other delegates were the Prime Ministers of their country.[56]

In spite of his official status, the Hon. Srinivasa Sastri put up a strong case on behalf of the Indians in some of the Crown Colonies and in South Africa. He pleaded for the extension of full rights of citizenship to Indians already fully domiciled in the Dominions and made it clear that India did not intend to go back on the compromise of 1918. He declared that it was a most urging and pressing matter that the Indian delegation be enabled to carry back a message "of hope, and good cheer".[57] Of the British Empire itself, Sastri said: "The supreme test of the Empire was whether it could be made something the world has not yet seen, viz., a united society of peoples in which faith, colour and language would not be a bar to full and equal citizenship."[58]

With this ideal the Colonial Secretary, Winston Churchill, concurred when he said "that the British Empire could only have one ideal in that connection, namely, that there should be no barrier of race, colour or creed, preventing any man, by merit, reaching any station if he were fitted for such a station."[59]

Despite the protests of the delegate from the Union of South Africa, General Smuts, who was the Prime Minister of the Union, Sastri received support from the Imperial Government and succeeded in getting a resolution adopted, which drew attention to "an incongruity between the position of India as an equal member of the British Empire, and the existence of disabilities upon British Indians lawfully domiciled in some other parts of the Empire . . .".[60]

The representatives of South Africa did not accept the resolution, and General Smuts, in spite of his "more kindly feelings towards the Indian population of South Africa", declared that inequality formed the basis of the political system in South Africa and that if the Indians were given any political rights the same could not be denied to the other non-whites in the country.[61]

Indians were grieved that no unanimity could be reached at the Conference on the question of Indians in South Africa – the only point on which there was any disagreement at the Conference. Commenting on the position, the *Indian Opinion* wrote: "The Indian community in South Africa now know which way the wind blows, and the opinion expressed by General Smuts in the course of an interview that 'Mesopotamia would be a better outlet for Indian immigration than South Africa' has rendered it still more easy for them to understand their position in this country." The journal exhorted the Indians to demand their just rights and to put up a struggle until they were obtained.[62]

The *Natal Advertiser* saw the crippling effects on the Empire of South Africa's stand and said that if all the Dominions were going to hold out for their pound of flesh on every matter that arose, "the very mirage of Imperial Union will recede further year by year".[63] The *Madras New India* wrote that in rejecting the resolution South Africa was undermining the foundations of the Empire.

The rejection by South Africa of the Resolution of 1921 meant that the relationship between the members of the British Empire in future years could never be what it was before 1921. It meant also that the policy of the Union Government remained unchanged even at the level of the Imperial Conference. If at such a level South Africa could not be persuaded to adopt a different attitude towards the Indian question the conclusion was that the Imperial Government and the other Dominion Governments were unable to bring their combined strength to bear on the issue. The Imperial Conference had no more influence than Great Britain acting alone had. Its place in the Empire was what General Botha had said it would be in 1911, i.e. not a place for resolutions. In such a situation there was no hope that an improvement in the South African Indian question would emerge from the external influences of the Imperial Conference. Even if India had full self-government there was little that this enhanced status would have served to gain for the South African Indians. The Imperial Conference in 1921 had proved that it was only a place where discussion and debates could take place. There was no extra-governmental way in which its resolutions could be enforced. The last part of the Resolution, however, kept the door open for any future negotiations between the Government of India and South Africa in order to resolve their outstanding differences. The Viceroy of India, Lord Reading, pledged his support to secure a settlement. He said that he would strive to secure a just settlement in keeping with "Indian pride and patriotism".

The South African delegates had stood firm at the Imperial Conference; but the rest of the Empire had accepted the principle that Indians were of equal status as citizens of the Empire. It followed that South Africa would go its way in the promotion of the way of life known and practised in the country. In March, 1922, the Natal Provincial Council passed three Ordinances which were in keeping with the official South African way of life. These were the Rural Dealers' Licensing Ordinance, the Townships Franchise Ordinance and the Durban Land Alienation Ordinance.

The first of the Ordinances removed the existing right of appeal in all cases from the decision of a licensing board to an appeal board and limited, instead, the right of appeal only on the grounds of the fitness of the person. The second Ordinance deprived Natal Indians of the Municipal franchise they had enjoyed since 1872. The third Ordinance, the Durban Land Alienation Ordinance, No. 14 of 1922 (Natal), gave the Durban Town Council the power of restricting the ownership or occupation, or both, of land to any particular race group by inserting in the title deeds or leases of such property the restrictive clauses. With the passing of these three Ordinances the recent anti-Asiatic agitation in the Transvaal seemed to be transferred to Natal, with this difference that the steps taken in the Transvaal to impose further restrictions on persons of Asiatic descent were comparatively milder than the steps now taken in Natal. These three Ordinances were ominous signs of the difficulties that lay ahead; they showed that the governments of South Africa – municipal, provincial and central were not planning to remove the old difficulties but were heaping new ones on them.

After the Natal Indian Congress protested against these Ordinances and called on the Minister of the Interior to recommend to the Government the use of the veto against the Ordinances, two of these Ordinances were rejected but the Durban Land Alienation Ordinance was sanctioned. The Minister informed the Congress that in giving approval to the Ordinance the Government was assured that Asiatics would be given reasonable opportunity of acquiring adequate residential sites.[64]

The Natal Provincial Council was disappointed that the two Ordinances moved by G. H. Hulett, M.P.C., were not approved by the Union Government. On the other hand, Indians were disappointed that their representations against the three Ordinances had resulted in the disallowance of two of them and the acceptance of the Durban Land Alienation Ordinance. The restrictions imposed by the Durban Land Alienation Ordinance were of a far-reaching nature. Indians were now not able to occupy or own land in certain areas so reserved by the Town Council. For the Indians, these restrictions, coming for the first time in this form in any part of Natal, represented the thin end of the wedge of segregation. The new restrictions were of sufficient proportions for the issue to be taken to India.

The position of Indians in South Africa was raised by a deputation which waited on the Viceroy, Lord Reading, on March 22nd, 1922, in New Delhi. The deputation comprised members of the Indian Legislature and five delegates from South Africa, viz., A. I. Kajee, A. M. Bayat, M. C. Patel, A. I. Gabru and P. K. Naidoo. The delegation asked the Viceroy to communicate with the Union Government on Indian grievances in South Africa.[65]

In his reply the Viceroy made a very important declaration of the principle of non-interference in the domestic affairs of a self-governing Dominion. The Indian delegation from South Africa also recognised the fact that it was to the Union Government that they had to look for the redress of their grievances. A. I. Kajee, one of the delegates, was to hold that view for many years after that. The Viceroy informed the delegates that he was pleased to learn that they held such views. He said that India would continue to do what she could to promote the aspirations of Indians in the Dominions towards their goal of free citizenship but in the matter of domestic difficulties redress should be sought from the government of the country concerned. Interference from India, he said, would tend to make the position of Indians in the dominions worse than it was.[66]

In the House of Commons, in reply to a question asked by the Labour M.P., Col. Wedgwood, whether the Colonial Secretary would do anything to prevent the enactment of three pieces of anti-Indian legislation of the Natal Provincial Council, Churchill replied that it was for the Union Government to decide whether assent was to be given. Colonel Wedgwood then asked whether Churchill could not advise the South African Government. Churchill refused to be led into a course of strife and friction with the Union Government. Thus, both from India and from Great Britain came the announcement at this time that no steps would be taken to interfere with legislation introduced in South Africa. There was, of course, the principle of reciprocity of treatment agreed upon in 1921.

It was not clear, as yet, what the Imperial Conference Resolution of 1921 would do to ease the position or what the Indian Government could or should do to ameliorate the lot of the Indians in South Africa. Neither was it clear how much any one of the above influences or both of them would cause the Union Government to depart from its defined programme. One definite attempt to come to grips with the Indian question in the Dominions was the impending visit of the Hon. Srinivasa Sastri to Canada and Australia. Invitations to Sastri to visit these Dominions had been extended during the Imperial Conference of 1921. No invitation was extended to him by the South African representatives and so the Union was not included in Sastri's itinerary.

In a Press interview in India, prior to his departure for the Dominions, Sastri said that his mission was to represent to the Dominion governments and parliaments the necessity of conferring the full franchise on the lawfully resident Indians. He said that though the Imperial Conference had adopted the resolution on reciprocity of treatment it was a matter for the Dominions to decide to remove the grievances of the resident Indians by effecting changes to existing legislation.

Sastri's tour of the Dominions was outside the pale of the Conference Resolution of 1921. He was going solely on a goodwill tour during which he would appeal to the legislatures and the governments of the Dominions visited to confer upon the resident Indians the full franchise. Many people had already ruled out the usefulness of this Resolution. But two Europeans who knew the South African Indian question well pleaded that the Resolution should not be treated "as a scrap of paper". The Rev. C. F. Andrews and H. S. L. Polak said in a joint statement that the time had come for the Government of India to make a clear declaration that it would not tolerate any racial inequality within the Empire; that the Colonial Office in London and the Union Government should be made to realise that in inflicting humiliations upon the Indians abroad they were "forcing an issue from which they themselves may well recoil".

But the appeal made by Andrews and Polak did not result in any improvement to the position. In South Africa Smuts replied by blaming the old Natal Government for the Indian problem the country was faced with. He explained that though he had nothing against the Indians, the duty of his government was to preserve white civilisation in South Africa; for this preservation, he said, "a great torch has been put into our hands by Providence". Smuts was not the first nor the last South African statesman to attribute to Providence the power and the privileges enjoyed by the government of the day in carrying out its chosen duty. This was a claim not easily defensible or justifiable. Even a European journal commenting on this said that white civilisation in South Africa would be judged by its record in dealing with the coloured races, not by attempting to make South Africa a white man's country.[67]

The South African Indian question had by this time travelled a long way on the international plane. From inter-governmental level it had passed to the Empire stage at the Imperial Conferences. Now it was to reach the international level at the League of Nations.

The question of the coloured races in South Africa, including the Indians, was one facet of the grave problem of the protection and fair treatment of minorities which confronted the infant League of Nations. Though this question specially concerned those European countries which had joined the Great War, an international organisation for peace, such as the League of Nations, could not ignore the treatment of racial minorities outside Europe. Thus in September, 1922, the South African racial situation came within the ambit of the international League of Nations.

The question of the proper treatment of minorities was not referred to specifically in the Covenant of the League of Nations itself. In President Woodrow Wilson's Second Draft the following clause on minorities appeared: "The League of Nations shall require all new States to bind themselves as a condition precedent to their recognition as independent or autonomous States to accord to all racial or national Minorities within their several jurisdictions exactly the same treatment and security both in law and in fact that is accorded to the racial or national Majority of their people."[68]

This clause was criticised widely and one reason for its criticism was that its application might not be limited to new States, but might be extended to some of the older States also. The result was that in the new draft of the Covenant produced on 3rd February, 1920, the clause took the shape of a general agreement by all members of the League guaranteeing religious toleration and equality. A few days later the clause was amended on a Japanese proposal. The additional clause ran: "The equality of Nations being a basic principle of the League of Nations, the high contracting parties agree to accord as soon as possible to all alien nationals of States members of the League equal and just treatment in every respect, making no distinction either in law or in fact on account of their race or nationality."

This was the position when Professor Gilbert Murray of South Africa introduced a motion in the Assembly of the League of Nations in 1921 on the treatment of minorities. This was withdrawn when the Council of the League of Nations adopted a new proposal on 25th October, 1921. This proposal was examined by Prof. Murray in the Debate of the Third Assembly of the League in 1922. Prof. Murray said that the old method of "discreet unofficial conversations" with the governments concerned had served to remove considerable grievances but was not the best method to deal with all the disputes that would arise from time to time.

It was to improve the position then existing in regard to the protection of minorities that two resolutions were submitted to the Sixth Committee of the League, one by Professor Gilbert Murray and the other by Dr. Walters, the Latvian delegate. The Committee adopted the principles on which Professor Murray's proposal was based.[69]

In a debate which followed in the Assembly, after the Report of the Sixth Committee was submitted to it, the delegate of India, His Highness the Maharajah of Nawanagar, said that Prof. Murray very wisely and very rightly pointed out that the question of minorities was not merely a humanitarian question but that it was also a political question and that the League should spread general contentment or the new distribution of Europe would not endure. The Maharajah had something to say about the minority questions outside Europe and the political order outside Europe where distributions were of older standing. He referred to the question of minorities in South Africa, the position of the Indians in the country. He appealed to the South African delegates, "the declared champions of the rights of minorities" to use their influence at home to obtain a satisfactory settlement of the minority questions in South Africa. Referring to the peculiar problems facing the British Empire, the Maharajah said: "We of the British Empire are a big family.

The British Mother has taken to her bosom the grizzly bear, the kangaroo, the lion and the ostrich, the tiger and the kiwi, and with a family of that description quarrels are bound to occur." He went on to say that if South Africa solved her problems, she would be more united; the British Empire would be relieved of a great political anxiety and India would also be satisfied.

Paying tribute to the South African delegates for their championship of minorities and to General Smuts, the Union's Prime Minister who "has himself in the past suffered experiences which must render him peculiarly appreciative of how poignantly a minority may resent its position", the Maharajah said that "other virtues besides charity may well begin at home". He outlined the Indian point of view thus:

> "We, in this Assembly, believe that one God made all men to walk erect on one earth; and we believe in one truth and one justice, universal for all men, and it is to this atmosphere and to this faith I make my appeal. But outside this Assembly there have often been two justices, one for the West and one for the East. It is for the League of Nations to engraft its own conception, the far higher, the far better conception, upon the universal practice of mankind. What is our ideal? What is our purpose? What is the very reason of our being? Let us have catholic justice and we shall have catholic peace."

The delegate from South Africa, Professor Gilbert Murray, spoke after the Maharajah. Referring to the particular points raised by the last speaker in connection with the treatment of minorities in South Africa, Professor Gilbert Murray said that the South African Government was not confronted so much with the difficulty of dealing with minorities as with having to deal with a number of races of varying levels of civilisation at different stages of development. He was satisfied that the fourth resolution afforded the protection of minorities which India sought.

At the end of the debate, five resolutions were unanimously adopted. Of these, the most significant, for this study, is Resolution IV which read as follows:

> "The Assembly expresses the hope that the States which are not bound by any legal obligations to the League with respect to Minorities will nevertheless observe in the treatment of their own racial, religious, or linguistic minorities at least as high a standard of justice and toleration as is required by any of the Treaties and by the regular action of the Council."

With the adoption of the Resolutions, particularly the Fourth Resolution in the case of South Africa, the question of the treatment of minorities became the concern of the League of Nations. From the inception, there was little hope that the League resolutions would go beyond the "benevolent" communication stage foreshadowed in the first resolution.[70]

The significance of the debate and the resolutions on the question of minorities in the Third Assembly of the League of Nations in 1922 was that the delegates from the Union of South Africa posed as the guardians of minorities and that the resolutions which were finally adopted were largely their work. Yet in 1921, the Union Premier, General Smuts, had refused to accept the Imperial Conference Resolution of that year which stated, *inter alia*, "that there is incongruity between the position of India as an equal member of the British Empire and the existence of disabilities upon the British Indians lawfully domiciled in some other parts of the Empire". The possible explanation for this lies in the fact that the visionary Smuts attached more importance to a favourable position for South Africa in the chambers of the League of Nations which, in any case, dealt almost exclusively with the problems of Europe than he did in the case of the Imperial Conference within the framework of the Commonwealth, at which conference he would be answerable to India and, to a lesser extent, to Great Britain for the policy of his government on the Indian question.

The position at the end of 1922 in regard to the Indian question in South Africa was that there appeared little on the scene or on the horizon to suggest that any solution was at hand. White South Africa still clung tenaciously to the hope of finding an eventual solution to the question by repatriating the Indians. At the Pietermaritzburg Congress of the South African Party held on 20th December, 1921, General Smuts took this line when making a strong appeal to his supporters to take the "long view" with regard to the Indian question. He said that while Natal's white population had increased by 40 per cent since 1911, the Indian population had increased by only 5 per cent; there was no reason, therefore, for the white people to speak of an "inundation" of Asiatics in Natal. He reminded the Congress that any decision arrived at by Congress would have repercussions beyond Natal. He felt that the best thing that his supporters could do was to induce Indians to leave South Africa and to go back to their country, while the white population should be increased; that was the solution which he felt was fundamentally sound.[71]

White Natal saw some hope that the repatriation of Indians might solve the problem. It was not prepared to follow a policy of extending any further rights to Indians, even if, in terms of the Reciprocity Resolution adopted by the Imperial Conference of 1918, India were to use retaliatory measures against South Africa. An article in the *Round Table* emphasised this point: "Whatever ideas may be entertained about equality and reciprocity it is simply wasting time to ask the people of Natal to grant equal civic rights to the Asiatics, since it would virtually place the balance of power in their hands."[72]

Commenting on the possibilities of the use of the Reciprocity Resolution, the *Natal Witness*, in a leading article, hoped that the South African Indians would not be a party to that policy because that would prevent any conciliatory proposals being well received.[73] There was great need for conciliation before any progress could be made. The *Natal Mercury* saw the position in a most statesmanlike way when it reviewed the Indian question at the beginning of 1923. It called for a positive policy based on justice and realities. There was no point in turning backwards in repentant mood:

"... No solution of the problem can be found by merely following the blind impulses of race hatred. No solution can be satisfactory which does not start from recognition of the fact that it is no less impossible to extrude the Indian element from the population of South Africa than to expel the negroes from the United States. If we turn the clock back eighty years, it would be easy enough to say simply, we will not have an Asiatic problem in South Africa. But we cannot undo the mistakes of the past. The present and succeeding generations must face, with all the courage, goodwill and resourcefulness they can muster, the consequences of these mistakes."[74]

The editorial reviewed the position most ably. On the point of assimilation of the

Indians with the South African white population and Western civilisation, it was emphatic that the Indians had no just claims to such assimilation. The Indian, on the other hand, was developing in this direction, for the percentage of those whose birth-place was South Africa was on the increase. In 1921, 35 per cent of the Asiatic population of the Union of South Africa was born in India and 63 per cent in South Africa; in 1946 the figures were 9 per cent and 89 per cent respectively.[75]

What appeared to be irreconcilable at the moment was the insistence of the European in the country that the preservation of Western civilisation meant the exclusion of the Asiatic from the councils of constitutional government and the increasing claims of the Indians to some recognition in this respect based, firstly, on the grounds of birth and upbringing in a western climate, and, secondly, on the acquisition of western standards of civilisation by way of education and experience. Though the advance in educational progress was slow, very slow, the advance was there. The handicaps in the way of an increase in the pace of this advance were many and real, but temporary. The problem of removing illiteracy from the Indian population of Natal was summed up by the Superintendent of Education in his Report for 1926 when he said: "But that this Province, or any other territory, can afford to sustain deliberately a large section of its population in enforced ignorance is a statement so patently prejudiced and prejudicial as hardly to require refutation."[76]

With the removal of illiteracy the position was bound to change. The important thing was that officials, such as the Superintendent of Education in Natal, were taking stock of the position. But the officials could remain at the level of "stock-takers" if Government policy did not change. The Government had to consider the position of Indians in the country for, at the Commonwealth level, the issue was bound to be raised at the next Imperial Conference, scheduled to be held in London in October, 1923.

How far this Conference was to improve on the work of 1917, 1918 and 1921 was a moot point, though it was clear, even if General Smuts did not admit it was so, that, after the refusal of South Africa to accept the Resolution of 1921, matters would come to a head at the Imperial Conference of 1923. Whatever the Imperial Conference of 1923 decided upon, it was clear, too, that its decisions would not be binding, except in a moral sense. For, as a journal commented, "Where men of honour meet their word is their bond".[77]

With the conference date not far off, the Union Prime Minister, General Smuts, had an opportunity to deal with the Indian question at the South African Party Congress held at Pietermaritzburg on 16th July, 1923. Smuts told the Congress that he did not wish to engage in a general discussion on the Indian question as it was one which affected the relations between the members of the Empire "in a very dangerous and material manner". All that he would say was that the Government was bound to respect the European standards and protect the European civilisation in the country.

General Smuts took note of the fact that the South African Indian question was not a simple one: it had its external complications. These, he said, were further accentuated by the attacks made by Sastri in his speeches during his tour of Dominion territories. One of the chief reasons for Sastri's tour, it will be recalled, was the aim he set himself to appeal to the Dominions to confer full franchise rights on the resident Indians. Smuts criticised

Sastri for his attacks on South Africa and said that on the franchise issue he could draw no distinction between the Indians and the Africans.[78]

General Smuts' reasoning was perfectly correct. There was no reason for any distinction between Indians and Africans in South Africa, provided, of course, that all things were equal, that the standards of civilisation adduced from reasonable criteria permitted the extension of the franchise to all non-whites in South Africa and that such criteria were also invoked to test the eligibility of the white man for the franchise. There is something to be said for the imposition of distinctions when dealing with people of varying levels of civilization but in a multi-racial society, where barriers are broken faster than they are created, the test for determining eligibility should be that of testing an individual, not his race.

Sastri's tour of the Dominions, his championship of the franchise, South Africa's refusal to accept the Resolution of the Imperial Conference of 1921, India's plea to South Africa at the League of Nations to show a more generous spirit towards the question of minorities in South Africa, and South Africa's determination to preserve the standards of white civilisation in South Africa could all be traced, directly or indirectly, to the work and influence of the Imperial Conference of 1921. The next conference, because of the influences and attitudes set in motion by the last one, would be followed with keen interest.

South Africa was represented at the Imperial Conference of 1923 by General J. C. Smuts, the Prime Minister; the Hon. H. Burton, the Minister of Finance; and the Hon. N. J. de Wet, the Minister of Justice. India was represented by the Rt. Hon. Viscount Peel, the Secretary of State for India and head of the delegation; His Highness, the Maharajah of Alwar; and Sir Tej Bahadur Sapru.[79]

Prior to the Imperial Conference debate on the status of Indians, Smuts issued a Memorandum criticising Sastri's speeches during his Dominions' tour and expounding the argument that there were no equal franchise rights in the Empire. Sir Tej Bahadur Sapru described the Memorandum as "a document of remarkable subtlety – such subtlety as he had always been accustomed to associate with the name of Smuts".[80]

Introducing the subject of the status of Indians in the Empire at the Imperial Conference on 24th October, 1923, Lord Peel, the Secretary of State for India emphasised that a solution of the problem was essential to the preservation of unity in the Empire. Lord Peel recalled that India contributed 1 400 000 men and over £200 000 000 during the war and was accepted during the war as an equal of the other Dominions. Similarly, India was accepted by the League of Nations as one of the greatest industrial states. The intention and ambition of India, said Lord Peel, was to share in the glories of the British Empire. The scope of the Indian question in the Dominions, apart from South Africa, was not very great, there being about 2 000 Indians in Australia, 600 in New Zealand and 1 200 in British Columbia.[81]

Sir Tej Bahadur Sapru, explaining the position of India in the Empire, said: "I claim my right to take my seat as a member of King George's household. I shall not be content with a place in his outer stables."[82] Referring to the Imperial Conference Resolution of 1921, Sir Tej Bahadur Sapru said that there was a growing sentiment in India against emigration. "We don't want our nation outside India to appear as a nation of coolies. We have had enough of that." He said that there was plenty of scope for the energy of

Indians in India and that the Dominions need have no fear in that connection. Sir Tej Bahadur made the following proposals:

1. The Dominion Government concerned, and the British Government in areas under their direct control, such as Kenya and Uganda, should appoint Committees to confer with a Committee which the Government of India would send from India to explore avenues how best and soonest the principle of equality embodied in the 1921 resolution might be implemented.

2. He appealed to Smuts as a humanitarian to help to raise the status of Indians in South Africa and as an Imperial statesman to establish peace throughout the world, saying: "Is he going to exclude from that happy mission his country and mine?"

3. He hoped that Smuts would agree to the appointment of a diplomatic agent from India to protect Indians in South Africa and to act as an intermediary between them and the South African Government and to put the Government of India in full possession of the facts.[83]

Sir Tej Bahadur Sapru said that the Indians had as much right to be in South Africa as the Europeans had; that they, too, had made a contribution to the prosperity of South Africa and had made every effort to raise themselves culturally. They should not, consequently, be relegated to a permanent position of inferiority. Such a position, he said, would cause trouble not only in South Africa and India but in the Empire.

Smuts had a difficult position to meet at the conference. He dealt with the Commonwealth aspects of the South African Indian question when he said that a common British citizenship in the whole Empire did not invest the holder with full franchise rights. He illustrated the position by stating that if an Australian came to South Africa he could not claim franchise rights as a matter of course merely because he was a British subject.[84]

General Smuts then commented on the remark made by Sir Tej Bahadur Sapru that if no satisfactory solution were arrived at the Imperial Conference of 1923, India might take the matter up outside the area of the Empire and make it a matter of foreign policy. Smuts said that if India took such a step and appealed to any tribunal outside the Empire (such as the League of Nations) it would prejudice India's case and she could no longer use the argument of a common British citizenship.

General Smuts concluded thus: "They (the Indians in South Africa) have all the rights barring the rights of voting for Parliament and the Provincial Councils, that any white citizen in South Africa has. Our law draws no distinction whatever. It is only political rights that are in question. There, as I explained to you, we are up against a stone wall and we cannot get over it."

Smuts' conclusion was an over-simplified one and probably correct in the strict theory of the law. But to say that Indians had "all the rights", barring certain voting rights was to overlook all the discriminations practised against them in numerous ways in the country, from provincial barriers to segregated schools; from separate counters in public places to separate seating arrangements in cinemas and in the railways; and in every facet of South African life, only those rights and privileges and opportunities based on inequality and catered for by a pattern of discrimination and differentiation.

Sir Tej Bahadur Sapru did not accept General Smuts' version. He said that legally and in accordance with more recent ideas on the subject it was impossible to accept two kinds of citizenship in the same Empire: a higher and a lower. If an Indian went to South Africa and satisfied the requirements for the franchise he could not be denied this on the grounds that he was "an Indian subject of His Majesty". Sir Tej Bahadur Sapru said that Smuts made no mention of the many disabilities Indians suffered from in South Africa. Though he had received much support from the Imperial Government and from the other Prime Ministers he was disappointed that he had not received any co-operation or support from Smuts. He opposed Smuts' desire that the Resolution of 1921 should be repealed and said that the reputation of the Conference itself, that of the Dominion Prime Ministers and of the Imperial Government, too, were at stake on this issue. He said that there was more to be gained not by shelving the issues but by attempting to solve them.

Sir Tej Bahadur Sapru said, on the matter of treating the Indian question in South Africa as a foreign problem, that he was misunderstood by Smuts. What he meant to convey was that it was not difficult to foresee the stage being reached when even the Government of India might find it necessary to appeal to the British Government and say that one part of the Empire was standing against the other, "and it is for you and His Majesty's Government now to treat this problem, inside your own Commonwealth, as you would deal with a problem of foreign policy. This is what I meant, and I anticipate a stage like that being reached at no distant date in so far as the relations of India with South Africa are concerned". He said that General Smuts' speech was remarkably illusory and evasive and that the General had failed to answer his questions as regards the grievances of the Indians in South Africa. In disagreeing with General Smuts' views as to the rights of citizenship, Sir Tej Bahadur declared that India was not the only country which claimed all political rights on the basis of British citizenship. He charged General Smuts with confusing territorial law with personal law.[85]

General Smuts, asserting that the issue was not a political one but an economic one, fought hard to have the Resolution of 1921 reversed. It was a futile undertaking; his effort to prove that it was consistent to deny Indians civil rights was "torn to pieces" by Sir Tej Bahadur Sapru, and the final voting at the Conference left the Union in a minority of one, the Irish Free State "generously supporting the Indian claim as a matter of pure right". Keith makes the following observation: "General Smuts resented the conclusion and refused brusquely to accept the presence of an Indian official to act as an intermediary between the Government and the Indians, whom he unfortunately could only regard from the standpoint of the Transvaal denial of the equality before man or God of the coloured with the – alleged – white."[86]

The Imperial Conference of 1923 was not as cordial, from the standpoint of the South African and Indian delegates, as that of 1921 had been. Both General Smuts and Sir Tej Bahadur Sapru had been outspoken. The feelings at conference time can best be understood by considering the statements made by the delegates of the Union and of India after the conference.

When interviewed by Reuter after the conference, Sir Tej Bahadur Sapru expressed the opinion that General Smuts had heaped insult on the Government of India, and though he stood forth as the champion of the unity of the Empire, he had done more harm to it than anyone else by his attitude and obstinacy towards India. While he was prepared to make full allowance for the party politics in South Africa, he thought that it was the duty of the leading statesman to guide and control public opinion, and not merely to succumb to it. Looking into the future, Sir Tej Bahadur said that he was afraid there would be tremendous feeling in India; for it was clear that the policy of General Smuts was going to lead to very serious results. Though India was not then a self-governing country, Sapru said that it was much stronger and more united than it had been a few years before. He noted that it was clear there was not going to be peace between the two units of the Empire – India and South Africa. He foresaw that, however independent South Africa might be, a stage would be reached when the Indian question there would cease to be a question of foreign policy.

Again, speaking at a reception in London on November 13, 1923, Sir Tej Bahadur Sapru delivered a vigorous attack on General Smuts. While admitting that he had no grievance on social grounds, he complained that General Smuts had declined to move an inch in exploring avenues for a settlement of the Indian question in South Africa. General Smuts had said that the question was not one of colour but an economic one, but Sir Tej Bahadur's contention was that they were all subjects of the same King, and that India was not going to accept any lower kind of citizenship anywhere in the Empire. He said that some Indians spoke of going out of the Empire but he held that it was necessary to remain within the Empire until Britain herself said there was no place in it for the Indians.

In an interview with Reuter, General Smuts replied to Sir Tej Bahadur Sapru by stating he had tried, out of deep respect for the Indian people, to maintain the same feelings in his dealings with Sir Tej Bahadur Sapru but that the latter's press statements had done a great disservice to the cause of India. Smuts denied that he had insulted the Government of India in any way.[87]

The Imperial Conference of 1923 failed to improve Indo-Union relations; the resolution of 1921 remained on record. General Smuts had tried to have it rescinded but had failed. There was no gain to be counted for any side. The Europeans in the country looked upon General Smuts' stand as a continuation of the Government's policy of "political self-preservation"; a journal went so far as to state that India would do the same if threatened by a foreign power – such as Japan. The same journal wrote that though a measure of self-preservation was justifiable it was idle to pretend that an oligarchy functioning in the guise of a democracy would serve the interests of those who were excluded from participation in the Government.

The European Press in South Africa was generally agreed on the point of the South African Government's stand on the preservation of white supremacy in the country. They and the Europeans, saw it this way: ". . . it is our problem – not India's problem. It affects our future – not India's. And it must be settled in our way."[88]

The European community in South Africa in general saw the proceedings at the Imperial Conference from the point of view of the future of European supremacy in the country. The Indians saw a totally different picture. They had no political aspirations until Sastri raised the franchise question during his tour of the Dominions. Gandhi had remarked on the unimportance of political aspirations at the time of his departure from South Africa. In the main they complained of the numerous disabilities they suffered from, pleaded for their removal in the limited way open to voteless people. There was another side to the picture: the side which concerned India. One question now arose. How could India force the hands of the British Government and the governments of the Dominions, especially South Africa, to accept her status as an equal member of the Commonwealth? To do so, in practice, would mean giving some heed to the proposals made by India at the Imperial Conference of 1923: that steps be taken to realise the principle of equality embodied in the 1921 Resolution; the raising of the status of the South African Indians; the appointment of a diplomatic agent from India in South Africa to protect the interests of the resident Indians and to act as an intermediary between the two governments.

But none of these proposals received any immediate favourable attention. India and her people were disappointed that the Imperial Government had not been able to bring about a settlement in the differences between India and South Africa that strained the bonds of Imperial unity. A greater cause for disappointment was the consummate ease with which the South African Government rejected the pleas made at the conferences and set about in its determined way along its own course.

This course hit the headlines when the Union Government declared its next line of action. It announced that the Indian question was a domestic question and that no outside interference would be tolerated. In January, 1924, less than three months after the conclusion of the Imperial Conference of 1923, the Union Minister of the Interior, Patrick Duncan, announced the intention of the Union Government to proceed with legislation in the form of the Class Areas Bill to provide for the compulsory trading and residential segregation of Indians. Such legislation had been recommended by the Asiatic Inquiry Commission of 1921,[89] though the Commission had made no recommendation that segregation should be compulsory.

The announcement of the terms of the Class Areas Bill came as a great shock to the Indians, many of whom felt that the discussions at the Imperial Conference might have led to a change of heart and to some amelioration, but not to such deterioration in so short a space of time. General Smuts had, by this step, clearly capitulated to the anti-Indian demands in his country. Even such capitulation was not enough to sustain him in power. Such was the "diabolic anti-Indianism" in the Union at this time.[90]

Indians acted immediately in protest against the Bill. A mass meeting of some 3 000 Indians was held in Durban on 27th January, 1924, under the auspices of the Natal Indian Congress. The meeting adopted resolutions protesting against the Bill and supporting the steps taken by the Natal Indian Congress against it. A delegation comprising Amod Bayat, Albert Christopher, M. Beethasee Maharaj, B. A. Magrajh and V. Lawrence was appointed by the Natal Indian Congress to interview the Minister of the Interior in Cape Town. The Natal Indian Congress had already sent off an invitation to Mrs. Sarojini Naidu to come to South Africa from Kenya where she presided over the East African Indian National Congress on the 19th and 20th January, 1924. It was felt that her presence in South Africa during this critical phase in the life of the Indians would have a salutary effect on them. Mrs. Naidu accepted the invitation and signified that she would be in Natal about the end of February, 1924.

Meanwhile the Transvaal British Indian Association also moved into action with a mass meeting on 27th January, 1924 and resolved to collect over £10 000 to fight the Class Areas Bill. Indians in South Africa were terribly agitated by the Government's intention and were resolved to fight the Bill all the way, though even then there was little hope of success.

The action taken against the proposed (and other) legislation was not confined to protest meetings. A deputation from the Natal Indian Congress waited on the Minister of the Interior to protest against the Natal Township Ordinance of 1924 (which had been refused assent on three occasions before) which sought to deprive Indians of the township franchise. The Congress representations were upheld and assent was refused for the fourth time.

In the other representation made by the Congress delegation, supported this time by the Cape British Indian Council, the Transvaal British Indian Association, and the Natal Indian Congress to the Minister of the Interior in February, 1924, against the Class Areas Bill, there was no success. The Minister of the Interior, Patrick Duncan, pointed out to the deputation that it was the Government's intention to treat the Indians with fairness and justice. A factor to be considered in the policy of the Government was that the close association of Europeans and non-Europeans led to a certain measure of social friction and this could be obviated if they were separated. This applied to trading as well. The Minister stated that there was no intention of conveying a slur or stigma on Indians or to make them out as of a lower civilisation. "If you think", added Duncan, "that the Government are always going to impose upon you and use every possible means of injuring you, then there is no use arguing if you start from that point of view. But I ask you to look at the Bill from the point of view that the Government is here to see reasonable fair play, and that they will use all the power they have to see that the Bill is carried out with justice and reason."[91]

Several members of the delegation replied, the gist of their remarks being that Indians had no intention of challenging the supremacy of the European races; all that they wanted was to have a means of livelihood assured; judging by the way Indians had been treated since Union there were the strongest reasons for fearing what might be done in the future; promises made to the Imperial Government had not been kept; if there was friction this had not been initiated by Asiatics who have always been peaceful and law-abiding; they considered it debasing to be told to go and live in a particular place; segregation would be derogatory to their national honour; Continentals from Europe were better treated than the Indians who claimed to be better subjects. The representations made by the Indians failed to get the measure withdrawn. It was left to parliament to decide.

With the fate of the Class Areas Bill to be now decided in Parliament, Indians in South Africa welcomed the arrival in the country of the famous Indian poetess and politician, Mrs. Sarojini Naidu, at the end of February, 1924. Mrs. Naidu, like Prof. Gokhale in 1912, was expected to take an active part in the attempts to improve the lot of the Indians in the country. Mrs. Naidu's first important task was the Class Areas Bill which Gandhi, in a statement issued in India, called a breach of the compromise of 1914.

Mrs. Sarojini Naidu lost no time in attending to the task in hand. She interviewed the Prime Minister, the Minister of the Interior, the leaders of the Opposition and other prominent members of Parliament on the Class Areas Bill; she was present in Parliament while the Bill was discussed there. Mrs. Naidu was surprised, during the second reading of the Class Areas Bill, to find that responsible members of Parliament indulged in the art of misrepresenting facts, thereby misleading the House. She revealed her impressions in an interview published in the *Natal Advertiser*. In this interview Mrs. Naidu said, *inter alia*: "Some of the speeches were clever, but were full of blind prejudice, selfishness and ignorance of the facts concerning the entire problem, both here and outside, and the mentality of the speakers was as confused between the material and moral issues. Many things were absolutely mis-stated."[92]

The debate during the second reading of the Bill was an indication of the determination of Parliament to have the measure on the Statute Book. In the midst of the debate, a by-election defeat of the South African Party, then in power, at Wakkerstroom, caused General Smuts to drop a bombshell by declaring that he would advise the Governor-General to dissolve Parliament, not because he was asked by the Imperial and Indian Governments to withdraw the Bill but because of the loss of the South African Party seat at Wakkerstroom. The dissolution of Parliament did not give cause for rejoicing, for the Bill was almost certain to be re-introduced.

During this period of anxious waiting the second session of the South African Congress opened on 21st April, 1924 under the Presidentship of Mrs. Sarojini Naidu. The conference reviewed the South African Indian question in its entirety, dealing with all matters on this question involving South Africa, India, Great Britain and the Imperial Conferences. In terms of Resolution No. 28 (there were 35 resolutions in all) Congress approved of the suggestion of the President, Mrs. Naidu, that a Round Table Conference be held between representatives of the Union Parliament, of India and the Indian Government and of the S.A.I.C., "for the adjustment of questions involving the rights, liberties and responsibilities of Indians domiciled and born in South Africa".[93] From the international standpoint the important factor emerging from this conference was the suggestion that inter-governmental talks be held to attempt a solution which had even eluded the Imperial Conferences.

The South African Indian Congress elected Mrs. Sarojini Naidu as its next President. This brought the S.A.I.C. and the Indian National Congress closer as Mrs. Naidu was also an important member of the latter Congress, of which she was to be elected President in 1925, thus gaining the unique distinction of being President of the South African Indian Congress and the Indian National Congress at the same time. In her speech at a farewell meeting held in her honour in the Durban Town Hall on 22nd May, 1924, Mrs. Naidu brought new hope to her audience by calling the problems of the country only temporary ones. Looking penetratingly into them, she said that "the deeper mind tells me not to be disturbed because for a moment there seems to be something in Africa almost like a race conflict, almost like a colour war. It says these things are temporary, they have no abiding place in the evolution of Africa".[94]

After the departure of Mrs. Sarojini Naidu for India, the South Africans had not long to wait before their fate for the moment could be decided. In June, 1924, the election results were known. The South African Party led by General Smuts was defeated and General Hertzog returned from his period of voluntary exile for ten years in the political wilderness to be next Prime Minister of the Union at the head of a Nationalist – Labour Pact Government. General Smuts suffered a great personal defeat at the hands of Labour in Pretoria West.[95]

But for all that, there was nothing in the election results for the Indians to rejoice about. If anything, darker days lay ahead if the Nationalists now in power put into practice their preachings of the past. When the new government took its first stand on the Indian question the position would become clearer. Before this could be discerned, the Secretary of State for the Colonies, J. H. Thomas, arrived in South Africa on a mission to see things for himself. He arrived in Durban on 30th August, 1924. Speaking at a public reception in the Town Hall in Pietermaritzburg on 5th September, 1924, Thomas referred to the Asiatic question. He said that the question was as much a problem for the Imperial Government as it was for South Africa. He boiled the whole question down to three important points and stated that no satisfactory solution could be arrived at that did not do substantial justice to each of the following points:

1. Europeans who demanded that the heritage which their fathers had built up should be secured for their children.
2. Indians who claimed consideration for the part which they had played in the development of the country.
3. African-born Indians who claimed that they knew no citizenship except citizenship of South Africa and of the British Empire.

To arrive at a solution Thomas advised that the leaders of all parties should be brought together and this included the representatives of India and of the Imperial Government. He warned South Africa not to drag herself and the Empire to ruin and disaster and said that "many of the views by some people (in South Africa) cannot be supported from the Imperial point of view".

How far and how seriously the Pact Government was to heed the advice given by Thomas remained to be seen. The first occasion given to the new Government to express itself on the Indian question was when it met a deputation from the Natal Indian Congress on 9th December, 1924, on the subject of the Natal Boroughs Ordinance of that year which sought to disenfranchise the Indians in the boroughs.

The Natal Indian Congress delegation consisted of sixteen representatives. The deputation was received in person by the Prime Minister, General Hertzog, who was accompanied by Dr. Malan, Minister of the Interior, Colonel Creswell, Minister of Defence and Labour, N. C. Havenga, Minister of Finance, P. W. Beyers, Minister of Mines, C. W. Malan, Minister of Railways, T. Boydell, Minister of Posts and Telegraphs, and Piet Grobler, Minister of Lands. Only two Cabinet Ministers, the Minister of Justice, Tielman Roos, and the Minister of Agriculture, General Kemp, who were engaged with other deputations, were not present. This large assembly of Cabinet Ministers was of particular significance for it indicated the Government's interest in the Indian question.

General Hertzog informed the deputation that it was hardly within the ambit of the Union Government to interfere with the rights of the Provinces and that Natal was acting entirely within its rights as the Ordinance had the support of the people of Natal. He promised to discuss the matter thoroughly within the Cabinet before coming to any decision.

After this there was little doubt what the decision of the Government would be. In fact in about a week's time the Government announced that it had advised the Governor-General to give his assent to the Natal Boroughs Ordinance. Indians protested strongly against this move. An executive meeting of the South African Indian Congress was held in Cape Town on 21st December, 1925, and resolutions were adopted supporting the intentions of the Natal Indian Congress, first to test the legality of the law in the highest courts of the Empire, and, failing this, to resort to passive resistance.

Protests against the action of the Government were widespread in South Africa and in India. India was aroused to protest strongly and to demand that the pledges of the past be honoured even at this late hour. The comments in the *Bombay Chronicle* give some idea of the position:

> "To the residents in Natal, it is wanton injury. Have the Imperial Government neither the will nor the strength to check a law of flagrant persecution against a law-abiding minority in a Dominion? Justice requires protest and veto. The measure is again quite in conflict with the assurances which Lord Sinha elicited from South Africa at the Imperial Conference of 1918."[96]

It seemed to be of no profit to be over-mindful of the pledges of the past; they were observed only in the breach. After the advent of Nationalist rule in 1924 and the coming into being in rapid succession of further deprivation of rights, the Natal Boroughs Ordinance, 18/1924 (loss of the municipal franchise in boroughs); the Natal Townships Ordinance, 3/1924 (loss of the municipal franchise in townships); Local Government (Provincial Powers Act), 1925 (loss of rights to serve on local health committees), not only were the resident Indians deeply troubled by these further disabilities but India, too, had to take note of the situation which was worsening.[97]

Inspired by the ideal of the maintenance of cordial relations between India and South Africa, the Indian Government sent a telegram to the Governor-General of the Union of South Africa on 8th April, 1925, stating that there should be a full, frank and personal discussion between representatives of the Government of India and the Government of the Union of South Africa in order to come to "a ready understanding of divergent points of view". The telegram referred to the suggestions in this regard already made by Thomas, the Secretary of State for Colonies when he visited South Africa in September, 1924. As to the venue the despatch suggested that the conference be held in South Africa, or failing this, in India or even in Geneva to coincide with the forthcoming session of the Assembly of the League of Nations.[98]

The despatch concluded with the wish of the Indian Government not to question the authority of the Union Government "on a point of domestic constitutional convention", though it could not help remarking that the Natal Boroughs Ordinance had far-reaching implications in that it affected the relations between the two countries adversely. The despatch stated that such measures needed adjustment in the "light of imperial and international considerations".

In his reply the Governor-General of the Union said that the Union Government was quite willing to have a friendly exchange of views between the governments concerned but made it quite clear that the political, economic and racial status of Indians in South Africa bore a direct relation to and was almost entirely dependent upon the effectiveness or otherwise of the repatriation of Indians. That was the only development which would satisfy European public opinion in the country.

The Indian Government's comment on this observation expressed a feeling of "profound disappointment" at the conclusion arrived at by the Union Government with regard to repatriation and stated that while repatriation might be usefully discussed at the proposed conference, it should not, and could not, be made obligatory and that the Indian residents should be encouraged to return voluntarily to India, "since nearly 63 per cent of the resident Indian population was born in South Africa and the majority of that element regard that country as their home, and are hardly likely to return to India unless compelled to do so".

Even such a candid statement that the majority of Indians in South Africa looked upon the country as their home could not deter the Union Government from introducing a Bill on 23rd July, 1925, which started from the premise "that the Indian, as a race in this country, is an alien element in the population, and that no solution of this question will be acceptable to the country unless it results in a very considerable reduction of the Indian population in this country".[99] Dr. Malan felt that the introduction of this Bill should not impede the prospect of continuing negotiations between the two governments.

Up to the time of the introduction by the Minister of the Interior of the Areas Reservation Bill, the Union Government had not informed the Government of India whether it had approved of the proposed round-table conference suggested by the latter Government. It was, therefore, with great concern that the Government of India received the first official intimation of the Bill in a letter dated 28th July, 1925. The decision in regard to the holding of a round-table conference was only communicated to the Government of India on 24th September, 1925, in which it was stated that the Union Government saw no reason to depart from their earlier stand: that the eventual repatriation of Indians from South Africa should form the basis for the holding of the conference; that anything less would be construed by the Europeans in South Africa "as an interference from outside". Once this was agreed upon the Union Government would be prepared to discuss the matter of providing suitable employment for Indians in South Africa, where such employment would not result in close competition between them and the Europeans and where some competition was unavoidable to make it "strictly equal and fair".[100]

In their reply, the Government of India stated that they had not intended it to be understood that the main object of the proposed conference was to expedite the repatriation of Indians. All that they had meant to convey was that "the existing scheme of repatriation on a purely voluntary basis might be re-examined with a view to ascertaining what difficulties had arisen in its working and how these difficulties could best be smoothed out". The Government of India was prepared to assist in the repatriation question as well as on the question of mitigating direct competition between Europeans and Indians. For their contribution to be worthwhile, they suggested that the Union Government agree to a deputation from India, which would collect information regarding the economic position of Indians in South Africa and investigate their general condition. The object of the deputation "would be to suggest an alternative solution of the Indian question to that embodied in the Areas Reservation and Immigration and Registration (Further Provision) Bill". The Government of India requested that the Bill be postponed for the time being.

Three days later the Government of India sent their considered opinion of the Bill. They questioned whether the Indian population, 60 per cent of whom were born in South Africa, could justly be regarded as an alien element; they reiterated their opposition to the principle of racial segregation; to prohibit the acquisition of agricultural land except in the case of existing Indian holders would increase the congestion in areas around Durban and at such places as Stanger; restricting the further entry of Asiatics lawfully resident in other parts of the Union into Natal and the Cape Province would seriously affect vested interests; the time-limit in respect of the entry into the Union of the wives and children of lawfully resident Indians was not in consonance with the terms of paragraph 3 of the Reciprocity Resolution of 1918. In the face of this criticism the South African Government could not agree to a postponement of the Bill. All that it was prepared to do was to receive a fact-finding deputation from India. This deputation would have plenty of time within which to complete its investigations and make its reports as the Bill would be sent to a select committee after the second reading.

An important stage had now been reached in the negotiations between the two governments for closer discussions. The suggestions of Sarojini Naidu and J. H. Thomas were coming nearer to realization. The Government of India appointed the following persons to constitute the deputation which was to sail from Bombay to South Africa by the s.s. *Karagola* on 25th November, 1925: G. F. Paddison, C.S.I., I.C.S., Commissioner of Labour, Madras, leader of the deputation; Hon. Syed Raza Ali, Member of the Council of State, member of deputation; G. S. Bajpai, C.B.E., I.C.S., Acting Deputy-Secretary to the Government of India, secretary of deputation, and C. S. Ricketts, assistant-secretary to the deputation. The third member of the deputation, Sir Deva Prasad Sarvadhikary, Kt., C.I.E., Member of the Council of State, recently dissolved, was to sail from Bombay by the s.s. *Karapara* on 9th December, 1925.

Before the Paddison Deputation reached South Africa, the South African Indian Congress, too, was actively engaged with the pressing issues. It assembled in conference at Cape Town on 9th November, 1925, rejected the Areas Reservation and Immigration and Registration (Further Provision) Bill, and called upon the Union Government to consent to a round table conference "to consider the whole position of the Indians here and arrive at an honourable solution". A deputation of the Congress waited on the Minister of the Interior on 16th November, 1925. The leader of the deputation, Advocate J. W. Godfrey pointed out to Dr. Malan that the proposed Bill was a breach of the Smuts–Gandhi Agreement; that the Indians wished to be treated as South Africans in every respect. He said: "We live and think and move about exactly as the Europeans do."

Dr. Malan's reply to the points raised by the deputation touched on three aspects of the case: firstly, that it was definitely understood in the Smuts–Gandhi Agreement that all agitation against legislation would end; secondly, the undertakings of General Smuts at that time related only to the administration of the existing laws. "As far as I can see", said Dr. Malan, "no undertaking was given or could have been given by any Government that the laws would not be changed or that any laws with regard to any question would not in future be introduced". Thirdly, on the matter of vested interests, Dr. Malan recalled Gandhi's definition of this in the letter sent by Gandhi to the Secretary for the Interior on the 7th July, 1914, viz., "the right of an Indian and his successors to live and trade in the township in which he was living and trading no matter how often he shifts his residence or business from place to place in the same township". Dr. Malan said that vested rights were always protected, in Law 3/1885, in the Transvaal Gold Law of 1908, and in the Asiatics (Land and Trading) Amendment Act (Transvaal) 37/1919. So it was in the Areas Reservation Bill of 1925.[101]

Dr. Malan left no doubt on how far external pressures would be tolerated:

"I may say, in general, that the Union Government considers the Indian question to be a question which has to be solved by the South African Government and Parliament and people. This is not to say, of course, that we shall not welcome the representations made to us by people outside. We shall always be willing to receive representations but, after all, the question is a South African one and has to be solved and settled by the Government and the people of South Africa."

The interview helped to clear the air. There was no doubt about the stand taken by Dr. Malan and his Government; similarly, the Indian deputation expressed its case clearly and unambiguously. Godfrey stressed the point of Indian opposition to the measure. He drove the point home in certain terms: "We take up the attitude that on principle we could not agree to this Bill. I cannot think that my community would even submit to voluntary or compulsory segregation. No form of legislation will be accepted by them nor agreed to by them, so far as their agreement can be looked for, where it is sought to locate them into areas and so place upon them the brand of inferiority."

Advocate Godfrey made another point clear on the propriety of seeking outside assistance in a domestic matter. This is how he put it: "Why do we go outside with representations that we should make to you and to no other person; why do we seek advice from England? Because we are unrepresented. You prepare your legislation without consulting us. We prepare our resolutions which are ignored. So we refer the matter to those whom we have just because they might induce you to do what we think to be right."

As no concession was made by the Minister of the Interior, the South African Indian Congress proceeded with its next steps. At the Fifth Session of the Congress, from 9th to 12th November, 1925, it was decided, in terms of Resolution No. 5, that a deputation should proceed to India to further the cause of the South African Indians there. The members of the deputation were: Dr. A. Abdurrahman (Cape), leader, A. A. Mirza (Transvaal), Amod Bayat, V. S. C. Pather, Sorabjee Rustomjee, J. W. Godfrey, and Pundit Bhawani Dayal.[102]

But in view of the decision of the Indian Government to send the Paddison deputation to South Africa, the Indian Government cabled the South African Indian Congress asking whether Congress would not defer or cancel the projected visit of its members to India. The S.A.I.C. replied with a resumé of the latest developments, including the recent interview with the Minister of the Interior, and concluded that the interests of the South African Indian community could best be served if the Government of India deputation deferred sailing until the S.A.I.C. deputation reached India. The Indian Government held that postponement of the visit by the Paddison deputation would not serve the best interests. Both deputations organised their trips in opposite directions. Thus it came about that a most significant and historic event in the annals of the South African Indians took place when the S.A.I.C. deputation sailed for India on 23rd November, 1925, and the Paddison deputation sailed for South Africa on 25th November, 1925.

While the Paddison deputation was busy in South Africa, the South African Indian Congress deputation was busy in India. The deputation remained in India for about two months and it had an interview with the Viceroy of India during which it presented the case of the South African Indians to him; the members of the deputation attended the Fortieth Session of the Indian National Congress at Cawnpore and put before the Congress the case of the South African Indians. The President of the Indian National Congress was Mrs. Sarojini Naidu who had been in South Africa in 1924 and was also President of the South African Indian Congress. Mrs. Naidu made reference to the deputation in her Presidential Address. She said:

"Our brothers in South Africa have sent their ambassadors to us in their hour of agony. They have come to the last desperate stage when they cannot stand alone and they come to you with hands of supplication saying: 'Oh, rise out of slavery because your slavery is the guarantee of our death in that country; your freedom is the prophecy of our honour in the eyes of the world! . . .' In South Africa where your people by the sweat of their brow and blood of their lives have built up that beautiful Natal, they say to us: 'You shall not trade here; you shall not live here; you are the Asiatic menace that we must cut off from our lives'; and we, with all the tyranny of our social system, with all the curse of disunion, with all the dishonour of our bondage, have not the power of authority to say to them: 'Thus far and no further, because the million-armed and free India stands before her stricken children in South Africa.' "[103]

An important point made by Mrs. Naidu was that India's subjection to foreign rule was largely responsible for the untenable position in South Africa. It was necessary, therefore, for India to become free first and then come forward in defence of the rights of the Indians in South Africa. Another notable feature was that in holding the dual position Mrs. Naidu was as much the spokesman for the South African Indians as she was for the people in India. The cause of both was interlinked. The cause of the South African Indians would now feature more prominently in the affairs of India. The members of the deputation in India addressed many meetings in the important centres in India. All funds for the expenses of the deputation during their stay in India were provided by the Imperial Indian Citizenship Association at the request of Mrs. Sarojini Naidu.[104]

The deputations to and from India had prepared the ground well for the next developments; the first of these were the interim conclusions and recommendations of the Paddison deputation. The deputation reported that they had been unable to find any justification for the general opinion held by Europeans in Natal that Indian competition in trade was increasing and was closing fruitful avenues of employment to Europeans; nor was there any justification for the assertion that Indians had displaced Europeans in skilled or semi-skilled occupations. The deputation then considered the three aspects in the Areas Reservation Bill and gave their opinion on each. These considerations, together with the Paddison deputation recommendations, were:

1. Commercial separation: this was already the case as a result of municipal administration of existing licensing laws.
2. Residential segregation: the condition of many localities occupied by Indians caused the Indian community to fear that the creation of any class area for them would have the same result.
3. Restriction provided for in Clause 10, i.e. the prohibition in the acquisition of immovable property in the Cape and Natal by certain persons. In the case of Natal,

immovable property could be acquired by Indians in the coast belt, to a distance of thirty miles from the coast. The deputation said that the effect of Clause 10 would be to drive the Indian market gardeners into the coast-belt; Indian market gardeners, who were tenants of Europeans, would be deprived of their means of livelihood; Indian traders outside the coastal belt would be driven into the belt on the expiration of their leases. This would not only impose great hardship on Indians but many Europeans would suffer as well for when the Indians found that they were shut off from the land they would turn for a living to the skilled trades in which the position of the Europeans would be further threatened. In view of these observations, the deputation was convinced that a round table conference would be the most satis- factory method of dealing with the situation.

The Union Government saw no reason to depart from its earlier decision that there was no need for a round table conference but made an important concession to Indian wishes when it suggested that the Areas Reservation Bill be sent to a Select Committee so as to enable the Paddison deputation to argue on the principle of the Bill. After its appearance before the Parliamentary Select Committee and discussions with the Union Ministers, the Government of India deputation succeeded in getting the Union Government to agree to the holding of a round table conference between the two governments. The Select Committee approved of the holding of such a conference with the object of settling the Asiatic question in South Africa consistent with the maintenance of western standards of life.

The negotiations between the two governments with regard to a round table conference between them had certain significant features; firstly, the cordial and courteous manner of dealing with each other is evident in the official records studied; secondly, they marked an advance in inter-governmental negotiations as they were conducted without the aid and intervention of Great Britain; thirdly, in spite of the protestations of the Union Government that the South African Indian was a Union national and therefore could not appeal to outside powers for assistance, the round table conference which commenced towards the end of December, 1926, was of sufficient importance for the conclusion to be reached that there was a moral obligation on the part of the Union of South Africa to hold discussions with India over the South African Indian question in view of the peculiar circumstances which led to the presence of Indians in South Africa.

There was a genuine desire on the part of the Indian Government to assist the Union Government to find a solution to this vexatious problem which had troubled South African, Indian and British statesmen on international platforms over the past sixty-five years. This desire was further seen in the invitation extended by the Government of India to the Union Government to send a representative Parliamentary delegation to India to establish "the fullest mutual understanding"; to meet prominent Europeans and Indians "and to study at first hand present-day conditions in India".[105]

This the Union Government readily accepted and while General Hertzog was attending the memorable Imperial Conference of 1926 in London, out of which was to emerge the Balfour declaration that Great Britain and the Dominions were "equal in status, in no way subordinate one to another", the Union's Parliamentary delegation was in India. This was the first occasion when an official delegation of the Union visited India. The delegation was headed by F. W. Beyers, the Minister of Mines, and had as its other members, J. S. Marwick, G. Reyburn, A. C. Fordham, W. H. Rood and M. L. Malan. Its secretary was J. R. Hartshorne, the Commissioner for Asiatics and Immigration Affairs.

The members of the delegation were supporters of segregation and of the repatriation of Indians. On their return from India they admitted that their horizon was broadened and said that they had discovered a good market in India for South African goods. But there was no indication that this visit would result in any change of policy at home. In fact, the new Pact Government had its own programme which would mean an acceleration of the process of safeguarding "white South Africa". This process meant the introduction of further difficulties for the resident Indians. When the Pact Government was returned to power there were already many difficulties. One of the urgent problems for Indians was that of housing. The housing conditions in 1925 were very bad; overcrowding was worst in the case of Asiatics. The average number of occupants per room in all urban areas of Natal was 1,07 for Europeans, 2,11 for Africans, 1,79 for Coloureds, but 2,44 for Asiatics. In Durban alone, in a survey of dwellings in 1921, it was found that the average number of occupants per dwelling was 5,55 for Europeans, 3,80 for Africans, 6,90 for other non-Europeans, but 9,52 for Asiatics. Linked with overcrowding were the insanitary living conditions of the bulk of the Indian community.[107]

The problem of Indian housing was very acute. The Durban Town Council put the blame on Indians for not co-operating. The Indians complained that the 14 Municipal lands were all sold to Europeans, that they were asked to accept land in Cato Manor which was outside the Borough boundaries, "and therefore it was highly probable that it would be neglected in the provision of civic amenities and would degenerate into a slum area". The position outside Durban, in any case, was worse than that inside Durban, for here 30 918 Asiatics were concentrated, a proportion of 3174,4 Asiatics per 1 000 Europeans.[108]

Though the Indian housing position was very acute at this time, and has continued to be so for a long time, another difficulty inflicted upon the Indians was the Mines and Works Amendment Act, 25/1926, known as the "Colour Bar Act". This Act empowered the Governor-General to make regulations about the grant of certificates of competency to certain classes of skilled workers, such as mechanical engineers and engine drivers, to Europeans, Cape Coloureds, Cape Malays and Mauritius Creoles. Indians were excluded. This was, in effect, a "civilised labour" policy and its effects on Indian employment in Government departments can be seen in this example. In 1924 there were some 1 800 Indians employed on the railways. By 1936 the number had fallen to 562.[109]

To add to the difficult times which the Indians were going through during the early years of the Pact Government, the Transvaal Dealers (Control) Ordinance, 11/1925 was passed. This Ordinance sought to place the Transvaal Indian traders in the same position as their Natal counterparts.

Nor did it stop at that. In 1926 the Liquor Bill was introduced. Sections 107 and 144 of the Bill dealt a serious blow to the hundreds of Indians employed in the brewery trade by refusing to allow them to be employed even as drivers of liquor vans as they were now denied access to licensed premises.

Such was the position of Indians in South Africa when the round table conference was held in 1926–7. Many people held that the Areas Reservation Bill which had led to the convening of the conference was not any harsher on the Indians than the Mines and Works Amendment Act, 25/1926. This Act was looked upon as the very epitome of white supremacy and domination in South Africa as seen and planned by the Pact Government. In spite of the protestations of General Smuts, the law was passed. Such protestations can be most profuse when they come from the Leader of the Parliamentary Opposition. Smuts affirmed that the Bill laid down a precedent of injustice, inequality and unfair dealing, which would recoil upon the Europeans. He recalled the words of Mahatma Gandhi to him in their earlier negotiations that "we recognise that there is a difference between you and us, and that distinction must be made, but don't cast a stigma on us in the laws of your country". Smuts pleaded eloquently for its rejection in words which did little to clear the heavy air of distrust and doubt before the delegates of the two countries met in Pretoria. This is what Smuts said:

"To cast a stigma on the Asiatics in our legislation was the very thing the Minister did. We were gathering on our heads the hatred of the whole of Asia from one side to the other. All Asiatic people were branded by the Bill, and we should feel the weight of their hatred for years to come."[110]

How could Asiatic feeling against the anti-Asiatic laws of South Africa be brought to the attention of the law-makers? What were the larger issues at stake in the important question which the round table conference was to help to resolve? The passing of these laws had local and international implications, as Miss Corbett observes:

"Thus there were the larger issues behind the problem of 161 339 Indians in South Africa, which gave it its significance. Within South Africa there was the larger issue of the colour problem, the question of the supremacy of the white race, which made it difficult to deal completely justly with those Indians. Without South Africa there was the larger issue of the relations between India and South Africa, even of the future of the British Commonwealth of Nations, if South Africans did not deal justly with her Indian community."

India saw the need and the wisdom to speak for the Indians whom she had sent out to South Africa who, since 1896, were voteless in Natal and since the advent of Union, in the whole country. "Once, however, they were absorbed into the body politic of South Africa, and granted the vote as South African citizens, India could cease to concern herself with their welfare, and this would become purely a domestic issue."[111]

If it was honour and prestige – "Izzat" – for the Indians, it was, as General Smuts said, "For South Africa, for white South Africa, it is not a question of dignity but a question of existence. . . ." And how could national honour and self-preservation, justice and expediency find a common solution on the green tables of diplomacy? To find a solution a heavier burden rested on South Africa, for it was South Africa's problem, it was to be solved in South Africa, and it was the South African Government that had suggested the formula for the Conference.

With this analysis and description of the background to the conference, the work of the First Round Table Conference between the representatives of the Government of India and of the Government of the Union of South Africa on the Indian question in the Union must now be dealt with. The conference opened in Cape Town on Friday, 17th December, 1926. Those representing the Government of India were the Honourable Khan Bahadur

Sir Muhammad Habibullah Sahib, K.C.I.E., Member of the Governor-General's Executive Council, who was the leader; the Hon. G. L. Corbett, C.I.E., Indian Civil Service, Secretary to the Government of India, who was the deputy leader; the Hon. V. S. Srinivasa Sastri, P.C., Sir D'Arcy Lindsay, Kt., C.B.E., Member of the Legislative Assembly; the Hon. Sir Phiroza C. Sethna, Kt., O.B.E., Member of the Council of State; Sir George Paddison, K.B.E., C.B.E., Member of the Legislative Assembly; Mr. G. S. Bajpai, C.I.E., C.B.E., Deputy Secretary of the Government of India, who was the secretary to the Indian delegation.[112]

Those representing South Africa were the Hon. J. B. M. Hertzog, M.L.A., Prime Minister; the Hon. Dr. D. F. Malan, M.L.A., Minister of the Interior; the Hon. F. H. P. Creswell, D.S.O., M.L.A., Minister of Defence; the Hon. F. W. Beyers, K.C., M,L.A., Minister of Mines and Industries; the Hon. T. Boydell, M.L.A., Minister of Labour; Mr. C. F. Schmidt, Secretary for the Interior; Mr. E. Brande, Principal Immigration Officer, Cape; Mr. H. Pring, Chief Clerk, Department of the Interior.

In his opening remarks to the Conference, General Hertzog said that the people of South Africa were not ill-disposed towards the Indians in the country but that a "feeling" had been created because of the danger to white civilisation present in the large native population in the country. To this population was now added a considerable number of the lower class of Indians. General Hertzog made heavy use of the word "feeling" which, as a euphemism, certainly served its purpose. The word was soon well worn and as the General warmed up the true surface appeared. He went on to say:

> "I wish once more to make this assurance that although in South Africa there is a prejudice against the Indian here – no one in this Conference should take that prejudice as a feeling of hostility against India on the part of the people in this country. The prejudice is in the first place one on economic grounds and in the second place it is unfortunately added to by a prejudice which, let me honestly say, is a prejudice common in South Africa, namely, the prejudice of colour."

General Hertzog made a candid admission that the Indian problem standing by itself was no problem at all. "It is a great misfortune", he said, "that we in South Africa have to deal with the Native and the Indian in juxtaposition such as they are. It is really only those who are closely associated with South Africa who feel how much the whole question of the natives and Indians here is complicated. The whole question of the existence of the white man and his civilisation is complicated by those two factors being here at the same time."

For his part, General Hertzog outlined the position in South Africa as it affected the Europeans. Voluntary repatriation, he said, was the main factor in the solutions to be arrived at. The leader of the Indian delegation, Sir Muhammad Habibullah, said that his delegation was not committed to any particular solution; that his delegation was greatly impressed by the atmosphere of great natural friendliness: "Feeling this as strongly as I do I am sanguine enough to look forward with confidence to the final issue of these negotiations."

The Conference decided on the following agenda:

(a) *Limitation of Indian Population*
   (1) Examination of the existing scheme of repatriation to ascertain what difficulties

have arisen in its working and how close these difficulties can be smoothed away.

(2)   Restrictions on migration:

(i) External;   (ii) Inter-provincial.

(b)   *Examination of ways and means to enable Indians resident in the Union to conform to western standards of life with special reference to:*

(a)   Sanitation;   (b)   Education.

The Conference sat for fifteen days, from 17th December, 1926 to 12th January, 1927, on four days of which the two sub-committees set up by the delegations met. Throughout the proceedings an atmosphere of understanding and friendliness prevailed. The tone for the whole Conference was set by General Hertzog on the first day. In their report-back Memorandum the Indian delegation remarked on this point as follows: "The Prime Minister's speech, which was animated by convincing friendliness and good-will, set the tone of the subsequent proceedings."

This friendliness prevailed till the end. On the last day of the Conference, that is, on 12th January, 1927, Dr. Malan, who had acted as Chairman of the Conference, said:

"I think that the reason why we have come to such a satisfactory solution is certainly, in the first place, because at the very outset we determined to be good friends and to remain good friends throughout, and, in the second place, because we did not think that this problem was a South African problem alone. We recognised that it was as much the problem of the one country as the problem of the other; we recognised that in the solution of this problem there was between us a community of interests, and we viewed this problem and grappled with this problem as a common one between us."

Dr. Malan was optimistic that the friendship cultivated at the Round Table Conference would last. He said: "Between South Africa and India there lies what we and what you generally call the Indian Ocean . . . when the waves of the Ocean lap our shores it will remind us of a friendly nation on the other side."[113]

Sir Muhammad Habibullah reciprocated the sentiments and certainly approved of the friendly atmosphere in which the discussions were held. What the leaders said would have had added significance if their work had stood the test of time. For the moment to some they appeared to be empty expressions; to others they were significant remarks for the reason that they boded well for the future, at least as far as the statesmen could see. The hopes for the future were built on the foundations of the work done by the Round Table Conference in Cape Town, the results of which were embodied in the Summary of Conclusions reached on the Indian question in South Africa, more popularly known as the Cape Town Agreement.

The main points in the Cape Town Agreement were the following: a scheme of assisted emigration was devised, in keeping with the first item on the Agenda of the Conference, viz., the limitation of the Indian population; the entry of wives and minor children in keeping with paragraph 3 of the Reciprocity Resolution; the upliftment of the Indian community, the first clause of which reads:

"The Union Government firmly believe in and adhere to the principle that it is the duty of every civilised Government to devise ways and means and to take all possible steps for the uplifting of every section of their permanent population to the full extent of their capacity and opportunities, and accept the view that in the provision of educational and other facilities the considerable number of Indians who remain part of the permanent population should not be allowed to lag behind other sections of the people."[114]

To give the Cape Town Agreement a fair trial, the South African Government agreed to withdraw the Class Areas Bill.

The Cape Town Agreement met with a mixed reception. There were some who said that the Agreement offered the best available solution; others felt that there was little hope that the Union Government would implement all the clauses of the Agreement. For its part, the South African Indian Congress passed a resolution at its Seventh Session on 12th March, 1927, accepting the Agreement "as an honest attempt to find a solution to the Indian problem" though it criticised certain features of the Agreement like restrictions on land sales; the failure to restore the municipal franchise; the continuation of the Mines and Works Act.

Dr. Malan himself saw many anomalies in it which were subject to a variety of interpretations. He himself interpreted the Agreement as nothing more than a repatriation agreement. In a statement which appeared in the Johannesburg *Star* on 12th April, 1927, he observed:

"The whole object of the Agreement is to get as many Indians repatriated as possible, and the energies of the Conference were bent in that direction namely, to draw up a satisfactory scheme with the help of the Government of India."

It is significant that Dr. Malan made no mention about the other clauses in the Agreement, particularly the Uplift Clause. Indians would cling as tenaciously to this clause as the Union Government would to the Assisted Emigration clause. Here, too, the odds were against the Indians, for what did westernisation offer? Miss Corbett gives a shrewd analysis of this point in her thesis:

"Westernization could not succeed as a solution. For education, tending to greater equality of civilization between Indians and Europeans, would intensify competition and the fear of colour. The ultimate aim of the policy of westernization, as advocated by the Indians, was equality of rights, based on equality of civilization. Westernization would make assimilation of the Indians in South Africa's western civilization possible. But equality of rights and assimilation were just what the Europeans above all were set to avoid. If the menace of a lower civilization was removed, the menace of colour would be intensified. . . ."[115]

Such were the heavy odds against the success of the Agreement. However, an important stage in the political relationship between India and South Africa had been reached by the convening of the Round Table Conference and by the results of its work. The test of time, of sincerity of purpose and good intentions, remained. These were to be seen in the working of the Cape Town Agreement.

FOOTNOTES

1. Government of India, *Papers Relating to the Round Table Conference*, 1926–7, p. 40.
2. C. F. Andrews, *Documents Relating to the Indian Question*, pp. 16–17 and *Indian Opinion: Souvenir of the Passive Resistance Movement in South Africa*, p. 29.
3. *Indian Opinion: Souvenir of the Passive Resistance Movement in South Africa*, p. 21.
4. Walker, *A History of Southern Africa*, p. 559.
5. *Indian Opinion*, 12th January, 1917. *Vide Ibid.*, 26th January and 2nd February, 1917 for articles by Sergt.-Major Albert Christopher on the Indian Bearers in E. Africa.
6. *The Dharma Vir*, 22nd March and 6th December, 1918.
7. Natesan, *Congress Presidential Addresses*, pp. 397–8.
8. *Indian Opinion*, 9th March, 1917.
9. M. Ollivier, *Colonial and Imperial Conferences*, Vol. I: *Colonial Conferences*, Introductory page and W. H. Atteridge, "The Problem of Imperial Organisation with special reference to the place of the Imperial Conference" – unpublished M.A. thesis, Univ. of Pretoria, Chap. V (*b*), pp. 1–29.
10. A. B. Keith, *Responsible Government in the Dominions*, pp. 1189–1190.
11. W. H. Atteridge, "The Problem of Imperial Organisation", pp. 10–11 citing Keith, *Selected Speeches*, Vol. II, pp. 297–8.
12. M. Ollivier, *Colonial and Imperial Conferences*, Vol. II, p. 359.
13. *Indian Opinion*, 24th January, 1919.
14. C. F. Andrews, *Documents Relating to the Indian Question*, Appendix C, p. 19.
15. Smith, *The Oxford History of India*, p. 780.
16. The following table illustrates the position:

Year	Europeans	Asiatics	Percentage Asiatic to Europeans
1911	1 280 381	152 583	11,92
1932	1 859 400	193 900	10,43

A small percentage of the Asiatics were Chinese. *Vide* South African Indian Congress, *Statement to the Indian Colonization Enquiry Committee*, 9th January, 1934, p. 5.
17. South African Indian Congress, *The Asiatic Land Tenure (Amendment) Bill: A Brief Survey of the Bill, with statements and extracts on the subject in relation to Indian rights to trade, occupation and residence in the Transvaal Province*, p. 22.
18. *Indian Opinion*, 31st January, 1919.
19. *Ibid.* Sir S. P. Sinha had a distinguished career: he matriculated at 14; was a brilliant scholar at Lincoln's Inn, London. At 23 he joined the Calcutta Bar; at 26 was Advocate-General of Calcutta; was President of the Indian National Congress when 52. Attended the Imperial War Conference in 1917 and was appointed K.C. in 1918, became Privy Councillor in 1919 and Under Secretary of State for India in 1919. He represented India at the Peace Conference at Versailles in 1919. The appointment of Sir. S. P. Sinha to the post of Under Secretary was a unique one. He was the first Indian to hold office in the British Cabinet.
20. C. F. Andrews, *Documents*, pp. 19–20.
21. *Indian Opinion*, 24th January, 1919.
22. *Indian Opinion*, 15th November, 1918.
23. Report of the Asiatic Inquiry Commission, U.G. 4/1921, p. 20.
24. *Ibid.*, p. 19. The definition of "vested rights" has been the subject of much dispute. Dr. Krause, on behalf of the Indian community, said before the Select Committee of the House of Assembly in 1919 that it was not confined to rights actually acquired at that date but included the inherent right appertaining at that time to all Asiatics to lease and occupy, as well as to trade upon, stands and premises on proclaimed land. The Asiatic Inquiry Commission of 1921 stated: "From Mr. Gandhi's own definition, however, as given in his letter of the 7th July, 1914, it would appear that no more was intended than that the vested rights of those Indians who were then living and trading in townships, whether in contravention of the law or not, should be respected." *Vide* p. 20 of the Report.

25. *Indian Opinion*, 25th July, 1919.
26. Report of the Asiatic Inquiry Commission, U.G. 4/1921, p. 22. The following return, published in the report of the Select Committee of the House of Assembly in 1919 shows the number of private companies, registered under the Transvaal Companies Act (No. 31 of 1919), all the shareholders of which were Indians:

Year	No. of Companies	Normal Capital
1913	3	£7 500
1914	9	£13 150
1915	38	£84 274
1916	103	£132 255
1917	91	£118 229
1918	114	£113 319 7s.
1919	12	£10 600 12s.
Totals	370	£479 327 19s.

Vide Report of the Asiatic Inquiry Commission, U.G. 4/1921, p. 21.
27. P. N. Agrawal, *Bhawani Dayal Sannyasi: A Public Worker of South Africa*, p. 48.
28. *Dharma Vir*, 17th January, 1919. At a mass meeting of Natal Indians held in Durban the following were elected as delegates to the meeting: Messrs. M. C. Anglia, Osman Ahmed, Mohamed Ebrahim, M. Rooknoodeen, P. S. Aiyar, Essop Bapu, R. B. Chetty, B. L. E. Sigamoney, A Christopher, J. N. Francis, M. Beethase, M. L. Sultan, G. D. Lalla and S. C. Pather.
29. *Dharma Vir*, 31st January, 1919.
30. Report of the Asiatic Inquiry Comm., 1921, p. 23; S.A.I.C., Asiatic Land Tenure Amendment Bill, 1930, Appendix D, p. 41.
31. *The Dharma Vir*, 13th June, 1919.
32. *The Dharma Vir*, 19th September, 1919.
33. *Vide* First Annual Report of the South African Indian Congress, 21st April, 1924, in S.A.I.C. *Emergency Conference*, 1926.
34. *The Dharma Vir*, 18th April, 1919.
35. C. F. Andrews, *Documents*, p. 21.
36. *Indian Opinion*, 22nd August, 1919.
37. C. F. Andrews: *Documents Relating to the New Asiatic Bill and the Alleged Breach of Faith*, pp. 21–2.
38. *The Dharma Vir*, 5th September, 1919.
39. *Indian Opinion*, 31st October, 1919.
40. *Indian Opinion*, 31st October, 1919.
41. *Indian Opinion*, 21st November, 1919.
42. *Estimated Number of Indians in each Province in East Africa, 1920:*
Zanzibar, 10 000; Tanganyika, 3 000; Uganda, 2 500; Nyasaland, 2 000; Portuguese East Africa, 2 000; Rhodesia, 3 200. *Vide Indian Opinion*, 14th May, 1920. Figures by Rev. C. F. Andrews.
43. *Indian Opinion*, 21st May, 1920. The Asiatic population of the Union in 1921 was 165 731, of whom 35 per cent were born in India and 63 per cent in the Union.
44. *Indian Opinion*, 18th June, 1920. In a tribute paid to the Rev. C. F. Andrews, at a farewell dinner in Durban in August, 1927, the agent for India in South Africa, Mr. Sastri, said, *inter alia*: "To the Indian community he has been a standby second to none, to the Indian community not only in South Africa, but everywhere in the world. I do not know a single place in the wide Empire where Indians live where Mr. Andrews has not also been to live." *Vide* S. R. Naidoo and Dhanee Bramdaw (Edited), *Sastri Speaks*, pp. 62–65 for the full speech. *Vide* also Dr. Mabel Palmer, *The History of the Indians in Natal*, Note on C. F. Andrews, pp. 99–101.
45. J. E. Corbett, "A Study of the Capetown Agreement" – unpublished M.A. thesis of the University of Cape Town – pp. 41–2.
46. U.G. 4/1921, p. 49.

47. G. H. Calpin, *Indians in South Africa*, pp. 39–40, quotes.

48. Report of the Asiatic Inquiry Commission, U.G. 4/1921, p. 1. The personnel of the Commission was: Chairman, J. H. Lange; Members: J. S. Wylie, H. J. Hofmeyr, and W. Duncan Baxter.

49. *Ibid.*, p. 54. At the time of the Report, i.e. in 1921, Indians in the Cape Province enjoyed the parliamentary franchise; in Natal, the municipal franchise; but in the Transvaal, neither.

50. Report of the Asiatic Inquiry Commission, 1921, *Summary of Recommendations*, pp. 63–4. Paragraph 222 referred to administrative functions, together with all official records relating to Asiatics. This included all statistics, arrivals and departures, trade licences, and purchase of land and property. *Vide Ibid.*, p. 62.

51. *Indian Opinion*, 18th March, 1921, quotes.

52. *Indian Opinion*, 1st April, 1921.

53. *Indian Opinion*, 13th May, 1921.

54. *Indian Opinion*, 24th June, 1921.

55. *Indian Opinion*, 1st July, 1921.

56. W. H. Atteridge, "The Problem of Imperial Organisation with special reference to the place of the Imperial Conference". Unpublished M.A. thesis of the University of Pretoria, Chap. V, p. 24.

57. *Indian Opinion*, 1st July, 1921.

58. *Ibid.*, 8th July, 1921.

59. *Ibid.*, 1st July, 1921.

60. A. B. Keith, *Responsible Government in the Dominions*, pp. 1203–4.

61. Joshi, *The Tyranny of Colour*, p. 104.

62. *Indian Opinion*, 12th August, 1921.

63. *Natal Advertiser*, 10th August, 1921.

64. S.A.I.C., Emergency Conference, 1926: Letter No. C.T.64, pp. 16–18. The Durban Land Alienation Ordinance, No. 14/1922 was promulgated on 27th July, 1922.

65. *Indian Opinion*, 7th April, 1922.

66. *Indian Opinion*, 12th May, 1922.

67. *Indian Opinion*, 22nd September, 1922, quoting the Johannesburg *Star*.

68. Sir John Fischer Williams, *Some Aspects of the Covenant of the League of Nations*, pp. 189–190.

69. League of Nations, *Records of the Debates of the Third Assembly*, p. 17 and pp. 171–172. These records were traced by the Public Inquiries Unit of the United Nations and sent to the writer in the form of photostat copies.

70. *Ibid.*, pp. 174–186. The Government of India and the Indian politicians themselves placed little faith in the efficacy of the League. "The dominant elements in Indian political life did not have a consistent attitude towards the League of Nations throughout the period of its working. In the early stages they had no confidence in it; indeed many were very sceptical . . .". *Vide* The Indian Council of World Affairs, *India and the United Nations*, p. 3.

71. *Round Table*, No. 46, March, 1922, pp. 446–7.

72. *Indian Opinion*, 12th January, 1923, quotes.

73. *Natal Witness*, 4th January, 1923.

74. *Natal Mercury*, 23rd January, 1923.

75. *Official Year Book*, No. 24, 1948, p. 1090.

76. Kailas P. Kichlu, *Memorandum on Indian Education in Natal* (South Africa), p. 4.

77. In a reply to the Honorary Secretaries of the Natal Indian Congress, Smuts said, on 13th July, 1923, that there was no good purpose in receiving a deputation from the Congress on the question of Indians in the Dominions as he was not aware, at that time, whether the question of Indians in the Dominions would come up at the Conference to be held that year. *Vide Indian Opinion*, 20th July, 1923.

78. *Indian Opinion*, 3rd August, 1923.

79. W. H. Atteridge, "The Problem of Imperial Organisation with special reference to the place of the Imperial Conference", Chap. V, p. 29.

80. *Indian Opinion*, 9th November, 1923.
81. *Indian Opinion*, 9th November, 1923.
82. Dhanee Bramdaw, *Out of the Stable*, p. 8.
83. *Indian Opinion*, 9th November, 1925.
84. C. F. Andrews, *Documents Relating to the New Asiatic Bill*, pp. 22–23.
85. *Indian Opinion*, 16th November, 1923.
86. A. B. Keith, *Responsible Government in the Dominions*, p. 1209, and pp. 834–5.
87. *Indian Opinion*, 23rd November, 1923.
88. *Indian Opinion*, 23rd November, 1923, quotes the Johannesburg *Star*.
89. *Vide* Report of the Asiatic Inquiry Commission, U.G. 4/1921, pp. 55–7.
90. Joshi, *The Tyranny of Colour*, p. 108.
91. *Hindi*, 22nd February, 1924.
92. *Hindi*, 11th April, 1924.
93. S.A.I.C., *Emergency Conference Agenda Book*, 1926; Resolutions of 1924, pp. 1–12.
94. G. A. Natesan, *Speeches and Writings of Sarojini Naidu*, p. 428.
95. Smuts accepted the safe Standerton seat which he represented in Parliament until he not only lost another election in 1948 but also his Standerton seat. At about this time, i.e., 1924, the Natal Colonial Born Association was formed through the instrumentality of S. L. Singh of Durban.
96. *Hindi*, 23rd January, 1925.
97. In the case of Abraham *v.* the Durban Corporation which was argued before the Appellate Division in April, 1927, Chief Justice Solomon held that the Natal Boroughs Ordinance, 19/1924, was *ultra vires* the powers of the Natal Provincial Council. *Vide* S. R. Naidoo, "The Problem of Franchise" in Natal Indian Congress, Agenda Book of Provincial Conference, 1944, p. 5. *Vide* also Dr. Mabel Palmer, *The History of the Indians in Natal*, p. 93. Dr. Palmer states that in 1953 there were 11 Indians on the Durban municipal voters' roll. In July, 1954, only 4 had re-applied for registration. There are also some 60 Indians on the Stanger municipal voters' roll. Stanger has an Indian councillor who was elected to the Stanger Town Council and is at present, i.e. 1962, in office.
98. *Important Correspondence* between the Government of India and the Government of the Union of South Africa on the Class Areas Bill, 1924, and Areas Reservation Bill, 1925, and negotiations leading up to the Paddison deputation and the Cape Town Conference (1926–27), Telegram No. 14–C., 8th April, 1925, pp. 5–7. This is cited hereafter as *Important Correspondence*.
99. C. F. Andrews, *Documents Relating to the New Asiatic Bill and the Alleged Breach of Faith*, Speech of the Minister of the Interior, Dr. D. F. Malan, p. 13.
100. *Important Correspondence*, pp. 10–11. Telegram from the Governor-General to the Viceroy, 24 September, 1925.
101. Statement Submitted by Deputation of South African Indian Congress to the Minister of the Interior, S.A.I.C. *Emergency Conference Minutes*, Sixth Session, 1926, pp. 1–7.
102. Interim Report of the Hon. General Secretary to the Sixth Session of the South African Indian Congress, held at Durban, 6th and 7th December, 1926, S.A.I.C. *Agenda Book of Emergency Conference*, 1926, pp. 2–4.
103. G. A. Natesan, *Congress Presidential Addresses*, p. 760.
104. Interim Report of the Hon. Gen. Secretary of the S.A.I.C. presented to the Sixth Session of the S.A.I.C., 1926, p. 3.
105. *Important Correspondence*, p. 28. Telegram to the Governor-General of the Union, No. 389, 31st May, 1926.
106. Walker, *History of Southern Africa*, pp. 607–608.
107. J. E. Corbett, "A Study of the Capetown Agreement", pp. 8–9. It is interesting to note what the Thornton Commission, set up in 1928 to enquire into housing conditions, had to say about the Durban Town Council in the matter of providing housing for Indians: "Whereas the Council has done a great deal for the better housing of Europeans in its area, little or nothing in this respect has been done for the Indian population other than for those actually in Municipal employment."

The Commission found that since the passing of the Durban Land Alienation Ordinance 14/1922 and up till 1928, 14 Municipal land sales were held, all of which were reserved for Europeans. During this period only 16 building sites were sold to Indians in the Old Borough of Durban. *Vide* A. I. Kajee and others, *Treatment of Indians in South Africa, A Memorandum of Facts*, p. 39.

108. Corbett, "A Study of the Capetown Agreement", pp. 10–11.
109. A. I. Kajee and others, *Treatment of Indians in South Africa*, p. 57.
110. *The Indian Review*, Vol. XXVI, April, No. 4, p. 311. The Bill, which was introduced by the Minister of Mines and Industries, Mr. F. W. Beyers, had its second reading on the 25th February, 1925. It became law almost a year later. It is interesting that after a few months of its becoming law the architect of the measure which was calculated to deprive thousands of Indians of a livelihood – a contemporary estimate of the number was 10 830 – was leader of the Parliamentary Delegation to India during the latter part of 1926. *Vide* also *Indian Review*, Vol. XXVII, No. 5/1926, pp. 292–3. In terms of the Act certificates of competency would not be given to Asiatics or Africans in the following callings: Mine Managers, Mine Overseers, Mine Surveyors, Mechanical Engineers, Engine Drivers, Miners entitled to blast, and "such other classes of persons employed in, at or about mines, works, and machinery as the Governor-General may from time to time deem it expedient to require to be in possession of certificates of competency". In the Act the definition of the words "Mine" and "Works" was so comprehensive and all-embracing that no Asiatic or African could be employed in a large number of industries in any other capacity than that of a common labourer. *Vide* Statement by the S.A.I.C. on the Bill, submitted to the Paddison deputation, S.A.I.C., *Emergency Conference Agenda Book*, 1926, pp. 1–7.
111. Corbett, "A Study of the Capetown Agreement", p. 37.
112. Government of India, *Papers Relating to the Round Table Conference*, 1926–7, p. 1. This is cited hereafter as Government of India, *Papers*, 1926–7.
113. Government of India, *Papers*, 1926–7, pp. 285–7.
114. Government of India, *Papers*, 1926–7, p. 344.
115. Corbett, "A Study of the Capetown Agreement", p. 40.

CHAPTER FOUR

THE BEGINNING AND THE END OF REPATRIATION: THE SECOND PHASE, 1927–1939

The path of the Cape Town Agreement was not an easy one. Its success depended upon the willingness of its architects on both sides of the Indian Ocean to give and take. As the Hon. Srinivasa Sastri said of it: "It is a compromise, as you all know, and compromise is the very soul of political progress. Now, in a compromise no party carries away the entire honour of the negotiations. Each party gives in a little and takes a little from the other side."[1]

How much of this was done remains to be seen. The Cape Town Agreement was announced on 21st February, 1927. In April, 1927, the Minister of the Interior introduced the Immigration and Indian Relief (Further Provision) Bill to give effect to the Cape Town Agreement. The second reading of the Bill started on 9th May, 1927, and was concluded on 23rd June. The South African Indian Congress made representations to the Minister of the Interior on certain unsatisfactory features in the Bill, particularly against Section 5 which empowered Immigration Officers and the Boards to whom appeals had to be made to cancel the registration certificates or certificates of domicile of any person whose document was proved to have been obtained by fraudulent representations made by him or on his behalf. This clause was inserted to close a loophole which arose out of a decision of the Transvaal Supreme Court to the effect that, under the law as it stood in 1926, a certificate of registration once granted could not be cancelled even if it were proved or admitted to have been fraudulently obtained.[2]

Though the Minister of the Interior gave a verbal assurance to the deputation of the South African Indian Congress that there would be no rounding up of those who were in possession of fraudulent certificates of registration, Congress was not satisfied with the assurance and appealed to the Minister to amend Section 5 so as to make only those certificates of registration fraudulently obtained after the passing of the Bill null and void. No such concession was made. Section 5 of the new Bill was not in accordance with any decision taken during the Round Table Conference. Another disability in the Bill which was, as in the case of Section 5, a source of offence to the Transvaal Indian community was the provision regarding the admission of a minor child only if accompanied by the mother. This was in accordance with the provisions of the Cape Town Agreement and, therefore, much exception could not be taken to it.[3]

The Bill became law in the form of Act 37/1927, with effect from 5th July, 1927, seven days after the arrival in the Union of the first Agent of the Government of India in the Union, the Right Hon. V. S. Srinivasa Sastri, P.C., who had ahead of him the difficult task of helping to implement the terms of the Cape Town Agreement. The Government of India viewed the appointment of an agent in South Africa with approval. Through such an official the Government of India would receive "regular, timely and first hand information" about Indian affairs in the Union. The agent would also act as a channel of representation for the Indian Government. This official would also be of help to the Union Government in the administration of their Asiatic policy as he would have a wider Indian experience and better knowledge of the Indian mind. As the first incumbent of this office, Sastri had a formidable task before him.

Not the least difficult of his tasks was to bridge the gap between the South African Indian political leaders. As from 8th May, 1927, the Transvaal British Indian Association, which had been founded by M. K. Gandhi in 1903, seceded from the South African Indian Congress "for flouting and ignoring the Transvaal Indians", particularly in respect of the representations made to the Government in connection with the Immigration and Indian Relief (Further Provision) Bill. Sastri addressed a crowded public meeting in Johannesburg on 12th October, 1927, and explained the points at issue, viz., the position of a minor child seeking entry into the Transvaal, and Section 5 of Act 37/1927. After this the supporters in the Transvaal of the reunion policy called a mass meeting and set up a new body called the Transvaal Indian Congress on 18th December, 1927. This body affiliated with the South African Indian Congress and, for the moment, Indian unity in South Africa remained intact.

As the Cape Town Agreement was an important experiment in inter-governmental negotiations, this study will now make a survey of the main events in South Africa relative to the Agreement and bearing on the international aspects of the Indian question in South Africa.

The spirit of the Round Table Conference was transferred to the Departments concerned with the Indians in the Union. The General Secretary of the South African Indian Congress wrote, in his Report to the Conference of the S.A.I.C. on 2nd January, 1928, that the heads of the Department of the Interior were most co-operative in dealing with matters concerning the Indians. Administratively, therefore, the Agreement had got off to a good start. Its success in any measure would, however, be dependent on the co-operation and support received from Natal.

But this Province, where Indians were most predominant, did not agree with the Government policy as embodied in the Cape Town Agreement. On 10th May, 1927, C. F. Clarkson, M.E.C., who was later to become the Minister of the Interior in Smuts' Government, moved a motion which was carried by 17 votes to 3 in the Provincial Council of Natal which expressed misgivings with regard to the Agreement. It deplored the fact that Natal had not been consulted before the Agreement was finalised and expressed the opinion that the Agreement would not solve the Indian question nor would it give the Europeans any protection against Asiatic encroachment.[4]

Though the fears in the motion relating to the "relaxation of existing licensing legislation", were unfounded – all that the Cape Town Agreement stated on this point was that when the time came for the revision of the licensing laws the grounds for refusal should be stated, such reasons should be recorded, and a right of appeal should be permitted – those in regard to increased educational facilities had some foundation, for the Indian delegates at the Round Table Conference were quite emphatic that if one of the corner stones of the Agreement was to be the emigration of Indians to India or elsewhere, the other corner stone should be the upliftment of those who remained behind. Such upliftment could only be brought about through educational facilities.

Though the Natal Provincial Council was hostile towards the Agreement, the persistence of the agent, the Hon. V. S. Srinivasa Sastri, the exploratory work of the Rev.

C. F. Andrews, the assistance of the Mayor of Durban and other influential persons and the co-operation of the Administrator of Natal, resulted in the appointment of the Natal Commission on Indian Education on 17th November, 1927. In accordance with their undertaking in this regard in the Cape Town Agreement, the Government of India deputed K. P. Kichlu, Deputy Director of Public Instruction in the United Provinces of Agra and Oudh, and Miss C. Gordon, lecturer in kindergarten methods at the Government Teachers' Training College, at Saidapet in Madras, to assist the Commission, the membership of which comprised Messrs. J. Dyson, M.E.C., Chairman, F. H. Acutt, M.P.C., C. F. Clarkson, M.E.C., F. W. Fell, M.E.C., F.C. Hollander, M.E.C., J. A. Lidgett, M.P.C., A. L. Pretorius, M.P.C., with C. A. B. Peck, as Secretary. The Commission was instructed to enquire into and report on various aspects of Indian education in Natal. K. P. Kichlu prepared a comprehensive Memorandum for the Commission. The Commission reported on 16th May, 1928. Its report found much to be desired in Indian education in the Province.

It recommended that Grant-aided Schools be extended; that Government Schools be provided in the larger centres; that aided schools be graded by average attendance and that the financial aid should be in the direction of a provincial responsibility for the total cost of the teachers' salaries; that salary scales and other conditions of service be improved; that a Teacher Training College be established; that the Administration accept the gift of the Rt. Hon. V. S. S. Sastri of a fully equipped training college; that the Union Government subsidy be increased and that the full subsidy be used for Indian education.

The recommendations of the Dyson Commission were put into effect with most heartening results. The improvement to Indian education in Natal was one of the brightest features of the post Cape Town Agreement period for, since 1928, the whole of the subsidy received from the Union Government for Indian education was spent on Indian education; expenditure rose from £28 430 in 1926–27 to nearly £60 000 in 1930–31, and the estimated expenditure for 1931–32 was £65 000; the number of Indian schools increased from 52 in 1928 to 78 in 1931; a training college, named after Sastri, who had been responsible for initiating the project in August, 1927, with a call for donations from the Indian community to the extent of £20 000, was built in 1929. It was officially opened by Sastri's successor, Sir Kurma Reddi, on the 1st February, 1930.[5]

If the provision for improved educational facilities, agreed upon at the Round Table Conference, was implemented in the period following the Cape Town Agreement, the same was not true with regard to housing and sanitary matters also mentioned in the Uplift Clause of the Agreement. To give effect to the recommendations of the Round Table Conference to investigate the sanitary and housing conditions in and around Durban, the Union Government appointed the Executive members of the Central Housing Board, E. N. Thornton (Chairman), J. Lockwood Hall and R. S. Gordon, on 19th September, 1928, to carry out the investigations. The Thornton Committee reported on 8th December, 1928. It stated that the Durban Corporation had done little or nothing to provide better housing for Indians. It suggested, as a first step, that of the sum of £50 000 which was earmarked under the Housing Act for Indian housing, an amount of £25 000 be made avilable to the Durban Council for erecting, under a scheme to be carried out on a suitable site at the Eastern Vlei, two-and three-roomed cottages to let or for sale on easy terms to Indians, at a place called Cato Manor, several miles outside the boundary of Durban. It was only in 1938 – ten years after the Thornton Commission Report – that the Durban City Council made a start with the building of 50 economic and sub-economic houses at Cato Manor; this was after Dr. Malan had threatened to withdraw the £50 000 set aside for Indian housing if no immediate start was made. The Eastern Vlei site recommended by the Thornton Commission was not used and now forms part of the Windsor Golf Course for Europeans.[6]

Education, housing and sanitary provisions were all confined to Natal. As for the rest of the Indian community in the country the important matters attended to by Sastri were the Condonation Scheme and the Liquor Act, both examples of the good intentions of the Union Government to carry out the letter and the spirit of the Cape Town Agreement.

The most difficult problem which the agent had to deal with during his early years was the problem of regularising the position of Indians who had entered the country illegally so as to have their illegal entry condoned. It was this matter which had caused the Transvaal British Indian Association to break with the South African Indian Congress. The former had charged the Congress with failing to press for a statutory amnesty in preference to an administrative scheme of individual condonation.[7] By the end of 1927 the Minister of the Interior had refused to make any alteration to Section 5 of Act 37/1927 but signified his willingness, "as an act of grace to mark the appointment of the Right Honourable V. S. S. Sastri, P.C., as the first Agent of the Government of India in the Union," to refrain from putting into effect Section 5 of Act 37/1927 against any illicit entrant whether in possession of a document or not, and whether in the Transvaal, the Cape or Natal, who proved to the satisfaction of the Minister that he had entered such a province prior to 5th July, 1924. The Minister's offer was conditional on his receiving on behalf of the Indian community an assurance that such illicit entry would be discountenanced in the future. The Minister's offer was made in May, 1927.

The assurance on behalf of the Indian community was only given on 6th January, 1928, after the annual conference of the Congress was held in Kimberley. It was embodied in a resolution which was conveyed to the Secretary of the Interior.

The scheme was gazetted on 29th July, 1928. Applications for condonation were to be received by the Department of the Interior by 30th September, 1928, the cases of applicants then in India were to be held over for decision till their return to South Africa, subject to a maximum delay of six months.[8]

Applications for condonation certificates came in very slowly. The chief opposition to the scheme came from the leaders of the South African Indian Federation, which was formed on 28th December, 1927, to "function exclusively for a revision of the Indo-Union Agreement which is of no practical advantage to the community in this country". By 20th September, 1928, some six hundred applications only had been received. But in the last ten days applications came in "in the nature of a stampede", making a total of 1 616 applications, of which number 1 333 protection certificates were issued under the scheme, 110 had been refused or not claimed (the figure included 85 Chinese cases) and the balance of 173 were awaiting disposal at the end of 1928.

The granting of a condonation certificate was a gesture of goodwill on the part of the

Union Government. So was the action of the Government in withdrawing Section 104 of the Liquor Bill. Had the clause remained, some 3 000 Indians throughout the Union would have been affected as they would have been debarred from working on licensed premises.[9]

In India, the news of this withdrawal was received with great relief. Sir Muhammad Habibullah, member of the Viceroy's Executive Council and leader of the Indian delegation in South Africa in 1926 and 1927, expressed the appreciation of the Government of India of this fresh manifestation of the friendliness of the Union Government, and his personal gratitude to the members of the Union Government for the generous manner in which they had dealt with the Government of India's representations. He added that the decision was sure to guarantee a continuance between India and South Africa of the friendly understanding established on the firm basis of the Cape Town Agreement. He paid tribute to the important part played throughout by V. S. Srinivasa Sastri, whose tact and persuasiveness proved of the utmost value.[10]

The post Cape Town Agreement period had resulted in some improvement in the position of the South African Indians; the improvements, sympathy and understanding shown during this period were a happy augury of the good relations between India and South Africa at this time. These developments were recalled when the anniversary of the Agreement was celebrated at Cape Town on 21st February, 1928. Sastri praised the Union Government for the success which the Agreement had enjoyed and called the Agreement itself "one of the most statesmanlike things that have happened within the British Empire in the past few years".[11]

For South Africa, the Prime Minister, General Hertzog, said that the good feeling between the two countries would last and that if South Africa had not done all that was desired she had at least tried to remove some of the hardships of the Indian community. The Minister of the Interior, Dr. D. F. Malan, who had himself played a big part in the drawing up of the Cape Town Agreement, was satisfied with the success it had achieved. He remarked on the understanding between the two countries by saying that "South Africa has discovered India, and India has discovered South Africa".[12]

General optimism pervaded that at long last a great problem had been solved. But, as it turned out, these hopes were misplaced for they were soon dashed on the bedrock of repatriation. The success of the Cape Town Agreement was to be judged, from the angle of the Union Government, by the number of Indians repatriated; from the angle of the South African Indians, by the efficacy of the Uplift Clause; and from the angle of the Indian Government, by both these points. The assisted emigration scheme came into operation in July, 1927. By the end of that year 1 655 Indians had taken advantage of it. In 1928 the number of assisted emigrants rose to 3 477. In 1929 it fell to 1 314, the total for the first six months of 1929 being only 822 as compared to the corresponding period in 1928 when the number of repatriates was 1 841.[13]

In 1929 a South African born Indian, Bhawani Dayal Sannyasi, founder of the journal, the *Hindi*, and Vice-President of the Natal Indian Congress, President of the All-India Emigrants Conference and member of the South African Indian Congress deputation to India in 1925, published a report on the subject of the repatriation scheme in which the following conclusions were made:

(1) The repatriation scheme had failed because it brought great misery upon the repatriates, especially those born in South Africa who were accustomed to a different standard of living.

(2) The caste system in India presented great difficulties to repatriates born of inter-caste marriages in South Africa.

(3) The Indian Government had been able to help a few repatriates in South India but hardly any in North India.

(4) Foodstuffs in India were very costly. The repatriates would be better off financially in South Africa.

(5) The repatriates, especially the skilled workers, found it very difficult to settle happily in India because of climatic conditions and low wages.

(6) The repatriation scheme would become increasingly unpopular as the true facts became known.

(7) It was morally wrong to encourage unsuspecting persons to take advantage of this scheme and thereby find themselves in great difficulties in return for which those left behind would be uplifted. It was selfish for those in South Africa to benefit at the expense of the repatriates as it was immoral for India to support the scheme without ensuring the total assimilation of the repatriates into Indian society.[14]

The indictment was a formidable one and could not be ignored. The Union Government, too, must have known by 1930 that there was no future in the assisted emigration scheme and, consequently, in the Cape Town Agreement as they understood it. This was mentioned by Sir Kurma Reddi, the new Agent in South Africa as from 1929, in his report for that year: "The decrease in the number of persons availing themselves of the assisted emigration scheme has caused the greatest anxiety both to the Agent and to the Union Government. For there can be no doubt that Europeans in South Africa judge the success or failure of the Cape Town Agreement by the working of this scheme."

It was too early to pass final judgement on the working of the Cape Town Agreement, especially in regard to the repatriation scheme, though it was becoming abundantly clear that the different hopes held out in the Agreement were not being realised sufficiently enough. Bhawani Dayal had complained about the repatriation scheme and its effects in India. Closer home, in the Transvaal, certain litigations drew attention to the fact that some Indians were occupying premises illegally for purposes of trading, and in certain developed townships (like Springs) the restrictive provisions of the Gold Law of 1908 did not apply to prevent Indians from occupying premises for the purposes of carrying on trade. In January, 1930, the Minister of the Interior, Dr. D. F. Malan, set up a Select Committee to inquire and report on the position created by these decisions and on the question how far the intentions of Parliament, as embodied in Act 37/1919, were being given effect to and whether an amendment of that Act was desirable.

The evidence submitted to the Select Committee was representative of both the European and Asiatic communities; the Transvaal Indian Congress tendered evidence; so did the Acting Agent of the Government of India, J. D. Tyson, in the absence of the Agent-General who had returned to India owing to illness. In his evidence Tyson said that it was a well-established principle, especially with regard to laws restrictive of the ordinary rights of citizenships, that the law allows what it does not prohibit; that if Indians had, even after Act 37/1919, formed companies to own land in a manner which did not constitute an infringement of that statute, it would be only fair and just that such companies, having been formed on a basis which was not at the time illegal, should be protected in any further restrictive legislation. As regards the holding of land through trustees, this was not and never had been illegal; if this was to be made illegal for the future, the existing interests should be protected.[15]

With regard to the occupation of premises, Tyson said that personal interrogation at 201 shops inside and outside Johannesburg showed that out of 201 licences, 72 were protected by Act 37/1919, 121 were unprotected and 8 were doubtful. The Government had done nothing to prevent the growth of these interests; indeed it had benefited by way of revenue from the licence fees.[16]

The Select Committee recommended:

(1) Asiatics to be prevented from acquiring any property in any form in the future outside areas set aside for them.

(2) Sections 130 and 131 of the Gold Law to be strictly enforced after 1st May, 1930, even in townships like Springs which were held to be outside the Gold Law.

(3) Trading licences to be issued only to Asiatics who were lawful owners of the premises occupied.[17]

The recommendations of the Select Committee were embodied in the Transvaal Asiatic Land Tenure (Amendment) Bill which was introduced by the Minister of the Interior in May, 1930. The Bill raised a storm of protest. Even the ailing agent, Sir Kurma Reddi, hastened back to South Africa when the Bill was presented to Parliament. The English and Indian press comments in South Africa were against the Bill, criticising the far-reaching restrictive measures contained in it, especially because it was introduced so soon after the Cape Town Agreement; the Bill was dubbed to be one which neglected the rights promised to the Indians. It was bound to open the old troubles with India and was looked upon as an example of South Africa's "readiness to treat its own covenants as scraps of paper".[18]

The atmosphere of great tension and distrust that prevailed before the Cape Town Agreement was revived by this Bill. Local opposition was mobilised when the South African Indian Congress held an Emergency Conference in Johannesburg on 5th and 6th October, 1930, to formulate its opposition. The agent to the Government of India, Sir Kurma Reddi, addressed the meeting but did not disclose the line of action of his Government as this was still under consideration.

The Conference passed a resolution stating that the Bill was a violation both in letter and in spirit of the Cape Town Agreement; that it imposed disabilities upon the Indians in regard to their trade, residence and occupation and deprived them of their vested rights in the Transvaal; that it aimed at their compulsory segregation and their ultimate ruin in that Province. The Conference called upon the Union Government to withdraw the Bill; in the event of the Government declining to do so, the Conference urged the Government of India to press for a Round Table Conference to review the position. In the event of this failing, Conference called upon the Government of India to withdraw its agency in South Africa as a protest against the Bill.[19]

The Government of India first protested against the Bill in a telegram to the Governor-General of the Union on 9th August, 1930, in which it was suggested that representatives of the two governments take advantage of the coming Imperial Conference to have conversations regarding the working of the assisted emigration scheme, the provisions of the Transvaal Asiatic Land Tenure Bill, and any other points that might occur. The Union Government replied that the Bill could not be held to stand in any relation to the Cape Town Agreement and that at the end of the last Parliamentary session an assurance was given and accepted that the Bill would be introduced at the beginning of the next session in an unaltered form; consequently any conversations in London would have a restricted significance.[20]

Finally, the two governments agreed that their representatives should have informal talks in London in concert with the office of the Secretary of State to discuss matters affecting Indians in South Africa, Canada and Australia. On 28th October, 1930, the representatives of India, Sir Muhammad Shafi and Bajpai, had informal talks with the Union Premier, General Hertzog. Referring to the scheme of assisted emigration, General Hertzog pointed out that there was a marked falling off in numbers. To this the Indian representatives replied that Dr. D. F. Malan, the Minister of the Interior, should visit India and form an independent judgement of the effectiveness of the existing machinery. As the climate in India was alleged to be one of the reasons for the drop in the number of Indian emigrants, the Indian representatives suggested that the two governments should conduct a joint examination to settle the assisted emigrants in Tanganyika. But India's helpfulness in making the scheme a success depended entirely upon the support of Indian opinion both in South Africa and India. To obtain this support, the Transvaal Asiatic Land Tenure Bill should be suitably modified. General Hertzog gave a sympathic hearing to the arguments set out by the Indian representatives and agreed to persuade Dr. Malan to visit India. He was, himself, quite prepared to accompany Dr. Malan.

Bajpai, one of the Indian representatives, advised the Government of India to instruct their agent in South Africa to make an appeal jointly to Dr. Malan and General Hertzog to get the Bill amended. He advised that the "representations should take the form of an appeal to the friendliness of Ministers rather than of arguments based on law or even equity". Bajpai was particularly anxious that General Hertzog should be invited to India. He said of General Hertzog: "He is well disposed towards India and as he is a man of generous instincts it is desirable to secure his friendship as a permanent asset."

On 28th January, 1931, the Indian Government asked for a postponement of the Bill.[21] In response to this request, further consideration of the Bill was postponed till after the meeting of representatives of the two governments to review the work of the Cape Town Agreement at the end of five years. The Indian delegation to this meeting landed in South Africa on 4th January, 1932. The delegation comprised the following members: Sir Fazli Hussein, Leader, the Rt. Hon. V. S. Srinivasa Sastri, Mrs. Sarojini Naidu, Sir Geoffrey Corbett, Sir d'Arcy Lindsay, Sir Kurma Reddi, and Mr. G. S. Bajpai, Secretary. The Union delegation comprised the following members: Dr. D. F. Malan, Leader, Mr. O. Pirow, Minister of Lands, Mr. E. G. Jansen, Minister of Native Affairs, Mr. Patrick Duncan, and Mr. G. H. Nicholls, the two representatives of the Smuts' party – the South African Party.

Any hopes which the South African Indians had of a favourable outcome from the impending Round Table Conference were dashed when Sir Fazli Hussein, leader of the Indian delegation, said at Kimberley in reply to the Mayor's welcome: "Both my Government and yours have agreed that none of our people should permanently settle in this country, and having agreed to this and with goodwill on both sides, we hope to reach a satisfactory settlement." This statement committed the Government of India to a particular line of policy which was unacceptable to the permanent Indian population in South Africa.

The second Round Table Conference opened in Cape Town on 12th January, 1932. The leader of the Indian delegation was absent from the opening owing to illness. The Prime Minister, General Hertzog, in his opening remarks, said, *inter alia*:

"Let us not forget that we are pioneers in the task of cultivating friendship and establishing active national relationship between South Africa and India, and that here as everywhere else the path of the pioneer is strewn with difficulties and dangers of the most unexpected nature. Whatever these may be let us determine especially at this Conference not to lose courage but to persevere in our endeavours."

When these endeavours were really under way the leader of the Union delegation and the chairman of the conference, Dr. Malan, said that the Cape Town Agreement was not primarily intended to improve the international relations between India and South Africa. Its real value, said Dr. Malan, was the extent to which, during the five-year period, it had contributed towards the solution of the Indian problem in South Africa. Dr. Malan said that the success of the Cape Town Agreement depended upon the success of the assisted emigration scheme. But, though 9 260 emigrants had left during the period of four years and four months following the Cape Town Agreement, the balance of emigration over immigration was approximately only 1 285 per annum, i.e. 107 per month, as 200 emigrants had returned and 3 224 were new entrants.[22]

Dr. Malan went on to say that from 1926 to 1930 the Indian population had increased by 11,18 per cent, while from 1926 to 1931 the European population had increased by only 10 per cent; consequently, on the ground of numerical increase the presence of the Indian continued to be regarded as a menace. His conclusions were that the Cape Town Agreement had not only failed in the matter of the assisted emigration scheme but had also failed to fulfil the expectation that it would be a means to improving inter-racial relations as a large section of the Indian population had always looked upon the Agreement with suspicion and had even openly rejected it. "The Cape Town Agreement has consequently failed as a settlement in any true sense of the word," he said.

Dr. Malan, who had lauded the work of the First Round Table Conference and had spoken in glowing terms of the Cape Town Agreement, had now undergone a complete *volte face*. For this development the failure of the assisted emigration scheme was responsible. For Dr. Malan the assisted emigration scheme was the Cape Town Agreement. There was nothing else to it. Its failure meant that the Agreement had failed.

If Dr. Malan saw in the Cape Town Agreement the assisted emigration scheme, the South African Indians saw in it something else. The South African Indian Congress stated that the assisted emigration scheme was accepted by the Indians of South Africa as the means for providing assistance to those who comprised the floating population of South Africa; it was accepted in the belief that it would be helpful to those who were actually desirous of leaving for India. But the voluntary nature of this emigration was vitiated by the increase in inducements from £10 to £20 per head. The increase in the bonus meant that a lump sum of money was available to those with a very low earning capacity, a sum which they would never possess for many years to come. Another factor which violated the voluntary character of the emigration scheme was the employment by the Department of the Interior of agents whose work was to induce people to take advantage of the scheme. Congress said, for these reasons, "We ask for the complete abandonment of the Assisted Emigration Scheme as enunciated in the Cape Town Agreement of 1926 and ratified by Act 37 of 1927".[23]

In this request, and in the opinion about the assisted emigration scheme held by the Union Government Delegation, lay the beginning of the end of the Cape Town Agreement. A way out of the difficulty was suggested by the Rt. Hon. V. S. Sastri to the Conference on 15th January, 1932. Sastri said that his delegation agreed that the assisted emigration scheme would meet with very limited success. If the South African Government wished to explore the possibilities of settling Indians in other countries where Western standards were not required the Indian delegation would recommend this step for the favourable consideration of the Government of India.

The Union delegation was much taken up by the idea but there were some doubts which were expressed. Dr. Malan asked whether any colonisation scheme would attract the Indian traders from the country as the Europeans in South Africa objected primarily to the presence of Indian traders.[24]

Patrick Duncan inquired of Sastri whether there were any prospects of success of a colonisation scheme on a large scale. Sastri's reply was that though emigration was good for the Indians, public feeling in India was strong against emigration "because of the fact that we have suffered all over the world in status, in prestige and in consideration internationally because of the people whom we indiscriminately sent out and who have reduced our prestige all over".

On the fifth day of the Conference, Sir Geoffrey Corbett, of the Indian delegation, said that he was authorised by Sir Fazli Hussein, the leader of the delegation who was the member of the Government of India in charge of the Department which dealt with emigration, to say that the Government of India were willing to co-operate with the Union Government in exploring the possibilities of settling Indians in countries other than India itself. He said that the Indian Government had always appreciated the importance which the Government of South Africa attached to the question of reducing the number of Indians in South Africa, especially in Natal, for two reasons: firstly, to remove the cause of friction which might endanger the friendly relations between the two countries; secondly, because such a step was in the interests of the permanent Indian population of South Africa, for their numbers were really a handicap to them and tended to obstruct their social, economic and political progress. In any move to reduce the number of Indians the support of the local Indian leaders was absolutely necessary.[25]

With the approval of the Conference, the Indian delegation consulted with the leaders of the South African Indian Congress on whether Congress would support any colonisation scheme. On 26th January, 1932, that is on the seventh day of the Conference, Mrs.

Sarojini Naidu reported to the Conference that "out of patriotic motives, and to ascertain whether there exist any good opportunities for South African Indians in other countries, they are prepared to co-operate in exploring outlets for colonisation". The Congress, however, made it clear that this decision was not binding on them to support the assisted emigration scheme.

The Conference ended on 4th February, 1932, without any decision being taken on the question of the contentious Transvaal Asiatic Land Tenure Bill – it was suggested earlier by Dr. Malan that the Bill fell outside the purview of the Conference as he had to carry with him the Select Committee that had recommended the Bill. He suggested that the two governments concerned have direct negotiations in connection with the Bill.

The direct negotiations over the Bill took a long time and the Joint Communique on the work of the Second Round Table Conference was only released simultaneously in South Africa and in India on 5th April, 1932, almost two months to the day since the Conference had concluded its labours. The most important clause in the Communique dealt with the failure of the assisted emigration scheme "owing to the economic and climatic conditions of India as well as to the fact that 80 per cent of the Indian population of the Union are now South African born. As a consequence the possibilities of land-settlement outside India, as already contemplated in paragraph 3 of the Agreement, have been further considered. The Government of India will co-operate with the Government of the Union in exploring the possibilities of a colonisation scheme for settling Indians both from India and from South Africa, in other countries . . . "[26]

The good work that had been started in 1926 to attempt to solve the Indian question by personal contact between representatives of the two countries concerned had taken another step, whatever the direction of this step – it was another step – in the Communique of 5th April, 1932. The South African Indian Congress had agreed, on certain conditions, to co-operate in the colonisation scheme.[27]

It was apparent that the Union Government held out great hopes for the success of the projected scheme which was to take the place of the hopes they had invested in the assisted emigration scheme. On 18th April, 1932, the Secretary for the Interior wrote to the South African Indian Congress inviting Congress to nominate a member to represent the Indian community on the Colonisation Enquiry Committee. The Congress assembled in conference at Johannesburg in August, 1932, when a resolution was adopted to co-operate with the governments of India and South Africa in the colonisation scheme on the understanding that this was not being done because the Indians were undesirables in South Africa or in order to reduce the Indian population in South Africa but because of the reasons already given, and conveyed by Mrs. Sarojini Naidu to the Second Round Table Conference, namely, to ascertain whether good opportunities existed for settlement of South African Indians in any other parts of the world.

Congress decided to leave the appointment of a member representing the Indian community in the hands of the Congress Executive. The Union Government was informed of this decision in September, 1932.

Meanwhile, the Transvaal Asiatic Land Tenure Bill, stripped of some of its harsher features, became law in the form of Act 35/1932. The clause describing the intention of the Union Government to remove all Indians in illegal possession and to segregate them in special areas was abandoned. In its place the Minister was given power to withdraw certain areas, to be decided on later, from the operation of the Gold Law of 1908. Once these areas were demarcated it was proposed to condone the illegalities of which Indians were guilty and to allow them to continue in occupation. To determine those areas, to compile a register of legal occupation and to make recommendations to the Minister regarding individual cases in which hardship might be involved, a commission was appointed. It was called the Transvaal Asiatic Land Tenure Act Commission and was under Mr. Justice Feetham.[28]

Soon after the appointment of the Feetham Commission an economic depression led to the formation of a coalition government under General Hertzog, with Smuts as Deputy Prime Minister and J. H. Hofmeyr as Minister of the Interior in place of Dr. D. F. Malan who became leader of the Opposition. The new Minister of the Interior announced in the House of Assembly the appointment of the Indian Colonisation Enquiry Committee, comprising James Young, ex-chief magistrate in Johannesburg, Chairman; G. Heaton Nicholls, M.P., for Zululand; a representative of the South African Indian community; and P. F. Kincaid, Commissioner for Immigration and Asiatic Affairs, for the purpose of carrying out a preliminary investigation in respect of the colonisation scheme to settle Indians both from India and South Africa in other countries.

The Government of India agreed to place its agent, Kunwar Sir Maharaj Singh, who had succeeded Sir Kurma Reddi in August, 1932, at the disposal of the Colonisation Committee for giving any informal help required. The Executive of the South African Indian Congress met in Durban and decided to nominate S. R. Naidoo as a member of the Committee of Enquiry. Naidoo was then the Joint Secretary of the South African Indian Congress. At the Executive meeting a difference of opinion arose, one section holding that a principle was involved and that the present enquiry was a distinct departure from the Communique in that under the original enquiry the initiative was to be taken by the Government of India. All but two of the executive members felt that co-operation was right and that they were bound by an honourable undertaking.[29] The Executive decision was ratified by the Emergency Conference held on 19th and 20th August, 1933. Albert Christopher, Manilal Gandhi and P. R. Pather who were most active in the condemnation of the appointment of S. R. Naidoo as a member of the Committee of Enquiry declined to attend the meeting though they were invited to do so. By 63 votes to 8 the appointment of Naidoo was carried.[30]

Immediately after the Conference the opposition organised a series of meetings in Durban and other parts of Natal. At first the Congress held counter-meetings. But when it was seen that these meetings ended in disorder and only served to accentuate feelings which were already bitter, Congress abandoned the counter-meetings.

One of these rowdy meetings took place in the Durban Town Hall on 24th August, 1933, when "over 4 000 men who had yelled and scuffled among themselves for three hours were silenced and shamed by a woman – the Kunwarani Lady Maharaj Singh". The meeting was also addressed by the agent, Kunwar Sir Maharaj Singh, who told the opposition members: "You talk of non-co-operation but two can play that game. You can refuse to co-operate with the Government and it can refuse to co-operate with you.

If this colonisation scheme ever comes about it will be voluntary and if you do not want to go you need not."[31]

The meeting ended with the crowd about evenly divided on the issue. A more violent meeting took place in Pietermaritzburg when the opposition, newly formed into the Colonial Born and Settlers Indian Association, were present in full force. It was stated that some of the Indians present in the hall were armed with knives, knuckledusters, bicycle chains and iron rods. Violent speeches were made by both sides and finally the police had to break up the meeting.[32] It was in such a dangerous atmosphere that the Colonisation Enquiry Committee conducted its investigations. The Indian community was divided on the issue and whatever the report of the Committee it was bound to meet with hostility from one side.

The South African Indian Congress presented a comprehensive statement to the Committee in which they adduced facts to show that the fear which the white man had that he would be swamped by the Indian was unjustified; fears of competition on the labour market were also without foundation; the number of Indians employed in industrial occupations outside agriculture was so small as to be negligible; the number of licences to trade held by Indians was on the decrease; the moral stability of the Indian was a point in his favour. In this statement the Congress set out to show that the percentage of Indians in the population was small and on the decrease; that Indians were rapidly assimilating western standards of life; that they were not a menace or obstacle to the progress of the Europeans. It took a firm stand against the colonisation of South African Indians in other countries and pleaded that:

> "South Africa is our birth place and our home and it is our sincere conviction that if we are given the fundamental rights and privileges of South African citizens not only will our small population be rapidly absorbed but also we shall prove of real value to the Community as a whole."[33]

After this most unequivocal statement, the recommendations of the Indian Colonisation Enquiry Committee, dated 26th February, 1934, that British North Borneo, British New Guinea and British Guiana were countries which offered the best prospects for the operation of a colonisation scheme came as an anti-climax. No one took serious heed of the recommendations and the work of the Indian Colonisation Enquiry Committee expired from the thoughts of men without any expressions of regret or disappointment.[34]

The failure of the colonisation scheme to receive any substantial support from the resident Indian population in South Africa in 1934 did not mean the end to the assisted emigration scheme sponsored by the Cape Town Agreement. Emigration to India continued in meagre and decreasing numbers hardly justifying the hope of the Europeans that it would reduce the Indian population in South Africa.[35] When its operation was suspended during the war years any attraction that it held out to would-be emigrants was well worn; settled families hardly took any notice of it. The scheme remained on the statute book in the form of Act 37/1927. But for the Indians in South Africa it might as well have been non-existent.

Its failure marked the failure, too, of the international negotiations and conferences set afoot by the first Round Table Conference of 1926–7 which culminated in the Report of the Indian Colonisation Enquiry Committee in 1934 and the rejection of this report by the resident Indian population in South Africa. At international level the experiment of Round Table Conferences to solve the Indian question ended in failure. The experiments were over but the problems remained. The position had to be reviewed *de novo*.

The Indians in South Africa claimed that this country was their home; the governments of India and South Africa accepted this claim and even embodied it in the Communique of 1932. For the present, both these governments had to treat the position as such. The years between the end of the international experiments on the South African Indian question and the outbreak of war in 1939 represented a period of comparative calm in matters relating to this question: an uneasy calm during which it was generally accepted that the South African Indians belonged here; their welfare was to be provided for here; their problems were to be solved here.

Their problems continued to increase. At one time these were put down to their insanitary habits and strange mode of life; then the matter of trade loomed large; after this a cry went up against their acquisition and occupation of land. Now all these and more were to follow. And in all the new developments, up to the outbreak of the World War in the first instance, the Indian Government maintained a benevolent watch over the interests of the South African Indians, intervening here and there, protesting when necessary, making representations, appearing before Select Committees and Commissions, doing everything possible that an overseer, without the power to alter the course, could do. In all such activities, India worked through its agency; and the Indians in South Africa, too, looked upon this agency for support and guidance not only against restrictions imposed upon them but in their internal political conflicts.

In this watching and active brief kept by the Government of India, the main centre was the Transvaal, and the main point at issue here was land tenure. In 1932 the Transvaal Asiatic Land Tenure Act Commission (popularly known as the Feetham Commission) was appointed to enquire into the occupation of proclaimed land by Coloured persons and to compile a register of persons in legal or illegal occupation.

The Commission was boycotted by the Transvaal and South African Indian Congresses but the Agent-General of India, Kunwar Sir Maharaj Singh, presented a memorandum to the Commission in which he pointed out that any trader had to follow his market and could not "erect his shop in a vacant area and expect houses and potential customers to grow around him". The fact that the Indian trader had survived, said the Agent-General, in spite of anti-Asiatic legislation, was conclusive proof that he had been of service to the country.[36]

The Commission reported that it did not find that the number of persons who were in illegal occupation of land was a large one; neither was the volume of Indian wholesale trade as great as it was made out to be. The Commission recommended the exemption of some 202 acres of land on the Rand for occupation and ownership by Indians. These lands were occupied by Indians on 1st May, 1930.[37]

Both Indians and Europeans protested against the recommendations. The former claimed that too little was being given to them and the latter that too much was being given and that the infringements of the Indians were being condoned. The result was that when Hofmeyr, the Union Minister of the Interior, announced a Bill to give legal form to the recommendations, there was such an outcry from all sides that he was forced to send the Bill to a select committee even before it came up for the second reading. The Agent-General protested against this step. The protests were echoed in the Legislative Assembly in India and an unsuccessful bid was made to adopt retaliatory measures against European nationals from South Africa who were then in India. The general fear was that the Parliamentary Select Committee would bow to the wishes of the European opposition to features favourable to the Indians in the recommendations.

The Agent-General for India, Sir Syed Raza Ali, tendered evidence before the Select Committee. Unlike his predecessors, Sastri and Kurma Reddi, who had opposed segregation, Sir Syed expressed himself (and thereby involved his Government, too) in favour of voluntary segregation. In doing so, the Agent-General earned the displeasure of the Indian community in South Africa, brought the agency into disrepute in the eyes of this community and made the sincerity of purpose of its principal, the Government of India, suspect. The agency was criticised for having taken this line in defence of those who were out to protect their self-interests. The Agent-General was reminded that he "had to view the future of Indian nationals in this country from a higher plane".[38]

By the actions of the Agent-General, it was clear that the Indian Government was working towards any slight gains to be had. These materialised in the form of the provisions in the Transvaal Asiatic Land Tenure Amendment Act, 30/1936, empowering the Minister of the Interior to exempt further areas for Indian occupation, it being agreed that, subject to confirmation by both Houses of Parliament, Indians might be granted title in freehold in these areas.[39]

The Government of India, as expected, expressed its approval of the Act. Though there were gains to be measured, there was also the acceptance of the policy of segregation which was opposed in many quarters. The Government of India was criticised for its unreserved acceptance of the Act. The *Hindustan Times* in India wrote that "for the Government of India to go into ecstacies over what are trifling gains, and advertise the results as a big event, is something inexplicable".[40]

What seemed to be explicable in the policy of the Government of India was the deep desire to maintain friendly ties between the two governments. On the crest of its enthusiasm for the latest Act, the Indian Government made an official request that the South African Parliamentary delegation to India – the second one in over ten years – which was to be headed by Jan Hofmeyr – was to be accorded full honour and the best hospitality during its forthcoming visit to India. At a banquet arranged by the Transvaal Indian Congress in honour of the delegation in Johannesburg on 28th August, 1936, Hofmeyr said that in the past the people of South Africa had a one-sided view of India: they knew too little of the culture and civilisation of India. "There was the other India, of which South Africa knew all too little . . . [41]"

The delegation was certain to see much of the new India. Further constitutional changes were being contemplated; the freedom struggle was becoming more intense; the Indian National Congress was playing a leading role in this struggle; more and more Indian women were entering the political field. Over and above all this, the delegation would see the numerical strength of the Indian population, which represented the majority in the entire British Empire, an estimated population of 365 000 000 out of an estimated total of 494 770 000. All these facts were bound to have an important bearing on the complete picture the delegation was to see. This picture, in turn, would influence its conclusions on the future of the Indian question in South Africa.

The delegation returned to South Africa after spending twenty-six days in India. Dr. N. J. van der Merwe, a member of the delegation, who was also the Free State leader of the Nationalist Party, said on his return that the delegation was satisfied that there was not the least hope for many Indians to leave South Africa for India under the repatriation scheme; the other important conclusion was that the days of British rule were numbered in India.

This last observation was based on the developments set in motion by the India Act of 1935. This Act gave to almost one-sixth of the adult population of India the right to vote; women were granted the franchise on the same terms as men. In the Central Government, the Governor-General retained control. The Secretary of State was retained. The federal system was introduced, in which the British maintained their control in the Central Government but lost their influence in the provinces where the British-appointed governors were the last vestiges of Imperial power. In the provincial elections of February, 1937, the Indian National Congress Party gained resounding victories. Congress ministries were established in seven out of the eleven provinces. The outstanding Congress premiers were C. Rajagopalachari, G. B. Pant and B. J. Kher. In the Central Assembly, Congress held 44 out of 104 elective seats from a total of 144. The leaders of the Congress did not assume office in the provinces. Their power was transferred to the Congress "High Command" – the Congress Working Committee or "cabinet" which was the highest authority in the Congress movement. The chief influence here was that of Mahatma Gandhi, who held no office in the Committee. Next came Pandit Jawaharlal Nehru who was elected President of the Congress in December, 1936. Other leading nationalist members of the Committee were Rajendra Prasad, Sardar Vallabhai Patel and Subhas Chandra Bose.[42]

The significance of all this, as the delegation observed, was that full responsible government in India and complete national independence were very near of achievement. This was bound to have its effects on the international relations between India and South Africa. These relations were already threatened by the deliberations in the United Party congress in South Africa in October, 1936, when the Government was requested to confine Asiatic trading to locations; to prohibit mixed marriages and the employment of white girls by Asiatics.

These decisions were taken one step further when General J. C. Pienaar (U.P. Marico) introduced the Mixed Marriages Bill early in 1937 prohibiting marriages between Asiatics and Europeans and Africans. The Minister of Public Health, J. H. Hofmeyr, said he was against mixed marriages but that this could not be controlled by legislation. "Many social evils," he said, "when dealt with by legislation, are only forced underground." Hofmeyr had recently returned as leader of the Union Parliamentary Delegation to India. He saw, therefore, another difficulty in the Bill. The relations between India and South Africa would be affected by this Bill through the insult implied in it to India's millions. The Bill was defeated.

Nor did the anti-Asiatic expressions rest at that. General J. J. Pienaar and J. H. Grobler who were unsuccessful in getting the Mixed Marriages Bill passed introduced two new Bills seeking to empower the Transvaal Provincial Council to refuse trading licences to all non-Europeans who employed white people in their businesses and to deny the right of owning property to any white woman who was married to a non-European – the Provincial Legislative Powers Extension Bill and the Transvaal Asiatic Land Bill, respectively. These private Bills created a crisis in the cabinet and a split was averted when they were referred to select committees. Hofmeyr, who threatened to resign if the cabinet accepted the Bills, was prevailed upon to remain until, as he said, the Government revealed an attitude which he regarded as a repudiation of himself. At this time, too, the Marketing Bill was introduced, which debarred Indians from holding seats on the regulatory boards because, as Eaton, M.P. for Durban County, said, "they did not play fair". The Minister of Agriculture, Col. Denys Reitz, told an Indian delegation which waited on him to protest against the Bill: "Gentlemen, you must realise that you Indians in South Africa will ever be a tragic community because of the temper and temperament of the people of South Africa."

The South African Indian Congress lodged strong protests against the three Bills; in India questions were raised by Indian members of the Legislative Assembly as to what steps were being taken by the Government of India to safeguard the political and social status and rights of the Indians in South Africa. The answer given was that the Government of India would present its case through its Agent-General before the Parliamentary Select Committee.

Even in the matter of giving evidence obstacles appeared in the way of the Agent-General, Sir Syed Raza Ali. He requested permission to attend all sittings of the Select Committee. This was refused, only Hofmeyr and Derbyshire were in favour of this being granted. The Agent-General then requested permission to attend when the South African Reddingsdaadbond gave its evidence; this, too, was refused. Finally, the Agent-General asked to be supplied with the Reddingsdaadbond evidence. This was also rejected. Hofmeyr and Derbyshire nearly always voted in a minority of two.

The stand taken by the Agent-General on mixed marriages for the convenience of land ownership by Asiatics and the employment of white girls by Asiatics followed that of the South African Indian Congress: that voluntary action to remove these objections should be allowed to take the place of the proposed legislation. The South African Indian Congress, through its Secretary, A. I. Kajee, gave an assurance that European employees working for Indians would be dismissed by their Indian employers. This assurance was accepted and the proposed measure was dropped.

In all these developments it was quite evident that white South Africa was not prepared to tolerate any situation in which the European was in any way subject to the control or influence of the Asiatics. This situation made it even more necessary for the Agent-General of India to take a clear line of action in defence of the interests of the Indians in South Africa. But the agency, thus far, had succeeded in achieving much less. The Rev. Mr. C. F. Andrews criticised the agents for not taking "their jobs seriously" not because the agents were themselves responsible for this but because the Government of India at this time did not instruct them to do so. Sir Syed had himself admitted in a speech to Rotary: "I wish I could speak frankly and strongly on this subject (of race prejudice), but unfortunately my lips are more or less sealed."

The Agent-General in South Africa could only go as far as his principal, the Government of India, would allow him to go. Some Indian observers in South Africa were now of the opinion that it was a wasteful expenditure for the Government of India to maintain its agency in that form here. The liaison was not serving any good purpose. It was better to maintain direct links with India and for the Indian nationals in India to keep in contact with South African affairs in other ways, such as by direct visits. On 16th December, 1937, one of these visits took place when Seth Govind Das, the Congress member of the Central Legislative Assembly in India, came to South Africa to study the position for himself and to report back to the Indian National Congress and to the Central Assembly. A foretaste of the international complications created by such visits was clearly in evidence when the visitor was refused permission to use a lift when he reported to pay a courtesy call on J. H. Hofmeyr, the Minister of Mines, at the Standard Bank Buildings, Pretoria, on 17th December, in spite of the fact that the Minister's private secretary was with him at this time and explained to the liftman who the visitor was. The sequel to this incident was the arrival of a letter of apology from the assistant-general manager of the Standard Bank.

Seth Govind Das observed the position of the South African Indians. His advice to them was that they should not accept a qualified franchise; that they should practise the principle of self-help in all matters. He said that though India would do all she could to assist the South African Indians she was quite weighed down by her own fight for freedom.

The divergence between the viewpoints held by the Congress members in India and the Government of India on the Indian question in South Africa was revealed in one way at this time. Seth Govind Das counselled against the acceptance of the qualified franchise; the out-going Agent-General, Sir Syed Raza Ali, advised the Indians at a farewell reception in his honour that they should accept such a franchise. Not many Indians paid any heed to the agency in South Africa as the feeling was that it had failed in its duties.

Another Congress leader to visit South Africa was the great philosopher, Sir Sarvapillai Radhakrishnan, who put his views across in a broadcast from Durban on 10th April, 1939. Sir Sarvapillai said: "To weld together into an organic state the European and the Native, the Coloured and the Asiatic is a formidable task, but it is not insuperable. The differences need not be fused, but they need not conflict. . . . No State can acquiesce in maladjustments of wealth and labour, leisure and opportunity and endure for long."

The formidable task of which Sir Sarvapillai had spoken was all too clearly before the statesmen of the country; they were at grips with the task – in their own way. At the level of international negotiations this is best seen in the form of the Agent-General's representations to the South African Government and this Government's legislative programme. It is also seen in the radical changes in the political groups among Indians in the country, changes often violent in their nature which called for the intervention of the Agent-General.

The Agent-General's representations to the Union Government are to be seen in matters relating to the work of two Commissions at this time. The first of these was the Transvaal Asiatic Land Laws Commission appointed on 3rd February, 1938, to report on any evasions by Asiatics of restrictive measures concerning their use, occupation or ownership of land other than proclaimed land.[43] The Transvaal Indian Congress submitted a memorandum to the Commission requesting that it recommend the repeal of all disabling legislation; it stated that there was no penetration by Indians into European areas; that the alleged evasion by Indians of the letter or spirit of any existing law was of an insignificant nature and not sufficient to justify any legislation. In his Memorandum, the Agent-General supported the contention of the Transvaal Indian Congress and traced the cause of all the troubles in the Transvaal to Law 3/1885. He ended with a plea for its repeal.

In its Report presented to Parliament the Commission stated that it did not find evasions on a large scale, though a few contraventions existed. On the matter of evasions resulting from marriages, the Commission was not satisfied that the object of such unions was the evasion of the law. In its recommendations, the Commission stated that if the statutory disabilities were to remain, they should be enforced by some special Department of State. In his minority report, B. Bloemsma said that all evasions of the law should be punished; he called for disabilities to be imposed on Europeans who contracted mixed marriages.[44]

The work of this Commission was one of the matters which engaged the attention of the Indian Government; the other Commission was the Mixed Marriages Commission under the chairmanship of Charles de Villiers, K.C.

The Commission was to report on whether such marriages were on the increase or sufficiently numerous to be detrimental to the welfare of the Union. The South African Indian Congress submitted a memorandum to the Commission pointing out that the small number of mixed marriages involving Asiatics did not justify the introduction of any legislation while the Government of India took slight notice of the Commission. In its report for the years 1937–8 the Government of India stated that such information as was available showed that mixed marriages were very rare among Indians in South Africa.[45]

The Report of the Mixed Marriages Commission appeared on 19th August, 1939. In the majority report four commissioners stated that a law should be introduced to make mixed marriages impossible and illicit miscegenation a punishable offence. Mrs. Spilhaus disagreed with the majority report and said that in her opinion mixed-marriages were due to the shortage of European women. She suggested the importation of young European women of good type.[46]

The Government did not act on the Report of this Commission only because of the war which intervened. The Asiatic Land Laws Commission and the Mixed Marriages Commission provided proof of the intense feeling against the Asiatics in the Transvaal at this time when it was clearly known that the assisted emigration scheme of the Cape Town Agreement was virtually at an end. The Indians in South Africa, recognised as South Africans, were now, especially in the Transvaal, treated as if they were still "forcing themselves upon a community reluctant to accept them". The Feetham recommendations granting areas for Indians on the Witwatersrand were not yet approved by Parliament. The last date for this – April 30th, 1939 – was drawing near.

The Union Government took the matter in hand by introducing the Transvaal Asiatics (Transvaal Land and Trading) Bill on 4th May, 1939, which provided for protection to Indians in exempted areas for another two years; the refusal of trading licences or transfers except under the authority of the Minister of the Interior; Asiatics outside the bazaars not to occupy land not occupied by them on 30th April, 1939, without ministerial consent; the Minister was empowered to make exemptions in regard to trading and occupation. The Bill was to take effect as from 1st May, 1939. Though, as Hofmeyr said during the House of Assembly debates on the Bill, its direct effects were not great, the indirect effects were of greater consequence. He had in mind not only the relations between Europeans and Asiatics in South Africa but the relations between the governments of India and South Africa. He said that as the measure was an interim one, it did not commit the House to the principle of segregation.

Leslie Blackwell echoed the fears of Hofmeyr that the Bill was dangerous in its effects on India. And not only on India, but on the Commonwealth in the dark days of 1939 – with the threat of war so near and so real. Blackwell said: "Yet it is in this year 1939, in the world as we know it today, that we are choosing as the time to antagonise the people of India and to stir up all trouble that this Bill will bring in its train." He called for the Bill to be rejected, except for the clause giving protection to the Indians till 1941.[47]

In the Senate, Senator Brookes appealed to the Minister not to adopt any permanent policy of segregation. The Minister replied "that without the imposition of any stigma upon anyone, the two races can be kept apart".[48]

It was difficult to see how the Minister's claim could be upheld. In India, the publication of this Interim Bill caused great anxiety. Swami Bhawani Dayal started a campaign against the Bill. He addressed various meetings and received the support of the Imperial Indian Citizenship Association and the Indian National Congress and from such individuals as Mahatma Gandhi and Mrs. Sarojini Naidu.[49] The Government of India, too, lodged its protest against the Bill and asked that consultations be held between the governments concerned. Gandhi and Jinnah, leaders of the Hindus and Muslims, respectively, in India, sent in their protests.

The Union Government rejected all the appeals made at home and abroad that the proposed measure be withdrawn. The Bill finally became law in the form of Act 28/1939, and the Government stated that it would be prepared to have consultations with India before the problem was settled permanently. This slight acknowledgement of India's role in the matter did nothing to appease the Indians in the Transvaal who were now in a state of great agitation. The Transvaal Indians were divided on what steps to take. The old group of the Congress opposed any vigorous measures of protest, still hoping that the Feetham recommendations would be accepted by Parliament. The other group led by the militant Dr. Y. M. Dadoo decided upon a line of passive resistance against the measure. Their decision received approval from Gandhi and Nehru in India. On 4th June, 1939, the two groups clashed in what turned out to be a most gory affair. Nine persons were seriously injured, one subsequently died. All of these were supporters of Dr. Dadoo. The result was that opinion in the Transvaal swung to the side of the young nationalist group led by Dadoo.[50]

These events found their echoes in India. On 24th June, 1939, the Indian National Congress criticised the Union Government for violating the obligations undertaken in 1914, 1927 and 1932 by the Smuts-Gandhi Agreement, the Cape Town Agreement, and the Feetham Commission Report. It approved of the decision of the Transvaal Indians to launch a passive resistance struggle. At home, a decision was taken to launch this campaign on 1st August, 1939. It was only the timely request from Gandhi in India that the campaign be postponed as the prospects of favourable settlement seemed near at hand that averted the commencement of another great struggle for the vindication of honour and rights.[51]

The period between the two world wars saw many things happening on the national and international fronts. For the South African Indians the starting point was the Smuts-Gandhi Agreement. It was a kind of manifesto to which appeals were persistently made. But so much happened during the inter-war years that even this Agreement was subsumed by the rapid changes and events. Now that another world war had broken out, introducing the element of uncertainties that wars always do, it would be instructive to recapitulate the main trends in national and international politics in so far as they affected South African Indians in the 1914–1939 period.

During this period the most important development after the Smuts-Gandhi Agreement was that of the Imperial Conferences and the hopes that were held out for a solution from this source. Where the Imperial Government had ceased to be a potent factor in 1914 it was felt that this Government, in concert with the other members of the Commonwealth, would strive with determination to resolve the problems of the Empire as they affected the relations between India and South Africa. These hopes were nullified by the failure of these Conferences to play any important part other than that of discussing, debating, criticising and resolving. An important opportunity was lost when the brotherhood created by the exigencies of war failed to transcend the prejudices of peace times. The League of Nations, too, was no more useful than the Imperial Conferences. In any case its interest lay in the West.

The inter-governmental negotiations between 1925 and 1932 established the right of India to have a say in the affairs of South African Indians, only because no other direct channels were available. When the channel of the Indian Agency in South Africa was created the need for direct negotiations at Conference level would no longer be pressing. The introduction of this Agency in 1927 was perhaps the most lasting contribution of the Cape Town Agreement. Everything else, with the important exception of the Uplift Clause, were secondary features of this first experiment of round-table talks.

The experiment of the Cape Town Agreement failed because of the lack of compromise. With its failure, too, came the acceptance of the South African Indian as a permanent part of the population of the Union of South Africa, with the emphasis now on the search for a solution at home and not abroad. From abroad it was certain that greater pressure would come from National India, gradually going her way to complete independence but for the moment checked by the British influence in the Central Legislative Assembly and in the Executive. This latter influence was largely responsible for the failure of the agency to assert itself in South Africa in accordance with the wishes of National India.

At home the significant features in the affairs of the Indians during the period 1914 to 1939 were the absence of a great leader to take over from Mahatma Gandhi; the formation of the South African Indian Congress; the anti-Asiatic measures in the Transvaal; anti-Indian agitation in the Transvaal tempered by the action and utterances of European friends in the liberal tradition set afoot by Hofmeyr. There were gains but the way was still uphill.

FOOTNOTES

1. S. R. Naidoo and D. Bramdaw, Eds., *Sastri Speaks*, p. 33.
2. General Secretary, South African Indian Congress to the Secretary for the Interior, 7th May, 1927, S.A.I.C., *Agenda Book of Conference*, 1928.
3. Report of the Agent for India, 1927, reproduced in *Sastri Speaks*, p. 243.
4. Report of the Agent for India in South Africa, 1927, Appendix A., reproduced in *Sastri Speaks*, pp. 252–3.
5. *Papers Relating to the Second Round Table Conference* between the representatives of the Government of India and of the Government of the Union of South Africa on the position of Indians in the Union, 1932, p. 8. This is cited hereafter as Government of India, *Papers*, 1932. To give effect to the Kichlu Report six qualified Indian teachers were imported from India, who replaced the European staff appointed earlier. They were Messrs. A. Shakoor, M.A., L.T.; F. Khan, B.Sc., L.T.; P. K. Koru, M.A., L.T.; B. T. Trivedi, B.A., L.T.; G. Sinha, B.Sc., L.T.; and R. Nair, B.A., L.T.
6. A. I. Kajee and others, *Treatment of Indians in South Africa*, pp. 39–40.
7. Section 5 of Act 37/1927 dealt with illegal entrants. This section was inserted as a result of the Salojee case of 1924, decided in the Transvaal Supreme Court, the effect of which was to rule that where a person obtained a registration certificate by means of fraud knowingly he could not rely on his own fraud, and a Court would cancel a certificate so obtained; but where a person, for example, a minor, though in possession of a certificate obtained by fraud, was himself innocent of any fraud, his certificate would not be cancelled by the Courts. *Vide* Agent's Report for 1928, *Sastri Speaks*, p. 268.
8. South African Indian Congress, Documents Relating to Condonation, S.A.I.C., *Agenda Book of Conference*, 1929. The entire correspondence on this subject is published here.
9. Agent's Report, 1927, pp. 251–2.
10. S.A.I.C., *Agenda Book of Conference*, 1929, Liquor Act, p. 4.
11. *Indian Review*, Vol. XXIX, April, No. 4, 1928, p. 260.
12. S. R. Naidoo and D. Bramdaw, Eds., *Sastri Speaks*, p. 212–5.
13. Indians repatriated from the Union under Act 37/1927:

Year	Number	Year	Number
1927 (Aug. to Dec.)	1 655	1934	880
1928	3 477	1935	492
1929	1 314	1936	430
1930	1 012	1937	232
1931	1 961	1938	205
1932	2 881	1939	121
1933	1 493	1940	48

In 1941 the scheme was abandoned for the war years. *Vide* Corbett, "A Study of the Cape Town Agreement", p. 88. Mabel Palmer, *The History of Indians in Natal*, p. 105.
14. Government of India, *Papers*, 1932, pp. 6–7. Bhawani Dayal Sannyasi edited a book on *Public Opinion on the Assisted Emigration Scheme Under the Indo-South African Agreement*. The views expressed on the lot of the repatriates in India were substantially the same as those mentioned in Bhawani Dayal's report. The co-author of the book was Pandit Benaresi Das Chaturvedi, who was associated with emigrants from South Africa for over fifteen years.
15. These litigations were: The North Eastern Districts Association (Proprietary) Ltd., versus the Norwood Land and Investment Company, Ltd.; Town Council of Springs versus Fakir Moosa and Moosa Essop Sidat.
   Government of India, *Papers*, 1932, pp. 7–8. Mr. Tyson's full statement to the Select Committee appears in S.A.I.C., *The Asiatic Land Tenure Amendment Bill*, 1930, pp. 11–30.
16. Government of India, *Papers*, 1932, p. 9.

TABLE OF LICENCES

	Johannesburg	Outside	Total
Licences still protected ..	40	32	72
Unprotected licences	92	29	121
Doubtful	4	4	8
	136	65	201

TABLE OF STOCK CARRIED

	Under £500	£500–£1 000	£1 000–£5 000	Over £5 000
Johannesburg ..	21	21	26	15
Roodepoort ..	9	5	8	—
Krugersdorp ..	7	5	4	3
Nigel	3	—	5	—
Springs.. ..	5	—	5	—
Germiston ..	—	1	3	—

In Johannesburg the figures of 83 shops only are given – the rest being fruit shops.

PERCENTAGE OF STOCK OBTAINED FROM EUROPEAN FIRMS

	Under 50%	50%–90%	Over 90%	Total
Roodepoort ..	—	12	10	22 shops
Krugersdorp ..	—	12	7	19 „
Nigel	—	6	2	8 „
Springs ..	—	7	4	11 „
Germiston ..	—	3	2	5 „
Totals	—	40	25	65 „
Johannesburg ..	15	26	91	132 „

Vide Statement of the Acting Agent for India, reproduced in S.A.I.C. The Asiatic Land Tenure (Amendment) Bill, 1930, p. 24.

17. Government of India, *Papers*, 1932, p. 8. The Chairman of the Select Committee was Dr. D. F. Malan. Its report was dated 13th May, 1930.

18. Comments by the *Diamonds Field Advertiser* reproduced in S.A.I.C., The Asiatic Land Tenure (Amendment) Bill, p. 69. Other comments reproduced are from the *Cape Argus*, 19th May, 1930; the Johannesburg *Star*, 17th May, also of the 21st May; the *Natal Witness*, the *Indian Opinion*, of the 6th June, 1930. The last journal concluded thus: " . . . we have at long last to act, to assert our manhood, to demonstrate that we are not wholly dead to the calls of honour, dignity and self respect; that we have not sunk so low that Indians may be spat upon again and yet again with impunity and without asserting themselves in protest. We have our weapon always at hand. It is a weapon we have used before, one that never rusts, never grows obsolete; the weapon of self- sufferings, of civil disobedience. All the portents seem to point to its once more being called into action."

19. Report of the Joint Hon. Secretaries of the S.A.I.C., S.A.I.C. *Agenda Book of Annual Conference*, 29th–31st December, 1930, Item No. 7. The President of the S.A.I.C. was A. Christopher and the Secretaries S. R. Naidoo and E. M. Mall. A delegation of the S.A.I.C. called upon the Minister of the Interior on 7th October, 1930, to discuss the Resolution adopted by Conference.

20. Government of India, *Private and Personal Correspondence leading to the Second Round Table Conference at Cape Town* No. 730–5, 9th August, 1930. This is cited hereafter as Government of India, *Private and Personal Correspondence*, 1932.

21. Government of India, *Personal and Private Correspondence*, pp. 2–7.
22. Government of India, *Papers*, 1932, pp. 2–13.
23. Statement of the South African Indian Congress Submitted to the Government of India Delegation, 1932, pp. 21–24.
24. *Ibid.*, p. 36. It is interesting to note that of the 673 emigrants who left during the period August to December, 1927, there were no traders. *Vide Sastri Speaks*, pp. 254–5. Of the 1 436 who left in 1928 there were 35 hawkers, 3 greengrocers and 2 storekeepers and 2 fruiterers and 1 tobacco dealer, all for Madras, and 28 fruit hawkers, 9 hawkers, a pedlar, 5 storekeepers and 2 fishmongers, all for Bombay. *Vide Sastri Speaks*, pp. 284–5. The conclusion is that no big Indian traders took advantage of the assisted emigration scheme.
25. Government of India, *Papers*, 1932, p. 55 and pp. 93–4.
26. *Vide infra*, Appendix G, p. 520.
27. The undertaking was signed by the following: Jossub Ebrahim Gardee, Bernard L. E. Sigamoney, Pragji K. Desai, S. B. Medh, S. R. Naidoo, M. M. Gandhi, Shaik Ahmed, C. F. Andrews, Sorabjee Rustomjee, P. R. Pather, A. I. Kajee, Hajee Cassim Adam, A. Christopher, V. S. C. Pather, A. Ismail, A. D. Motala. *Vide* Report of the Indian Colonization Enquiry Committee, U.G. 23/1934, p. 5.
28. Union Government Information Office, New York, *The Indians in South Africa*, p. 31.
29. S.A.I.C., *Emergency Conference Agenda Book*, 1933, p. 5.
30. Report of the Agent of the Government of India in South Africa, 1933, p. 8.
31. *Natal Mercury*, 25th August, 1933.
32. *Natal Witness*, 5th September, 1933.
33. In 1932 the European population of Natal was 181 300; the Indian population was 163 000: the percentage of Indians to the total of the two races was 47,34 per cent. *Vide* S.A.I.C., Statement submitted, 9th January, 1934, pp. 6–15.

RETURN OF LICENCES IN THE BOROUGH OF DURBAN
1st January, 1933, to 28th November, 1933

Government Licences			*Corporation Licences*		
Europeans	..	2 901	Europeans	..	1 116
Asiatics	..	2 552	Asiatics	..	393

Ibid., p. 9.

CONVICTIONS FOR SERIOUS CRIME BY RACE PER 10 000 OF POPULATION

	1926	1927	1928	1929	1930	1931	Total	Average
Europeans ..	15,21	15,72	18,15	17,62	13,39	12,59	92,68	15,45
Asiatics ..	18,19	18,21	19,42	13,90	10,70	11,76	92,38	15,40
Bantu	32,82	34,15	35,69	35,54	25,95	28,66	192,81	32,13
Other Coloured	67,18	73,28	82,43	75,31	43,98	47,27	390,25	65,00

34. *Vide* Report of the Committee, U.G. 23/1934, p. 14.
35. Report of the Indian Penetration Commission, U.G. 39/1941, p. 5.
36. Report of the Transvaal Asiatic Land Tenure Act Commission, U.G. 7/1934, p. 243, para. 3. Parts I and II of the Report appeared in 1934 and Part III (U.G. 22) appeared in 1935.
37. Kajee and others *Treatment of Indians in South Africa*, p. 34.
38. *Indian Opinion*, 24th July, 1936.
39. Muriel Horrell, *Indians in Pretoria*, p. 3.
40. *Indian Opinion*, 7th August, 1936.
41. *Ibid.*, 4th September, 1936.
42. Smith, *Oxford History of India*, pp. 809–819.

43. The chairman of the Commission was Justice J. M. Murray and the members were Harry Britten, Nimrod Smit and B. Bloemsma. *Vide* Report of the Asiatic Land Laws Commission, U.G. 16/1939.
44. Report of the Asiatic Land Laws Commission, U.G. 16/1939, pp. 42–6 and 48–9.
45. *Indian Opinion*, November 18th, 1938. The statistics are as follows:

MARRIAGE BETWEEN

Year	European males and Asiatic females	Asiatic males and European females	European males and African females	African males and European females	European males and Coloured females	Coloured males and European females	Total
1926	1	2	20	5	66	15	109
1927	—	5	61	3	66	18	153
1928	—	5	35	7	76	12	135
1929	—	3	15	1	64	16	99
1930	—	5	16	1	60	15	97
1931	1	3	7	1	59	14	85
1932	—	6	6	—	63	7	82
1933	—	7	9	—	57	10	83
1934	2	3	7	—	47	13	72
1935	2	1	7	—	66	15	91
1936	1	7	6	—	36	17	67

(Report of Mixed Marriages Commission, U.G. 30/1939, p. 3.)

46. *Vide* Report of the Mixed Marriages Commission, U.G. 30/1939, p. 3, pp. 39–40.
47. House of Assembly Debates, No. 12, 1939, pp. 4062–3, and No. 13, p. 4240.
48. Senate Debates, No. 6, 1939. Senator Brookes, pp. 1000–1 and the Minister of the Interior, pp. 1003–4.
49. Agrawal, *Bhawani Dayal Sannyasi*, A Public Worker of South Africa, p. 128.
50. Report of the Agent-General for India 1939, the events of 4th June.
51. Joshi, *The Tyranny of Colour*, pp. 250–60. Nothing came of the hopes cherished by Gandhi. It is worthy of note that in South Africa Mr. Jan H. Hofmeyr and Mr. Leslie Blackwell were expelled by the United Party causus for their support of the Indians in South Africa.

CHAPTER FIVE

THE SIGNIFICANCE OF THE WAR YEARS, 1939–1945

"In no other country in the world is it possible for a group to have its own prejudices legalised and turned into a powerful weapon for serving its own interests at the cost of deadly harm to some other group . . . It may well be that the struggle to win a social order in which human values and not colour-bars are supreme will be a sterner fight than the bloodiest onslaught of tank and bomb."

RT. REV. S. W. LAVIS
(Coadjutor Bishop of Cape Town)

On 1st September, 1939, Germany invaded Poland; two days later Great Britain and France declared war on Germany. These fateful events marked the beginning of World War II. In South Africa the coalition ministry was split over the war issue and ceased to exist as from 4th September. General Smuts became the country's new Prime Minister. With this political change South Africa became involved in the war struggle.

The outbreak of war was bound to have serious effects on the question of Indians both in India and in South Africa. In India the important question of participation in the war was to develop into a constitutional issue, especially after the recent Congress gains in the Provinces. This would in some way affect the South African Indian question. During the war years, therefore, the reactions of Indians to the issue of war; their participation therein; their contribution; their agitation in side issues; the reactions of the Governments in India and in South Africa to such agitation; and, finally, the political organisation of the Indians in India and in South Africa would seem to be the important developments.

To begin with the last aspect (as it affected the South African Indians), one sees that in the Transvaal the militant nationalist-bloc of the Transvaal Indian Congress, led by Dr. Y. M. Dadoo, had greater support in that Province than the officials then in power. In Natal the duality of Indian political organisation was found in the existence of two rival bodies, the Natal Indian Congress and the Colonial-born and Settlers' Indian Association, since 1932. It needed all the tact and persuasion of the eminent Indian philosopher and statesman, Sir Sarvapillai Radhakrishnan to unite these two groups. This amalgamation was effected on 8th October, 1939, when it was agreed that one body, the Natal Indian Association, be formed.[1] This unity was short-lived and three months later A. I. Kajee and Swami Bhawani Dayal established a splinter group into the "Natal Indian Congress", a body which carried the name of the organisation which had been founded by Gandhi in 1894.[2]

Natal was divided into two political camps but both of them supported the war effort of the Union Government, hoping, no doubt, that when the war ended a more acceptable settlement of the South African Indian question would emerge. On the issue of war the South African Indians looked towards India for guidance. This is explained by the coolness evinced during the early days of the war and the enthusiasm of a later period. This

151

is exactly how India reacted. Though there was general moral support in India for the cause of the Allies there was also a reluctance to act immediately in active support of the war struggle. The familiar expression of "no taxation without representation" was now interpreted as "no popular war effort without responsible government". When the Government of India decided to participate in the war the Congress ministries in the Provinces resigned. The Viceroy, Lord Linlithgow, found himself without a responsible ministry. He appealed to the legislatures and held consultations with the Indian leaders. The Muslim League ministries and the princes agreed to support the war but the Congress held out for an immediate declaration of independence. The Viceroy compromised on 17th October, 1939 "by affirming dominion status to be the goal of constitutional development, action to be taken after the war. . . ."[3]

This offer did not placate the Congress. The fall of France and the grave threat to Great Britain which followed this fall "softened" Congress hostility. On June 1st, 1940, Mahatma Gandhi wrote: "We do not seek our independence out of British ruin." There was more active support now for the war effort. Congress demands for immediate independence continued throughout the war and the British war cabinet declared in August, 1940, "that the post-war constitution was to be drawn up by an Indian constituent assembly". This meant that independence would surely come at the end of the war and that when this happened Congress would dictate the terms, being the strongest political body in India.

With the initial period of refusal to support the war effort over, Indian troops distinguished themselves in the desert campaign of 1940–1 and in the Middle East operations, and finally in the various campaigns against the Japanese.[4] The Indian soldiers were mentioned in despatches. In one of these, the Army Council in the Western Desert wrote to the British Commander-in-Chief as follows: "The British soldier is proud once again to have gained the victory side by side with his Indian brother-in-arms. . . . The Indians took their full share in the capture and destruction of the Italian forces on Egyptian soil." In recognition of India's contribution to the war struggle she was appointed a full member of the British War Cabinet when Sir A. Ramaswami Mudaliar was appointed India's representative in October, 1942. This was an improvement on India's position in 1917 when her representatives were not full members of the War Cabinet but mere advisers to the Secretary of State for India.

India's example was followed in South Africa. Though certain individuals and groups opposed participation in the war at first, Indians in the country threw in their lot. By 1941, some 1 200 Indians, mostly from Durban, joined the transport corps. The Mayor of Durban, Councillor Rupert Ellis Brown, when welcoming the South African Indian and Malay Corps, saw the need to call for old differences to be forgotten in the common struggle. In this respect he recalled the words of an Indian in India, V. N. Chandavarkar, President of the National Liberal Federation in India: "We must not allow a domestic quarrel between India and Great Britain to queer the pitch for action against the common enemy of mankind. This is as much our war as Britain's."[5]

This was a reasonable plea. But the important thing was whether the brotherhood created by the common project and towards a common goal would result in a lessening of the tension in the South African Indian question of recent years, very much in evidence in the Transvaal where restrictive measures had found their way into the Asiatics (Transvaal Land and Trading) Act, 28/1939.

Already at the time of the outbreak of war rumblings were heard in high and low places that the fate inflicted on the Transvaal Indians in the form of Act 28/1939 was to be extended to Natal where it was now alleged that Indians were penetrating into European areas. Though it was war-time, the Union Government did not allow this external influence to deter it from its ordinary programme at home. Before the Government took any drastic measures the Natal Indian Association interviewed the new Minister of the Interior, H. G. Lawrence, and gave an assurance that the Association would do its best to prevent the purchase of property by Indians in predominantly European areas. It agreed to co-operate with an *ad hoc* committee of the Durban City Council in this and other related matters. The assurance was on the same lines as that given by A. I. Kajee to the Natal Municipal Association in 1936.

The sequel to the assurance given was the inauguration of the Lawrence Committee on 14th March, 1940, the function of which was to prevent the acquisition by Indians of property within the borough of Durban, occupied for residential purposes by Europeans. It was agreed that Committees would be appointed by the Durban Borough Council and by the Natal Indian Association to co-operate by joint consultation to further the aims and objects of the Lawrence Committee. The Natal Indian Association was represented by six members. In the early months of its existence the Lawrence Committee did useful work; the Indian members were commended for their good work. This is reflected in a resolution of the Committee passed on 18th April, 1940.[6]

The smooth functioning of the Lawrence Committee gave promise that the war years would not be made any more difficult for the Indians in Natal. But this promise was not given sufficient scope to develop into something lasting. As the months went by certain pitfalls appeared because members of the Lawrence Committee held irreconcilable views with regard to the scope of the Committee. The Indian representatives held the view that in dissuading Indians from acquiring properties in predominantly European areas they hoped that the Durban City Council would provide Indians with sites which would enjoy the same views and civic amenities as were available to the European residents of Durban. These hopes remained unfulfilled. The Durban City Council for its part held the view that these expectations were not intended in the machinery created by the Lawrence Committee. Because of these diametrically opposite views a deadlock soon resulted. This necessitated the personal intervention of the Minister of the Interior on 7th November, 1940. The Minister pointed out to the Committee that the Indian members were justified in their expectations and that the City Council "should not leave the Indian community in the lurch".

These, then, were the important events in South Africa in relation to the Indian question. At the international level the important considerations would appear to be the effect of the war on the social and political aspects of this question; the steps taken by the Union Government to uphold the work for which the Lawrence Committee was created; the intervention by India in the affairs concerning Indians in South Africa. In giving consideration to this last aspect it is necessary to review the position of the Indian Agency in South Africa during the early months of the war. As from 1st January, 1941, the status of the Agent-General was raised to that of High Commissioner. This change was a significant one. In recent years the Agency of the Government of India in South Africa had come in for much criticism both inside and outside Parliament. In some quarters the Agent-General was looked upon as a symbol of India's interference in the domestic affairs of South Africa as the office had been created with the object of seeing to the fulfilment of the obligations undertaken by the Union Government in terms of the Cape Town Agreement, especially the Uplift Clause of that Agreement. It was believed at that time that an Agent coming from the public life of India would be better able to convey the viewpoint of India in matters relating to the Indians in South Africa and would also speak on behalf of the Indian community in South Africa. With the new status the High Commissioner's right to speak for the Indians in South Africa was restricted. This right which was exercised by Sastri and his successors was resented by official circles in South Africa, especially after 1935 when Sir Syed Raza Ali assumed the position of Agent-General in South Africa. Sir Syed's criticism of the Union Government and his repeated plea for the restoration of the franchise to the Indians were unpalatable to the Government. It was an "open secret" (the *Leader* reported) that the Union Government had asked that Sir Syed's successor should not raise embarrassing issues. The Indian Government acted in accordance with the request of the Union Government and appointed Sir Rama Rau, a member of the Indian Civil Service, to fill the position.

The higher status of High Commissioner debarred the holder of this office from criticising the Union Government; he was to be the sole channel of communication between the Union Government and the Government of India in all matters. To the Union Government this change was an indication of the growing importance of the office. General Smuts, in his message of congratulation to the first High Commissioner, Sir Rama Rau, said: "The Union Government desire not only to emphasise the importance of the post in itself but also and more especially to express to the people of India their sympathetic interest in their progress towards the attainment of free and equal partnership in the British Commonwealth of Nations."

Indians in South Africa and in India saw the new status and its implications from a different angle. In South Africa they saw it as an attempt "to silence India's representatives in the Union and to prevent a public recital of grievances of the South African Indians". In India, a South African-born Indian and former president of the Natal Indian Congress, Swami Bhawani Dayal remarked that the new status virtually amounted to the diplomatic termination of the Cape Town Agreement now that India's representative would no longer look after its provisions. "The Cape Town Agreement", he said, "is no longer a living issue; it is dead".

If, as some critics asserted, the Cape Town Agreement was at an end, then the interest of the Government of India in the affairs of the South African Indians was also at an end. But nowhere was it stated that the new status would bring this about. The new office did impose limitations on the incumbent's activities in regard to the domestic affairs of the South African Indians but it did not restrict the voice or the actions of the Government of India in New Delhi. This was supported by the remarks made by the retiring High Commissioner, Sir Rama Rau, at a farewell reception in the Durban City Hall in 1941: "India will never forget the descendants of those who left her shores many years ago . . .

and will never rest satisfied until an honourable solution of your problem has been reached."

In actual practice the change meant that South African Indians and their political parties would no longer be able to look to the office of High Commissioner for support or for leading any deputation to the Union Government. In spite of what Sir Rama Rau, the first High Commissioner, himself said that the new position had no mystery about it and did not affect any duties of the official arising from the terms of the Cape Town Agreement, the change did affect the duties of this official in a broad way. We see the new position in the remarks of the second High Commissioner in South Africa, Sir Shafa'at Ahmad Khan, who was not an I.C.S. man but a former Professor of History at Allahabad, when he spoke at Newcastle in Natal in 1942: "I am not here to ventilate the grievances of the Indian community. It is impossible for me to do that because of my position as the High Commissioner. I am not supposed to lead the Indian community publicly; in that respect my predecessors were more fortunate."[8]

With that review of the position of India's representative in the country, it is time to consider the international effects of the war in so far as the local South African field was affected. Indian troops passing South African ports in transit presented no small embarrassment to the Government authorities. Indians who sat as full members of the British War Cabinet would, in the normal course, come under the differential laws of South Africa. General Smuts saw the seriousness of the position and appointed Douglas Buchanan, K.C. as the Union Liaison Officer in Cape Town, whose duty it was to receive Indian passengers who were on their way to India via Cape Town owing to the diversion of sea traffic from the United Kingdom to India. The Liaison Officer was to ensure that these Indians received the utmost courtesy during their short sojourn in Cape Town.

In Natal no such appointment was made till 1942. In that year the Union Government realized that Durban was as important as Cape Town and appointed Major Stead to the Staff of the Natal Command with the duties of catering for visiting Indian troops and civilians. Major Stead and Douglas Buchanan made arrangements for Indian officers to obtain services in the hairdressing saloons of a European firm with businesses in both cities. This was a change in the ordinary pattern of South African life and was due entirely to the exigencies of war.[9]

This change, however, applied to Indian officers only. By and large, the other ranks as well as civilians felt the force of South African life most sharply. Towards the end of 1942 a formidable array of Indians from England in the category of the intelligentsia: doctors, lawyers, scientists, technicians, educationists – with an imposing string of British degrees and diplomas – sent a letter to the *Leader* in which they pointed out how the "Colour Bar" in South Africa stared them in the face wherever they went – in cafes, cinemas, railway carriages, shops, post offices and public libraries. The letter went on to say that they were "amazed to find that this could exist at such a time when we are supposed to be fighting for democracy. . . . What hope is there for mankind if Fascist forces are destroyed in Europe only to preserve them in South Africa?"[10]

Situations such as this certainly accentuated the colour problems of South Africa and gave greater prominence to the existence of colour barriers because, at this time, it was felt in larger circles that there was no room for such barriers at home when the object was to mobilise all possible strength to defeat the common enemy. Indians in South Africa, in spite of difficulties at home, enlisted in the armed forces with the Indian Malay Corps whose headquarters was at first at the Crown Mines, Johannesburg and later in Ladysmith, Natal. There were difficulties in this Corps in regard to food supply and in regard to the religious and social susceptibilities of the Indians. The High Commissioner for India, Sir Shafa'at Ahmad Khan, decided that the best incentive to promote Indian support for the war would lie in the creation of a separate Indian army. The High Commissioner's suggestion was accepted by the Director of the Non-European Army Services. A separate Indian battalion was created under the command of Major J. H. B. Knox, M.C., who had served in the Indian army in the last war. The site of the camp was contiguous to that of the Indian Malay corps camp in Ladysmith. Recruiting for the Indian Battalion started in November, 1942. By the end of the year 86 recruits had been obtained, 62 of whom enlisted during the month of December alone.[11]

Though the support for this battalion was less than was expected, the effort was still creditable and the numbers gradually increased with the advent of new recruits and with transfers from the Indian Malay Corps. It was not difficult to understand why a spontaneous and hearty support for the war effort was not forthcoming. It was difficult to rally to the call made on patriotic grounds when the country concerned was not even prepared to accord to the Indians the most elementary rights due to true patriots. In India the very same situation gave rise to the "Quit India" resolution adopted by the All-India Congress Working Committee at the request of Mahatma Gandhi on 7th August, 1942, after the failure of the Cripps Mission to work out a programme for the independence of India after the war.

The Cripps Mission to India was followed with keen interest in South Africa. When it failed the English press criticised the Indian political leaders for what they considered to be their lack of political realism. The Nationalist press, on the other hand, sympathised with the cause of the Indians. *Die Transvaaler*, for example, wrote that the English adopted the same tactics in India as they had in South Africa. In India the English were foreigners and the Indians were completely justified in agitating for complete independence. The newspaper went on to state that both the English and the Indians in South Africa were foreigners here with dual loyalties.

The war developments were giving rise to the charge that Indians in South Africa were guilty of serving "dual loyalties". In the reasoning advanced by the Nationalist press only the Afrikaner was free of this charge. Though the historical fact, of course, is that from 1652 to 1860 three important streams of immigration brought to this land the Dutch, British and Indian immigrants, many of whom made their permanent home in South Africa. The charge of "dual loyalties" against the Indians was an old charge and it gained momentum whenever a fresh crisis developed. The war was in itself a period of great crisis but there was more to it than the mere issue of war. There were great constitutional strides being made in India; there was the failure of the Cripps Mission; there was also the introduction of the "Quit India" campaign to confuse the picture. Above all this, there was the ever present threat of a Japanese invasion and conquest of India and the political implications of such an eventuality. These events were not without their interest for South Africa in view of the close relation between India and South Africa in the affairs of the South African Indians.

In spite of her own struggle for independence at home, India continued to look after the interest of Indians in South Africa. War or no war this interest was maintained and would be maintained (as the High Commissioner for India, Sir Shafa'at Khan, said) until the franchise was restored to the Indians in South Africa and they were granted parliamentary representation. This interest, it was explained, was not to be construed as interference in the domestic affairs of South Africa. It was necessarily heightened during the war years for, as the High Commissioner for India reported, the "colour bar in Durban, Cape Town and other ports along the coast subjected the cream of Indian leadership in war time in the defence forces of our government, en route to and from India, to humiliations on many occasions. There have been some very ugly incidents. . . . Indian high-ranking officers and others found for the first time such a thing as a colour bar, and have been astonished at the patience and fortitude with which the Indian community in the Union has borne these humiliations for the last 80 years."[13]

South Africa followed the internal developments in India with an eye to possible repercussions in this country. In the Union House of Assembly J. H. Grobler asked General Smuts whether he would inform the British Government that the acceptance of the Cripps proposals by India would not involve South Africa in any obligations or make any difference to existing legislation. The Prime Minister did not reply to the question. He was, no doubt, aware of the international implications of the Indian question, more especially during the war years.[14]

There was no easing-off in the tension built up in recent years. The restrictions of old were not only not relaxed but were enforced with the same strictness of old. The war had really done nothing to improve the position at home. This is reflected in the following incident, in no way an isolated one: An incident took place in Pietermaritzburg which an Indian journal reported on its front page in the following terms: "South Africa's 'Storm Troopers' in Action – Indians fisted and booted at Air Display in P.M. Burg – Maritzburg wants Government Enquiry." The headlines referred to unpleasant incidents in which Indians from the city who had gathered to witness an air display were manhandled by European soldiers. Various correspondents wrote to the *Leader* and other newspapers giving first-hand accounts of the incidents. One such correspondent recalled the words spoken by Field-Marshal Smuts in Pietermaritzburg only a few days after the incidents at the air display when the Prime Minister said that the Europeans were being trained to tolerance, forbearance and Christian feeling, which attributes alone made life worth living. Smuts called for fair play and said: "We ought to see that every section – and let me go further, every colour – has justice."

This incident and Smuts' speech were the very epitome of South African contradictions between practice and precept. The difference on this occasion was that the contradiction received much publicity and even drew into the picture the Acting High Commissioner for India, J. Muir, who travelled to Pietermaritzburg in order to make an on-the-spot investigation; he reported his findings to the Prime Minister who agreed to arrange for a thorough investigation of the complaint.[15]

The Government appointed a Court of Inquiry. Though the inquiry was concluded in October, 1941, it was only towards the end of March, 1942, that General Smuts issued a statement refusing to reveal the findings of the military court of inquiry. In his Report for

1941 the High Commissioner stated that he was informed that though the Military Court found that the conduct of the police was not what it should have been they were unable to convict any particular member of the force of acts of violence or of impropriety.[16]

This incident went a long way towards drawing attention to the disabilities to which the Indians in the country were subjected. The position in Natal where the bulk of the Indians lived was no worse now than it was before. Nor was it any better. There was a general desire among the Indian leaders for the franchise on the common roll. There was some conjecture also whether the type of political campaign being waged at that time in India would not bring about good dividends in South Africa. Senator Edgar H. Brookes considered these questions when he opened the annual conference of the Natal Indian Congress in September, 1941. He said that the claim for the common roll was thoroughly justified for it was the only kind of franchise "completely right in principle". But holding out for it (especially when the same consideration applied to the African) meant putting the proposition "half a century ahead". Drawing a comparison between the situation in India and South Africa, Senator Brookes said that in India the no-compromise policy was applied "by a sage and saint of his time". In India the policy succeeded to a point because the people on whose behalf it was adopted constituted a great majority whereas in South Africa the Indians represented the smallest minority. "Non-co-operation", said Senator Brookes, "is infinitely better than either violence or slavish acceptance of injustice. But it is not as good as co-operation."[17]

Many things are certainly gained by co-operation and conciliation. In the war struggle the Indians of South Africa were co-operating to a reasonable extent. This attitude was also present in their role on the Lawrence Committee. Conversely, it is necessary to give some attention now to the policy of the Union Government on the acquisition and occupation of properties by Indians in so-called European areas in order to see how much of co-operation and conciliation emanated from this source.

When the Lawrence Committee was set up in 1940 it was the first step taken by the Union Government in the direction of "pegging" the position of acquisition by Indians of property in Durban. This Committee, however, was not invested with any statutory power and this factor was the bedrock on which the Committee finally floundered. On 9th December, 1941, the Durban City Council's representatives on the Committee recommended to the City Council that a resolution be adopted stating that the Lawrence Committee would not be able to achieve any useful result in regulating or controlling the acquisition and occupation by Indians of property in predominantly European areas in the city unless the Committee was "given some powers in the matter over and above the powers of persuasion of its members. . . ." The resolution also called upon the Government to introduce legislation which would make it a prerequisite in property transactions between people of the different races that the approval of the Lawrence Committee be obtained. These recommendations were adopted by the City Council.

The Indian representatives on the Committee opposed the above recommendations on the grounds that the Committee was created to work on non-statutory lines; that the investing of the Committee with statutory powers would constitute an attempt at segregation which the Indians were opposed to. In any case, the Indian members stated, the

Durban City Council had failed to keep its side of the bargain in making suitable sites available to the Indians.

The Indian representatives then outlined a plan for the smoother functioning of the Lawrence Committee and expressed their hopes that the future boded well for the Committee. These hopes were somewhat far-fetched for the Durban City Council had no intention of giving way to the suggestions or to the requests made by the Indian representatives. Six months later, in July, 1942, a further deadlock in the working of the Committee resulted when the Durban City Council proposed a scheme to expropriate the Riverside, Merebank and Sydenham areas. The Indian representatives told the Lawrence Committee that the Durban City Council was doing nothing more for Indian housing than creating an agitation. They stated that they were no longer prepared to act only as "policemen" and that Europeans had to be blamed for selling to Indians, thus creating a situation which gave rise to complaints of penetration into European areas.

The Indian representatives of the Lawrence Committee were not the only persons to protest against the City Council's expropriation scheme; a Durban Joint Council of Action was formed to oppose the scheme. Senator Edgar Brookes was one of the speakers at a protest meeting organised by this Council. He said that the proposed expropriation was "an effort to introduce segregation under the guise of slum clearance".

The City Council's scheme even led to the Indian High Commissioner, Sir Shafa'at Ahmad Khan, paying a personal visit to Durban to acquaint himself with the proposals. Prior to the High Commissioner's visit, the Minister of the Interior, H. G. Lawrence, sent the members of the Central Housing Board to Durban to examine the proposals and to try to arrange a modification of the scheme which would meet the objections raised by the Indians. Though the Board recommended that the Riverside area be expropriated for both Indian and European housing, the High Commissioner opposed the scheme because he felt that the less desirable part of the locality would be set aside for the Indians.[19]

The upshot was that the Durban City Council abandoned its expropriation scheme for the Riverside area. Of greater significance at this time was the ungracious demise of the Lawrence Committee. This important experiment on non-statutory lines had failed. The Committee failed because it was unable either to control Indian penetration or to provide satisfactory housing schemes for Indians. On the European side the Committee failed because of the attitude of the Durban City Council which was reluctant to provide adequate Indian housing in the more suitable areas. On the Indian side the Committee failed because the Indian representatives who were drawn from the Natal Indian Association were unable to claim to be the representatives of the entire Indian community. Some of the more wealthy Indians who were outside the pale of the Association could not be prevailed upon to refrain from making purchases of property in European areas.

Because of the divergent views and attitudes of its members, the Lawrence Committee was dissolved in 1942 and the Minister of the Interior announced that an Indian Advisory Board would take its place. The failure of the Committee put an end to the hopes of preventing penetration by the method of co-operation. Though the Government was, at the time the Committee was first set up, in the thick of the early months of war, its great concern over the complaints by Europeans that Indians were penetrating into European areas led to the appointment of the Indian Penetration Commission on 15th May, 1940, under the chairmanship of Justice F. N. Broome, to enquire and report on the extent of India penetration since 1st January, 1927, for trading or residential purposes in predominantly European areas in Natal and in the Transvaal (excluding proclaimed lands) and to give the reasons for such occupation and acquisition.[20]

The appointment of the Commission at such a time is adequate proof that the government considered the matter to be of such grave importance that it could not be postponed even during war time. It was a definite victory for those Europeans who protested so vigorously against Indian penetration into European areas. The Natal Indian Association even appealed to the Government to suspend the Commission and to allow the Association to concentrate its energies in the organisation of an Indian Service Corps rather than in the preparation of evidence to be submitted before the Commission. The request was refused.

The appointment of the Commission was an indication, too, that the Union Government had come to the point where it was determined to act firmly against the Indians: war or no war and in defiance of the call for patriotic action by a common brotherhood against a common enemy. It was also in defiance of the words recalled to mind by Councillor Rupert Ellis Brown, Mayor of Durban, that nothing should be done "to queer the pitch for action". The international "pitch" during war time would be far less friendly after this appointment.

Indians in South Africa were opposed to the steps taken by the Union Government in setting up the Commission because they claimed that it was their indisputable right to reside and trade according to their choice and wisdom in any locality. They also put forward their own points. They were opposed to segregation in any form; the Government had taken the first step towards further restricting their rights; the Government was fighting for democracy on one front and yet practised an undemocratic policy towards the Indians; the move was against the letter and spirit of the Cape Town Agreement; and, finally, the appointment of the Commission "was humiliating to Indian nationhood" because the Indian community was singled out for the first time "for investigation with a view to segregation".[21]

The setting up of the Commission embittered those persons in the Transvaal and in Natal who were not happy that Indians should support the war while such measures were being taken by the Union Government. The Nationalist blocs in the Transvaal Indian Congress and in the Natal Indian Association – the younger and more militant politicians who were rapidly gaining ground towards the eventual leadership of these political bodies – called upon Indians to boycott the Commission and appealed to the Government of India to express its strong disapproval. The Union Government took action against some of these persons under the War Measures Act.[22]

Finally, however, the Commission received co-operation from the Transvaal Indian Congress, the Natal Indian Assocation and the Natal Indian Congress, to which bodies the Commission expressed its indebtedness and in particular made mention of the good work done by S. M. Nana of the Transvaal Indian Congress, Sorabjee Rustomjee and S. R. Naidoo of the Natal Indian Association and A. I. Kajee of the Natal Indian Congress.[23]

The Report of the Commission was made public on 11th October, 1941. In the case of the Transvaal the Commission found 339 cases of penetration from 1927 to 1940; 246 cases being for trade and 93 for residence. Of the 232 cases of urban penetration, 111 occurred in the unproclaimed portion of the Johannesburg municipal area. But for the 111 cases in Johannesburg alone, the Commission reported, the number of cases in the Transvaal would not have been impressive. And of the 111 cases, 50 occurred in Doornfontein which was a predominantly European area in 1927 but lost its European character since then because of a common characteristic of urban development particularly in new countries – migration. On whether or not the figures revealed a situation to be alarmed at, the Commission reported that the facts did not disclose "a situation which can by any stretch of imagination be described as critical".[24]

In its Report the Commission considered the reasons for Indian penetration. It began by rejecting the view that there was any general desire among the Transvaal Indians to live among Europeans. It also rejected the view that European exodus from towns such as Doornfontein was caused by Indian infiltration into such areas. The Commission concluded that European exodus preceded the entry by Indians. The Commission then advanced three factors that contributed to penetration in urban areas. In areas other than Johannesburg and Pretoria, centralisation of trade was taking place in the larger centres through improved means of communications; smaller centres appeared less attractive to the trader. The second factor was the Cape Town Agreement and its emphasis on the western way of life. The traditional family system was changing and some sons were branching off on their own after marriage and more and more Indian traders were living away from their shops. All this meant an increased demand for residential premises. The third factor was the acquisition of immovable property by companies in which Indians held a predominant interest or by Cape Malay women married to Indians: once *de facto* Indian ownership was established, Indian occupation followed.

The Commission then concluded with what it considered to be the main reason for Indian penetration in the Transvaal: ". . . nothing more than the normal desire among Indians to acquire wealth. The bulk of the Transvaal Indians are Mohammedans. Their forefathers were traders and they are naturally predisposed to become traders themselves." The Commission's Report was a clear vindication of the Transvaal Indian and it showed that there was nothing unusual, abnormal or damaging in what had taken place in respect of penetration. Far from the European being aggrieved, the Commission found that "Truly the Transvaal Indian is between the horns of a cruel dilemma".

After this the Commission considered the position in Natal. It divided Natal into two parts: Natal, excluding Durban, and Durban alone. In the first part the Commission found 328 cases of penetration for residential and trading purposes and 80 cases for agricultural purposes. Having regard to the Indian population in this area, viz., 103 175 in 1936, the Commission found that the position did not appear to be serious, being "little more than a trickle".

The Commission then dealt with the position in Durban in two parts: the Old Borough up till 1932 (which consisted of approximately 13 square miles) and the Added Areas since 1932 which extended the Old Borough of 13 square miles to the new Municipal area of 67 square miles). In the Old Borough the Commission found 512 cases of penetration by Indians into predominantly European areas, of which 150 sites were acquired and occupied and 362 sites were acquired but not occupied. In the Added Areas the Commission was unable to establish what portions were predominantly European in 1927 as it did not receive any information from the Durban City Council on the position prior to 1934. Of the 1 759 divisions acquired by Indians since the beginning of 1934 the Commission found that 730 of this number actually adjoined sub-divisions which were already in Indian ownership on that date. The Commission found that the greater part of the Added Areas was not predominantly European in 1927 and it concluded that the position in the Added Areas was not acute.

It remained for the Commission to give what reasons it could to explain Indian penetration in Natal. It found that the desire to make investments was the most important single reason for penetration in Natal and that the Indians of the wealthier class had only two avenues of investment that appealed to them, trade and the acquisition of immovable property. The Commission found this to be true of the less wealthy class Indians too, and commented that for this class of Indian land occupied the same position as did cattle for Africans.

In its over-all findings the Indian Penetration Commission exploded two commonly-held fallacies of that and of an earlier time: that there was inordinate Indian penetration in predominantly European areas in the Transvaal and in Natal and that one of the reasons for this penetration was the desire of Indians to live among Europeans. In its concluding remarks, the Commission said: ". . . before we leave the subject we desire to repeat that we do not believe there is any general desire on the part of Indians to live among Europeans. Where they have acquired properties in European areas they have been actuated by the desire to make money, or by the desire to live in areas that are more attractive to them for reasons other than the presence of Europeans there."

The findings of an impartial judicial Commission showed that the allegations made against Indians were largely unfounded. These allegations were treated with the greatest respect by the Union Government because even the dangers of war and the fact that Indians here and abroad were comrades-in-arms failed to put the Government off. It was a reasonable expectation that the Government would take serious note of the true position and act in support of the Commission's findings. But the Government was an all-white Government and not morally bound to follow the lead of a Commission of Enquiry. There was the electorate to consider. What the Europeans generally felt about the Commission's Report can be summed up by the statement made by one of their representatives: "The Broome Commission showed that there were 570 odd cases of penetration inside Durban, and I am quite prepared to say that is penetration, even if the Commission is not prepared to say so."

The atmosphere against the Indians was still very tense and the general European attitude still inflexible; there was, consequently, little hope that the tempering effects of the Commission's Report would change this atmosphere or attitude. There was one exception to this position which offered a faint glimmer of something beneficial to the South African Indian out of the existing political situation in South Africa. The outgoing Indian High Commissioner, Sir Rama Rau, pointed out what this was when he said on his return to India that "Europeans in South Africa now realized better than at the beginning of the war, racial questions would have to be considered from a different standpoint. The present Government in South Africa was very sympathetic towards the Indian problem, and the presence of Mr. Hofmeyr in the Cabinet was a guarantee that the Indian problem would not only be dealt with sympathetically but also liberally".

These remarks revealed an optimism in which it was difficult for the South African Indians to share, in the absence of cogent proof that the Government was in fact "liberal". There was, of course, the sympathy and understanding of Hofmeyr and Lawrence but these two men did not make up the Union Government. This Government had still to show that it was concerned about the damaging results its policy towards the Indians had on the international field, especially in the relations between South Africa and India. Far from evincing any concern, the Union Government took a number of steps during the last three years of the war which not only aggravated the position but clearly showed that the hopes of Sir Rama Rau were misplaced.

The first of these steps was the appointment of an Asiatic Affairs Advisory Board in February, 1943, to take the place of the defunct Lawrence Committee. The Board was to comprise four European and four Indian members, with a European chairman. The first signs were that the Board would have an uneasy existence. The unhappy fate of the Lawrence Committee of 1940–2 was not yet forgotten; nor did the Indians see how the Board would succeed where the Committee had failed. The first breach in the working of the Board was caused when one of the Indian members, Sorabjee Rustomjee, declined to accept the appointment because of doubts concerning the attitude of the Durban City Council, especially after the experience of the Lawrence Committee. Rustomjee said that he doubted whether the Board would be able to serve any useful purpose until the Durban City Council was "prepared to do justice to the Indians as citizens and not act in a partisan spirit".

This first step of the Union Government was a positive step and might have realised some good with a fair trial and with honest intentions prevailing. But if this move had any positive value in it, this was soon undone by the second step which was the appointment of another Commission of Enquiry in the person of a single commissioner, Justice F. N. Broome, to enquire into acquisitions of sites by Indians in the municipal area of Durban since the 30th September, 1940, in those areas which the previous Commission (the Indian Penetration Commission of 1940) found to be predominantly European on the 1st January, 1927.[26]

In taking the step to appoint a Commission to go into the matter of penetration by Indians in European areas between 1940 and 1943 the Union Government clearly indicated that it was not satisfied with the findings of the Commission of 1940 that there was no justification for the complaints made by Europeans that penetration was taking place at a rapid pace in Durban mainly because Indians wanted to live next to Europeans. After the Indians had been absolved from the charge of penetration by the Commission of 1940, it was obvious that the appointment of the latest Commission would not serve to improve relations between India and South Africa. Already the relations were deteriorating and this was in evidence when the Central Legislative Assembly in New Delhi passed the Indian Reciprocity Act in March, 1943. This Act aimed at imposing the same restrictions on South African Europeans in India as were imposed on South African Indians in South Africa. In terms of the Act it was possible for such Europeans to be declared undesirable elements in India, to be denied permanent residence in India, to be required to deposit £100 before entering India, to be denied contact with Indian women, to be segregated in post offices, railways, public places and to occupy seats especially reserved for them. The Act was placed in the Statute Book to be enforced if and when necessary.[27]

Though the Act was not yet enforced, and it was not even clear how its enforcement would result in improving the position in South Africa, it was clear that the political atmosphere in Pretoria and New Delhi had become heavier. The statement by the Minister of the Interior, H. G. Lawrence, in Senate on 22nd March, 1943, did nothing to improve the atmosphere. He said that if the Report of the Second Indian Penetration Commission upheld the allegations of the Durban City Council the Government would have to act and that any legislation introduced would have retrospective effect as from 22nd March, 1943. The Minister mentioned that feelings were running so high that racial riots were possible in Durban.[28]

The High Commissioner for India, after reading the press reports of Lawrence's Senate speech, informed the Minister on 24th March that the Government and the people of India would strongly oppose any statutory solution of the Indian question in Natal which involved the segregation of Indians in prescribed residential areas. The High Commissioner asked to be informed of the Union Government's intentions before any irrevocable steps were taken. On 26th March Sir Shafa'at Ahmad Khan saw Field-Marshal Smuts who was non-committal on the matter. On the following day the High Commissioner informed Lawrence that he had been instructed by the Government of India to repeat the objections against any segregation measure. The High Commissioner also said that the possibilities of a racial war were greatly exaggerated and that a very large portion of Durban Europeans lived in suburbs fully protected by anti-Asiatic clauses.

The report of the Second Indian Penetration Commission was dated 25th March, 1943, and was made public on 6th April. The High Commissioner again reminded the Minister of the Interior on 30th March that the Government of India had asked for an opportunity to be informed of the proposals of the Union Government in order to make their representations before any final decision was taken. The following day a copy of the report was telegraphed to the Government of India.

The report vindicated the allegations of the Durban City Council that penetration on a large scale was taking place in Durban. Between October, 1940 and February, 1943, it found 326 cases of penetration.[29] The Commission found that the number of sites acquired during 1942, the last complete year in its enquiry, was $2\frac{1}{2}$ times greater than the highest previous yearly total, viz., that for 1939; that during the first two months of 1943 Indians paid more for sites in European areas than during any complete year dealt with by the previous Commission, and that the amount so paid by Indians during the 29 months covered by the present Commission did not fall far short of the total amount so paid during the whole of the 13 complete years covered by the previous Commission.

Though the Commission was not requested to go into the reasons for the acquisition by Indians of properties in European areas, it did not, in its investigations, exclude the reasons advanced by certain witnesses. In glossing over some probable reasons, the Commission said that the abnormal conditions brought about by the war restricted the trade facilities enjoyed by the wealthy Indians in Durban with the result that they invested their money in immovable properties. The Natal Indian Congress claimed that there was a general acceleration in the direction of acquiring properties and this applied to European purchasers as well. It asserted that properties were also changing hands from Indian ownership to European. The Commission, however, found that this process was of a lesser extent in that only 16 properties were so acquired as compared to 326 sites acquired by Indians from Europeans.

Having shown that there was no general changing hands of property, the Commission went on to consider the other reasons for the rapid penetration since 1940. One of these was the mistaken impression created by reading only the summary of the first Indian Penetration Commission Report, which conveyed the mistaken idea that no Indian penetration had taken place since 1927. The Indian community, which shared this mistaken impression, felt that having been acquitted of the charge of "penetration" they were free to penetrate further. Finally, the Commission said that a possible reason was the desire of the Indian community "to pass through the door while it is still ajar".

Whatever the reasons for this phenomenon, none were called for and therefore none mattered. One thing was quite clear. The Report would be accepted by both the Union Government and by Parliament as complete justification for restrictive legislation. The Union Cabinet met on April 6, the day on which the Report was published, to discuss the nature of the proposed legislation. On the next day the newspapers carried news of a Cabinet crisis in which J. H. Hofmeyr threatened to resign because of his disagreement with the suggested legislation.[30]

On 7th April, 1943, the draft Bill covering both Natal and the Transvaal was published. The purpose of the Bill was to make provision for restrictions on trading by Asiatics in the Transvaal and the occupation by them of land in that Province, and to impose restrictions on the acquisition and occupation of land in Natal. In the Transvaal the Interim Act, the Asiatics (Transvaal Land and Trading) Act 28/1939 as amended by Act 28/1941 and extended till 1943 was to be renewed for a further period of three years, that is up till the 31st March, 1946. In Natal, the position in Durban was to be pegged so that no Indian would be permitted to occupy or acquire property occupied or owned by a European before March 22nd, 1943. Similar provision could be applied at any time to the rest of Natal by proclamation following the report of an *ad hoc* committee. The proposed legislation was non-discriminatory in form in that Europeans were disqualified from acquiring property in Indian ownership or possession on March 22nd. The provisions were to cease to have effect on 31st March, 1946, but could be extended or revived by resolution of Parliament.[31]

The announcement of the provisions of the Bill created great concern in India and among the Indian community in South Africa. The Government of India issued a Press communique on 8th April in which they emphasized their interest in the proposed legislation and expressed their regret at the failure of the Union Government to give them an opportunity to comment on the proposals. The Government of India sent a further urgent communication to the Union Government. In this note the Union Government was reminded of its decision in October, 1939 not to proceed with Indian legislation during the war, having regard to the feeling and friction which such legislation would inevitably cause. The Government of India requested the Union Government to re-examine the position and to try to arrive at a scheme for the voluntary restriction of inter-racial purchases of property. In passing the Union Government was informed that the Reciprocity Bill had been passed into law with the unanimous approval of the Indian legislature.[32]

In their reply the Union Government referred to their 1939 decision and explained that it was taken because of their genuine desire to acknowledge the support that was forthcoming from the Indian community at the time for the maintenance of the *status quo*. The hopes expressed by the Government at that time had not been realised and the position had deteriorated. It was necessary, therefore, to introduce legislation to check the recent developments. The Government pointed out that the happier position obtaining in the Transvaal was due to the existing legislation which it was proposed to extend for three years. In a memorandum attached to the note the Government stated that unless control was exercised racial feelings would be fanned to such a pitch that it would be impossible for the Indian community to have its claims for housing and other civic amenities examined in a calm and dispassionate atmosphere. It was the intention of the Union Government to appoint a Commission on which Indians would be asked to serve to make recommendations generally as to what steps were necessary to implement the Cape Town Agreement of 1927 in Natal. As regards the Transvaal, the memorandum quoted the number of cases of potential infiltration prevented by the control exercised by the Interim Act.

In spite of the protests and the pleas of the Government of India and of the Indians in South Africa, the Union Government was not deflected from its resolute course. The Bill was introduced and given its first reading on the same day – April 10th – a day after a deputation of sixteen members of the Natal Indian Congress waited on the Minister of the Interior and presented to him a comprehensive memorandum in which the Indian case was set down with great clarity. It was pointed out in the memorandum that the Report of the Second Penetration Commission did not draw a distinction between ownership and occupation and that if this had been done, 326 cases of acquisition would have been set out in correct perspective showing only 54 cases of ownership for purposes of actual occupation.[33]

The Congress memorandum went on to state that in the second report, the Commissioner had appended a map showing acquisitions in "Block A.L." This map dealt with a small part of Durban's residential Berea. The pictorial presentation of the map showed at a glance the accelerated pace of Indian purchases – from two sub-divisions in 1927, twenty-five from 1927 to 1940, to seventy-seven in the twenty-nine months of the war. In its statement the Natal Indian Congress touched on one important fact which highlighted the one-sidedness of the map "Block A.L." The building societies in Durban had held a meeting and decided that no loans would be granted by them to Indians for the purpose of assisting them to acquire property in areas which were considered to be predominantly European. This decision was conveyed to the Durban City Council. Yet from May, 1942, onwards the building societies continued giving loans on properties acquired by Indians in the western portion of "Block A.L.", and this facilitated the acquisition of properties by Indians. The majority of the 77 sub-divisions were purchased by Indians after May, 1942. This policy indicated that the building societies considered the western portion of "Block A.L." one in which Indians should be allowed and assisted to purchase property.

The Natal Indian Congress pointed out that the total number of 838 acquisitions since 1927, coupled with the 204 acres which were deemed to be predominantly Indian in 1927, added up to a total of 359 acres which constituted only 4 per cent of the total acreage of the Old Borough of 8 274 acres. Drawing a comparison between Johannesburg and Durban, Congress said that while the Feetham Commission had recommended the exemption of 202 acres of land in the city of Johannesburg for occupation and ownership by an Indian population of 10 000 in that city, the Durban City Council was content to confine its 25 000 Indians in an area of the same size – 204 acres. It went on to reveal some interesting figures concerning Indian housing in Durban up till 1943: that while 50 economic houses had been built by the City Council at a cost of £26 708 and 225 sub-economic houses at a cost of £117 000 for an Indian population of 90 000, 705 houses costing £659 882 had been built for a European population of 102 000; and while 1 100 sites had been sold to Europeans, only 16 were sold to Indians.

Another important submission in the memorandum was the distinction between acquisition for investment and acquisition for occupation; that purchase of a property did not necessarily mean that it would be occupied by Indians, that in most cases the purchase was purely for investment. In the case of flats acquired in European areas no Indian occupation could ever take place because of the operation of the "Licence" system. Licences for the occupation of flats were issued by the City Council with restrictive rights. The permits clearly specified that the flats were for occupation by Europeans or Indians only.

Referring to the case presented by the Durban City Council on Indian penetration, the Natal Indian Congress memorandum claimed that the City Council had magnified the position out of all proportion; that the value of property held by Indians in the Old Borough was £4 million compared to a European holding of £35 million; Indians owned 1 783 sites as against 12 782 owned by Europeans. If Indian holding in 16 years had increased by £2,7 million of which £1,7 million was in Indian areas – European holding had increased by £15,6 million in the same period; of a total acreage of 8 274, Indians held 359 acres or 4 per cent of the total.

Finally, the memorandum addressed an appeal to the Union Government to formulate its policy towards the Indians in accordance with the principles enshrined in the Atlantic Charter and in keeping with the Cape Town Agreement. It ended with the following strong plea:

> "If ethical considerations are to be the governing factor then the classroom arithmetic of so many acquisitions justifying legislation should not be the determining influence in the enactment of legislation which curtails the liberty of action and freedom which is the inherent right of a free citizen in a free democracy."

Following the submission of this statement to the Minister of the Interior, copies of a booklet containing the memorandum were sent to all members of the Senate and the House of Assembly, together with an open letter to each member. In the open letter the members of the Natal Indian Congress deputation made a fervent plea for the Bill to be rejected:

"Finally, we urge you to reject this further repressive racial legislation which separates us from the national stream of South Africa and forces us into opposition when our desire is to take our full responsibility in the nation's development."

Attached to the open letter was a joint petition from the Natal and Transvaal Indian Congress requesting that they be allowed to appear at the Bar of the House either in person or by Counsel. An open letter was also issued and distributed by the Transvaal Indian Congress. Referring to the claims of the Minister of the Interior that the position in the Transvaal was kept in check only through legislative restrictions this letter said that the 1 300 odd trading permits to Indians in the last four years and the 583 refusals were no justification for the extension of the Asiatics (Transvaal Land and Trading) Act. The issue of 1 300 permits did not mean that new licences had been granted; the majority of the 1 300 permits represented the transfer of existing licences from one Indian to another in premises situated in exclusively non-European areas.

On the same day as the release of this open letter, the Government of India sent a further note to the Union Government stating that there was nothing in the Second Penetration Report to suggest the extension of the Transvaal legislation to Natal and that the refusals of permits referred to would in any case have received similar results through the actions of the licensing authorities. It welcomed the proposal of the Union Government to appoint a Commission to go into the question of Indian housing needs in Natal but felt that the proposed legislation would not provide the right atmosphere for the work of the commission. The Government of India suggested that pending the report of the proposed judicial Commission all intended transfers of land between Europeans and Asiatics should be made subject to prior publication before confirmation, and objections should be heard by a Joint Committee on the lines of the Lawrence Committee which would not have statutory powers but would be at liberty to publish its recommendations. The Government of India reminded the Union Government that both Governments were signatories to the Cape Town Agreement and that the Government of India would be grateful for further information regarding the proposed judicial Commission which the Union Government intended to set up to implement the Agreement.[34]

The Indian Government's note was handed to the Secretary for External Affairs on the morning of 14th April and was in the hands of the Prime Minister and Lawrence before the debate on the second reading of the Bill began. Neither the note nor the representations made by the Natal and Transvaal Indian Congresses affected the final course of the Bill. No internal or external plea or pressure was allowed to even modify the course.

The Government of India tried its best to alter the course in some way; its representative in South Africa, Sir Shafa'at Ahmad Khan, too, in spite of the limitations placed on his office, worked strenuously against the proposed measure in South Africa. In Natal, he helped to combine the Indian opposition to the "Pegging" Bill by forming a committee of twelve made up of six members each from the Natal Indian Congress and the Natal Indian Association. This was the first step taken towards ultimate unity between the two political organisations in Natal. Sir Shafa'at addressed this committee with deep emotion when he referred to the proposed measures.

The introduction of the Trading and Occupation of Land (Transvaal and Natal) Restriction Bill, referred to more commonly as the "Pegging Bill" in spite of all the protests against it marked the beginning of grave international complications in the political and economic relations between India and South Africa.

Speaking on the Second Reading of the Bill the Minister of the Interior, H. G. Lawrence, who introduced the Bill, said that he realised how deeply the Indians felt about the measure and that he appreciated their protests as well as the representations made by the Government of India on their behalf. But he urged them to take the long view and "to realise that this position which has arisen, if not dealt with now, can only lead ultimately to their detriment".[35]

The Minister of Finance, J. H. Hofmeyr, did not see the matter in quite the same way. He announced in the House of Assembly that he had tendered his resignation to the Prime Minister because of disagreement over certain provisions in the Bill, especially concerning the Transvaal. Outlining his objections to the Bill, Hofmeyr said that what appeared to him to be indefensible about the Bill was the fact "that the findings of the Judicial Commission are accepted when they suit one's own point of view. Of course, we as a European community are in a position of ascendancy in South Africa. There is nothing really to stop us from having it both ways . . . but that is a course of action which one's reason cannot commend, nor one's sense of justice approve."[36]

Hofmeyr's appeal was for justice to all people. There were other speakers, too, who thought of justice but from a different angle. The Leader of the Opposition, Dr. D. F. Malan, for instance, did not see the propriety of interference by the Government of India in the internal affairs of South Africa and for the South African Indians to appeal to India. He called for the termination of the Cape Town Agreement.

The Prime Minister, General Smuts, expressed surprise that the "father of the Cape Town Agreement", Dr. Malan, should have suggested the termination of that Agreement, the intention of which was to give the South African Indians, "our own fellow citizens, a square deal". General Smuts was an international figure, a military leader, leading his country during war time. He could not afford to take an illiberal attitude at this time. It would be most impolitic. He regretted that his Government had to introduce this measure but he saw no other way to deal with the situation: "We have no choice in the situation", he said, "which has been forced on us". And though he admitted that the Bill was an affront to India – a common ally – the path taken by his Government, he felt, was the right one because the Indian question "is in its nature almost insoluble but on every occasion by give and take" a *modus vivendi* had been worked out.

General Smuts' speech, except for his failure to understand why South African Indians appealed to India in times of trouble (for the simple truth was they had no local, provincial or national representation in the political machinery of the country to make their appeals effectively heard or felt, with the emphasis on "effectively" as distinct from the theoretical opportunities present in interviews, memoranda, petitions and such representations) was a most generous and statesman-like evaluation of the position. He had gone far enough to plead on behalf of the Indians. But he could go no further. For the Indians what really mattered was not a *de facto* plea on their behalf but a *de jure* translation of the plea into a tangible reality. Hofmeyr had tried to achieve this reality by submitting his resignation. The exigencies of war prevented its acceptance but Hofmeyr's stand was not without its value. As deputy-leader of the governing party there was the possibility that one day he would be the nation's Prime Minister and when that happened his policies were bound to be accepted. His utterances and actions were, therefore, followed with great interest.

Except for the solitary stand of J. H. Hofmeyr and for the opposition by the three African representatives, the House of Assembly was quite unanimous in its acceptance of the provisions of the "Pegging" Bill.

On April 22, the day on which the Bill received its first and second readings in the Senate, a last representation to the Union Government was sent by the Government of India. In this the Government of India suggested that if the Union Government found it necessary to pass the Bill, a clause should be added empowering the Governor-General to bring the operative sections of the Bill into force on such date as he might think fit. In the meantime the machinery suggested by the Government of India in their note of April 14th, or any other acceptable non-statutory approach should be tried out, with the legislation in the background in the event of failure. The Union Government's reply was only communicated after the Bill had passed through Senate. It rejected the proposals made.

In the Senate, Senator Brookes presented a petition from the Natal Indian Association asking for the Bill to be rejected. Edgar Brookes referred to the matter of interference by India. He felt that India had the right to make representations to the Union Government on issues which affected her internal situation. The position of the South African Indian was of interest to the Nationalist group in the Indian Legislative Assembly and this interest brought about conflict between the members of that Assembly and the Government of India. Senator Brookes conceded to the Indian Government the right to make representations but not the right to dictate. The South African Indians appealed to India because, the Senator said, fair treatment was not given to them: "Indians will behave as sons of South Africa", he said, "when South Africa ceases to treat them as step-sons. You cannot ask an Indian to feel the same unfeigned loyalty to South Africa which a member of the more privileged classes, unhampered by legal restrictions, feels."[37]

Indians in South Africa and in India protested against the measure from its inception. Both the Natal Indian Association and the Natal Indian Congress presented petitions to be heard at the Bar of the House through private Members (Morris Alexander and Mrs. Ballinger) but as they were relegated to a low place on the Order Paper they were not reached. The Indian leaders interviewed Ministers and Members of Parliament and A. I. Kajee addressed a meeting of Natal M.P.s. Similarly, the Transvaal Indian Congress presented a memorandum to the Minister of the Interior.

The Pegging Bill received such international attention during the war that it even brought forth denunciations from the Axis radio stations – Berlin, Tokyo and Rome – and those associated with it, such as Saigon. According to the *Leader* radio reporter, Berlin said that the first instalment of the application of the Atlantic Charter was given to the minority Indians in South Africa by General Smuts. Berlin contended that Britain had no right to declare war against Germany when she invaded Poland, for, according to General Smuts, each country could deal with its own affairs and treat its own inhabitants in its own way. And Tokyo stressed the fact that Asia should be for the Asiatics as the European was squeezing the Indian out of Africa.

The events in South Africa could no longer be strictly confined to the borders of the country. They were finding echoes even in the war-torn areas of the world. This was a significant development which could not be ignored in the future. Closer home, a mass meeting of Indians and other races numbering almost 5 000 was convened under the auspices of 25 Durban organisations, 17 of which were trade unions, to protest against the Bill. And at another meeting held in the City Hall, Durban, Sorabjee Rustomjee tore up a copy of the Atlantic Charter with the words:

> ". . . the Charter had no place for the minority group in South Africa, its sanctity amounted, as far as South Africa was concerned, to no more than a scrap of paper and the best place for it was the rubbish heap. In the name of God, I say that the Charter has become first-class mockery. . . ."[39]

The protests of the South African Indians against the Pegging Act were soon aimed in the direction of making common cause politically, educationally and economically with the Africans and other non-Europeans of South Africa. This step was to be promoted in a resolution to be moved by Councillor A. Ismail of Cape Town and seconded by A. I. Kajee of Durban at the next session of the South African Indian Congress in Johannesburg.

The Pegging Act, by accident and not by design, was serving to bring the Black peoples of South Africa together. This was a development not anticipated in the strict legal design of the Act. It could very well be included among the unpredictable things the famous historian, Lipson, wrote of when he said of the 1848 revolts in France: "It is the fatal vice of revolution that one can never foretell its course or predict its issues . . .". The Act was to bring in its train some aspects which at the time of its creation were unforeseen. One of these was the proposed "common cause" among the Black peoples. The other was a thorough discussion on their position by the members of the Natal Indian Association Committee. The important question which was foremost among Indians at this time was the justification or not for taking the case of the South African Indian to India. There were divergent points of view that emerged and it is important to consider some of these. Albert Christopher, R. K. Naidoo, P. S. Aiyar and P. R. Pather took the view that as Indians in South Africa were South African nationals they should not turn to India for help. On the other side, A. K. M. Docrat, Ashwin Choudree, Sorabjee Rustomjee and S. R. Naidoo took the view which is well summed up in the words of S. R. Naidoo: "The question of our nationality has not yet been decided and as we are treated like the step-children of the country we must appeal to the outside world."

On the question of the right and need to appeal to India, the *Leader* editorial wrote that precedent for such appeal was to be found in the Round Table Conference between India and South Africa and that such appeal was therefore in order.[40]

The Pegging Act provided the opportunity and the excuse for much comment and criticism. In the Delhi Assembly debates on the Indian question in South Africa, subsequent to the passing of the Pegging Act, suggestions were made to enforce economic sanctions against South Africa. The Reciprocity Amendment Act was put on the Statute Book by the Indian Central Legislature at the request of the Government of India. Reciprocal action on the part of the Government of India was generally regretted and was condemned by the *Natal Witness* and *Natal Daily News* as likely to worsen a situation which was already bad enough. These papers expressed the view that retaliatory action would damage India much more than South Africa.[41] Indeed, statistics adduced lead to the same conclusion and reflect a favourable balance of trade for India.[42]

The point of the passing of the Reciprocity Amendment Act and the serious talk of economic sanctions against South Africa lead on to the study of the developments in India directly attributable to the "Pegging" Act of 1943. These developments will now be treated in some detail as they serve to indicate the serious international repercussions arising from the introduction of this Act. A significant feature of the opposition to the measure in India was the agreement between the Indian leaders and the Government of India as to the steps to be taken (although there was, as will be shown later, much reluctance on the part of Lord Wavell to take any kind of action against the Smuts Government).

The Indian leaders of all parties and from all walks of life spoke out clearly against the Act. At a mass meeting at Bombay, Sir Chimanlal Setalvad said that all the talk about the fine performance by Indian troops in the war meant nothing when in South Africa Indians were to be subjected to "this obnoxious piece of legislation". He said that the Indians were growing sceptical of the promises made by the United Nations that the war was being fought for the freedom and the liberty of all people. M. S. Aney, Member of the Viceroy's Council, said that the determination of the South African Government to keep any city in South Africa as a purely European city could not be justified either by prudence or by reason. He said that such a move was "the spirit of racial arrogance run amok". He wondered how a statesman of the international reputation of Field-Marshal Smuts could have anything to do with such a measure. At a meeting of the Muslim Chamber of Commerce, Khan Bahadur G. A. Dossani said that Indians in South Africa had every right to live where they were and that India resented any legislation stipulating anything to the contrary. An ex-judge of the Indian Appeal Court and a member of the Privy Council, Dr. M. R. Jayakar said that one of the most important results of the "Pegging" Act in India was the effect it had in uniting and bringing together on the same platform the important political and other groups. He said that the measure would dissolve the Empire much sooner than any hostile agitation in India; that it was bound to raise the cry that Asia was for the Asiatics and that in the Asiatic Federation to come there would be no place for Europeans. Faith in the British Empire, he said, was fast diminishing in modern India and would completely vanish if the measure was allowed to pass.[43]

If the utterances of the Indian leaders served as a barometer reflecting the feelings aroused in India against the Pegging Act, then the actions as well as the utterances of high-ranking officials of the Government of India were not less so, especially as a united front against the Act had been formed.

The Department of the Government of India which was responsible for Indians overseas was called the Indians Overseas Department and was headed by a member of the Viceroy's Council. In May, 1943, Dr. N. B. Khare, former Prime Minister of the Central Provinces and Berar (who was *persona non grata* with the Congress Working Committee, having been expelled from the Indian National Congress in 1938), took charge of this Department. With the approval of the Viceroy, Lord Linlithgow, he convened a conference of prominent Indian leaders to discuss the situation which had developed in South Africa as a result of the passing of the "Pegging" Act. Among those invited to attend the conference were the following: former Agents-General in South Africa, Rt. Hon. V. S. Sastri, Sir Kunwar Maharaj Singh and Sir Raza Ali; Rt. Hon. M. R. Jayakar, former judge of the Federal Court; Pundit Kunzru, President of the Servants of India Society; Sir Purushottamdaas Thakurdas, President of the British Imperial Citizenship Association; Sir Jagadish Prasad, former Minister-in-charge of the Indians Overseas Department; M. A. Jinnah, President of the All-India Muslim League; Bhuluhbai Desai, leading Congress figure; V. D. Savarkar, President of the Hindu Maha Sabha; Tara Singh, leader of the Sikh group in the Central Legislative Assembly; Sir Frederick James, Leader of the European group in the Central Legislative Assembly; Sir Henry Richardson, another leader of the European group in the Assembly; Professor V. G. Kale, authority on Indian overseas affairs; Seth Ramkrishna Dalmia, industrialist; Kumararataja of Chettinad, commercial magnate. The Congress and Muslim League representatives did not attend the conference.[44]

The conference resolved that the Government of India should take steps to vindicate the self-respect of Indians domiciled in South Africa. Dr. Khare acted on this recommendation by amending the Indian Reciprocity Act of March, 1943 (which he was informed could not be brought into force because of certain technical legal difficulties) on 26th July, 1943. With the passing of the amended Act, the Government of India decided in August, 1943, to enforce economic sanctions against South Africa; the sanctions were not to apply to war materials. This exception provided a difficult problem for the Government to decide which goods or material were necessary for the prosecution of war and which were not necessary.[45]

The question of enforcing economic sanctions against South Africa became more difficult when Lord Wavell succeeded Lord Linlithgow as Viceroy in October, 1943. The new Viceroy informed Dr. Khare that he was not prepared to approve of steps against the Union Government because of his close association with General Smuts nor was he prepared to enforce the decisions taken during the term of office of Lord Linlithgow. Dr. Khare states in his Memoirs that "though the bitterness in India against South Africa was rising in tempo, I could not do anything to satisfy the Indian feelings on account of the stonewall in the shape of Lord Wavell". However, when a motion was tabled in the Central Legislative Assembly censuring the Government of India for failing to take steps against South Africa, Lord Wavell approached Dr. Khare to see that the member concerned withdrew the motion as it would embarrass the Government. Dr. Khare agreed to do so provided the Viceroy undertook to enter into personal correspondence with General Smuts in order to find some solution to the pressing problems. This was a political manoeuvre, as Dr. Khare admits, to get the Viceroy involved in the issues in question – not that any hope was cherished that the personal correspondence would be productive of any good.[46]

The Viceroy kept to his part of the undertaking but no reply was received from General Smuts. Consequently, Lord Wavell consented that the Executive Council could deliberate on the retaliatory measures. His hands were at last being forced in spite of his reluctance to act against the Smuts Government. Lord Wavell had not only to contend with pressure from the Indian nationalists on the Viceroy's Council but also from the members of the Central Legislative Assembly where a full debate was held on the "Pegging" Act. Here, too, the debate was initiated by Dr. Khare who said: "Had India been independent, she would have considered this a *casus belli* against South Africa." He called for action – even symbolic action – against South Africa and reminded the British Government of its moral responsibility towards the Indians. Sir Henry Richardson, Leader of the European group, suggested that the British Government should request the Union Government to invite a delegation from India to discuss the future of the Indian community in South Africa. Other speakers strongly criticized the British Government for failing to protect the interests of the Indians in South Africa. Among them was Liaquat Ali Khan, Deputy Leader of the Muslim League, later to become the first Prime Minister of Pakistan, who said that if the British Government had exerted any pressure he was sure the South African Government would have stayed their hands. Khan said that the war could not be made an excuse for delaying any action, for the war itself was being fought for preserving the honour, liberty and self-respect of humanity. The Central Legislative Assembly adopted the following motion:

"The position arising out of the recent Pegging legislation in South Africa be taken into consideration with a view to enforcing the Reciprocity Act and adopting measures to redress the grievances of Indians in South Africa."[47]

In the face of such outspoken criticism, Lord Wavell could no longer brush the issue aside. The opposition against the "Pegging" Act was now directed towards ways and means of employing retaliatory measures. The Indian Reciprocity Act of March, 1943 was amended in July to make enforcement possible. The Viceroy had till then delayed the actual enforcement. The relations between South Africa and India were getting worse by the day. General Smuts could not remain unmindful of the unsettling effect this rift had on the war situation. At home he blamed the agitation of the Indians in South Africa for the passing of the amendment to the Indian Reciprocity Act. Because of this he even refused to meet a delegation from the South African Indian Congress. This refusal brought into prominence the two standards of treatment which were represented in the policy of Smuts. The *Natal Witness* wrote that the difficulties concerning Indians should be approached with statesmanship and courage. "They will not be overcome by denying outright for domestic application the principles the Prime Minister advocates for world acceptance."[48]

India with her growing nationalism and her impending independence would no longer accept the two-standard policy of General Smuts. In the Indian Parliamentary debates it was being suggested that the Indian High Commissioner in South Africa be withdrawn as a mark of protest against the "Pegging" Act, for that office after 1941 was little more than "a mere post office". It was suggested, too, that the South African Trade Commissioner in India should return to South Africa.

The "Pegging" Act had created a great upheaval and it was difficult to see how it would serve to maintain a period of calm for three years when in less than three months of its being such great internal and external complications had set in. In India the Government and the people were opposed to it. In South Africa it served to bring about the amalgamation of the Natal Indian Association and Natal Indian Congress. These two bodies had branched off in 1939. On 18th July, 1943, the Unity Agreement was drafted by which the political groups affiliated as one to the Natal Indian Congress which had been established in 1894 by M. K. Gandhi. The High Commissioner for India, Sir Shafa'at Ahmad Khan, took part in the discussions leading to the amalgamation; he presided over the inaugural meeting of the new Natal Indian Congress. With this amalgamation ended the friction for the time being between the Indian political leaders in Natal so that they might concentrate their interest and their energy in the fight against the "Pegging" Act.[49]

This "fight" was not long in coming and it brought with it unfavourable publicity for the Union Government. In November, P. R. Pather (one of the Secretaries of the newly-formed Natal Indian Congress) was prosecuted under the Act for occupying his house in Moore Road after 22nd March, 1943. Pather was sentenced to a fine of £5 or seven days' imprisonment. Pather, who had been a member of the Lawrence Committee, refused to pay the fine. His prosecution was the subject of questions asked in the House of Commons.

The Government of South Africa had to counter the unfavourable publicity which the operation of the Act was bringing. The Minister of the Interior, Senator C. F. Clarkson, delivered an address to the Natal Municipal Executive in Pietermaritzburg in which he pointed out that Natal and the Transvaal would have to face the question of restoring some form of franchise to the Indians. "We cannot expect the Indian population", he said, "which now equals the European population in Natal, to be voiceless in the control of Municipal and State affairs."[50]

The Minister also arranged a meeting between the Natal Indian Congress and the Natal Municipal Association. This meeting failed to result in any improvement as Congress maintained that Europeans should object only to juxtapositional residence between Europeans and Indians while the Association contended that Europeans objected to both acquisition by Indians as well as to occupation. No amount of local effort on the part of the Government, like the well-meaning gesture by Senator Clarkson, would serve any useful purpose until by and large Europeans in the country (especially in Natal) would accept the changes and improvements suggested.

Senator Clarkson's efforts to improve the internal situation, abortive though they were, were revived when the Government announced the appointment of the Commission of Enquiry into Matters Affecting the Indian Population of the Province of Natal, commonly referred to as the third Broome Commission. The appointment of this Commission had been promised by the Minister of the Interior, H. G. Lawrence, during the debates on the "Pegging" Bill. It was to go into all matters pertaining to Indians in Natal and especially to report on how best to implement the "uplift" clauses of the Cape Town Agreement. The members of the Commission were Justice Broome (Chairman); W. M. Power, M.E.C., Natal; Senator D. G. Shepstone; A. L. Barns; A. I. Kajee and S. R. Naidoo – the two last-named representing the Natal Indian Congress. The Indian members made it clear that they regarded themselves as free to continue to work for the repeal or the withdrawal of the "Pegging" Act.[51]

Before the Commission began its public sittings, another move was made and accepted to minimise the drastic measures in the "Pegging" Act. This was the acceptance of the famous Pretoria Agreement. On 29th March, 1944, the South African Indian Congress presented a memorandum to the Prime Minister, General Smuts, in which it was pointed out that the effect of the "Pegging" Act had been to freeze the elementary right of ownership and occupation of property. The memorandum admitted that "though unreasonable there is on the question of living in close proximity between Europeans and Indians a problem on which issues should be joined and to which a solution should be found". It suggested that the "Pegging" Act be annulled and that, for Durban, its place should be taken temporarily by a Board or Committee of two Europeans and two Indians with a chairman with legal training. This Board or Committee should have the power to issue licences for occupation of houses in areas where there was "a sharp racial distinction of residential property occupation". In this way it proposed to solve the problem of juxta-positional living.[52]

Arising from the suggestions made by the South African Indian Congress, the Prime Minister and the Minister of the Interior met the Administrator of Natal and D. E. Mitchell, M.E.C., Senator D. G. Shepstone and the following representatives of the Natal Indian Congress: A. I. Kajee, P. R. Pather, S. R. Naidoo, A. B. Moosa, T. N. Bhoola, M. Ebrahim and S. M. Paruk in connection with matters arising out of the application of the "Pegging" Act in Natal. At the end of the meeting, held in Pretoria on 18th April, 1944, the Prime Minister issued a press statement in which the proposals of the South African Indian Congress of 29th March were embodied together with the addition that the Board would be constituted in terms of an Ordinance to be introduced by the Natal Provincial Council, whereupon the "Pegging" Act would be withdrawn by proclamation.[53] After this meeting General Smuts sent a cable to Lord Wavell, Viceroy of India, informing him of the constitution of the board of five members and of the agreement which "provides a fair solution of the trouble which has arisen in connection with the Pegging Act and will, I trust, be as welcome to Your Excellency as it has been to me".[54]

The troubles were far from over. General Smuts' optimism was misplaced. For one thing the Pretoria Agreement received a mixed reception. A section of the Indian community denounced it as a betrayal by their leaders in that it was a voluntary acceptance of segregation; the rank and file of the Indians suspected that the wealthy Indians would use the agreement to invest their wealth in the purchase of property in Durban. In their eyes, those Indians who had negotiated the agreement were "wealthy Indians". The Europeans opposed the Pretoria Agreement because those primarily concerned, viz., the Durban City Council and the burgesses of Durban were not consulted at all. Their attitude, as the Commission put it, was: "We have got the Pegging Act; why should we surrender any of its protection without being consulted in the matter at all?"[55]

Though the Pretoria Agreement met with a great measure of local opposition, it was an attempt at modifying the provisions of the "Pegging" Act and to that extent it received the support of the Government of India.[56] In terms of the Agreement the Natal Provincial Council was empowered to introduce an Ordinance which would create a Board to prevent juxtapositional living. The Natal Provincial Council drafted an Ordinance which was rejected by the Natal Indian Congress as being contrary to the agreed terms. A second Ordinance called the Draft Occupational Control Ordinance was introduced and was accepted by the authorities concerned, both Central and Provincial, as being in accordance with the Agreement on all essential points. But the second Ordinance met with firm opposition from the Europeans and the Provincial Council referred it to a Select Committee which submitted an entirely new Draft Ordinance called the Residential Property Regulation Draft Ordinance.

The Natal Indian Congress claimed that the latest draft was in conflict with the Pretoria Agreement in many respects. It made provision for the control of acquisition of residential property whereas the Pretoria Agreement was concerned only with the occupation of individual dwellings; the scope of the new Draft Ordinance was not limited to Durban; it gave statutory legality to voluntary agreements arrived at between local authorities and local Indian communities; it interfered in the sphere of property transactions; it made provision for the European members of the Board to be drawn from persons nominated by local authorities and the views of the town councils or town boards had to be taken into account.[57]

The Residential Property Regulation Draft Ordinance was not an off-shoot of the Pretoria Agreement. It was one of four Ordinances which were, at the time, interdependent and "designed to relegate the Indian community to certain specific areas" – a principle which Indians had always opposed. The three other Ordinances were the Natal Housing Board Ordinance, the Provincial and Local Authorities Expropriation Ordinance and the Town Planning Ordinance.

The Natal Indian Congress refused to accept the Draft Ordinance and carried its protests from the Provincial level to the Prime Minister. One of its officials, A. I. Kajee, even appeared at the Bar of the Provincial Council on 30th October, 1944.[58]

The Natal Indian Congress had by now put its case before the Natal Provincial Council; it had conveyed its protests to the Administrator and to the Prime Minister. In spite of all this, the Draft Ordinance passed through all its stages by 2nd November, 1944. Simultaneously with this Ordinance, two other Ordinances, the Natal Housing Board Ordinance and the Provincial and Local Authorities Expropriation Ordinance were also passed. These Ordinances gave rise to yet another bitter agitation among the Indian community in South Africa and in India. The atmosphere was so charged with racial bitterness that the third Broome Commission, which had hitherto been working in an atmosphere of goodwill and co-operation from the Indian community, decided on 3rd November, 1944, not to continue its public sittings.[59] Three weeks later, on 28th November, 1944, the Natal Indian Congress deputation met the Prime Minister to protest against the three Ordinances recently passed. After the interview the Prime Minister announed that the Pretoria Agreement was "stone dead" and that the first objectionable Ordinance would not be assented to as long as the "Pegging" Act remained unrepealed.[60]

The Pretoria Agreement, like its forerunner the Lawrence Committee, was now no more. The Agreement had aimed at modifying the "Pegging" Act but had failed to do so. It had, however, the indirect result of bringing into power the more militant nationalist group of the Natal Indian Congress, the Anti-Segregation Council, which came into being on 7th May, 1944, under the leadership of Dr. G. M. Naicker to protest against the Pretoria Agreement.[61] The Council finally ousted the old Congress leadership of the Kajee–Pather group and took over the reins of the Natal Indian Congress on 21st October, 1945.

All these were the direct results of the passing of the "Pegging" Act in 1943 in the war-time atmosphere of a troubled world. The Government of India, ever since the beginning of the Wavell administration, had hesitated to act against South Africa. The failure of the Natal Provincial Council to carry out the terms of the Pretoria Agreement, the appearance of the three objectionable Ordinances, the adjournment of the third

Broome Commission, the introduction of pressure from within the Viceroy's Council, especially from Dr. N. B. Khare, Member in charge of the Indians Overseas Department, finally compelled Lord Wavell to agree to the holding of an Executive Council meeting on 2nd November, 1944, to discuss the South African Indian question. On that day the Viceroy summoned a private meeting of his four Councillors on the Viceroy's Council, Sir A. Ramaswami Mudaliar, Sir Sultan Ahmed, Sir Azizul Huq and Dr. Khare. He suggested to the meeting that a delegation from India comprising Sir Ramaswami and Dr. Khare should wait upon the British Government with regard to the South African Indian question and take the advice of this Government especially as it was war time. Until then the Government of India should not debate the South African Indian question. Sir Ramaswami agreed to the proposals but Dr. Khare objected for the reasons that the British Government had been responsible "for all the insults, miseries and misfortunes suffered by the Indians in South Africa" and that they were fully aware of the facts. "There is nothing new that we can tell them", said Dr. Khare. "They are not at all inclined to help us." Dr. Khare refused to be a member of any delegation to England.

At the Executive Council Meeting the Viceroy's proposal was turned down and a rider was added to it that if the British Government wanted such a deputation from India it would be sent. Not long afterwards the British Government informed the Government of India that it was opposed to the sending of a delegation to England from India to discuss the South African Indian question. Dr. Khare pressed for the enforcement of economic sanctions against South Africa and the Executive Council agreed to it. On 4th November, 1944, the *Extraordinary Gazette of India* published news of the enforcement of the Indian Reciprocity Amendment Act against South African Europeans. The Act provided for the treatment in India on a reciprocal basis of persons of non-Indian origin domiciled in other British possessions in regard to the entry into, travel, residence, acquisition or holding of property, enjoyment of educational facilities, holding of public offices, the carrying on of any occupation, trade, business or profession. The Act had three sets of rules: (a) the Reciprocity (South Africa) Rules under which all persons of non-Indian origin domiciled in South Africa were declared prohibited immigrants and as such were not allowed to enter or reside in India without obtaining exemptions or entry permits; (b) the Reciprocity (Natal and Transvaal) Rules under which persons of non-Indian origin domiciled in the Transvaal and Natal could not acquire any property without a permit from the Government of India or occupy any land or premises in India which was not occupied by a South African before 1st December, 1944; and (c) the Reciprocity (South Africa) Local Franchise Rules which debarred persons of non-Indian origin domiciled in the Union, excepting the Cape Province, from the franchise of a local authority in India unless already on the electoral roll before the commencement of the Act.[63]

Following on the announcement of 4th November, 1944, came the meeting of the Central Legislative Assembly on the 6th November, 1944. At this meeting Dr. Khare said: "Our patience is now completely exhausted and the whole nation is in the mood of desperation. We have already told the Government of the Union of South Africa in the plainest and most unequivocal terms that the Government of India now hold themselves free to take such counter measures as they can." The Central Legislative Assembly adopted a motion stating that economic sanctions against South Africa be enforced and that the Government of India exercise its powers under the Reciprocity Act. "Thus it was", said Dr. Khare, "for the first time in the history of British rule in India that the principle of retaliation was adopted and enforced by the dependent Government of India against an independent fellow member of the British Empire."[64]

The enforcement of the Reciprocity measure was not expected to solve the burning problems in South Africa. Indeed, even Dr. Khare compared it to "a baby's bottle with only the rubber teat and no milk". But it was a symbolic expression of India's determination to take action at last, even though the remedies available were insignificant in the overall picture: such incidents as two Europeans from South Africa landing at Karachi, who, fearing deportation, left hurriedly for home again and a board at the Taj Mahal Hotel, Bombay, reading "South African Europeans not allowed" – insignificant in themselves – were nevertheless India's latest reply (and its most militant thus far) to the problems existing in South Africa.

Nationalist India, on the eve of V-Day, was evolving a "victory" of its own kind. This was to be seen in its enthusiastic and lively agitation against South Africa. The third Broome Commission criticised this agitation especially where misrepresentations were disseminated but found that there was nothing wrong with India being interested in the welfare of her descendants in South Africa. In its Interim Report the Commission recommended that the Union Government invite the Government of India to send a delegation to the Union, made up substantially of Indians to discuss all matters affecting the Indians in South Africa; that the invitation be sent early by the Union Government; that the Commission be adjourned while the negotiations were taking place and that upon the acceptance of the invitation the Commission be dissolved.[65]

The Commission felt that the Indian question in South Africa after the introduction of the "Pegging" Act was so serious that inter-governmental negotiations between India and South Africa should be resumed. The war was reaching its end, giving victory to the Allies, of whom the Indians were a part. Their contribution in India, overseas and in South Africa, was lauded on many occasions.[66]

Though the war served to focus further attention on the increasing constitutional reforms in India and gained for Nationalist India the promise that at the end of the war full independence would be accorded to India, in South Africa the internal situation was not altered in any significant way by the advent of war. If anything, the cry of penetration was South Africa's battle-cry and the Indian was public enemy No. 1 as far as this cry was concerned. The Government could not be put off even by a common struggle from tackling the issues in dispute. War-time South Africa was bold enough to appoint three commissions under the charge of a single commissioner to enquire into the Indian question in the country. South Africa was emboldened to act in terms of the second Report – the most convenient one – and to place on the Statute Book the much hated "Pegging" Act which was to have a torrid effect on the national and international scenes.

Except for the war itself and the international complications resulting from the visits of Indian soldiers and civilians to South Africa in transit to and from Great Britain and India, the most important single landmark in the study of the Indian question in South Africa from an international standpoint during the war years was the passing of the "Pegging" Act. This Act received echoes in London, New Delhi and the capitals of many cities on the Allied and enemy sides. It brought together the rival Indian political parties in Natal; had the same effect in India with this difference that it served to weld the people and the Government together into a united front. It resulted in the passing of the Indian Reciprocity Act and its amendments and led to bitter denunciations of the Governments of South Africa and Great Britain.

South Africa tried to redeem herself during the war years by the experiments of the Lawrence Committee and the Pretoria Agreement. But the non-statutory provisions characteristic of them had no place in a hostile atmosphere where protection was sought not by the force of reason, by the virtue of justice, but by the letter of the law.

India's position on the international plane had important consequences for the internal situation in South Africa. The Quit India programme of 1942 did not pass off lightly in this country. The militant attitude of the Indians Overseas Department, headed by Dr. N. B. Khare, had much to do with the acquiescence by the British Viceroy, Lord Wavell, a friend of Smuts, with the policy of retaliation. Though this policy was not productive of immediate and tangible gains the obvious conclusion was that as Nationalist India came nearer to the day of ultimate and complete independence, more forceful steps would be taken against South Africa.

During the war years the Union Government had signified its intentions to keep South Africa safe for the Europeans. On the other hand the Indians, whilst not challenging the propriety of this aim, were themselves interested in safeguarding their own interests in the country. They continued to appeal to India and India continued to answer their call. Great Britain was no longer in the picture, though as "trustee" of India she was rightly the trustee of India's descendants. Great Britain was no longer interested in the South African Indian question and even refused to receive a delegation from India on this issue.

A few months remained for the "Pegging" Act to reach the end of its three years' run. The Government of India was anxious that something better should take its place and consequently summoned its High Commissioner, Ramrao Desmukh, to India for consultations with the Government.

India's concern over the lot of the South African Indians as well as that felt by the local Indians is understandable when it is recalled that even such a time as war time failed to earn a measure of respite for the greatly-troubled Indian community of South Africa. The pattern of South African life since the early days of Law 3/1885 of the Transvaal had now taken a full turn when in Natal, too, the acquisition and the occupation of property were to be regulated by law – even though it was "pegged" for the moment. The question which the Indians in South Africa could very well ask now was: If so much during war time how much more when the world would be free after the dawn of peace?[67]

FOOTNOTES

1. The name of this body was suggested to and agreed upon by Mahatma Gandhi. The first officials were: President, Hajee A. M. M. Lockhat; Joint Secretaries, Sorabjee Rustomjee and P. R. Pather.
2. Shafa'at Ahmad Khan, *The Indians in South Africa*, p. 312.
3. Smith, *The Oxford History of India*, p. 825. Chapter 7, pp. 820–828 deals with India and the War, 1939–1945.
4. *Ibid.*, pp. 821–3. At one time there were more than 2 million Indians in the armed forces.
5. *Leader*, 22nd February, 1941, 4th January, 1941, 5th July, 1941 and 24th October, 1942.
6. Natal Indian Association, *Statement to the Minister of the Interior on Alleged Indian Penetration*, p. 4. This is cited hereafter as *Statement*. The chairman and secretary of the Lawrence Committee were the Mayor and the Town Clerk of the Durban City Council respectively. In 1941 the Indian representatives were A. Christopher, J. W. Godfrey, A. S. Kajee, P. B. Singh, P. R. Pather and Sorabjee Rustomjee.
7. *Leader*, 28th December, 1940; 11th January, and 18th January, 1941.
8. *Leader*, 18th January, 1941, 21st June, 1941 and 24th October, 1942. Members of the I.C.S. were very much in disfavour among the Indians both in India and in South Africa as they were servants of a bureaucracy which was resented at this time. The charge against the I.C.S. was "that the government servants will merely dance to their master's tune".
9. Report of the High Commissioner for India, 1942, pp. 5–6.
10. *Leader*, 16th January, 1943.
11. Report of the High Commissioner for India, 1942, pp. 4–5.
12. Report of the High Commissioner, 1942, p. 9.
13. Sir Shafa'at Ahmad Khan, *The Indians in South Africa*, pp. 88–9. *Vide* also pp. 104 and 117.
14. *Leader*, 11th April, 1942.
15. *Ibid.*, 6th September, 1941. The incident is described in the Annual Report of the High Commissioner for 1941 on p. 4. On the 25th August, 1941 the Air Commando visited Pietermaritzburg to give a display of aeronautics. No proper arrangements were apparently made for the spectators: European and non-European spectators crowded on to the ground. "The military police cleared the ground and in doing so appear to have used a certain amount of violence and a great deal of bad language to the non-Europeans, many of whom were Indians."
16. Report of the High Commissioner for India, 1941, p. 4.
17. *Leader*, 20th September, 1941.
18. Natal Indian Association, *Statement*, Appendix D, pp. 16–17.
19. Report of the High Commissioner for India, 1942, p. 10.
20. Report of the Indian Penetration Commission, U.G. 39/1941, p. 1.
21. Joshi, *The Tyranny of Colour*, pp. 270–2.
22. *Ibid.*, pp. 272–4. Some of those arrested were Dr. Y. M. Dadoo, H. A. Naidoo, C. I. Amra, R. K. Naidoo, K. S. Pillay, and D. A. Seedat.
23. Report of the Indian Penetration Commission, U.G. 39/41, Chap. III, pp. 12–16, and Chap. IV, p. 18.
24. Report of the Indian Penetration Commission, U.G. 39/1941, Chap. II, pp. 40–41. The 339 cases of penetration may be classified as follows:

	Trade	Residence	Total
Urban	150	82	232
Rural Township	40	3	43
Rural	56	8	64
Total	246	93	339

25. *Leader*, 5th July, 1941.
26. Report of the Second Indian Penetration (Durban) Commission, U.G. 21/1943, p. 1.
27. *Leader*, 13th March, 1943.

28. Report of the Indian High Commissioner, 1943, p. 6.
29. Report of the Second Indian Penetration Commission, U.G. 21/1943, p. 3. A detailed table of the 326 cases is as follows:

	No. of sites	Purchase price £	Rateable value £
1940 (Oct.–Dec.)	12	10 370	7 550
1941	77	153 045	116 560
1942	195	336 500	241 200
1943 (Jan.–Feb.)	42	101 470	64 550
Total, Oct. 1940 to Feb. 1943	326	£601 385	£429 860

30. Report of the High Commissioner for India, 1943, p. 7.
31. The Trading and Occupation of Land (Transvaal and Natal) Restriction Bill 35/1943, and Report of the High Commissioner for India, 1943, p. 7. All acquisitions or occupations were to be controlled by permits from the Minister.
32. Report of the High Commissioner for India, 1943, p. 7.
33. Natal Indian Congress, *Statement on the Alleged Question of Indian Penetration to the Hon. The Minister of the Interior*, pp. 4–7.
34. Report of the High Commissioner for India, 1943, p. 8.
35. House of Assembly Debates, Vol. 46, 1943, p. 5394.
36. *Ibid.*, pp. 5394–5400.
37. Senate Debates, Seventh Session, Fourth Senate, 1943, pp. 2085–6.
38. Report of the High Commissioner for India, 1943, p. 10.
39. *Leader*, 1st May, 1943.
40. *Leader*, 29th May, 1943.
41. Report of the High Commissioner for India, 1943, p. 13 and Bhawani Dayal Sannyasi and others, *Economic Sanctions Against Africa: Their Need and Feasibility*, Foreword.
42. Information extracted from the Official Year Book of the Union of South Africa, 1940, relating to figures for the year ending 1939, shows:

Imports into South Africa

Total: £91 321 226   From India: £2 257 058
                           From British Commonwealth: £49 252 016

Exports from South Africa

Total: £34 162 744   To India: £388 257
                           To British Commonwealth: £17 768 653

Vide Bhawani Dayal Sannyasi and others, *Economic Sanctions Against South Africa*, pp. 8–9.

Indo-South African Trade

	Exports	Imports	Balance of trade in favour of India
1941–42	Rs. 5,88,49,218	Rs.1,23,86,764	Rs.4,64,62,454
1942–43	Rs.10,49,38,162	Rs.2,24,97,516	Rs.8,24,40,646

43. *Leader*, 24th July, 1943.
44. N. B. Khare, *My Political Memoirs*, pp. 155–6.
45. Khare, *My Political Memoirs*, p. 157.
46. *Ibid.*, pp. 158–160.
47. *Leader*, 2nd October, 1943.
48. *Leader*, 14th August, 1943, quotes *Natal Witness*, 12th August, 1943.
49. Report of the High Commissioner for India, 1943, p. 18 and pp. 13–14.
50. Natal Indian Congress, Agenda Book of Provincial Conference, 1944.
51. Interim Report of the Commission, U.G. 22/1945, pp. 5–8.
52. S.A.I.C., Memo submitted to the Prime Minister, 29th March, 1944.

53. S.A.I.C., Press Statement by the Prime Minister, 18th April, 1944.
54. S.A.I.C., *Documents*, Statement on the Residential Property Regulation Draft Ordinance.
55. Interim Report of the Third Broome Commission, U.G. 22/1945, p. 6.
56. Khare, *My Political Memoirs*, p. 166.
57. Interim Report of the Third Broome Commission, pp. 6–7.
58. S.A.I.C., *Documents*, A. I. Kajee's Speech, 30th October, 1944.
59. Interim Report of the Commission, p. 8.
60. *Leader*, 9th December, 1944.
61. *Leader*, 13th May, 1944.
62. Khare, *My Political Memoirs*, pp. 160–1.
63. Kondapi, *Indians Overseas*, pp. 494–5.
64. Khare, *My Political Memoirs*, pp. 164–7.
65. Interim Report of the Commission, p. 9 and pp. 18–19.
66. India's war effort can be gleaned from the following comparative table:

COMMONWEALTH, 1939–1943

Country	Killed	Missing	Wounded	Prisoner of War	Total	Percentage
U.K.	120 958	29 489	93 822	143 947	387 995	53,2
U.K. (Civilian)	49 730	—	59,371	109 101	—	—
India	5 912	17 819	12 238	78 848	109 800	16,4
Australia	12 292	11 887	18 383	28 789	74 338	11,1
New Zealand	5 829	884	11 315	7 898	25 717	3,8
Canada	8 709	2 745	3 983	4 380	19 697	2,9
South Africa	3 132	279	6 473	1 398	23 825	3,6
Colonies	1 635	15 130	1 803	7 213	25 786	3,8
Total	158 741	78 204	159 219	270 995	667 159	

Vide Leader, 10th June, 1944.

67. Representatives of the Government of India in South Africa:
    Agents:
    1. V. S. S. Sastri, 1927–1929.
    2. Sir Kurma Reddy, 1929–1932.
    3. Kunwar Sir Maharaj Singh, 1932–1935.
    Agents-General:
    4. Sir Sayed Raza Ali, 1935–1938.
    5. Sir Bengal Rama Rau, 1938–1941.
    High Commissioners:
    6. Sir Shafa'at Ahmad Khan, 1941–1945.
    7. R. Desmukh, 1945–1946.
    Vide Report of the High Commissioner for India, 1945, p. 11.

CHAPTER SIX

THE ROAD TO UNITED NATIONS, 1945–1946

"If it be accepted that the primary value of the U.N. is to serve as an instrument for negotiation among Governments and for concerting action by Governments in support of the goals of the Charter, it is also necessary, I believe, to use the legislative procedures of the U.N. consistently in ways which will promote these ends. In an organization of sovereign States, voting victories are likely to be illusory unless they are steps in the direction of winning lasting consent to a peaceful and just settlement of the questions at issue."

MR. DAG HAMMARSKJOLD
(Late Secretary-General of United Nations)

The Second World War, "fought against the deification of the nation state",[1] was an event of great moment for the freedom-loving peoples of the world, who combined their resources for a common cause under the banner of the "United Nations". South Africa and India were two of the many members of this "coalition of victors". Beneath the surface old differences remained. Both of them were vexed by the question relating to the Indian population. In the first country it centred largely on the issue of acquisition and the occupation of property which, for the moment, transcended all other issues; in the second it was a matter of obtaining complete political independence already enhanced by the war fought in the name of freedom.

One of the results of the war was the birth of the United Nations Organisation. The organisation had its origins on 1st January, 1942, when the representatives of 26 nations, including South Africa, made the declaration by United Nations which was signed in Washington. The term "United Nations" was suggested by Franklin Delano Roosevelt, President of the United States of America, and was accepted at the San Francisco Conference when the Charter was signed on 26th June, 1945, as a tribute to the late President who died shortly before the United Nations Organisation was finally established.[2]

The draft constitution for the United Nations Organisation was formulated in the Dumbarton Oaks Proposals for the Establishment of a General International Organisation, on 7th October, 1944. At the Crimean Conference on February 11th, 1945, at which were present delegates from the U.S.A., the U.K., and the U.S.S.R., headed respectively by President F. D. Roosevelt, W. S. Churchill and Marshal J. V. Stalin, the foundations laid at Dumbarton Oaks were considered further and an agreement was reached that a conference of United Nations should meet at San Francisco on April 25th, 1945, to prepare the charter of such an organisation along the lines proposed at Dumbarton Oaks.

South Africa was signally honoured when her Prime Minister, General Smuts, who had been co-founder of the League of Nations, was invited to write the preamble to the Charter of the United Nations. The Charter of the United Nations was signed at San Francisco on June 26th, 1945. Thus another world organisation had come into being, offering new hope for the future. The coming years would show what part the new world organisation would play in the affairs of South Africa for the Indian question was rapidly outgrowing the confines of the South Africa-India orbit. There was need for an international solution. Every opportunity was being utilised to discuss the conflict and to try to find a solution. The issue was even raised at the Commonwealth Relations Conference in London in March, 1945. An Indian judge, Sir Muhammed Zafrullah Khan, led the case for the South African Indians in the discussion on the question of relations between Indians and Europeans in South Africa. A former Agent-General for India in South Africa, Kunwar Sir Maharaj Singh, was the deputy leader. He told the conference that if the Commonwealth was to continue as such all forms of racial discrimination should cease. He said that the only difference between the Commonwealth practice and the Nazi theory of race superiority was that in the Commonwealth it was practised but not openly professed.

A memorandum on the South African Indian question was submitted to the Indian delegation by the Natal Indian Congress. The up-and-coming Anti-Segregation Council of the Natal Indian Congress sent a telegram to the Indian delegation congratulating it on its "uncompromising stand against the bestial forces of colour, oppression and Fascist-like treatment of your brethren in South Africa".[3] A delegation headed by the Labour Member of Parliament, Fenner Brockway, representing the Indian Freedom Campaign, also informed the delegates attending the Conference about the lot of Indians in South Africa.

Meanwhile, in India, the Government was censured by some members for not imposing economic sanctions against South Africa. Dr. Khare, the member for Commonwealth Relations, said that the enforcement of economic sanctions required careful consideration and he hoped the House would give the Government of India some discretion in the matter of carrying out further measures. He said that as regards the imposition of restrictions on residence, the number of South Africans in India was too small for India to apply those restrictions against them. Dr. Khare agreed that there was some delay but said that everything possible was being done.

With all these developments taking place in various quarters there was some hope that the official government attitude in South Africa would change in the near future. The *Manchester Guardian* speculated that if the South African liberal, Jan H. Hofmeyr, became the country's next prime minister race and colour questions would create fewer problems under his leadership.

But General Smuts was still in office and the official United Party attitude was as before. On 21st January, 1946, the Prime Minister made an announcement in the House of Assembly on the proposed measure which would take the place of the "Pegging" Act which was due to lapse on 31st March, 1946. General Smuts said that it was the intention of his government to introduce a Bill during that session of Parliament to deal with land tenure in Natal. This would have retrospective effect as from the date of his announcement.[4] The Government of India was taken unawares by this announcement which envisaged the acquisition by Asiatics of property in exempted areas only, for before the Indian High Commissioner had left for India he had called on General Smuts in December, 1945, and the Prime Minister had indicated to him the legislation he had in mind to take the place of the "Pegging" Act. After consultations with his government, the Indian High Commissioner called on General Smuts again and made representations on the contemplated legislation.[5] After these representations, the declaration of the Union Government came as a surprise to the Indian Government as they were given to understand that in the Housing (Emergency Powers) Act and the Natal Housing Ordinance a solution of the Indian problem had been found. The Government of India therefore instructed their High Commissioner to urge upon the Union Government that the legislation should be postponed and that the recommendation of the Broome Commission that representatives from the Government of India and South Africa should meet to explore an alternative settlement of the question be followed. These recommendations were rejected by the Union Government.[6]

The Prime Minister's statement caused an upheaval among Indians in South Africa. The Indian Congresses throughout the country were alerted to act quickly in protest against the proposed measure. The Natal Indian Congress sent a telegram to the Government of India, which read in part:

"Honour of India at stake. The situation demands immediate action to uphold the honour and dignity of Indians abroad. Urge Government of India should raise the question at the General Assembly of UNO."

Congress sent a cable overseas making a similar plea.

A call for aid to world leaders, including the Viceroy of India, Lord Wavell, and to parliamentary and party leaders in India and Britain was sent out by the Transvaal Indian Congress. This call, *inter alia*, pleaded for the exertion of pressure on South Africa to agree to a round table conference.

In India an admission of failure was sounded by Dr. N. B. Khare, member of the Viceroy's Executive Council, Indians Overseas Department, when he told the Legislative Assembly at New Delhi: "As far as I personally am concerned, I am convinced that all our efforts will fail. I have no doubt that in spite of all we do the Government of South Africa is not going to listen to us." He said that the High Commissioner, R. M. Desmukh, was returning to South Africa with instructions from India.

In South Africa a mass meeting of Indians was held in Durban to protest against the Prime Minister's statement. Four days later an official statement released in Pretoria stated that the Union Government had decided to extend the franchise to the Transvaal and Natal Indians on a communal basis – the very basis which the Broome Commission had advised against. Local Indian opposition to the proposals was as keen and animated as that which was being mobilised in India.

On 11th February, 1946, a deputation from the South African Indian Congress waited on the Prime Minister. The South African Indian Congress was in conference in Cape Town at this time. The delegates at the conference decided to make one last appeal to the Prime Minister to postpone the legislation and to arrange for a round table conference with India. Over fifty Indians, headed by A. I. Kajee and Sorabjee Rustomjee, waited on General Smuts. Calpin writes as follows on this interview: "The interview was an uncomfortable experience for all concerned. Some bitter things were said which are best forgotten. General Smuts is slow to anger, and most silent when he is angry. The deputation left, and reported to the conference that their appeals were in vain."[7]

The South African Indian Congress resumed its conference in the knowledge that General Smuts was determined to proceed with the legislation he had in mind. The High

Commissioner for India delivered an important speech to the conference, which outlined India's role in the developments. The speech, because of the aspects covered therein, is given in some detail. Desmukh explained India's stand as follows:

"India's object is to promote good relations, and she is inspired by no desire to interfere in the internal governance of the country. When she is critical of the administration and policies of the country, it is because of the obligation imposed on her under the contract between the two Governments which brought Indians to South Africa's shores.

"This is an obligation imposed on all Governments to protect their countrymen overseas, particularly when those countrymen have not been accorded, in their new country of residence, the full rights of citizenship which would enable them to protect their own interests.

"Moreover in the circumstances of modern times, there is an obligation imposed on all Governments, called on to take part in the counsels of nations, to see that minority groups are accorded that fair treatment which ensures international harmony."[8]

India was striving resolutely to find an honourable solution to the important questions concerning the South African Indians. This was an uphill task for if the "Pegging" Act could make its appearance in the difficult days of the war and if the recommendations of the third Broome Commission calling for a round table conference could be ignored then the appeals engineered by the Indian members of the Viceroy's Council and the Central Legislative Assembly in the peace-time climate of 1946 were capable of achieving less.

The local Indians, however, would not accept failure without a strenuous fight on their part. On 12th February, 1946, the South African Indian Congress took an important decision to mobilise all the resources of the Indian people in South Africa to secure the lapsing of the Pegging Act and to oppose the proposed legislation of the Government by sending a deputation to India to urge the Government of India to convene a round table conference between the governments of India and South Africa and failing which to request the government to withdraw its High Commissioner and to apply economic sanctions against South Africa; and also to carry out a propaganda campaign in India to receive general support from the Indians. Congress also decided to invite Indian leaders to South Africa and to send deputations to America, Britain and other parts of the world. Internally, Congress resolved to prepare the South African Indians for a prolonged resistance against the new measure proposed by the government.[9]

The delegation to India was to comprise Advocate A. Christopher, Sorabjee Rustomjee, S. R. Naidoo, M. D. Naidoo, A. S. Kajee, A. A. Mirza and S. M. Desai, the last named from the Transvaal. The delegation to visit Britain and America comprised A. I. Kajee, Dr. Y. M. Dadoo, A. M. Moola, Rev. B. L. E. Sigamoney and P. R. Pather. Dr. G. M. Naicker who was the president of the Natal Indian Congress declined nomination.

M. D. Naidoo, a joint hon. secretary of the Natal Indian Congress, in a letter to Sorabjee Rustomjee, refused to be associated with the S.A.I.C. delegation to India. He feared that a compromise solution on the lines of the Pretoria Agreement would be accepted. He stated that it was a calculated insult to Natal to be given one delegate out of seven and to have had Natal's proposal for the inclusion of A. I. Kajee and A. I. Meer in the delegation to India turned down. The old problem of in-fighting, group thinking and personality clashes would appear from time to time. It was inevitable that this should happen where important issues were concerned. Their timing was often very unfortunate.

The next phase in the struggle was the introduction of the Asiatic Land Tenure and Indian Representation Bill in the House of Assembly on 15th March, 1946. The following day the first counter-move by the Government of India was announced in the form of a notice of trade sanctions to the Union Government.[10]

Though the Asiatic Land Tenure and Indian Representation Bill falls within the ambit of local affairs, like its forerunner, the "Pegging" Act and its successor, the Group Areas Act, it comes more appropriately within the exclusive group of matters local in origin and character but international in effect and magnitude, necessitating a more than cursory treatment if the international aspects are to be emphasised correctly. For these reasons, therefore, certain details have had to be included.

The Bill followed the Pegging Act very closely in that it applied to both occupation and acquisition of property throughout Natal in urban and rural areas. Two kinds of areas were created: the Controlled Areas and the Uncontrolled Areas. The Controlled Areas were non-Asiatic areas except for properties which had been owned or occupied by Asiatics prior to 21st January, 1946. In these areas an Asiatic might not occupy any property, even his own if such property had not been in Indian occupation prior to 21st January. In these areas no Asiatic might purchase a property from a non-Asiatic and vice versa, save under permit.

The Uncontrolled Areas were set aside by schedules attached to the Bill and were commonly termed free or exempted areas. In these areas there were no restrictions on acquisition or occupation of properties. These areas were already, for the most part, owned and occupied by Asiatics.

In the Controlled Areas, all transactions between Europeans and Asiatics were prohibited unless authorised by permit granted by the Minister of the Interior upon the recommendation of a specially constituted Land Tenure Advisory Board of five members, of whom two might be Indians. The chairman was to be a legal man of at least ten years' standing.[11]

The second chapter of the Bill was devoted to political representation of Indians. The basis was to be communal: two Europeans would represent Transvaal and Natal Indians in the Senate and three Europeans in the House of Assembly. Two members, who might be Indians, were to be elected to the Natal Provincial Council. The qualifications under the Bill for Indian voters were a minimum age of 21 years, Union nationality, Standard VI education and either an income of at least £84 a year or ownership of immovable property valued at not less than £250, over and above any mortgage thereon.

The objections of Indians to the proposed measure were well summarised by Ashwin Choudree and P. R. Pather in their booklet: *A Commentary on the Asiatic Land Tenure and Indian Representation Act* in which they stated that the Act took away from the Indians their inherent human rights to acquire and occupy property anywhere they chose; that for the first time in the history of Indians in Natal areas had been demarcated for acquisition and occupation by Indians; that the motive behind the legislation was to compulsorily segregate the Indians; that it was galling to the Indian community of South Africa and an insult to the national honour of India; that its purpose to control mortgage bonds was an attempt to strangulate the Indian community economically; that the effects of segregation were well known in South Africa and elsewhere and examples of the shocking conditions in which the Indian and coloured people lived in the Transvaal were not uncommon in places such as Benoni, Boksburg, Germiston, Vrededorp, Pretoria Asiatic Bazaar, where civic amenities, if they did exist at all, were in the most primitive stage and where dilapidated wood and iron shanties served as housing for the non-European people; that the offer of communal franchise was only a sop for taking away a right; that communal franchise had been found to be detrimental to the interests of any country wherever it had been tried; that the present legislation abrogated unilaterally the bilateral Cape Town Agreement.[12]

This measure, like the "Pegging" Act before it, aroused a storm of protest from Indians in South Africa and in India. These protests will be considered after the main debating points in the Union legislature are dealt with. The Bill was introduced in the House of Assembly on the 15th March, 1946. It became law in the form of Act 28/1946 on 3rd June, 1946, after a debate which went on record as the longest ever held in the House of Assembly. This fact in itself is an indication of the contentious nature of the proposed legislation and of its far-reaching effects internally and externally.

The Prime Minister, General Smuts, who in the eyes of all his opponents and some of his supporters now appeared as the benefactor of the Indians, was in no easy position in regard to the new measure which was in reality one of racial discrimination and opposed to the idealism of the United Nations whose preamble he had drawn. The Prime Minister insisted that the matter was for the Union to decide; he would brook no interference from outside as the Indians in South Africa were part and parcel of the permanent population of the country. He rejected any suggestion of a round table conference between India and South Africa as there now existed a medium for inter-governmental negotiations through the Indian High Commissioner in South Africa.[13]

The Deputy-Prime Minister, Mr. J. H. Hofmeyr, contrary to expectations in certain circles, gave his support to the measure because it conceded political rights to the Indians and was therefore different from the treatment given to the Indian question in the past where the emphasis had been on "the whittling away of their rights".[14]

The leader of the Dominion Party, Colonel C. F. Stallard, said that he could see no objections to representations being made by India on behalf of the South African Indians and that South Africa should not be "too squeamish" in considering her domestic affairs. However, in regard to the possible appeal to the United Nations for relief, he said that the South African Indians were treading on dangerous grounds as this could lead to their displacement from South Africa.[15]

For the African representatives, Mrs. Ballinger said that in the past when people considered the problems before the country (for which there was no precedent anywhere to guide the country) there was "too little thought and far too much emotion". What was needed, she said, was a formula under which the country could be governed "by consent and not by bludgeon".[16]

The Leader of the Opposition, Dr. D. F. Malan, opposed the measure because of the implications in the second part of the Bill by which the six non-European representatives would hold the balance of power and act as "arbiters between European and European".[17]

No amount of opposition could prevent the Bill from passing the stages in the Assembly. In the Senate, too, strong speeches were made against it by Senators Basner and Brookes. The former presented a petition to be heard at the bar of the House.

On 3rd May, 1946, M. D. Barmania, one of the secretaries of the South African Indian Congress, appeared on behalf of the petitioners and addressed the House for fifty minutes. This was only the second time in 32 years that such a privilege had been granted to appear before the highest tribunal in the land. The petitioners objected to the restrictions on the purchase and occupation of property as well as to communal franchise.[18]

The chief government spokesman, Senator D. G. Shepstone, supported the Bill because it gave the Indian tangible proof that he was a part of the permanent population of South Africa. Shepstone maintained that the Bill offered channels to the Indian which were hitherto closed. He said: "Is it to be wondered at that in his time of trial and stress he turns to India in order that his case may be placed before the South African Government and in order that his rights may be protected? I see nothing wrong in his appealing to India, for the simple reason that he has no channels open to him in this country whereby he can appeal through those channels which are open to every other section of the community, including the Bantu people."[19] Now, of course, with the coming into being of this measure no such appeal was necessary. White support for this measure was prompted, as Senator Edgar Brookes pointed out, by public opinion which in turn was swayed by fear.[20]

No amount of opposition against the Government was strong enough to hold up the measure. After five days of fiery debate in the Senate, the measure was approved. It was a far-reaching one for Indians and it was natural that they would express strong disapproval both in India and in South Africa. On 31st March, 1946, a procession estimated at 6 000 people marched down West Street, Durban, demonstrating against the Bill. The speakers at this demonstration were Dr. G. M. Naicker, for the Natal Indian Congress; Mr. H. I. E. Dhlomo, for the African National Congress; and Mr. L. A. Smith, for the African Peoples' Organisation. The meeting endorsed the decision of the Natal Indian Congress conference "to launch a concerted passive resistance struggle for the defeat of this measure".[21]

It was announced that the passive resistance campaign would open on 13th June – ten days after the measure became law. At this time, too, the government announced the setting up of the Land Tenure Board. The Commissioner for Immigration and Asiatic Affairs, J. H. Basson, asked the Natal Indian Congress for nominations for the two posts reserved for Indian members at a salary scale of £1 500 per annum. Congress rejected the offer and informed Basson that "your request, coming as it does after such unequivocal demonstration of outraged Indian feelings anent the very principles of the 'Ghetto' Act, is deliberately adding insult to injury".[22]

The most significant internal development arising from the Act was the inauguration of the passive resistance struggle. The first phase in this struggle started on 13th June, 1946, with the occupation of a vacant site in Gale Street, Durban, and continued for many months thereafter. Batches of Indians, including some educated Indians of the professional classes – doctors and lawyers – courted arrest and were sent to prison. Even the president of the Natal Indian Congress, Dr. Naicker, was sent to prison. Indian women joined the struggle. Prominent among them were Dr. Goonam and Miss Fatima Meer. Dr. Mabel Palmer states that it is "estimated that nearly two thousand Indians went to prison, offering no resistance either to their arrest or to their treatment in prison".[23]

The significance of the resistance struggle could not be localised. As Calpin says: "It would be a mistake to ignore its significance on other counts. The presence of 2 000 resisters in and out of gaol was an embarrassment to the government and particularly to General Smuts. It carried tremendous propaganda value in England, and in the United States where other people's causes find a quick response, especially when they lie within the framework of what is still described as British imperialism."[24]

Neither was the agitation and protest confined to the domestic scene. The South African Indian Congress delegations set up at the conference at Cape Town in February, 1946, were busy with their respective tasks. On the 12th March, 1946, the delegation to India comprising S. Rustomjee, S. R. Naidoo, A. A. Mirza and A. S. M. Kajee submitted a statement to the Viceroy of India, Lord Wavell. After giving a résumé of anti-Indian developments in South Africa, the delegation said: "We have come all the way from South Africa not to seek protection of individual or property rights, dear as both are, but we have come definitely to ask your Excellency and the people of the Mother Country to appreciate the fight for equality of status, which is theirs as much as ours, and to give us as much help as possible for you and them to give."[25]

The statement of the Congress delegation to the Viceroy was supported by the Aga Khan who headed an associate deputation comprising Sarat Chandra Bose, Leader of the Opposition in the Indian Central Legislative Assembly, Mrs. Sarojini Naidu, representing the Indian National Congress, Homi P. Moody, representing the Imperial Indian Citizenship Association and M. H. Hasham Premji, President of the Indian Merchants' Chamber, Bombay.[26] South African and Indian forces were combining their resources in a common struggle.

On the same day as the Congress deputation interviewed Lord Wavell, i.e. the 12th March, an announcement was made in the Indian Council of State by Dr. N. B. Khare and in the Central Legislative Assembly by R. N. Banerjee to the effect that the Government of India had decided to apply economic sanctions. Dr. Khare reported that all efforts made by the Government of India to arrange for a round table conference between the two countries had failed.[27]

The voice of Mahatma Gandhi was also raised against the measure. Writing in *Harijan* on 24th March, 1946, he said that the course of events had raised at the highest level the question of the policy of the South African Government. He said that, unseen, the policy held the seeds of world war and though India would help more in a moral sense the main brunt would have to be borne by the South African Indians. He recalled their use earlier on of *Satyagraha* and called it their only and ultimate source of power. Addressing the whites of South Africa, Mahatma Gandhi said: "Does real superiority require outside props in the shape of legislation? Will they not see that every such wall of protection weakens them, ultimately rendering them effeminate. The lesson of history ought to teach them that might is not right. Right only is might."[28]

The premier political organisation in India joined in the struggle. In a resolution the All India National Congress proposed counter-measures against the Union. The Congress

Committee could not agree that the Anti-Asiatic measure in South Africa was a domestic affair. It clearly saw that internationalism was the order of the day.

Mr. Nehru, too, threw in his support. As India's future Prime Minister, his part in the struggle is of great significance. He said that he did not expect India to go to war with South Africa on this issue: "I do expect UNO and the rest of the British Empire, if they are in earnest about it, to dissociate themselves from South Africa and cut her away from the family of nations if she follows the Nazi doctrine. If UNO, Europe or America do not do that the time will soon come when all Asia may do that, and so might Africa."[29]

Addressing the South African Indian delegation in the Central Legislative Assembly, Nehru urged that the Indians in South Africa should look at their problem not only as a local issue or one for India but in its widest context as an issue affecting all the oppressed peoples of the world. He asked the delegates to press for the recognition of the rights of all peoples of the world. Indians in South Africa should co-operate with the African people for, "if you consider yourselves their superiors, then others will consider themselves your superiors".[30]

The Asiatic Land Tenure and Indian Representation Act of 1946 had aroused general opposition to its restrictive clauses. National India, on the eve of her independence, could not allow the Act to remain on the South African statute book without arousing the sympathy of the civilised world for the cause of the South African Indians. The member of the Viceroy's Council in charge of the Indians Overseas Department, Dr. N. B. Khare, told the Viceroy that as the war had ended there was no longer any reason to delay the enforcement of economic sanctions against South Africa. He suggested, too, that the Indian Government should show their disapproval of the latest Act by recalling their High Commissioner from South Africa. But Lord Wavell, the Viceroy, was not prepared to act in the manner suggested by Dr. Khare and said that Dr. Khare should visit South Africa for talks with General Smuts before taking any drastic steps against South Africa. Dr. Khare was not prepared to go to South Africa unless he was invited by General Smuts. This was hardly possible at this time as the Union Prime Minister had indicated his stand in the matter by rejecting the recommendation of the third Broome Commission that round table talks should be held between India and South Africa.[31]

The Government of India acted against the Asiatic Land Tenure and Indian Representation Act by resolving, both in the Central Legislative Assembly and in the Council of State, that economic sanctions against South Africa should be enforced and that the High Commissioner should be recalled. These steps were taken against the wishes of the Viceroy himself and they were to date the most drastic measures taken by India against South Africa; their timing coincided with the termination of the war. A promise had been made by the British Government that full national independence would be accorded to India once the war was over. The realisation of this promise was now almost a *fait accompli*. The influence of the British Government could no longer decide the bigger issues in India though it was known as early as March, 1946, that the British Government was opposed to the suggestion mooted by Dr. Khare that the South African Indian question should be placed before the United Nations as such a step would "amount to a radical blow to the very conception of the Empire".[32]

The position had now reached a very serious stage at international level. It did not rest at that for the Indian delegation in Great Britain, comprising Ashwin Choudree and P. R. Pather, were hard at work. From their headquarters in the Strand Imperial Hotel, London, Choudree and Pather issued an interesting and informative booklet: *A Commentary on the Asiatic Land Tenure and Indian Representation Act and A Short Survey of the Indian Question in South Africa*, on 1st May, 1946. They addressed various public and private meetings. Among the organisations whose support they solicited were the India League, Royal Empire Society, the Royal Institute of International Affairs, the Society of Individualists and National League for Freedom, the Society of Friends, the Fabian Society, the National Peace Council, the International Missionary Council and the Women's International League.[33] Resolutions were adopted at the meetings addressed by the delegates condemning the proposed measure and asking that it be abandoned. One of the largest of these meetings was that held on the 5th May, 1946, convened by the National Council of Civil Liberties, embracing some 800 trade unions and other industrial and co-operative organisations, at Grosvenor Place.[34]

The delegation to Britain, as in India, had a successful trip from the point of view of informing overseas opinion and soliciting support against South Africa. When the delegation from Britain returned it was able to say: " . . . we found encouragement and support for our cause from every shade of public opinion. We return profoundly impressed with the deep interest and concern shown by the British people in the treatment by the Union Government of her Indian population".[35]

But the Union Government remained unshaken till the end. It had decided on a programme of work and was not to be deterred in its accomplishment by any measure of opposition or protest. If it had succeeded in placing the Asiatic Land Tenure and Indian Representation Act on the Statute Book it had by no means solved its problems. It had merely gained the verdict in the first round of the struggle, for the struggle was not, and could not be, localised. There were rumblings in the distance that the edifice of UNO was to be the final tribunal: that the voice of internationalism had to be heard. South Africa, before it could claim to have won the fight, had to face UNO and all the members who comprised it. Therein lay the newness in the fight; for the novelty without it would have been, by 1946 at least, well worn. Nearly every aspect of negotiation from 1860 to 1946 in dealings between the South African (and, before that, Natal) Government and the Indian Government had been tried and exhausted. A settlement was still far from being reached. The failures of the past invested UNO with greater responsibility than would have been the case had there been some successes to relieve the position.

In this short chapter which covers the period spanned by the closing months of 1945 and the first half of 1946 some momentous developments had taken place both nationally and internationally. The war had ended and the South African Government no longer felt any constraints in its policy regarding the Indian question (not that the war had in any case imposed any undue restraint on the emotions and the complaints that had led to the "Pegging" Act). The "Pegging" Act expired in March, 1946, and the Union Government placed the Asiatic Land Tenure and Indian Representation Act in its place. There was nothing new in the first part of the Act which was no more than a perpetuation of the legislation dealing with Asiatic land tenure in the Transvaal since 1932 (although in so far as the Act was extended to Natal it was a new thing for which Natal was first prepared when the "Pegging" Act had made its appearance in 1943). The second part offering communal franchise to Indians with white representation in Parliament was the slight improvement which General Smuts' international reputation (recently lauded when he was called upon to draw the Preamble to the United Nations Charter) dictated. Indian political leaders in South Africa rejected this arrangement which was the first attempt at restoring a part of what had been lost in 1896 and 1924 when the parliamentary and municipal franchise, respectively, had been withdrawn. If in India communal franchise on Hindu-Muslim lines had been offered and accepted during an earlier period, there was some wisdom in accepting the second part of the 1946 Act, albeit as a stepping stone and under protest if necessary. But to have rejected it *in toto* was to have believed overmuch in the political predictions which reserved the premiership in the future for Jan H. Hofmeyr and not Dr. Daniel F. Malan. Had the leaders who opposed the limited franchise measures in the second part of the Act foreseen the debacle of the United Party in 1948 the counsels might have been different. What had been offered to the Africans since 1936 should have been accepted by the Indians in 1946 not as the final thing but as the first stage on the road to political equality. Whatever could have been said for a qualified acceptance of the second part of the Act, the first part was totally unacceptable. But as this was a package deal it was a case of all or none.

The enforcement of economic sanctions against South Africa; the recall of the Indian High Commissioner and the submission of the Indian case to UNO were all directly attributable to the Act of 1946. The international relations between South Africa and India had at last reached a breaking point. The final breach or the lasting solution remained. There was no middle course in the issue at stake. The world now cast its hope in the direction of UNO and the next chapter is devoted to this international institution. Before we turn to the next chapter to review the work of UNO in relation to South African affairs, it seems appropriate to end this one with the knowledgeable observations of a white South African and former President of the Institute of Race Relations, Maurice Webb, who had in 1946 spent nearly a year in relief services in various countries of Europe. Webb said that we lived in a time of social upheaval when vast forces for good and for evil were astir. Over vast areas the mechanism of civilisation had been destroyed. People had lost confidence in themselves and in one another, in goodness and the purposes of life. But there was also another picture which he very vividly described as follows:

"On the other hand there is also in our world a great stirring of new hope, a desire for a fuller and a freer life. There is a resentment of restraints upon the human person, a straining at old bonds. The coloured peoples everywhere are challenging the long accepted position of the white peoples, claiming that worth should rest on merit, not on pigmentation. The poor, the weak, the despised, the oppressed, . . . have glimpsed a vision, if dimly, have set their faces towards the rising sun of hope."

In the future, said Mr. Webb, the forces of despair had to give way to those of hope, for despair stemmed from isolated nationalism whilst hope came from the power of internationalism set up in the name of UNO. Mr. Webb saw this hope (as did the South African Indians and all oppressed and unhappy peoples) in the following words: "We have come to a situation in which world opinion and the aspirations of many people are centred at UNO. The force of world opinion will become more powerful as it is coordinated and given organised expression. The eyes of millions of people are turned to UNO. It is there that they focus their dreams."[36] The future would tell whether or not this hope was misplaced.

FOOTNOTES

1. Nicholas, H. G., *The United Nations as a Political Institution*, p. 1.
2. *Year Book of United Nations*, 1946–1947, p. 1., and *United Nations in the Making: Basic Documents*, p. 9.
3. *Leader*, 10th March, 1945.
4. Union of S.A. Government Information Office, *The Indians in South Africa*, p. 27.
5. Report of the Indian High Commissioner, 1945, pp. 14–15.
6. Government of India, *Question of Treatment of Indians in the Union of South Africa. Documents and Proceedings*, Document A/68, p. 11.
7. G. H. Calpin, *The Indians in South Africa*, p. 219, and *Leader*, 16th February, 1946. *Vide* Union of South Africa Government Information Office, *The Indians in South Africa*, pp. 27–8 for Premier's reply to deputation.
8. *Leader*, 16th February, 1946.
9. S.A.I.C. *Conference Agenda Book, 1946*.
10. *Ibid.*, 23rd February, 1946. There were changes in the personnel of the delegations that finally left. On the 23rd March, Messrs. A. I. Kajee, Ashwin Choudree, P. R. Pather, Sol Paruk and Rev. Sigamoney left by air. A. M. Moola was to join the delegation in England. Dr. Y. M. Dadoo did not go, preferring to remain behind to conduct and direct resistance. Messrs. Sorabjee Rustomjee, S. R. Naidoo, A. A. Mirza and Ahmed S. M. Kajee went to India. It was necessary for a three-months' notice to be given before trade sanctions could be operative.
11. *Vide* Ashwin Choudree and P. R. Pather, *A Commentary on the Asiatic Land Tenure and Indian Representation Act*, pp. 1–10, and George Singh, *The Asiatic Act: A Brief Survey of its Background, Terms and Implications.*
12. *Ibid.*, pp. 8–9.
13. Union of South Africa, Government Information Office, *The Indians in South Africa*, pp. 39–40.
14. House of Assembly Debates, No. 10, 1946, pp. 4433–4.
15. *Ibid.*, p. 4307.
16. *Ibid.*, pp. 4314–5.
17. Calpin, *Indians in South Africa*, p. 231.
18. Senate Debates, Third Session, Ninth Parliament (Fourth Senate), 1946–1947, pp. 1270–5.
19. *Ibid.*, p. 1746.
20. *Ibid.*, p. 1716. For the text of the full speech by Senator Brookes of the 8th May, 1946, *vide* pp. 1713–1735. This is what Sir Shafa'at Ahmad Khan, former High Commissioner for India had to say about Senator Brookes' speech: "Senator Brookes' was disappointing, though his references to the part which Indians had played in building up Natal's prosperity will be appreciated by the Indian people. His objection to the Indian case being placed before the United Nations Organization has no force or validity, as the Government of India did their best to get the question settled by direct negotiation between the two Governments." *Vide* Khan, *The Indians in South Africa*, p. 560.
21. *Leader*, 6th April, 1946.
22. *Leader*, 8th June, 1946.
23. Palmer, *The History of the Indians in Natal*, p. 139.
24. Calpin, *Indians in South Africa*, p. 243.
25. *Memo to His Excellency, Field-Marshal Viscount Wavell, Viceroy and Governor-General of India, New Delhi, 1946*, by the S.A.I.C. delegation. Obtained from the S.A.I.R.R., Johannesburg.
26. *Ibid.*
27. Sir Shafa'at Ahmad Khan, *The Indians in South Africa*, pp. 479–480.

28. *Ibid.*, pp. 489–490.
29. *Leader*, 13th April, 1946.
30. *Ibid.*, 20th April, 1946.
31. Khare, *My Political Memoirs*, pp. 170–1.
32. *Ibid.*, pp. 172–177.
33. *Leader*, 27th April, 1946.
34. *Ibid.*, 11th May, 1946.
35. *Ibid.*, 1st June, 1946.
36. Maurice Webb, *South Africa Faces UNO*, p. 31.

CHAPTER SEVEN

THE UNITED NATIONS, 1946–1950

"The world is facing imminent peril on account of mounting racial antagonisms. It looks to the United Nations for leadership based on a recognition of the maintenance of standards and values. We are on trial today. Let us not fail ourselves."

VIJAYALAKSHMI PANDIT
(Leader of the Indian Delegation, speaking at the United Nations)

On 24th October, 1945, the United Nations became an accomplished fact when the majority of its member states, including the Big Five, ratified its Charter. With the establishment of this international organisation, the world had now travelled a long way towards finding the elusive guardian of international peace and security, of harmony among nations both large and small and among the peoples of the world – of all races, kinds and creeds.

It was inevitable that the South African Indian question (which since 1860 had gradually assumed the proportions of a major problem for South Africa and which had since then been debated at every national and international level) would find its way to UN, for better or for worse.

Viewed in retrospect in 1961, the distant days of 1946 and the turbulent years which followed reveal that on the international scene, though much of great significance had occurred, the Indian question of South Africa (and its related issues) was treated like so many "Davids" before the "Goliaths" of our age: a comparatively little thing straining at the bonds surrounding it; cropping up annually but like the hardy annual remembered more when absent and looked on with indifference when present. There is a singular monotony pervading the South African Indian question at the United Nations between 1946 and 1961 that one is seriously tempted to ask whether the question justifies any detailed study. For the student of history who has set himself the task of looking at all sides of the subject from the international standpoint, there appears no good reason why a study of the South African Indian question at the United Nations should not take the form of a chronological approach, with emphasis on the salient features. On a mature consideration and in the interests of the study undertaken it is this form and pattern which the succeeding pages take. This issue is not as insignificant on the international plane as it first appears to be. Like the puny "David" it might yet worry the mighty "Goliath" as minority questions have a peculiar way of becoming worrisome.

In the history of the South African Indian question a great moment dawned when the leader of the Indian delegation to the United Nations wrote to the Secretary-General on the 22nd June, 1946, requesting that the question of the treatment of Indians in the Union of South Africa be included in the provisional agenda for the second part of the first session of the General Assembly.[1]

In this letter Sir A. Ramaswami Mudaliar gave a brief résumé of the points on which the Indian delegation based its case. These were discrimination against Indians and

197

denial of elementary rights to Indian settlers ever since 1885, such as the lack of parliamentary and municipal franchise, restrictions on rights of ownership and occupation of property, restrictions on trading, on employment in public services, and in travel, and lack of educational facilities; the situation created as a result of the passage by the Union Government of the Asiatic Land Tenure and Indian Representation Act which constituted a unilateral repudiation by the Union Government of the Cape Town Agreement and the joint statement by the Union and Indian Delegations at the Round Table Conference of 1932; the termination of the trade agreement between the two countries and the recall of the Indian High Commissioner for consultation. In view of these points, Sir Ramaswami claimed a situation had arisen "which is likely to impair friendly relations between India and South Africa".[2]

The Union Government, when informed of the contents of Sir Ramaswami Mudaliar's letter by the Secretary-General, Mr. Trygve Lie, instructed the South African Minister in Washington to convey to the Secretary-General the intentions of the Union Government to be present at the second part of the first session of the General Assembly as well as the objection of the Union Government to the jurisdiction of the General Assembly on the ground that the matter at issue was essentially within the domestic jurisdiction of the Union of South Africa in terms of paragraph 7 of Article 2 of the Charter.[3]

As Article 2 (7) forms the crux of the Union Government's case at the United Nations, it is necessary to recount the words of this clause at this early stage:

"Nothing contained in the present Charter shall authorize the United Nations to intervene in matters which are essentially within the domestic jurisdiction of any state or shall require the Members to submit such matters to settlement under the present Charter; but this principle shall not prejudice the application of enforcement measures under Chapter VII."[4]

With the basic views of the Indian and South African Governments now lodged with the Secretary-General, the principal parties commenced the important task of preparing their respective cases to be presented later in the year in the forums of the United Nations. Meanwhile, in South Africa, Indians who had begun a feverish campaign of protest against the Asiatic Land Tenure and Indian Representation Act, intensified their agitation against the Act by inaugurating a passive resistance campaign[5] which was reminiscent of the Passive Resistance Movement which had first been launched by M. K. Gandhi in the troublous days of Responsible Government Rule in the Transvaal in 1907 but which now sadly lacked the leadership and the magnetism of a Gandhi of the Mahatma stamp. Indians in the country resolved to observe June 13th, 1946, as a Hartal Day – a day of mourning. India, too, geared herself for the struggle by announcing the severance of her diplomatic relations with the Union during the second week in June, although her High Commissioner in South Africa, R. M. Desmukh, had left the Union three weeks before.[6]

What India did in the name of the South African Indians was not likely to go unnoticed by the member states of the United Nations. But what happened in South Africa was certain to attract greater attention. For the present the centre of interest was the political agitation against the Asiatic Land Tenure and Indian Representation Act in the form of passive resistance.

The Passive Resistance campaign of 1946 was controlled and organised by a Joint Passive Resistance Council, which decided on sending Ashwin Choudree, an Indian lawyer, and Sorabjee Rustomjee, an Indian businessman, as delegates of the Council to advise the Indian delegation at the United Nations in New York. But with the incarceration of the latter for a period of three months for a passive-resistance offence, Ashwin Choudree had to leave for New York as the sole delegate of the Passive Resistance Council, whose campaign had the desired effect of focussing world attention on South Africa's Indian question, particularly because those who now participated in the campaign, unlike their predecessors of the period 1907 to 1913 under the leadership of M. K. Gandhi, were South African citizens with a South African interest in South Africa. The case of one of them, J. M. Francis, an ex-sergeant in the Union Defence Force, illustrates the position quite graphically. On 23rd May, 1945, Sergeant Francis had received the following letter from Field-Marshal J. C. Smuts, Prime Minister of the Union of South Africa and Commander-in-Chief of the U.D.F.: " . . . I wish to express to you the thanks of your country for the part you have played in this great world struggle . . . You made the sacrifice for South Africa and for the wider cause of world freedom. . . . You and your comrades upheld the honour and the interests of South Africa. . . . For all this I express our warm thanks to you." And on the 5th July, 1946, ex-sergeant Francis was sentenced to two months' imprisonment for a passive resistance offence. In a statement to the Court, Francis said that he was disillusioned to find on his return from the army that the man who had promised so much during the war was himself the pilot of the Asiatic Land Tenure Act of 1946.[7]

If South African Indians were disillusioned, Indians in India also felt the reverberations of this disillusionment. India had at last sallied forth into her *de facto* independence with the formation of the Interim Government in 1946. The new India which would be greatly strengthened when the *de jure* position of independence followed would not like to be humiliated in her new status on the score of the position of the South African Indians. The Vice-President of the newly inaugurated Interim Government in India, Mr. Jawaharlal Nehru, said in his first broadcast in this official capacity: "We hope that India will have friendly and co-operative relations with England and the countries of the British Commonwealth, but it is well to remember what is happening in one part of this Commonwealth – in South Africa racialism is the state doctrine – if this racial doctrine is going to be tolerated it must inevitably lead to vast conflict . . . "[8]

Both the national and international fields were gradually preparing themselves for the "conflict". In South Africa, the South African Indian Congress, in terms of a resolution adopted in February, 1946, announced that a congress delegation comprising Sorabjee Rustomjee, A. I. Kajee and P. R. Pather would leave for New York on 21st September to present the case of the South African Indian Congress to the Indian delegations at the United Nations.[9]

But before this could materialise the age-old canker of the duality of Indian opposition in South Africa, the internal rivalry between the different political groups and the personal differences between the political leaders, found expression once again in the internal disputes which followed. The executive of the South African Indian Congress, apparently desirous of satisfying all the Provincial units, decided on a more bulky delegation to proceed to New York and nominated A. I. Kajee, P. R. Pather, Advocate Albert Christopher, Sorabjee Rustomjee (all from Natal); Hajee M. H. Joosub (from the Transvaal) and C. Palsania (from the Cape). S. R. Naidoo, a joint secretary of the S.A.I.C., declined nomination on the grounds that the delegation was already too big and that the expenses involved would be too great.[10] In any case, a delegate of the Passive Resistance Council, Ashwin Choudree, was already in New York for some months and was expected back in the Union on the 25th September.[11] At this stage it was announced that H. A. Naidoo, an official of the S.A.I.C., who was then in Paris, was proceeding to New York to join the S.A.I.C. delegation there. The matter of the South African Indian delegations was further confused when a quarrel between Sorabjee Rustomjee and P. R. Pather resulted in a serious cleavage when Rustomjee and H. A. Naidoo announced their resignation from the S.A.I.C. and their decision to represent the Joint Passive Resistance Council of Natal and the Transvaal. The Joint Passive Resistance Council now disowned the S.A.I.C. delegation as not being representative of local Indian opinion and interests.[12]

It was quite clear to all concerned that the instability of Indian unity at a crucial phase in the struggle was not only damaging the case of the local Indians but was also weakening that of the Indian delegation from India and Pakistan. The Vice-President of the Interim Government of India, Mr. Nehru, stepped into the picture and intervened in the South African Indian political unrest through the Indian High Commissioner's office. He stated that the Government of India would recognise the decisions of the S.A.I.C. only if they were endorsed by the Natal and Transvaal Indian Congresses.[13] This endorsement hardly seemed likely at the time since the Natal and Transvaal Indian Congresses, whose officials constituted the Joint Passive Resistance Council, and the parent body, the South African Indian Congress, were mutally *personae non gratae*.

Thus the duality of Indian opposition in South Africa persisted till the end and the local Indians had to be content with two official delegations proceeding to New York in the same plane, carrying with them the same picture of the South African scene, but yet insistent on presenting this picture separately, at great harm to the unity and the prestige of the South African Indians and at equally great expense to the Indian pocket. P. R. Pather and A. Christopher finally went as delegates of the S.A.I.C. and Sorabjee Rustomjee as a delegate of the Joint Passive Resistance Council.[14]

With the time drawing near for the second part of the first session of the General Assembly, other delegations also converged in New York. The delegation of the Union Government was headed by the Prime Minister, Field-Marshal Smuts, fresh from his latest honour of drafting the preamble to the Charter of the United Nations, and last-surviving founder of the defunct League of Nations, with his deputy in Heaton Nicholls, who, as Administrator of Natal, was well versed with the Indian question which was essentially Natal's question. The delegation from India was headed by Mrs. Vijayalakshmi Pandit, sister of the Vice-President of the Interim Government of India. Fifty-four delegations from member states were present at this important session of the General Assembly.

Prior to the opening of the General Assembly, the Government of India communicated to the Secretary-General a memorandum on the position of Indians in the Union of South Africa.[15] This memorandum is in three parts: Part I deals with the "History of Indian Immigration into South Africa"; Part II with "Treatment of Indians in South

Africa: History of Discriminatory Measures Against Them"; and Part III with "Disabilities to which Indians are subject in the Union of South Africa". As the substance of this memorandum is essentially a resumé of Indian history in South Africa from the first attempts to bring Indians to Natal around 1855 till the position as it obtained in 1946 and as the main points are covered in the earlier chapters of this study, it is not considered necessary to reproduce the contents here.

The Union Government countered with a Memorandum on the Subject of Indian Legislation[16] and a Further Memorandum on the Subject of Indian Legislation.[17] These memoranda contained the case of the Union Government, the crux of which was that this Government viewed the issue from the angle which pointed to the ultimate repatriation of Indians to India, maintaining that Indians were in South Africa on a temporary basis.[18] It was stated that the racial policies of South Africa were based on the principle of "unity in diversity", which was the only way for the multi-racial people of South Africa to "march together without conflict".[19]

It now remained for the General Assembly of the United Nations to judge the issue. Before the verdict could be obtained, the full machinery of the General Assembly had to be set in motion. This started in the General Committee of the Assembly. It is one of the functions of the General Committee to recommend to the Assembly the approval of items on the provisional agenda and allocate such items to the various committees. South Africa, as a vice-president of the first session of the General Assembly, was represented *ex officio* on the General Committee. When the item tabled by the Government of India came up for approval, Field-Marshal Smuts moved that it be removed from the agenda on the grounds that the matter at issue was, in terms of Article 2 (7) of the Charter, outside the competence of the General Assembly. In terms of the Committee's Rules of Procedure, the delegate of India was then invited to present to the committee his delegation's case for inclusion of that item on the agenda. In the subsequent discussion, Smuts agreed to a suggestion by the delegate of the United Kingdom that the item be referred first to the sixth committee of the Assembly (the Legal Committee) for consideration. Finally the General Committee decided by a majority vote that the item be referred separately to the first committee (the Political Committee) and the sixth committee, rejecting a proposal that it be referred to joint meetings of the first and sixth committees. But as the South African and Indian delegations mutually agreed upon the joint meetings earlier rejected, the General Assembly adopted the proposal.[20]

The Joint Committee held six meetings to discuss the whole issue. Mrs. Pandit (India), in a historical resume, pointed out that the victims of the Union's policy were mainly people who had been born in South Africa, who had contributed towards its economic progress and were entitled to the protection of the United Nations Charter and of the principles set forth in its preamble. The case before the committee was therefore a case of violation of the fundamental principles of the Charter. Mrs. Pandit went on to say that the Government of India maintained that the question was a political and not a legal one. It was not even a question that concerned two countries only; its potential consequences made it a world problem. The only means of solving it was for the United Nations to exercise their collective wisdom and to employ their moral sanction in the interests of justice.[21]

For the Union of South Africa, Field-Marshal Smuts stressed the fact that the exploitation of domestic issues by foreign states as a political weapon would determine to a large extent the future issues of peace and war. He said that the principle involved in Article 2 (7) was the recognition of the fact that within the domain of its domestic affairs a state is not subject to control or interference and its action could not be called into question by any other state. There was an exception to this contention which brought into operation the enforcement measures in Chapter 7 of the Charter to prevent the impairment of friendly relations between states and to guard against any threat to the maintenance of international peace and security. Another exception was present in the form of treaty obligations. In that connection he stated that the so-called Cape Town Agreement of 1927 between the Government of India and the Government of the Union of South Africa, and the joint communique issued by those governments in 1932 were not instruments giving rise to treaty obligations.[22] In this respect, Field-Marshal Smuts quoted the words of Sir Geoffrey Corbett, who had attended the 1926/7 conference as a deputy leader of the Indian delegation, and who was also a delegate to the 1932 conference, who had said in 1932:

"Do you not feel that too much has been made of the understanding we had in 1926–1927, by calling it an agreement? As I understood it at the time, the agreement proper was 6 or 7 clauses merely embodying a declaration of policy on behalf of your Government, and a declaration of policy on our side. The agreement clauses were limited to the effective co-operation in carrying out the policy which was yours. That is how I have always read it, and not as a Charter which will handicap you in dealing with the Indian population."[23]

A third exception to the rule of domestic jurisdiction, said Field-Marshal Smuts, might be sought in the direction of human rights and fundamental freedoms, such as the right to exist, the right to freedom of conscience, and freedom of speech, and the right of free access to the courts. In the absence of any internationally recognised formulation of such rights, and as the Charter itself did not define them, Member States did not have any specific obligations under the Charter.[24]

In conclusion, Smuts said that without admitting the right of the United Nations to intervene in the matter he had no objection to the case being fully discussed. As the present case would form a precedent for the future, he would formally propose that at the conclusion of the debate, the Joint Committee should recommend to the General Assembly that an advisory opinion be sought from the International Court of Justice upon the question whether the matters set forth by the Government of India and replied to by the Government of the Union of South Africa were, under Article 2 (7) of the Charter, essentially within the domestic jurisdiction of the Union of South Africa.[25]

Forty-five other speeches, following those made initially by Mrs. Pandit and Field-Marshal Smuts, were made during the course of the Joint Committee meetings. Elaborating on the points introduced by Mrs. Pandit (India), Mr. Chagla (India) said that since 1860 there had been a painful history of broken promises. He said that in 1913 Indians had become citizens of the Union of South Africa, bearing the burdens of citizenship without the right of franchise. In view of these circumstances of taxation without representation the Government of India had always considered it a duty to look after the interests of Indians in South Africa. The South African Government had always accepted this policy. Until the present debate, it had never treated the Indian problem in South Africa as a domestic problem. The Indian case was that the South African Government by its general policy and by the enactment of the Asiatic Land Tenure and Indian Representation Act of 1946 had violated the Cape Town Agreement of 1927 and the fundamental principles and purposes of the Charter. Referring to the Cape Town Agreement of 1927, Mr. Chagla said that any solemn agreement between States constituted a treaty. A telegram from the Governor-General of South Africa to the Governor-General of India, dated 16th February, 1927, had stated that his ministers wished him to communicate the fact that they had formally approved the Cape Town Agreement. The agreement was solemnly ratified by the legislatures of both countries; it had never been terminated. It had been reaffirmed in 1932. Quoting Field-Marshal Smuts that the signature of the Charter had resulted in the "contraction of the domain of essentially domestic matters", Chagla said that the Charter would become merely a scrap of paper if any signatory could, with impunity, violate its terms without the United Nations having any right to take action.[26]

For the Union of South Africa, Mr. Heaton Nicholls, dealing with the factual aspects of the Indian complaint, said that the Indian problem in South Africa had reached its present dimensions as a result of its being exploited as a political weapon in order to further India's political aims. He said that the bulk of the Indian population in the Union of South Africa enjoyed a higher standard of living than their kin in India. However, they were still subject to the same caste distinctions as the corresponding classes in India. They still spoke four different languages and their education was delayed by the necessity of studying English as a medium of instruction. Education had been slow in Africa but this was due to many technical difficulties. The problem of the Indian community was superimposed on the problem of the native population.

Mr. Nicholls said that the Indians were always regarded as temporary residents in Natal; that the Cape Town Agreement was of domestic character and had never been registered as a treaty as enjoined by the Covenant of the League of Nations. It was never signed and was merely a statement of good intentions. He could not agree with the claims of certain delegates that the mere fact of discrimination of any kind constituted a violation of the Charter. Political rights, he said, were not fundamental. If it were so, it was tantamount to saying that the most progressive races should be retarded by the less progressive if, in fact, they constituted a majority. Whole clauses in the trusteeship agreements would have to be struck out on the ground of discrimination, if that argument held. Equality in fundamental rights and freedoms could only be assured in a multi-racial state by a measure of discrimination in non-fundamental rights. In conclusion, Mr. Nicholls asked that the great experiment in human government which had been made in South Africa should be properly understood.

With this reiteration of their respective cases by the delegates of India and the Union of South Africa, it is not necessary to follow the views of other delegates in the forty-three other speeches which followed or preceded those made by Chagla and Nicholls. The other delegates, in any case, were either for one or the other principal party or for no party at all. Their stand is reflected sufficiently in the voting analysis.

During the proceedings of the Joint Committee, India withdrew her resolution submitted at the opening of the meeting in favour of one sponsored by France and Mexico. The Franco–Mexican resolution stated that the treatment of Indians in South Africa had impaired the friendly relations between India and South Africa and that unless a satisfactory settlement was reached the relations would be further impaired. It called for the treatment of Indians in South Africa to be made to conform to the treaty obligations of the past, taking into account also the Charter of the United Nations.

Similarly, South Africa withdrew her original resolution in favour of an amendment to the Franco–Mexican resolution tabled jointly by the United States, the United Kingdom and Sweden, calling upon the International Court of Justice to give an advisory opinion on the question whether the issue was within the domestic jurisdiction of the Union of South Africa in terms of Article 2 (7).

Voting in the Joint Committee gave victory to the Franco–Mexican Resolution, supported by India, with a tally of 24 votes for the resolution, 19 against it, with 6 abstentions and 5 absent, over that of the joint amendment sponsored by the United States, the United Kingdom, and Sweden and favoured by the Union of South Africa.[27]

The Joint Committee had now arrived at a decision by which it called upon the South African Government to take heed of their international obligations in respect of the South African Indians and to ensure that the treatment of the Indian people in South Africa should be in accordance with the terms of the Charter of the United Nations. It rejected an amendment which requested that the issue be submitted to the International Court of Justice for an advisory opinion on competence. It remained now for the General Assembly to consider the report of the Joint Committee.

General Smuts moved an amendment in the General Assembly and pointed out that the vote on the resolution was in effect indecisive, that of a total of fifty-four members of the two committees it received only twenty-four votes. He urged that the Assembly was in all justice and fairness bound to pass its own judgement on the matter.[28] The amendment moved by Smuts was essentially the same as that submitted by the United States, the United Kingdom and Sweden in the Joint Committee, asking for reference of the matter to the International Court of Justice for its advisory opinion on the issues of law involved. The Joint Committee, under its voting procedure, did not deal with this matter at all but the General Assembly was competent to deal with it in the form of an amendment. Smuts said that the South African delegation had no intention of again raising the merits of the dispute. It only asked that the proper constitutional legal procedure should be followed to provide an answer to the question whether South Africa had broken any international treaty obligations or violated fundamental rights or freedoms enjoined upon her by the Charter.[29]

Mrs. Pandit (India), appealing to the General Assembly to adopt the recommendation of the Joint First and Sixth Committee, said that as the Union Government had signed the Charter and as the Prime Minister of South Africa was himself the author of the Preamble, the South African Government was bound to honour the obligations imposed by the Charter. Mrs. Pandit said that the issue no longer rested with India or with South Africa but with the United Nations which stood for "the defence of the law, ethics and morality of nations".[30]

Mrs. Pandit appealed to those representatives who had voted against the Franco–

Mexican Resolution in the Joint Committee, particularly to the United Kingdom and to her Dominions, to reconsider their stand, and ended with an impassioned plea that the member states should create for the United Nations the confidence of the common people in it as a defender of justice, public law and morality. "I ask," she said, "for the verdict of this Assembly on a proven violation of the Charter; on an issue which has led to acute dispute between two Member States; on an issue which is not confined to India or South Africa . . . ".[31]

There were fewer speakers in the General Assembly than in the Joint Committee. Excluding the Rapporteur, eighteen speeches were made in all and on the 8th December, 1946, the decision of the General Assembly was made known. The South African resolution asking that the meeting refer the dispute to the International Court of Justice was defeated by 31 votes to 21 with 2 abstentions; the Franco–Mexican Resolution, as recommended by the Joint Committee, was adopted by 32 votes to 15, with 7 abstentions. The details of the voting as well as the resolutions introduced are necessary in order to follow subsequent developments.[32]

With this decision of the General Assembly, the first on the South African Indian question, an important milestone was reached in the history of the South African Indians. The issue in question was deemed to be of sufficient importance to find a place, indeed among the first matters of international proportions to be placed on the first agenda of the first General Assembly of the United Nations, in the forums of the new world body. Now that the South African Indian question had reached the United Nations it was implicit in this development that this issue was one of the problems of the world.

Though this was a logical inference, what was not equally clear was how was this world body to resolve the dispute between South Africa and India? The Charter had made much of the human problems and human rights the new organisation was to interest itself in. The Preamble to the Charter expressed the determination "to reaffirm faith in fundamental human rights, in the dignity and worth of the human person, in the equal rights of men and women and of nations large and small". Articles 55, 62 and 68 re-echoed this aim. As an ideal these aims were lofty, plausible and necessary. But in the world of reality a moot point was how was the practical side of it to match the idealistic side? In his study of the United Nations, H. G. Nicholas makes the following observation:

"The Charter does not . . . give to the world organization any power to impose a settlement of its members' disputes. It provides an elaborate adaptable machinery for settlement which it expects them to use, but no organ of the U.N., not even the Security Council, is empowered to impose a decision. In the event of the dispute developing into a threat to peace and security the Council can certainly act, but again not to impose a decision, but only to preserve the peace. The U.N. is not a world government."[32a]

There were serious limitations in the structure of the United Nations itself. There was little hope that in spite of this the world organisation would find an early solution to to a problem which had eluded a solution for the past 86 years. The South African Indians, however, were hopeful that some good would come from the intervention of the United Nations. Their representatives were present at the United Nations but as two groups were present this division and disunity did nothing to enhance the cause they were there to promote. It was reported that these representatives were engaged in a "cat and dog" fight among themselves. The leader of the Joint Passive Resistance Council delegation, Sorabjee Rustomjee, spared no effort in putting himself in a commanding position. Having come to New York directly from jail and having been associated with the Passive Resistance struggle, he had got the ear of the Indian delegation at New York. This was resented by the South African Indian Congress delegation which comprised the old and tried South African Indian political leaders, P. R. Pather and Albert Christopher, who were joined in New York by A. I. Kajee. The role which these and other men had played in South African politics was recounted by P. R. Pather when he told Mrs. Pandit, the leader of the Indian delegation, that for the past 25 years every speech, resolution or memoranda touching on South African Indian affairs were drafted by S. R. Naidoo, Albert Christopher, A. I. Kajee or P. R. Pather, whilst other leaders gained prominence and publicity without having done as much. This delegation made a worthy contribution by way of disseminating information on the South African Indian question when it produced a well-documented booklet in the name of the South African Indian Congress entitled *Treatment of Indians in South Africa: A Memorandum of Facts*.[33]

The key-man in this delegation was A. I. Kajee who regretted the fact that the South African Indian question had got out of the hands of the South African Indians and had passed into the hands of the United Nations. When he left the United Nations he was convinced that the best way to resolve the Indian question was by holding a round table conference between India and South Africa, at which local Indians would be present. His political opponents differed from him and placed their confidence "in a rapid decision of the United Nations".[34]

Though this confidence was quite widespread, there were many among the Europeans and the Indians in South Africa who had reason to be disappointed with the outcome of the United Nations deliberations on the Indian question. General Smuts expressed his disappointment in a broadcast to the nation on the 18th December, 1946, when he said that the General Assembly had denied the Union the fundamental right of access to the International Court of Justice and had proceeded to "assume implicitly the guilt of the Union". He said that the General Assembly had usurped the authority of that Court.[35]

Indians in South Africa, too, had little to be happy about. It was true that a resolution asking the Union Government to alter its policies was approved by the General Assembly. But the practical results were yet to be seen. Dr. G. M. Naicker, President of the Natal Indian Congress, cautioned the Indians that it was not time to gloat over any victory; instead, it was time to consider what steps should be taken next. This view found support in a *Leader* editorial which forecast more difficult days for the Indian people in South Africa. The editorial went on to state that the United Nations lacked an effective machinery to compel a member state to abide by its decision. At most, it stated, the Assembly decision was a grave moral censure and "moral censures have been disregarded with impunity by Christian South Africa".[36]

Though for the present the only aspect seemed to be the moral one, the important thing for the South African Indian question at international level was that the issue had been raised for the first time at the United Nations. Consequently some effective decision would have to be taken some day either in favour of the one or the other principal party.

The future of the United Nations, its prestige, its value as an arbiter in world problems, could very well be said to depend on how it handled the South African Indian question. No urgent or precipitate step was called for in 1946 as the issue could not be placed, at that time, among the problems which threatened international peace and security.

The Union Government, no doubt, realised that the United Nations could not force their hands. They re-affirmed their domestic policy when the Minister of the Interior, Senator Clarkson, announced that the Asiatic Land Tenure and Indian Representation Act would remain in operation and that in terms of the Act an Indian Advisory Board would soon be appointed. This announcement was met with opposition from the Indians who held a mass meeting in Durban on 9th February, 1947, to reject the proposed Advisory Board and to protest at the refusal of passports to Drs. Y. M. Dadoo and G. M. Naicker, Presidents of the Transvaal and the Natal Indian Congress, respectively, who applied for permission to travel to India in February, 1947, for consultations with the Interim Government of India and to attend the All-Asian Conference convened by Nehru and scheduled to take place in New Delhi on 24th March, 1947. Indians rejected the proposed Advisory Board because they felt that in accepting this and the communal franchise, they would strengthen the case of the Union Government when the Indian question was raised again at the United Nations.

In the announcement of the Minister of the Interior was to be seen the determination of the Union Government to proceed at full speed with its own programme. Whether it was wise policy to ignore completely the strictures of the United Nations was another matter altogether. The *Natal Witness* did not think so and wrote that it was "absurd to think that we can snap our fingers at world opinion, walk out of UNO in a huff, and expect to benefit from it in the long run".[37] The journal called on responsible South Africans to re-examine their attitude towards colour.

There was everything commendable in such an appeal. In fact, the Union Premier, General Smuts, himself felt the need for this on his return from the United Nations. He said at Pretoria on the 20th December, 1946, that there was too great a tendency in South Africa to look merely at a man's skin and to judge him on that. "Man," he said, "is not necessarily the same because he has the same colour of skin. A question to be seriously considered is whether we should not give a man of a different colour, who is highly educated and with outstanding qualities of leadership a chance. Why treat them all on the lowest level?"[38]

It was this very attitude now attacked by Smuts which was responsible for the South African Indian question being debated at the United Nations. General Smuts, who had had the opportunity of learning at first hand the reactions among the member states of the United Nations to the policies of the Union Government, must have realised that these policies would be unacceptable to the world organisation. His dilemma was how to introduce a change when this meant inflicting an innovation which would not go down well among most whites in South Africa. There was no question about the necessity for a change. All progressive people desired to see it brought about as soon as possible so that South Africa's racial policies might not again be attacked at the United Nations. The South African Indians themselves had a contribution to make towards the realisation of this change. But the way for them, too, was not clear. Their representatives at the last session of the United Nations were hopelessly divided among themselves. This division was carried further in the internal politics at home. There were two clear groups, the first of which represented the "new guard", militant young men whose leaders made up the Joint Passive Resistance Council and whose membership was drawn from the Natal Indian Congress and the Transvaal Indian Congress. Their leaders were Drs. Dadoo and Naicker. The second group represented the "old guard", the Kajee-Pather group which had lost its hold over the Natal Indian Congress and would soon lose its grip over the South African Indian Congress. At the international level these two groups were divided on the issue of finding a solution to their local problems. The first group held the view that local agitation such as a passive resistance campaign would project the South African Indian question in a dynamic manner on the world forum at New York, from which direction some assistance would be forthcoming. The second group felt that the local difficulties should be resolved between the Union and Indian governments without any interference from other sources. The first group was referred to as the "extremists" and the second the "moderates".

It was apparent that the extremists and the moderates could not meet in the same organisation, that is, in the Congress, for sooner or later the influence and predominance of the new leadership in the Natal Indian Congress would be extended to the South African Indian Congress.

Consequently, an informal meeting of representative Indians was held on the 23rd April, 1947, under the chairmanship of Hajee Ahmed Sadek Kajee, who was one of the delegates of the South African Indian Congress to India in 1946. A. S. Kajee explained what had transpired at a meeting with the officials of the N.I.C. on the 18th April, 1947, when the officials of the N.I.C. did not give a clear reply on the issue of accepting in principle the necessity for a round table conference between the Government of India and the Union Government. Speaking at this meeting, P. R. Pather said that on his return from the United Nations he had suggested that passive resistance should be suspended to pave the way for discussions between the two governments. Pather suggested three alternatives to the meeting: to go into the fold of the Natal Indian Congress which would mean fighting amongst themselves on questions of policy; to form a group on the lines of the Anti-Segregation Council which would again result in similar quarrels; or to form a body to speak for moderate Indians. The meeting adopted a resolution to convene a conference of representative Natal Indians to decide on what steps to take in the future.[38a]

The conference was held in Durban on 4th May, 1947, and a new political body called the Natal Indian Organisation was constituted. On 21st May, 1947, a delegation from the N.I.O. waited on the Prime Minister, General Smuts, in Pretoria. The N.I.O. delegation presented a memorandum to General Smuts requesting that he take immediate steps for the resumption of diplomatic relations between the Union and India and that he initiate discussion in accordance with the United Nations resolution of 8th December, 1946, between representatives of the Union and Indian Governments to arrive at a solution of all matters affecting Indians and in such discussions to allow South African Indians representatives to participate.[39] In respect of the Asiatic Advisory Board, the N.I.O. memorandum stated that the formation of advisory boards or similar bodies would tend to disintegrate the South African nation and to accentuate the racial differences.

In the Press Statement issued by the Prime Minister on the same day, the main business transacted with the N.I.O. delegation was mentioned. With regard to implementing the resolution of UNO, the Prime Minister stated that he had received a communication from Mr. Nehru and that he had replied requesting the Government of India to resume diplomatic relations with the Union by sending its High Commissioner back to South Africa for discussions. The reply that he had received from Mr. Nehru indicated that the Government of India was not disposed to adopt this course in the circumstances that prevailed. The Prime Minister agreed to make further representations to the Indian Government on that point and he urged the N.I.O. to use their endeavours in the same direction.[40]

On the question of the Indian Advisory Board, General Smuts said that he would not proceed with its appointment if it was not acceptable to the N.I.O. But as there were day-to-day matters of administration directly affecting the Indian people, he would like to have the views of the Indian community without the necessity of having to arrange large deputations. He suggested that the N.I.O. should appoint a small committee for this purpose without prejudice to its principle of representation on such basis as the community might claim.

The N.I.O. had made its debut in a most impressive manner. Within its fold it had tried politicians like A. I. Kajee and P. R. Pather, whose main policy at the time of the formation of the N.I.O. was to help towards the restoration of diplomatic relations between the Union Government and the Government of India and thereafter to work towards a round table conference between them. A start had been made in the direction of implementing the resolution of UNO of the 8th December, 1946, when, a day after the preliminary meeting that was to lead to the birth of the N.I.O., the Minister for External Affairs and Commonwealth Relations, Mr. Jawaharlal Nehru, wrote to the Union Prime Minister expressing the desire of the Government of India to implement the resolution of the United Nations of 8th December, 1946.[41]

Field-Marshal Smuts replied that the absence of the High Commissioner for India in South Africa was a difficulty that had prevented the Union Government from raising the matter of negotiations earlier. He said that correspondence between the two governments by cable or otherwise would mean delay and might not achieve their common purpose of finding a solution for their difficulties. The Union Government would, therefore, welcome the return of the High Commissioner for India.[42]

Nehru did not agree that the absence of the High Commissioner debarred the Government of the Union of South Africa from initiating and conducting discussions with the Government of India. He said: "The Government of India conceive the immediate tasks before our two Governments as the taking of appropriate and effective steps to implement the resolution passed by the General Assembly of the United Nations of December 8th, 1946."[43]

As this correspondence is of great importance in an understanding of the international dispute between India and South Africa, excerpts from it are reproduced in this study. Mr. Nehru's reply was quite explicit on the position of the High Commissioner:

"The High Commissioner for India to the Union was recalled for consultation, as a consequence of the deterioration in relations between our two countries, of which the General Assembly of the United Nations has taken note. The Government of India have to state with regret that these relations have not only not improved since, but have deteriorated further. The reasons which determined this course of action therefore continues. . . . They will gladly arrange for the return of their High Commissioner to South Africa as soon as such an improvement takes place . . . ".[44]

In his reply, Field-Marshal Smuts referred to the deputation of the N.I.O. that had called on him and had expressed concern at the continued rupture in the relations between the two governments; the South African Indian Congress had already appealed to the Indian Government to resume diplomatic relations with South Africa. Smuts went on to say:

"You will allow me to point out that the Union Government are under severe provocation to consider the attitude of the Indian Government in this and other respects less than friendly. The Indian Government have severed trade relations with South Africa and unilaterally applied trade sanctions to the Union, to the great injury of South African interests . . . ".

General Smuts again requested the return to South Africa of the Indian High Commissioner.[45]

A week later Nehru informed Smuts that his government was of the firm opinion that further discussions between the two governments could only be on the basis of the United Nations resolution and that these discussions should take the form of a conference of fully accredited representatives of both governments and not through the High Commissioner. However, he stated, if the Union Government accepted the United Nations resolution as the basis for discussion, the Indian Government was prepared to send their High Commissioner to South Africa to initiate the discussions.[46]

The reply of the Union Government was delayed for more than a month. When Smuts finally replied he was not prepared the concede that the implementation of the United Nations resolution of 8th December, 1946, should be made the basis for discussion between the two governments, for the Union Government had not broken any agreements and had not violated any principles of the Charter. "They are not even sure what agreements and principles are referred to, as their request for an advisory opinion by the International Court of Justice on the matter has been refused," he said.

Referring to the contentious Asiatic Land Tenure and Indian Representation Act, Smuts said that the Act did not substantially differ from the practice of other members of the United Nations in their policies to maintain peace between the different communities in their States. As one instance of this practice he mentioned the land purchase transactions between Jews and Arabs in Palestine.[47]

The negotiations came to an end with the despatch from Nehru, dated 8th August, 1947, in which he noted the inability of Field-Marshal Smuts to accept the implementation of the United Nations resolution of 8th December, 1946, as the basis for negotiations. Nehru went on to say that Field-Marshal Smuts seemed to regard the United Nations resolution as uncertain and obscure and the result of discussions which took place in a "highly-charged emotional atmosphere". He could not see how the return of the Indian High Commissioner would help to resolve the matters which the United Nations left "obscure and uncertain".[48]

Hopes of an early solution to the Indian question in South Africa were dashed with the deadlock in the negotiations between Smuts and Nehru, which were aimed at finding a common ground to implement the resolution of the United Nations of the 8th December, 1946. But this breakdown of negotiations did not affect the prominence given to the issue of the South African Indians in various parts of the world. The All-Asia Conference was held in March, 1947, and the South African Indian Congress delegates, Drs. Y. M. Dadoo and G. M. Naicker, were given passports at a late hour to attend the conference.[49] In London a special conference of the India League, organised by the South African Committee of the League, had also been held in March to consider the Asiatic Land Tenure and Indian Representation Act. The invitation to delegates attending the conference stated that the people of Great Britain and the world were equally entitled to declare their attitude towards legislation which violated the United Nations Charter.

The India League Conference was addressed by H. A. Naidoo, a former leading congress official in South Africa and delegate of the Joint Passive Resistance Council at the United Nations in 1946, and Reginald Sorrenson, Labour M.P. The latter said that if those present were sincere in their attacks against Fascism they should insist that the white people of South Africa should not betray them. They should believe in a common humanity if they were to have a common world or a number of conflicting fragments would lead them to war.[50]

But the white people of South Africa were afraid of sharing their power in a country where they were hopelessly outnumbered by non-whites. This fear and their traditional colour attitude made it difficult for them to be rational in their utterances and in their policies. One place where this was most obvious was the Parliament in Cape Town. In May, 1947, the Nationalist member for Moorreesburg, F. C. Erasmus, moved that the Government should take immediate steps to put a stop to Indian penetration into urban, village and rural areas in the Cape Province through the acquisition of land by Indians or otherwise. The Cape Province had hitherto not given much thought to the Indian "problem" as the Transvaal and Natal had done. The atmosphere there had always been congenial. Smuts realised this as he also did the force of world opinion. Being in the middle of his negotiations with Nehru, he was not disposed to disturb any more hornets' nests. In reply to Erasmus' motion, Smuts said that Parliament should be very careful when dealing with matters of that kind in order to avoid any provocative action.[51]

The Parliamentary Opposition did not agree with the views of the Prime Minister. The Leader of the Opposition, Dr. D. F. Malan, said: "UNO wanted to destroy South Africa's traditional policy and to end white civilisation in South Africa, but instead of looking to South Africa's interests the Prime Minister was looking to UNO."[52]

The difficulties of the Prime Minister were many and real. He was the only leading South African statesman who had had a lifetime of association in international circles. He realised the potency of international opinion and the value of international co-operation. He had been a leading figure in two world wars and knew the full meaning of international goodwill and understanding. His dilemma was that he was also a South African who was dependent on the white electorate of South Africa. This electorate saw little more than its own preservation and protection in South Africa. For this the only hope it saw was to stand four-square behind the bastion of South Africa's traditional way of life. It could not see that traditions, too, had to change to meet the requirements of a new age. The changing times showed that Canada had, at last, conferred the franchise on Indians. Indians in British Columbia, numbering about 1 700, were enfranchised by the Legislative Assembly of British Columbia. By this act they were placed on the same footing as other Canadian citizens.[53]

But the position of South African Indians was still in the melting pot. They were themselves politically divided. While Drs. Dadoo and Naicker were addressing mass meetings in India, the N.I.O. had been formed in Natal. A former Agent-General, Sir Syed Raza Ali, said of this formation: "The N.I.O. seemed to be the result of an unholy alliance between big Indian money and a resourceful Prime Minister, who knew how to extricate himself from a tight corner." He urged the Indian people to be patient for "old prejudices die hard and long-standing issues involving international complications cannot be expected to be settled in a few months".[53]

The international complications of the South African Indian question were becoming more and more involved. The resolution of 8th December, 1946, of the United Nations, calling upon the governments of India and South Africa to have discussions on this question failed to bear fruit when the Nehru-Smuts correspondence resulted in a deadlock. Protests and mass meetings in South Africa and in other parts of the world calculated to bring indirect pressure on the Union Government proved to be of no value. A new political body in Natal, the Natal Indian Organisation, dedicated to a programme of working towards a round table conference between the Union and Indian governments had also failed to bring this about. There was only a little hope on the international horizon that when India became fully independent some positive steps in the direction of a solution would be taken.

The long-promised independence to India was set in motion when the Indian Independence Bill was introduced in the British House of Commons on 4th July, 1947. It was aimed at creating two independent dominions to be known as India and Pakistan as from 15th August, 1947.[54] The Bill became law on 18th July, 1947; the Indian Central Government and legislatures came to an end on 15th August, 1947. And with this stage having been reached, the responsibility of British rule in India finally came to an end.[55]

With the creation of the independent dominions of India and Pakistan the question of Indians in South Africa took on a new colour and a new significance. It had always been contended by Indian nationals on many international platforms that India's subjection to British rule was an impediment to her real assistance to the South African Indians. A good example of this argument was the presidential address delivered by Mrs. Sarojini Naidu to the Indian National Congress in 1925, when she said, inter alia: "Oh, rise out of slavery because your slavery is the guarantee of our death in that country; your freedom is the prophecy of our honour in the eyes of the world. . . ."[56]

The time had now come to see what the independent dominions of India and Pakistan would do in regard to the South African Indian question which dependent India had failed to do. The first opportunity for this was not long in coming with preparations being made for the next session of the United Nations.

South African Indians, too, were preparing for the coming session. Sorabjee Rustomjee and A. I. Meer were elected to represent the Joint Passive Resistance Council in New

York, though there was a bitter controversy over Rustomjee's going as he had not accounted for his last expenses at Lake Success. Drs. Dadoo and Naicker were particularly opposed to his going.[57]

The Natal Indian Organisation, too, had plans to be represented by A. I. Kajee and P. R. Pather. Though the N.I.O. finally decided not to be represented by delegates in New York, they compiled a memorandum to be distributed among the members of United Nations.[58] In this memorandum, dated 10th October, 1947, the N.I.O. traced the grievances of Indians in South Africa and ended with the proposal that the best way to resolve the grievances was by way of a round table conference.

The time had now come for the United Nations to review the position again. The question of the treatment of Indians in the Union of South Africa came before the First Committee of the General Assembly on 12th November, 1947. The leader of the Union delegation was Mr. Harry Lawrence, that of India, Mrs. Pandit, and that of Pakistan, Sir Zafrullah Khan.

Two reports had earlier been submitted to the Secretary-General, giving information on the efforts made to implement the resolution of the General Assembly of 8th December, 1946. The Government of India stated that in the view of that government, the Union Government had completely ignored the United Nations' resolution in that they took no action to implement the resolution and refused to accept the terms of the resolution as a basis for discussion. The report stated that spokesmen of the Union Government, including their Prime Minister, had "in their statements impugned the judgement and impartiality of the United Nations, denounced its composition and subjected it to ridicule". It requested the United Nations to take appropriate steps to ensure the implementation of the resolution.[59]

The report of the Union Government stated that no progress had been towards a settlement of the existing differences because of the Indian Government's insistence that the Union Government accept "a condemnation said to be implied in the resolution" and because of the continuance of economic sanctions against South Africa. The Union Government expressed their willingness to work towards a friendly settlement and suggested that the two governments should agree to re-examine the policies announced during the time of the first and second round table talks in 1927 and 1932.[60]

Mr. Lawrence, South Africa, said at the meeting of the first committee that the intergovernmental discussions had failed because the Union Government had been unable to arrive at any agreement with the Indian Government as to the correct interpretation of the resolution of 1946 and because of the continuation of economic sanctions on the Union by the Government of India. He said that the Union Government was not prepared to admit that it had violated principles of the Charter and that it had committed a breach of international agreements. A strong point raised by the Union was in regard to the exact scope of the expression "human rights and fundamental freedom". Paragraph II of the Memorandum of the Union Government dealt with this important aspect. The Union Government's conclusion on this point was that it was not the purpose of the Charter to deal with every conceivable right but only with such rights as were fundamental and absolutely essential for the "dignity and worth of the human person" to be recognised "in all countries at all times in regard to all human beings".[61]

The Union delegate requested once again that the question of domestic jurisdiction in terms of Article 2 (7) should be referred to the International Court of Justice.

Mrs. Pandit, India, in her opening remarks referred to editorial comments which appeared in the English press in South Africa after the 1946 session of the United Nations in order to show that even in South Africa there were calls for the Union Government to change their policies. Mrs. Pandit quoted excerpts from these comments. One of the extracts quoted was from the *Cape Times* dated 11th December, 1946, in which the journal stated that truculent defiance would not help South Africa nor would negative policies be of any avail. South Africa, it said, had for too long lived in a fool's paradise and was brought back to reality by the challenge issued by the United Nations.[62]

Mrs. Pandit went on to show how the challenge was met. Field-Marshal Smuts had attributed the resolution of 1946 to ignorance. He had said that the question had been considered under the influence of a "flood of emotion and mischievous propaganda". On 20th December, 1946, the Prime Minister made two speeches in Pretoria in which "he denounced the United Nations as a body dominated by coloured peoples". He described the United Nations Assembly as "a company of politicians, partisans who are drunk with slogans". Mrs. Pandit pointed out that Field-Marshal Smuts had referred to the minds of the members of the United Nations as "fogged or benumbed". Finally, as late as 24th October, 1947, when the General Assembly was already in session for that year, Field-Marshal Smuts was reported to have said at a meeting of the United Party at the City Hall, Cape Town: "Why bother about the UNO may I ask? I have great respect for the UNO, but it is only an infant. People are talking about world conditions who do not know about world conditions." On the claim of equality by the Africans and Indians, Smuts was reported to have said: "Their cry for equal rights is a cry for the moon. European leadership will remain in the Union probably forever."

Mrs. Pandit then traced the history of the Smuts-Nehru correspondence and showed how and why the negotiations had failed. It was her conclusion that those who believed in the creation of a new world order were apprehensive about the danger of disharmony between races for such disharmony would result in conflict and disaster.

Mrs. Pandit moved a resolution calling upon the governments to hold a round table conference on the basis of the resolution of 8th December, 1946, and to invite the Government of Pakistan to take part in such discussions.

The leader of the delegation from Pakistan, Sir Zafrullah Khan, referring to the written statement of the Union Government of the 15th September, 1947, and the speech by Mr. Lawrence on the 12th November, 1947, said that they were full of irrelevancies which tended to confuse the issue. He said that discrimination against Indians in South Africa was admitted and because there were numerous cases of discrimination in other countries that was no reason to condone the discrimination in South Africa, for "two wrongs do not make a right". He supported the view that the three governments should begin negotiations to resolve the differences.[63]

After the proceedings had lasted four days and over fifty speeches were made on the issue, the first committee of the General Assembly adopted the draft resolution submitted by India by 29 votes to 15 with 5 abstentions calling upon the three governments to hold a round table conference on the basis of the General Assembly resolution of 8th December,

1946, and to report back to the United Nations at its next session. But when the draft resolution was submitted to the General Assembly it failed to get a two-thirds majority when 31 nations voted for it and 19 against it and 6 abstained. It was, consequently, rejected by the General Assembly.[64]

The Indian delegation was greatly upset by this defeat. For nearly thirty minutes after the voting was over the Russian delegate, Mr. Gromyko, who had been in the chair, addressed the Indian delegates in the writing lounge. Soon after supper Mr. Gromyko announced to the delegates that the Indians had introduced a new resolution on the subject. This announcement was met with great surprise and not a little bewilderment. Mr. Lawrence, who was at this time dining in a restaurant close by, was sent for by the South African liaison officer, Mr. R. B. Durrant. Lawrence protested against India's action in introducing a new resolution on an Assembly item which had been disposed of. South Africa was supported by the delegates of the United Kingdom and the United States. Mr. Gromyko said that although the earlier motion had been rejected, the question had not been eliminated from the Assembly's Agenda. The Assembly agreed to consider the legality of the new motion at a later meeting. The text of the new Indian resolution did not make any reference to the resolution of the 8th December, 1946, as constituting the basis for discussion.[65]

India hoped that by submitting a milder resolution and by not insisting that the conference between the two governments be on the basis of the resolution of 8th December, 1946, the new resolution would be sufficiently acceptable to the members of the United Nations to ensure a two-thirds majority. But the new resolution came too late in the day and was not considered. The result of the 1947 session was that with 31 members for, 19 against, and 6 abstentions, the majority fell short of the requisite two-thirds figure by three votes and the outcome was that on that occasion the General Assembly failed to make any further recommendations on the subject.

The leader of the Indian delegation sent a message of good cheer to the Indians of South Africa which said that the defeat in the General Assembly should not give cause for disappointment for the Indian delegation had gained a moral victory.[66]

There was nothing comforting in such a "victory" for the South African Indians. The disappointment was keener because so much was expected at the United Nations and so little was achieved. Too much of emphasis was laid on the "faith in U.N."[67]

For the Union Government, too, the fact that the 1947 resolution had failed to gain a two-thirds majority did not mean that the policies of this government were more acceptable to the member states of the United Nations. There was need to foster a policy of conciliation abroad and at home to improve the lot of the Indians so that the position of the Union Government at the United Nations in the future sessions would be strengthened.

As for the Indians in South Africa, the defeat of the Indian resolution in the General Assembly meant that their next steps had to take note of this defeat. The Natal Indian Congress announced plans to convene a national non-European conference, while the Natal Indian Organisation was to hold a conference on the 11th January, 1948, to discuss the advisability of sending a deputation to India.[68]

Before this conference could be held A. I. Kajee, the Chairman of the Committee of the Natal Indian Organisation, died early in January, 1948. Abdulla I. Kajee had had a long association with the political affairs of this country and had been a top official of the Natal Indian Congress, the South African Indian Congress and the Natal Indian Organisation. His most fervent desire during his last years was to bring about a round table conference between the Indian and South African governments. Only such a conference, he felt, could solve the question of the South African Indians. His passing away led to the postponement of his organisation's conference but not to the abandonment of his policy of a round table conference.

The proposal of the Natal Indian Organisation to send a deputation to India and the many appeals to India to intervene in the affairs of the South African Indians did not meet with approval especially among the members of the parliamentary opposition in South Africa. The Leader of the Opposition, Dr. D. F. Malan, moved a motion in the House of Assembly on 20th January, 1948, that Chapter II of the Asiatic Land Tenure and Indian Representation Act of 1946 (dealing with parliamentary representation of Indians) should be repealed. He said that the Act had not brought about the slightest change in the attitude of the Indians; they continued to defame South Africa abroad and were responsible for the matter being taken to the United Nations where South Africa stood as a condemned party, "a criminal in regard to the Indian question".

Replying to the motion, which was eventually defeated, the Prime Minister, Field-Marshal Smuts, sounded a warning that the debates in the Assembly were finding echoes in faraway places. He said that the world was listening in to the debates.[69]

The world was watching the events in South Africa. This Smuts realised and respected for he was an international figure himself. There were many whites in South Africa, however, who had no time for international politics and policies. Their horizon was limited to the borders of South Africa. Their short-sighted policy was out of step with the growing internationalism of the mid-twentieth century. Some Indian leaders in South Africa were determined to keep the Indian question in the international limelight. Five days after Dr. Malan's motion calling for the repeal of Part II of the 1946 Act, fifteen Indians from Natal crossed the Natal-Transvaal border at Volksrust to open the second phase of the passive resistance campaign.[70] Behind this was the Natal Indian Congress and the Joint Passive Resistance Council. About a month later Drs. Dadoo and Naicker were sentenced to six months' imprisonment without the option of fine for "aiding and abetting" Indians to cross the Transvaal border without permits. The South African Indian question was once again right in the forefront, internationally.

It was kept there when on the 29th January, 1948, a deputation comprising representatives of the Natal Indian Organisation, the Transvaal Indian Organisation and the Cape Indian Congress called on the Prime Minister in Cape Town. The deputation consisted of 34 members. With the Prime Minister were present the Minister of the Interior, Mr. H. G. Lawrence; the Minister of Posts and Telegraphs, Senator Clarkson; the newly appointed Administrator of Natal, Mr. D. G. Shepstone; the Commissioner for Immigration and Asiatic Affairs, Mr. J. H. Basson; the Chairman of the Asiatic Land Tenure Advisory Board, Mr. Van der Merwe.[71]

The secretary of the N.I.O., Mr. P. R. Pather, submitted a memorandum in which the deputation urged that the deadlock existing between the Union Government and the Indian and Pakistan Governments should be resolved and suggested that the best means of restoring friendly relations was by way of holding a round table conference between the governments at which all aspects of Indian life in the Union would be considered without prejudice to the stands hitherto taken by each government. Pather urged that pending the holding of the conference the Union Government should give careful attention to such matters as education, employment and measures designed for the social uplift of Indians.

The Prime Minister informed the deputation that his government was considering ways of bringing about a conference as suggested by the deputation and that he was most anxious to create the right atmosphere for such a conference. He accepted the offer of co-operation made by the deputation in their memorandum. The Prime Minister undertook to give careful consideration to the representations made in regard to welfare matters and he suggested the formation by the N.I.O. of a small committee, which would keep in touch with him and other Ministers to overcome day-to-day difficulties and to maintain the goodwill which he earnestly desired. The Prime Minister then made reference to the remarkable gift of the late Mr. A. I. Kajee and his devoted services to his community, and, at his request, those present stood in tribute to his memory. In conclusion, the Prime Minister agreed to meet a small representative committee the following week.[72]

On 7th February, 1948, the private secretary to the Prime Minister wrote to A. S. Kajee, the president of the N.I.O., confirming the views he had expressed at the recent interview and appealing to the Indian communities to assist in creating the right atmosphere for a conference between the Union and the Indo-Pakistan Governments. Actions such as the spreading of misleading propaganda and the passive resistance struggle, the letter went on to state, were not calculated to create the right atmosphere.[73]

The N.I.O. replied on 26th February, 1948, after its Provincial Committee had considered the whole matter, expressing its appreciation of the friendly attitude of the Prime Minister who, in order to resolve the deadlock between the Union Government and the Governments of India and Pakistan, was willing to hold a round table conference without insisting upon the return of the Indian High Commissioner to South Africa or the lifting of trade sanctions against South Africa as prerequisites to the holding of the conference. The N.I.O. pointed out that it could not control the actions of the extremists who were responsible for the passive resistance campaign but hoped that once the preliminaries for the proposed conference were concluded this campaign would cease.

The letter advised the Prime Minister that the South African Indian Conference composed of representatives of the Natal Indian Organisation, the Transvaal Indian Organisation and the Cape Province would be held in Durban on the 13th and 14th March, 1948, and that the conference would work towards finding ways and means to bring about the round-table talks between the Union Government and the Indo-Pakistan Governments.[74]

All this indicated that steps were now being taken in quick succession for the convening of a round table conference. The Union Government was more amenable in 1948 to the holding of such a conference than it had been in 1947 as the condemnatory resolution of the General Assembly of the 8th December, 1946, no longer stood in the way. As H. G. Lawrence had declared in London on 6th December, 1947, on his way back to

South Africa after that country's victory at the last session of the United Nations, South Africa was no longer in the position "of having a pistol at her head, or of being treated as the condemned party".[75]

Though this situation gave rise to more favourable prospects for the holding of talks between the governments concerned, the fact remained that the failure of the Indian resolution to get a two-thirds majority vote in 1947 did not invalidate the resolution of 1946; nor did it mean the repeal of the resolution.

Meanwhile the Natal Indian Organisation held its meeting and decided that five delegates should go to India at an "opportune time" to negotiate for a round table conference. This decision received widespread disapproval both in South Africa and in India. Typical of the reactions of many Indians was the comment by J. N. Singh, a top official of the Natal Indian Congress, who said in a speech at Pietermaritzburg that General Smuts was trying to send his envoys to India with proposals which would prove to be unacceptable to the Indian Government and that when the mission failed Smuts would report to the United Nations that the reason for the failure did not rest with his government.[76] In India a critic, Dr. Lanka Sundaram, said that as long as the Indians in South Africa were divided there was no good purpose to be served by the sending of deputations to India when such deputations represented "cliques of people who want to batten upon the credulity and loyalty of their fellows".[77]

Mr. P. R. Pather of the N.I.O. did not accept the views expressed by Dr. Sundaram and announced that the deputation, comprising Messrs. A. Ismail, A. I. Minty, A. M. Moolla, S. R. Naidoo and P. R. Pather, would leave for India towards the end of June, 1948. But before this could happen other developments, no less momentous for the future of the Indian and other black peoples in South Africa, were taking place. The country was in the throes of a general election. The Nationalist-Afrikaner pact of Dr. Malan and Mr. Havenga was given little hope of victory while the United-Labour pact was confident of victory. The Malan-Havenga group faced the election on the ticket of "Apartheid". In an election manifesto "The National Party's Colour Policy" was defined as one of separation between the white and black racial groups.[78]

Contrary to predictions, Dr. Malan's Nationalist and Mr. Havenga's Afrikaner Party won the general election by a narrow margin "to their own surprise and to the dismay particularly of those Ministers and their wives who had confidently left their belongings in their official residences while they went campaigning".[79]

Though Prime Minister for the first time in a long political career, Dr. D. F. Malan was no stranger to the Indian question in South Africa for, as Leader of the Union representatives and Minister of the Interior, he had presided at the First and Second Round Table Conferences in 1926–7 and 1932, the first of which had resulted in the Cape Town Agreement of 1927. He had definite views on this question, the gist of which is exemplified in the following excerpt from the Nationalist Election Manifesto: "The party will strive to repatriate or move elsewhere as many Indians as possible; the present ban on Indian immigration, inter-provincial movement and penetration will remain and be more stringently maintained."[80]

The officials of the Natal Indian Congress, in an over-zealous moment, which they later regretted, sent a telegram to the new Prime Minister on 28th May, 1948, congratulating him on his party's victory and reminding him of his past contribution to the Indian question in South Africa while at the same time asking that his party rule in the best interests of the whole of South Africa and its inhabitants.

At the Provincial Conference of the Natal Indian Congress held on 31st May, 1948, it decided to suspend the passive resistance campaign of the Natal and Transvaal Indian Congresses and to seek an interview with Dr. Malan in order to learn what the new government's policy was in regard to the Indians.

There was no need, however, to wait for an interview for that purpose as Dr. Malan covered the main points in a broadcast to the nation. Referring to the United Nations, he said that his government would brook no interference in the domestic affairs of South Africa. As for internal politics, he gave prominence to his government's policy of "Apartheid" and said that for the non-European this policy meant a large measure of independence "through the growth of their self-reliance and self-respect".[81]

The advent of the Nationalist Government has been treated in some detail as the policies and programme of this government would affect the international scene in no small measure. With this victory the Nationalists were at long last free to attend to the shaping of the destiny of South Africa as they saw it. As Dr. Malan said in his victory speech on 2nd June, 1948: "In the past we felt like strangers in our own country, but today South Africa belongs to us once more. For the first time since Union South Africa is our own."[82]

After this there could be no doubt as to the policy of the government on the main issues in South Africa and abroad. General Smuts, in the closing months of his term of office, was moving in the direction of discussions with the Governments of India and Pakistan. It remained to be seen what the new government's reactions would be to the holding of such discussions.

The N.I.O. wrote to Dr. Malan tracing their negotiations with his predecessor and enquiring whether the new Prime Minister would receive a deputation from the N.I.O. on the question of a round table conference and "also on several matters of import and urgency affecting the Indian people of South Africa". The letter was directed by the Prime Minister to the Minister of the Interior for attention and reply. On 23rd July, 1948, the private secretary to the Minister of the Interior wrote to the N.I.O. stating that the Minister was prepared to meet a deputation from the organisations of the N.I.O. as that body was "neither communistic in their orientation or leadership" and because it did not flout the laws of the country or appeal to outside countries for political aid. On the question of a round table conference, the Minister stated that his Government was prepared to hold one provided the agenda for such a conference would not include matters of domestic concern. "On the other hand, there seems to be no objection to such a Conference if it be held on the basis, subject to the restrictions, and with the objective of the prior Conference of 1927 and 1932."[83]

There was no doubt as to the intention of the proviso mentioned. The "objective" referred to could only mean one thing: repatriation of Indians. But as this had been tried and as its failure had been admitted in the Communique of 1932, there seemed little point in carrying on with the negotiations with the South African Government.

The N.I.O., however, in their reply dated 3rd August, 1948, clarified their position in regard to that part of the Minister's letter which dealt with appeals to outside countries for political aid. It pointed out that when a State failed to extend fundamental human rights of citizenship to a section of its subjects that section had the right to appeal to world opinion and that in the case of the South African Indians the governments of India and Pakistan had the right based on treaty obligations to protect the welfare of the local Indians.[84]

The South African Government was prepared to receive a deputation from the N.I.O. but rejected a similar request made by the Natal and Transvaal Indian Congresses. In a letter to these bodies the Minister of the Interior said that he was not prepared to extend that facility to any organisation of Indians which sponsored or associated itself with any organised flouting of the laws of the country. He also excluded organisations which were communistic in their orientation or leadership.[85]

While these negotiations were proceeding in South Africa, related matters were being taken up at international level. On 12th July, 1948, the Indian representative at the United Nations requested the Secretary-General to place the subject of Indians in the Union on the provisional agenda of the third session of the Assembly. The request stated that this matter continued to be a serious violation of the purposes and principles of the United Nations Charter and that the continuation of the policy of racial discrimination against Asians and other black peoples was the result of an assumption by the Union Government that the failure of the General Assembly to adopt an effective resolution in 1947 constituted a tacit approval by the United Nations of that policy.[86]

The Indian representative stated that further steps were being taken to amplify that policy. In August, 1948, the Prime Minister announced in the House of Assembly the Government's future plans to implement the policy of "Apartheid". These were: the repeal of Chapter II of the Asiatic Land Tenure and Indian Representation Act; the abolition of the representation of Africans in Parliament; the removal of the coloureds in the Cape from the common roll; the creation of separate segregated universities.[87]

The Prime Minister's announcement showed clearly that it was the intention of the new government to proceed with the implementation of its policy of separate development without regard to the force of world opinion, which was to be expressed in Paris in September of that year when the third session of the United Nations General Assembly opened. Preparations were afoot for local Indian leaders to represent their respective political parties in South Africa. Drs. Y. M. Dadoo and G. M. Naicker were delegated by the Transvaal and Natal Indian Congresses to proceed to Paris. Soon a new body was to be formed and it, too, would decide on a delegation to be present at the third session. On 11th September, 1948, at a conference held in Durban the South African Indian Organisation was formed. Its constituent bodies were the Natal Indian Organisation, the Transvaal Indian Organisation, and the Cape Indian Congress. Its first officials were, president, S. R. Naidoo; secretaries, A. M. Moolla and P. R. Pather; treasurers, S. M. Paruk and M. R. Parekh.[88] The moderate element in the Indian community had, by this act, created a platform for itself but in the process had divided the Indian community into two clear groups which were to survive for many years to come. The S.A.I.O. decided at this conference to send three members, one each from its constituent parts, to Paris to act as advisers to the Indian and Pakistan delegations. The three persons nominated were P. R. Pather (Natal), A. I. Minty (Transvaal), Ahmed Ismail (Cape).[89]

On the day of the formation of the S.A.I.O. a ban was imposed on Drs. Dadoo and Naicker, presidents of the Transvaal and Natal Indian Congresses, respectively. On the same day Dr. Y. M. Dadoo was taken off the aeroplane bound for Paris at the last minute and his passport was impounded. Subsequently these persons were informed by the Minister of the Interior that their passports had been confiscated because they were "communist agitators" and because they would indulge in "un-South African activities" abroad.[90]

In an editorial headed "The Government Blunders", the *Natal Witness* commented on this incident, stating that the Government had erred in taking action against Dadoo and Naicker; that two democratic rights were involved: freedom of speech and freedom of movement.[91]

If the leaders were prevented from leaving the country by government edict, the Indian people showed their sympathy for them and their confidence in them by overhauling the leadership of the South African Indian Congress at the eighteenth session of the S.A.I.C. held in Durban on the 18th and 19th September, 1948. The "no compromise" militants were voted into office, while none of the older officials of the S.A.I.C. was present. Dr. G. M. Naicker was elected president; Messrs. J. N. Singh and A. I. Meer were elected joint hon. secretaries; Dr. A. H. Sader and Mr. George Singh were elected treasurers.[92]

The new leadership of the S.A.I.C. meant that at the head of affairs in the most powerful Indian political body in the Union were men who were not prepared to compromise with the Government and whose declared policy was to work in collaboration with the other black peoples in the country.

A sample of the change was in evidence when the leader of the South African Government delegation to Paris, Eric Louw, arrived at Waterloo Station on 18th September, 1948, to find Indian demonstrators carrying black flags in silent protest against the action of the Union Government in refusing passports to Drs. Dadoo and Naicker.[93]

The government took a strong view of Indian leaders from South Africa carrying on or assisting in campaigns against the government overseas. In this regard it had not only prevented Dr. Dadoo and Dr. Naicker from leaving the country. It also denied passports to the S.A.I.O. delegation, moderate leaders whose avowed policy was to work for a round table conference between the Union Government and the governments of India and Pakistan. The S.A.I.O. applied to the Minister of the Interior for passports on 21st October, 1948. The next day the Minister informed the organisation by telegram that the application was refused.[94]

With the refusal of passports to the moderate S.A.I.O. delegation the new Union Government clearly indicated that it would not tolerate any representation by the South African Indians for support from external sources. Since the 1947 session of the United Nations the Natal Indian Organisation had worked towards bringing about the round table talks requested in the General Assembly resolution of 1946 and repeated in the unsuccessful resolution of 1947. The Indian question was now before the United Nations for the third time without any progress having been made.

On 22nd September, 1948, E. H. Louw of South Africa spoke in the General Committee protesting against the inclusion of the question of the treatment of Indians in South Africa on the agenda. He based his arguments on Article 2 (7) of the Charter. As there was no formal proposal to exclude the item, the chairman, Dr. Evatt, stated that its retention on the agenda would be recommended to the Assembly.[95]

The issue was, therefore, once again before the United Nations. What gave the issue added significance in 1948 was the fact that a determined Nationalist Party Government in South Africa was to appear to answer the charges levelled against it at the United Nations. The second question of some importance was what would the decision of the General Assembly be on this occasion after the defeat of India's resolution in 1947?

The next session of the United Nations promised to be an important one for the South African Indian question not only because of the above-named factors but also for the reason that the member states were bound to take note of the coming into being of the Union Act 47/1948, the Asiatics Law Amendment Act which repealed Chapter II of the Asiatic Land Tenure and Indian Representation Act of 1946.[96] This Act further aggravated the position of Indians in South Africa. Speaking in favour of the Act, Dr. Malan said that as the Indians in South Africa kept appealing to overseas countries, to India, and to the United Nations and stirred up opinion against South Africa, they had no right to consider themselves part of the permanent population of South Africa and should therefore be content to live in the country under restrictions.[97] The Leader of the Opposition, Field-Marshal Smuts, did not agree with Dr. Malan and said that the Indians were South Africans who were South-African born and had a South African outlook. They were not "temporary sojourners".[98]

If in South Africa the whites were divided in such a manner over the Indian question, it was to be expected that the United Nations would not find it an easy task to work out a settlement acceptable to all parties. The debates in the South African House of Assembly found echo in the chambers of the United Nations in Paris where the question of the competence of the General Assembly to deal with the question of the treatment of Indians in South Africa was raised by Eric Louw on 28th September, 1948. Dr. Evatt, the chairman, pointed out that under the Rules of Procedure it was left to the first committee to decide the question of competence. When the first part of the third session closed on 12th December, 1948, the first committee had not reached the Indian item on their agenda. The matter was therefore left over for consideration during the second part of the session which was to begin in April, 1949.[99]

Though the Indian question was not debated in the 1948 session of the United Nations, the adoption by the United Nations of the Universal Declaration of Human Rights at the plenary meeting of the General Assembly on 10th December of that year had some bearing on this question as this Declaration would certainly be invoked when racial issues were debated in the world organisation. Twenty-nine nations voted for it and seven abstained; twenty-two delegates were absent when the vote was taken. The Declaration contained a preamble and thirty articles. The last part of the preamble reads: "The General Assembly

    Proclaims the Universal Declaration of Human Rights as a common standard of achievement for all peoples and all nations, to the end that every individual and every organ of society, keeping this Declaration constantly in mind, shall strive by teaching and education to promote respect for the rights and freedoms and by progressive measures, national and international, to secure their universal and effective recognition and observance, both among the peoples of Member States themselves and among the peoples of territories under their jurisdiction."[100]

South Africa did not support the Declaration. The acting leader of the South African delegation, Harry Andrews, said in the Assembly: "In our country all the basic and elementary human rights and freedoms are enjoyed by all the people, irrespective of colour or sex. In that respect we do not take second place to any other state represented in this Assembly." The leader of the South African delegation at Paris, Eric Louw, speaking at Hermanus, Cape, said that if the Declaration of Human Rights was accepted by South Africa the European in South Africa could pack his possessions and leave the country. He did not see what advantages South Africa derived by being represented at the United Nations. It cost something like £150 000 for South Africa to be represented at that organisation where she was subjected to indignities.[101]

If the South African Government regarded the attacks at the United Nations as "indignities", the South African Indians on whose behalf these attacks were made in the first instance had reason to feel that certain "indignities" at home had contributed to the enlargement of the Indian question in South Africa to international proportions. And though the Union Government was first taken to task at the United Nations for its treatment of its Indian subjects, the complaints against the Government were soon to embrace the racial policies of the country in respect of all black peoples in the Union of South Africa. At home the racial problems of South Africa which were to have an important bearing on the international aspects of the Indian question erupted violently into prominence with the outbreak of racial riots in Durban on 13th January, 1949, resulting in loss of life and property. One hundred and forty-two people died (1 European, 50 Indians, 87 Africans and 4 not classified) and one thousand and eighty-seven were injured (32 Europeans, 11 Coloured, 541 Africans and 503 Indians). The buildings which were completely destroyed included a factory, fifty-eight stores and two hundred and forty-seven dwelling houses, while two factories, over six hundred stores and a thousand dwelling houses were damaged to varying degrees.

The Government set up a commission of enquiry under the chairmanship of Mr. Justice F. van der Heever, with Mr. Ryle Masson and Mr. W. Schulz, both chief magistrates as members, and Mr. B. C. van der Merwe as secretary, to report on the events which led to the riots, their causes, and to give the causes of any strained relations between Africans and Indians which existed before the riots.

The Report of the Commission dated 7th April, 1949, gave as the causes of the riots the increasing lack of discipline on the part of the African; bad precepts and bad examples; the character of the parties to the riots; increasing tension between the Indians and the Africans; unsatisfactory local conditions.[103]

However, for the purposes of this study, the contention advanced by Dr. Lowen who represented the Joint Committee of the African National Congress and the South African Indian Congress deserves particular mention. Dr. Lowen said that the root cause was the slum conditions for Indians and Africans alike; yet another cause, he said, was the racial antagonism, racial hostility, and racial hatred which had been propagated for years by the previous government and continued by the present government; that the speeches made by Cabinet Ministers had the effect of creating hatred in the European and in the African. All these factors combined, said Dr. Lowen, to bring about the tragic riots. The Commission, however, reported that it was unable to establish a causal connection between the public speeches complained of and the riots.[104]

This conclusion is not the full explanation for the explosive situation. There are other aspects which cannot be laboured here. Kenneth Kirkwood comments on certain characteristics of the report and on the shortcomings in it.[105] But for the international aspects of this study, influenced as they are by national factors, the most significant result of the Durban riots was the growth of a new understanding, a new pact, a reorientation in outlook and attitudes, in Indo-African relations in South Africa. January 13th 1949, was in essence the beginning of an era of understanding between Indians and Africans that was sorely wanting before. This understanding was in evidence when Dr. Lowen was briefed to appear before the Commission on behalf of the Joint Committee of the A.N.C. and the S.A.I.C.[106]

It was in evidence again when, on 6th February, 1949, the African National Congress and the South African Indian Congress formed a joint council "to advance and promote mutual understanding and goodwill among our respective peoples".[107]

With this new understanding cemented, the South African Indian Congress, whom the Union Government was not prepared to negotiate with, sent off M. D. Naidoo to India by the S.S. *Karanja* in March, 1949. His departure was a closely kept secret. It was only towards the end of the month that the S.A.I.C. announced that Moulvi I. A. Cachalia and M. D. Naidoo had been appointed accredited representatives of the S.A.I.C. in India.[108]

With the S.A.I.C. now officially represented in India, the Executive Committee of the S.A.I.O. decided on the 6th April, 1949, that Messrs. P. R. Pather, A. M. Moolla and A. S. Kajee should proceed to London where, later in April, the Commonwealth Prime Ministers' Conference was to be held. The delegation of the S.A.I.O. was of the opinion that the opportunity should be seized to seek the assistance of the Prime Ministers to bring about an amicable and lasting solution of the question of the treatment of Indians in South Africa.[109]

In reply to the application made by the S.A.I.O. for passports for its delegation, the private secretary to the Minister of the Interior wrote that owing to the short duration of the Union Prime Minister's visit to London a conference between him and the Prime Ministers of India and Pakistan could not be arranged. The letter went on to state that the Minister was amazed that the N.I.O., made up of South Africans, should blame South Africa exclusively for the failure to restore friendly relations between the Union, India and Pakistan.[110] In his reply the Minister admitted that the Indians were *South Africans*, something which he and the other members of the government had refused to acknowledge earlier. This admission was carried further when Dr. Dönges admitted in the Senate on 10th May, 1949, that the Indians were South African nationals.[111]

The S.A.I.O. delegation was refused passports to proceed to London but it sent cables to all the prime ministers urging them to use every endeavour to resolve the deadlock between South Africa and India and Pakistan. And on 25th April, 1949, the secretaries of the S.A.I.O. wrote to the Secretary-General of the United Nations sending copies of the correspondence with General Smuts, Dr. T. E. Dönges and the cables sent to the prime ministers in London. The letter urged that the copies should be circulated to all member nations and that when the matter came up for discussion every endeavour should be made to bring about a round table conference between the Union, India and Pakistan with a view to securing a lasting settlement of the Indian question in South Africa.[112]

The scene was now transferred to the second part of the third regular session of the United Nations where the discussions began in the first committee (Political and Security Committee) on 9th May, 1949. Eric Louw (South Africa) moved that the Committee should decide on the question of competence first before the complaint was discussed. Louw's motion was rejected by 33 votes to 7 with 10 abstentions.

Mr. Setalvad (India) was the first speaker. The gist of his argument was that human rights were being violated in the Union of South Africa and that it was the responsibility of the United Nations to secure respect for those rights in terms of the Charter and subsequent resolutions on the subject. He moved a resolution recommending that a three-man commission be set up to enquire into the treatment of Indians in South Africa.[113]

Louw said that he was not prepared to go into the substance of the matter at issue. He wished to raise an entirely separate issue, that of the competency of the United Nations, in relation to Article 2 (7), to consider the matter before it. He wanted a separate vote to be taken on that issue and emphasized the importance of the decision to be taken as member states who did not have the right of veto in the Security Council looked to the application of Article 2 (7) as their only protection. He pointed out that in certain respects the complaint of the Government of India was a new one and consequently the 1946 resolution was no longer binding on the Assembly. In the present instance India not only claimed to intervene on behalf of all Asians and other non-Europeans in the Union but they had further alleged that the Union was guilty of a violation of the purposes and principles of the Charter and of a denial of human rights and freedoms.

Louw submitted a draft resolution calling upon the General Assembly to decide that item 2 on the agenda – The Treatment of Indians in the Union of South Africa – was a matter which was essentially within the domestic jurisdiction of the Union of South Africa and that it did not fall within the competence of the Assembly. Louw stated, in conclusion, that he would not participate in the discussion on the substance of the Indian complaint because such participation would be an admission that the United Nations had the right to interfere in the domestic affairs of a member state. He would, however, be present at meetings without taking his seat at the committee table. Before the vote on the question of competence he would resume his seat to reply to arguments on that issue and to cast his vote.

Twenty-one representatives participated in the debate which followed, twelve of whom were of the opinion that the Assembly was competent to consider the matter and that Article 2 (7) had no application.[114] Of the representatives who supported the Union's view, only those from Denmark, Argentina and France stated that the Assembly was incompetent to deal with the matter. The representatives from New Zealand and Belgium were inclined to the view that as there were grave doubts regarding the actual scope of

Article 2 (7) it would be advisable to refer the matter to the International Court of Justice.

The representative from Canada felt that a distinction should be made between the right of the Assembly to discuss the problem and its competence to intervene. Nevertheless, he felt that the matter could best be solved by the two governments employing methods of their own choice. Australia, Peru and Greece supported the view that the two governments should be encouraged to settle the dispute themselves.[115]

The draft resolution submitted by the Union of South Africa was then put to the vote. It was rejected by 33 votes to 5 with 12 abstentions.[116] Two draft resolutions were finally adopted in the first committee; the first resolution was submitted jointly by France and Mexico. The resolution called upon the governments of India, Pakistan and the Union of South Africa to enter into discussions at a round table conference, having regard to the purposes and principles of the Charter and the Declaration of Human Rights. This resolution was adopted by 39 votes to 2 with nine abstentions, while the Indian resolution calling for a three-man commission was adopted by 21 votes to 17 with 12 abstentions. It was evident that the Franco-Mexican resolution had a greater chance of survival in the General Assembly.

The two resolutions were submitted to the plenary session of the General Assembly on 14th May, 1949, without any specific recommendations. In the plenary session, General Romulo (Philippines) appealed to India to withdraw the draft resolution in favour of the Franco-Mexican resolution. The Indian delegate admitted that his resolution did not stand a chance of obtaining a two-thirds majority and as he was anxious to seek a practical and quick solution he was prepared to withdraw his resolution.

Louw (South Africa) said that while the Franco-Mexican resolution was a tremendous advance when compared to the past resolutions it still entailed domestic interference in the affairs of a member state. He suggested that the concluding portions of the resolution referring to the "purposes and principles of the Charter" and the "Declaration of Human Rights" be deleted. Setalvad (India) argued that his delegation attached the greatest importance to the words referred to as they constituted a directive to the conference suggested.

At the end the Franco-Mexican resolution was adopted by the required two-thirds majority, by 47 votes to 1 with 10 abstentions.[117]

The most significant development during this session of the United Nations was South Africa's virtual withdrawal from the discussions on the substance of the Indian complaint. This was in accordance with the government's contention that no interference in her domestic affairs would be permitted, at least not with its own connivance. Louw's decision to withdraw from the discussions met with general approval from those who supported his contention that Article 2 (7) afforded protection against interference in the domestic affairs of member states. But whether the move was a wise one in the diplomatic sense of international politics was another matter altogether. The case of the South African Government since 1946 in regard to the Indian question rested on the broad base of non-interference in the domestic affairs of sovereign states as embodied in Article 2 (7) of the Charter. This article is one of the contradictions of the United Nations. The architects of the Charter, no doubt thinking of the recent war atrocities (brought to light by the Nuremberg trials), desired to ensure that fundamental human rights and the dignity and worth of the human person would not again be violated. But they also wished to ensure that the United Nations would not be transformed into an institution like the concert of Europe to interfere in the domestic affairs of independent nations. Just as Castlereagh, Canning and Palmerston, of Great Britain, had resisted the interpretation of Count Von Metternich of Austria so those who wished to see the sovereignty of states respected worked for the inclusion of Article 2 (7) in the Charter, though just how this sovereignty was to be respected if Article 2 (7) were to be ignored represented a serious contradiction. Legally, therefore, Louw's contention was justified; but to insist upon legal principles alone was to suggest that the case of the South African Government was weak and that there was something to hide. The discussion on the question of the competence of the General Assembly to include the item on the agenda was, as Nicholas states, a debate in some form of the item itself and though the substance of the case need not be dealt with at such a stage the stipulation was respected more in the breach than in the observance. The Union Government's insistence upon the legal interpretation of Article 2 (7) would, therefore, find little or no support at the United Nations so long as the issues of fundamental human rights, the dignity and worth of the human person and the Declaration of Human Rights stood opposed to those involved in Article 2 (7).[118]

When the third session of the United Nations General Assembly reached its end the position was that all the governments concerned were called upon once again to hold discussions in order to settle their differences on the Indian question. The first step towards implementation was taken by the Government of India on 4th July, 1949, when they enquired "whether the Government of the Union of South Africa were agreeable to a round table conference being convened as provided for in the resolution, and if so, where and when". It was suggested that the details of the agenda and other matters could be discussed later.[119]

Five days later the Government of India lodged a protest against the Asiatic Land Tenure (Amendment) Act, 1949, in terms of which an Asiatic would, after July 1, 1949, be prevented from occupying any land or premises even for the purpose of business or trade in areas in which ownership and residence had already been prohibited.[120]

The Government of India also informed the United Nations that they considered the new Act to constitute a fresh violation of the purposes and principles of the Charter of the United Nations and the Declaration of Human Rights.[121]

The South African Government expressed their willingness to hold discussions with the governments of India and Pakistan subject to the conditions that the South African Indian question was the domestic concern of the South African Government and that any solution arrived at with the co-operation of other governments must be acceptable to the South African Government; that in any discussions an exaggerated emphasis on the Declaration of Human Rights should not be made and that this declaration should not be accepted as the determining factor.[122]

Both these points contained the basis on which the South African Government was prepared to hold discussions with the governments of India and Pakistan. It was suggested in the telegram of the 13th July, 1949, that South Africa should be the venue for such talks. The Indian Government replied that India could no more interfere in the domestic affairs of South Africa than the South African Government could in the affairs of India but as the Indian problem in South Africa had to be viewed as one in which both governments were interested and that because of its racial implications it also had an international significance, the Government of India was taking steps towards finding a solution. The Indian Government was willing to hold preliminary discussions in South Africa.[123]

In the course of these exchanges the South African Government ventured to suggest that "success even of preliminary informal talks would be enhanced if trade sanctions are withdrawn voluntarily by India so as to allow the parties to negotiate on an equal footing".[124]

The Indian Government saw no reason to accede to this request but rather drew the attention of the South African Government to further examples of discrimination in South Africa; these were the refusal of renewals to Indian traders in African reserves; the deportation of foreign-born Indians on conviction for offences; the prosecution of Indians under the price control regulations even for minor irregularities; the examination of documents of Indian companies to check irregular and illegal occupation of fixed property; the refusal of transfer of licences even between Indians in the Pretoria Asiatic Bazaar; the refusal of building permits; the introduction of segregation in railway stations, post offices and buses in Cape Town. These new complaints were calculated to point out that such measures were not conducive to "a propitious atmosphere for the Round Table Conference" and it asked that they be postponed until the projected conference had reviewed the entire problem.[125]

For its part the South African Government also adduced points to show that the actions of the Indian Government were also creating an unfavourable atmosphere for the talks and in support of its allegations charges were made against the action of the Indian Government in arraigning the South African Government before the United Nations on the ground of its unwillingness to seek a solution while correspondence was still being exchanged between the two governments; that while the whole matter was *sub judice*, criticism by the Indian delegation at the United Nations of the progress of the negotiations was irrelevant and unfounded; that the maintenance of unilateral trade sanctions against South Africa was not justified; as also was the latest concern of the Indian Government with matters which were within the domestic jurisdiction of South Africa.[126]

In a war of attrition such exchanges could go on *ad infinitum* until the wood could not be seen for the trees. Both sides had strong debating points which would only subscribe to greater acrimony and delay. If the important thing was the projected conference everything else would have to be subordinated to it. In view of the charges and counter-charges it is a wonder that the discussions were held at all.

At this time Pakistan, the junior partner in the negotiations, was moving in the direction of re-opening trade relations with South Africa. But when it was announced that the three-power talks would begin in Cape Town on 6th February, 1950, Pakistan agreed to hold up the matter of resuming trade relations with South Africa pending the outcome of the talks.[127]

In a statement on the preliminary discussions the South African Indian Congress, welcoming the move, said: "Our only regret is that the announcement comes four years too late." Though late, there was still time to make up lost ground if only a common and mutually acceptable settlement could be worked out.

India was represented at the talks by Pandit Kunzru, leader, and Messrs. Y. D. Gundevia, and R. T. Chari who was secretary to the High Commissioner of India in South Africa.

The South African delegates were Dr. T. E. Dönges, leader; Mr. D. D. Forsyth, the Secretary for External Affairs; Dr. L. C. Steyn, senior law adviser; Mr. J. H. Basson, Commissioner for Immigration and Asiatic Affairs; J. H. N. van der Merwe, chairman of the Asiatic Land Tenure Board, while Pakistan was represented by Dr. Mahomed Hussain, leader; Messrs. Akhtar Hussain and Sajjad Hussain.[129]

When the preliminary talks opened Dr. Dönges, the South African Minister of the Interior, tried to make out that the discussions were not being held because of any resolution of the United Nations but had been made possible solely as a result of personal contacts established between Mr. Nehru, Prime Minister of India, and Dr. Malan, Prime Minister of the Union, in London. Dr. Dönges said that the scope of the discussions was limited by the correspondence exchanged between the governments prior to the talks. He said that the objective of the previous conference in 1932 had been the reduction of the Indian population in South Africa. The Cape Town discussions should carry on from that point.[130]

The leader of the Indian delegation, Pandit Kunzru, contended that India was entering the discussions solely because of the United Nations resolution and not because of the meeting between the prime ministers in London. He did not agree that the sole purpose of the 1927 and 1932 Conference was to discuss the question of reduction of the Indian population in South Africa. These diametrically opposed statements and objectives clearly showed that the main parties were far from treading on common ground.

When the three delegations got down to the drawing up of the actual agenda for the Round Table Conference, South Africa proposed the item: "Reduction of the Indian population in South Africa" to be entered on their behalf. India and Pakistan proposed the following item: "Removal of Political, Social and Economic disabilities of South African Nationals of Indo-Pakistan origin and the provision of opportunities for their fullest development." It was agreed that the ultimate wording of the communique should be such as not to wreck in advance the possibility of a successful discussion by undue criticism outside the conference, though privately the delegates should have an accurate idea of the points which might be discussed under the particular agenda heads.

The Press Communique dated 20th February, 1950, stated that the three delegations agreed to recommend to their respective governments that a round table conference be convened to settle the Indian question in South Africa and that in the holding of the discussions or the conference it was understood that there was no departure from the previous standpoints of the respective governments in the issue of domestic jurisdiction.[131]

The first hurdle was over, though there was very little to be sanguine about. No departure was made by either side on any important point. There could not, therefore, be any hope of success with the *status quo ante* prevailing.

Dr. Dönges, in a statement to the House of Assembly on 20th February, 1950, said: "It is with confidence that I commend to the House the decision to hold a round table conference on the agreed basis in the conviction that that decision will be regarded by us all in a truly national light."

Few observers gave the Conference any chance of success. The London *Statesman* wrote: "There is no indication that the Union Government has modified its opinion on racial matters; indeed the current recrudescence of racial turmoil is largely traced by Imperial observers to the attitude of the Nationalists. There is equally little reason to believe they (Nationalists) are impressed – though they are certainly annoyed – by world opinion."

In this category of world opinion could be included Indian opinion. The Government of Pakistan, however, remained conciliatory in their attitude. They decided to end the trade ban between Pakistan and South Africa, hoping, as they informed the Government of India, that their step would "go a long way towards securing a lasting settlement with South Africa which would satisfy the honour of Pakistanis and Indians domiciled in that country and ensure for them civic, political and economic rights".[132]

This was a laudable step, within the framework of conciliation and compromise, whose success depended upon the reaction it aroused from the other interested party, in this case, South Africa. But the reaction which it received was a most violent and uncompromising one. It got the Group Areas Act. It was this Act, more than any other, that has left in its wake immense tragedy and deep bitterness.

FOOTNOTES

1. *Principal Documents Relating to Consideration by the United Nations General Assembly of the Representations by the Government of India on the Treatment of Indians in the Union of South Africa 1946*, p. 1. This is cited hereafter as *Principal Documents*.
2. *Principal Documents*, p. 1.
3. *Principal Documents*, p. 1.
4. *The United Nations in the Making: Basic Documents*, p. 43. The enforcement measures referred to under Chapter VII deal with "Action with Respect to Threats to the Peace, Breaches of the Peace and Acts of Aggression" and are epitomised in Article 39 of Chapter VII: "The Security Council shall determine the existence of any threat to the peace, breach of the peace, or act of aggression and shall make recommendations or decide what measures shall be taken . . . to maintain or restore international peace and security." *Ibid.*, pp. 52–56.
5. Leo Kuper, *Passive Resistance in South Africa*.
6. *Leader*, 15th June, 1946.
7. *Leader*, 13th July, 1946. It is important to note that only 11,3 per cent of all Asiatics (including Chinese) were not born in South Africa. This means that 88,7 per cent of the Asiatic population of 282 539 were at this time Union nationals by virtue of their native birth. Of this total no less than 228 119 lived in Natal as compared with 232 923 Europeans living in that Province. *Vide Report of the United Nations Commission on the Racial Situation in the Union of South Africa*, p. 45, par. 342, and Ellen Hellmann (Ed.) *Handbook of Race Relations in South Africa*, Population, pp. 25–6.
8. *Leader*, 14th September, 1946.
9. *Leader*, 14th September, 1946.
10. *Ibid.*, 28th September, 1946.

11. *Ibid.*, 21st September, 1946.
12. *Ibid.*, 12th and 19th October, 1946.
13. *Ibid.*, 19th October, 1946.
14. *Ibid.*, 26th October, 1946. According to the information of the *Leader*, Rustomjee collected about £7 000 to cover the expenses of H. A. Naidoo and himself.
15. Document A/68, 26th August, 1946. The text of this document is reproduced as Annexure 2 in *Principal Documents*, pp. 6–23.
16. Document A/167, 31st October, 1946. This is reproduced as Annexure 3 in *Principal Documents*, pp. 24–43.
17. Document A/167, Add. 1, 15th November, 1946, reproduced as Annexure 4 of *Principal Documents*, pp. 44–53.
18. *Principal Documents*, p. 25, par. 8.
19. *Principal Documents*, p. 40, par. 74. A pamphlet entitled *The Indian in South Africa* issued by the South African Government Information Office in New York was also distributed.
20. *Principal Documents*, p. 2.
21. *Principal Documents*, pp. 54–55.
22. *Principal Documents*, p. 55.
23. *Principal Documents*, Annexure 6, p. 81.
24. *Ibid.*, p. 55.
25. *Ibid.*, pp. 55–6.
26. *Principal Documents*, p. 58.
27. *Principal Documents*, Annexure 8, *Analysis of Voting*, p. 105. The following analysis is important as an indication of the stand taken by Member States:
THE FRANCO-MEXICAN RESOLUTION: *For:* Byelorussian S.S.R., Chile, China, Columbia, Cuba, Czechoslovakia, Egypt, Ethiopia, France, Guatemala, Haiti, India, Iran, Iraq, Mexico, Philippines, Poland, Saudi Arabia, Syria, Ukrainian S.S.R., Uruguay, U.S.S.R., Venezuela, Yugoslavia. *Against:* Australia, Belgium, Brazil, Canada, Costa Rica, Dominican Republic, El Salvador, Greece, Iceland, Luxembourg, Netherlands, Nicaragua, Norway, Paraguay, Peru, Sweden, Union of South Africa, United Kingdom, United States. *Abstention:* Denmark, Ecuador, Honduras, New Zealand, Panama, Turkey. *Absent:* Afghanistan, Argentina, Bolivia, Lebanon, Liberia.
28. *Principal Documents*, Annexure 7, p. 84.
29. *Principal Documents*, p. 85.
30. *Ibid.*, p. 89.
31. *Principal Documents*, pp. 89–90.
32. *Principal Documents*, Annexure 8. Analysis of Voting, p. 105. The details of the voting are as follows:
SOUTH AFRICAN RESOLUTION IN THE ASSEMBLY: *For:* Argentina, Australia, Belgium, Brazil, Canada, Costa Rica, Denmark, Ecuador, El Salvador, Greece, Luxembourg, Netherlands, New Zealand, Nicaragua, Paraguay, Peru, Sweden, Turkey, Union of South Africa, United Kingdom, United States. *Against:* Byelorussian S.S.R., Chile, China, Columbia, Cuba, Czechoslovakia, Dominican Republic, Egypt, Ethiopia, France, Guatemala, Haiti, Honduras, Iceland, India, Iran, Iraq, Lebanon, Liberia, Mexico, Norway, Panama, Philippines, Poland, Saudi Arabia, Syria, Ukrainian S.S.R., Uruguay, U.S.S.R., Venezuela, Yugoslavia. *Abstention:* Afghanistan and Bolivia.
FRANCO-MEXICAN RESOLUTION IN GENERAL ASSEMBLY: *For:* Afghanistan, Byelorussian S.S.R., Chile, China, Columbia, Cuba, Czechoslovakia, Dominican Republic, Egypt, Ethiopia, France, Guatemala, Haiti, Honduras, Iceland, India, Iran, Iraq, Lebanon, Liberia, Mexico, Norway, Panama, Philippines, Poland, Saudi Arabia, Syria, Ukrainian S.S.R., Uruguay, U.S.S.R., Venezuela, Yugoslavia. *Against:* Argentina, Belgium, Canada, Costa Rica, El Salvador, Greece, Luxembourg, Netherlands, New Zealand, Nicaragua, Paraguay, Peru, Union of South Africa, United Kingdom, United States. *Abstention:* Australia, Bolivia, Brazil, Denmark, Ecuador, Sweden, Turkey.

Though the Resolution adopted by the United Nations General Assembly on December 8th, 1946, is the same as that adopted by the Joint Committee, a few minor stylistic changes in the form (though none in the essence) in the General Assembly necessitates a fresh reproduction here:

"The General Assembly having taken note of the application made by the Government of India regarding the treatment of Indians in the Union of South Africa and having considered the matter:

(1) STATES that, because of the treatment, friendly relations between the two Member States have been impaired, and unless a satisfactory settlement is reached, these relations are likely to be further impaired;

(2) IS OF THE OPINION that the treatment of Indians in the Union should be in conformity with the international obligations under the agreement concluded between the two Governments, and the relevant provisions of the Charter;

(3) THEREFORE REQUESTS the two Governments to report at the next session of the General Assembly the measures adopted to this effect."

Vide Principal Documents, Annexure 9, *Treatment of Indians in the Union of South Africa*, p. 106, Resolution No. 44 (1).

32a. Nicholas, *The United Nations as a Political Institution*, pp. 26–7.
33. *Leader*, 30th November, 1946.
34. G. H. Calpin, (Ed.) *A. I. Kajee*, p. 152.
35. *Leader*, 21st December, 1946.
36. *Ibid.*, 14th December, 1946; 8th February, 1947.
37. *Natal Witness*, 2nd December, 1946.
38. N.I.O., South African Indian Conference Records, quoted by A. I. Kajee in his speech to the Pietermaritzburg Rotary Club, 17th April, 1947.
38a. Natal Indian Organisation, South African Indian Conference Records, Formation of Natal Indian Organisation.
39. *Ibid.*, Memo to Prime Minister, 21st May, 1947, pp. 1–3.
40. *Ibid.*, Prime Minister's Press Statement, 21st May, 1947.
41. *Ibid.*, Smuts-Nehru Correspondence, No. 3217, Secretary to Government of India to Minister of External Affairs, Cape Town, 24th April, 1947.
42. *Ibid.*, Minister of External Affairs, Cape Town, to Secretary to Government of India, No. 76, 28th April, 1947.
43. *Ibid.*, Secretary to the Government of India to the Secretary for External Affairs, No. 3506, 6th May, 1947.
44. *Ibid.*
45. *Ibid.*, Secretary for External Affairs, Pretoria, to Secretary to the Government of India, No. 99, 18th June, 1947.
46. *Ibid.*, Secretary to the Government of India to Minister of External Affairs, Pretoria, 24th June, 1947, No. 4909.
47. *Ibid.*, Minister of External Affairs, Pretoria, to Secretary to the Government of India, No. 125, 28th July, 1947.
48. *Ibid.*, Secretary to the Government of India to Minister of External Affairs, No. 6422, 8th August, 1947.
49. *Leader*, 8th March, 1947.
50. *Ibid.*, 22nd March, 1947.
51, *Leader*, 10th May, 1947.
52. *Ibid.*
53. *Ibid.*, 31st May, 1947.
54. *The Annual Register*, vol. 189, 1947, pp. 511–513.
55. *Whittaker's Almanac*, 1948, p. 761.
56. Natesan, *Congress Presidential Addresses*, p. 760. Passive resistance was still in force in South Africa at this time. The following figures explain the position:

STATISTICAL ANALYSIS OF PASSIVE RESISTERS
June 13th, 1946, to June 13th, 1947

Total numbers of resisters imprisoned: 1 710 (1 431 men and 279 women). Natal: 1 386. Transvaal: 289. Cape: 27. Basutoland: 8. Vide *Leader*, 21st June, 1947.

57. *Leader*, 30th August, 1947.
58. *Ibid.*, 6th September, 1947. With Mr. Ashwin Choudree also in New York, the delegates of the Joint Passive Resistance Council now were Messrs. Choudree, Rustomjee and Meer. Vide *Ibid.*, 20th September, 1947.
59. Government of India, Question of the Treatment of Indians in the Union of South Africa, Verbatim Record of 106th to 112th Meetings of the First Committee held in November, 1947, p. 2, Document A/68.
60. *Ibid.*, p. 5, Document A/387.
61. *Ibid.*, p. 9. *Vide* also Union Government's Statement to the United Nations, 15th September, 1947, Document A/387, pp. 7–9.
62. Verbatim Record of 106th to 112th Meeting of the First Committee, November, 1947, pp. 12–14.
63. *Ibid.*, pp. 14–90.
64. *Leader*, 22nd November, 1947.
65. *Natal Witness*, 22nd November, 1947.
66. *Leader*, 6th December, 1947.
67. *Ibid.*, 29th November, 1947.
68. *Leader*, 6th December, 1947, and 3rd January, 1948.
69. House of Assembly Debates, Vol. 62, 1948, pp. 62–80.
70. *Leader*, 31st January, 1948; 28th February, 1948.
71. Press Statement by the Prime Minister, 29th January, 1948. N.I.O., South African Indian Conference Records.
72. *Ibid.* The members of the N.I.O. representing Natal on the deputation were Messrs. A. S. Kajee, P. R. Pather, S. R. Naidoo, A. M. Moolla, A. B. Moosa, Y. C. Meer, A. G. Bux, C. M. Anglia, C. M. Bassa and M. R. Parekh.
73. Letter P. S. 2888/44, Private Secretary to Mr. A. S. Kajee, 7th February, 1948, N.I.O., South African Conference Records, 1948.
74. Secretary of N.I.O. to Private Secretary to the Prime Minister, 26th February, 1948. *Ibid.*
75. Dr. Lanka Sundaram, writing in the *Pravasi*, reproduced in the *Leader*, 6th March, 1948.
76. *Ibid.*, 20th March, 1948.
77. *Ibid.*, 22nd May, 1948.
78. Report of the United Nations Commission on the Racial Situation in the Union of South Africa, 1953, p. 140.
79. Walker, *History of Southern Africa*, p. 772. Dr. Malan became Prime Minister and Minister of External Affairs; Mr. Havenga, the sole representative from the Afrikaner Party, was given the portfolio of Finance. The remaining members of the Ministry were: Dr. E. G. Jansen, Native Affairs; Mr. J. G. Strydom, Lands; Mr. P. O. Sauer, Transport; Mr. C. R. Swart, Justice; Mr. E. Louw, Economic Development and Mines; Dr. T. E. Dönges, Interior and Posts and Telegraphs; Mr. S. P. le Roux, Agriculture; Mr. F. C. Erasmus, Defence; Mr. B. J. Schoeman, Labour and Public Works; Dr. A. J. Stals, Education. *Ibid.*, p. 773.
80. *Leader*, 5th June, 1948.
81. *Ibid.*, 12th June, 1948.
82. *The Annual Register*, 1948, Vol. 190, p. 114.
83. P. R. Pather and E. I. Haffejee, Joint Hon. Secretaries, N.I.O. to Private Secretary to the Prime Minister, 17th June, 1948, in South African Indian Organisation, First Conference Records, 1951.
84. S.A.I.O., First Conference Records, 1951.
85. *Leader*, 7th August, 1948.
86. *The Treatment of Indians in the Union of South Africa:* Discussions and Proceedings in the United

Nations, Third Session, September, 1948, to May, 1949, p. 1. This is cited hereafter as United Nations, *Discussions and Proceedings*, 1948–9.

87. *Leader*, 14th August and 21st August, 1948.

93. *Ibid.*

94. Telegram PDA 423, 22nd October, 1948, S.A.I.O., First Conference Records. Dr. Dadoo left the country early in October, 1948, without a passport and later sued the Minister of the Interior successfully for the return of his passport.

95. Vide *Leader*, 23rd October, 1948. United Nations, *Discussions and Proceedings*, 1948–9, p. 1.

96. House of Assembly Debates, Vol. 65, 1948, p. 3047.

97. *Ibid.*, pp. 3054–5.

98. *Ibid.*, p. 3058.

99. United Nations, *Discussions and Proceedings*, 1948–9, p. 1.

100. *Leader*, 18th December, 1948.

101. *Leader*, 15th January, 1949.

102. Report of the Commission of Enquiry into Riots in Durban, U.G. 36/1949, p. 5.

103. *Ibid.*, p. 11.

104. *Ibid.*, p. 10.

105. Maurice Webb and Kenneth Kirkwood, *The Durban Riots and After*, pp. 20–1.

105. Maurice Webb and Kenneth Kirkwood, *The Durban Riots and After*, pp. 20–1.

106. The position is better illustrated by *Population Statistics* that bear out the significance of this new "alliance":

Year			Whites	Africans	Asiatics	Coloured	Total
1936	..	..	2 003 334	6 595 597	219 691	769 241	9 587 863
1946	..	..	2 372 044	7 830 559	285 260	928 062	11 415 925
1951	..	..	2 641 689	8 560 083	366 664	1 103 016	12 671 452

Union of South Africa, Monthly Bulletin of Statistics, Vol. XXXIX, No. 5, May, 1960, p. 2.

107. *Leader*, 13th February, 1949. The members of the Joint Council were: FOR THE A.N.C.: Dr. A. B. Xuma, President-General; Messrs. A. W. G. Champion; C. S. Ramahanae; R. G. Baloyi; H. Selby Msimang; J. B. Marks; J. Malangabe; G. Mkabeni; Moses M. Kotane; L. K. Ntlabati; O. R. Tambo. FOR THE S.A.I.C.: Dr. G. M. Naicker, President; Messrs. A. I. Meer; J. N. Singh; Dr. A. H. Sader; George Singh; I. A. Cachalia; T. N. Naidoo; V. Lawrence; I. C. Meer; M. D. Naidoo; Debi Singh; Nana Sita; Y. Cachalia; G. H. Pahad. OTHER INDIAN AND AFRICAN LEADERS WERE: Prof. D. D. T. Jabavu; Rev. Z. R. Mahabane; N. Mkele; D. W. Moshe; S. B. Ngcobo; S. R. Naidoo (Cape).

108. *Ibid.*, 2nd April, 1949. Dr. Naicker was, at this time, refused a passport to visit America to attend the Cultural and Scientific Conference for World Peace.

109. S.A.I.O., Report of the Joint Secretaries submitted to Conference, 20th–22nd April, 1951, p. 4.

110. S.A.I.O., First Conference Records, 1951, and *Leader*, 16th April, 1949.

111. *Leader*, 14th May, 1949. In terms of the Indian Immigration Bureau Bill introduced by the Minister of the Interior certain Natal (Colonial) Acts were to be repealed and the Indians were to be recognised as Union Nationals.

112. S.A.I.O., First Conference Records, 1951, Report of the Joint Secretaries, p. 5.

113. United Nations, *Discussions and Proceedings*, 1948–9, p. 6.

114. These were the U.S.S.R., Yugoslavia, Poland, Byelorussian S.S.R., Pakistan, China, Philippines, Siam, Cuba, Ecuador, Uruguay and the U.S.A.

115. United Nations, *Discussions and Proceedings*, 1948–9, p. 6.

116. *In Favour:* Argentina, Brazil, Greece, Netherlands, Union of South Africa. *Against:* Venezuela, Yemen, Yugoslavia, Afghanistan, Byelorussian S.S.R., Chile, China, Columbia, Costa Rica, Cuba, Denmark, Ecuador, Egypt, Haiti, Honduras, India, Iran, Iraq, Lebanon, Liberia, Mexico, Norway, Pakistan, Panama, Philippines, Poland, Saudi Arabi, Siam, Syria, Ukrainian, S.S.R., U.S.S.R., U.S.A., Uruguay. *Abstaining:* Australia, Belgium, Burma, Canada, Dominican Republic, France, New Zealand, Nicaragua, Peru, Sweden, Turkey, United Kingdom.

117. *Ibid.*, pp. 7–8, Resolution No. 265 (III).
118. Nicholas, *The United Nations as a Political Institution*, pp. 95–6.
119. Government of India, *Memorandum on Question of Treatment of Indians in the Union of South Africa – Exchange of Correspondence between the Governments of India and the Union of South Africa for holding a Round Table Conference*, submitted to the United Nations, 1950, p. 16. Telegram No. 30386, 4th July, 1949. This is cited hereafter as Exchange of Correspondence, India and South Africa, 1949–1950. Some of the telegrams in the memorandum are paraphrased versions of actual communications.
120. *Ibid.*, Telegram No. 30393, 9th July, 1949.
121. *Ibid.*, pp. 17–18, 11th July, 1949.
122. *Ibid.*, pp. 18–19, Telegram No. 15, 13th July, 1949.
123. *Ibid.*, pp. 19–20, Telegram No. 30399, 21st July, 1949.
124. *Ibid.*, pp. 24–5, Telegram No. 17, 14th September, 1949.
125. *Ibid.*, pp. 25–6, Telegram No. 30440, 22nd September, 1949.
126. *Ibid.*, pp. 26–7, Telegram No. 19, 11th November, 1949.
127. *Leader*, 14th January, 1950. Pakistan required a minimum of 180 000 tons of coal a month. This she got from India but there was some uncertainty whether such supplies would be continued, in which event she could obtain coal from Poland, Britain, France and other European countries. On re-opening trade relations with South Africa, she would, naturally, buy South African coal.
128. *Ibid.*, 24th December, 1949.
129. *Ibid.*, 28th January, 1950.
130. Exchange of Correspondence, India and South Africa, 1949–50, p. 6.
131. *Ibid.*, pp. 6–7.
132. *Leader*, 25th February, 1950.

CHAPTER EIGHT

THE UNITED NATIONS, 1950-1961

The origin of the Group Areas Act goes back to 26th November, 1948, when the new Nationalist Government appointed the Land Tenure Act Amendment Committee in Natal "to receive and consider proposals for the amendment of Chapter I of Act No. 28 of 1946" and in the Transvaal the Asiatic Land Tenure Laws Amendment Committee, with the same terms of reference.[1]

These Committees submitted a Joint Report, U.G. 49/1950, to Dr. Dönges, the Minister of the Interior, and on the basis of this report the Minister introduced the Group Areas Reservation Bill in May, 1950. The provisions of the Group Areas Bill were released in Cape Town on 27th April, 1950, in spite of a request from the Government of India on 5th April, 1950 that the introduction of further legislation be stayed pending the deliberations of the Round Table Conference.[2]

The Union Government turned down this request as it referred to a matter which was within the domestic jurisdiction of the South African Government.[3] At the same time it suggested that the Round Table Conference be held in October or November of that year "at a centre where all the three Governments are represented so that full use can be made of local staffs".[4]

When the provisions of the Group Areas Bill were announced they evoked a storm of protest both in South Africa and in India. On 22nd April, 1950, the South African Indian Congress asked whether the Round Table Conference would achieve any useful purpose "in the face of this most devastating racial Bill" and whether the Union Government were serious in agreeing to a Conference with India and Pakistan.

Four days later the South African Indian Organisation sent cables to Mr. Nehru and Mr. Liaquat Ali Khan, Prime Ministers of India and Pakistan, respectively, who were holding talks in Karachi on the grave situation facing the Indian people as a result of the Group Areas Bill. The cable stated that the introduction of the Bill contradicted the tripartite agreement to hold a Round Table Conference and seriously raised the question of the *bona fides* of the Union Government to solve the deadlock between the three countries.[5]

One of the immediate results of the Group Areas Bill was to knit together all opposition to it. Black peoples of all races closed their ranks. The Natal Indian Congress requested that the 1st May, 1950, be observed as a day of protest, a "Hartal Day", a day of mourning. On that day a large gathering of Indians, Africans and Coloureds, described as one of the largest, assembled at Nichol Square to denounce the Group Areas Bill.[6] It was becoming increasingly clear that the introduction of this Bill, badly timed as it was, would have serious repercussions at home and abroad. As for the proposed talks between the Governments of South Africa and India and Pakistan, the very foundations for them were now being undermined.

However, the Pakistan Government, in an effort to salvage whatever hopes remained of a Round Table Conference, sent a telegram to the Union Government on 9th May, 1950, suggesting that the Conference could be held in Karachi and asking the Union

Government to postpone the Group Areas Bill pending the forthcoming Conference. The telegram reminded the Union Government of the Pakistan Government's action in lifting the trade ban on the eve of the last talks in order to create the right atmosphere.[7]

But the introduction of the Group Areas Bill had damaged the atmosphere irretrievably. On 6th June, 1950, the Indian Government informed the Union Government that they had decided not to participate in a Conference which would be one-sided in view of the Union Government's determination to go ahead with their policy of apartheid – a policy which the Indian Government had always opposed.[8]

The negotiations had at last broken down. What followed is of no importance as the main aspect and hope had fallen. The Union Government expressed surprise at the decision of the Indian Government since, it claimed, the Indian Government had been informed through Pandit Kunzru of the intention of the South African Government to introduce legislation of the kind that was now a reality.[9]

The Indian Government, however, denied any prior knowledge of the Bill,[10] and each side was left with its own version. It does appear that as the version of the Indian Government was backed by the testimony of the leader of the Pakistan delegation at the preliminary talks at Cape Town, these two delegations were not aware of the Union Government's intentions to introduce the Bill. It does not appear logical that the two Eastern delegations would have acquiesced in such an intention and Pandit Kunzru's version seems acceptable. On the other hand there is no denial on any side that Dr. Dönges did make mention of the fact that apartheid "would place all the races on the same footing and remove the stigma of inferiority".[11] If by this Dr. Dönges meant the Group Areas Bill and the Indian leaders understood it to mean something else it was a case of an unfortunate misunderstanding with serious implications for all parties concerned.

The Bill became law as the Group Areas Act No. 41, 1950, when it was assented to on the 24th June, 1950.[12] Mr. P. R. Pather gave a five-point summary of the effects of the Group Areas Act on the Indians. It would compulsorily segregate the Indian people; it would bring with it its attendant evils (such as the absence of civic amenities and slum conditions, to mention only two) apart from the insult to the national honour of the Indian nation; it would interfere with trading rights; Indians would be denied rights to any land for industrial purposes in industrial areas; loans would be denied on Indian properties outside the Indian group area.[13] If any single Act could have been said to be aimed at the crippling of the Indian economy, of Indian livelihood, of peace and security for the Indians in South Africa, aimed at taking away from them that which they valued and toiled for most, it was the Group Areas Act. In it there was no longer any security of tenure or assurance of just returns. It aimed at economic strangulation under the guise of social separation.

The effect of the Group Areas Act on international affairs was seen immediately in the cancellation of the Round Table Conference between the Union Government and the Governments of India and Pakistan. Before the next effects could be ascertained the attention of the United Nations was directed towards Korea where, early in August 1950, conflict between the North and South soon developed into an international conflict with United Nations troops participating in the struggle. The Indian question in South Africa receded into the background though it was by no means forgotten.

On 10th July, 1950, India requested that the question be placed on the provisional agenda of the fifth session of the General Assembly. The General Assembly agreed to include the item in the agenda and to refer it to the Ad Hoc Political Committee. The Indian delegation was led by Mrs. Pandit and the South African delegation by Dr. Dönges.

On 20th November, 1950 the Ad Hoc Political Committee adopted a draft resolution after both Mrs. Pandit and Dr. Dönges had addressed the Committee and after the issue of competence had been decided by 35 votes to 3, with 17 abstentions. The resolution requested the three governments to proceed with the holding of a round table conference on the basis of their agreed agenda and recommended that in the event of this conference not taking place before 1st April, 1951, a commission of three members be established to help the parties in their negotiations. The resolution appealed to the South African Government not to proceed with the implementation of the Group Areas Act while the negotiations were taking place.[14]

The draft Resolution was adopted by the Ad Hoc Political Committee by 26 votes to 6, with 24 abstentions. It was adopted by the General Assembly by 35 votes to 13, with 12 abstentions.[15]

The significant result of the work of the Fifth Session was that the policy of apartheid of the Union Government, which was blown into a new dimension through the introduction of the Group Areas Act, was severely criticised at the United Nations. The Union Government was requested to stay the enforcement of the Act pending the conclusion of the Round Table Conference between the parties concerned. Indeed, there was still some hope in spite of the abortive negotiations of 1950 that the Conference could come about.

Whatever the force and frequency of these criticisms, the limitations of the United Nations in the matter of helping the parties find an amicable solution were becoming more and more pronounced with the passing of time and with the passing of resolutions of almost the same tenor year in and year out. The important question for the Indian people of South Africa to answer now was that posed by Senator E. H. Brookes: "What good can such support do you with either the governing classes of South Africa or the majority of the United Nations?"[16]

If there was nothing for the South African Indians to gain through the intervention of the United Nations, there was also not much to lose (except perhaps the goodwill of a few South African Whites who did not approve of appeals against their country). The adverse effects on the Union Government of the hardening world opinion were greater. Though the same arguments were repeated at the United Nations every year, as the *Natal Witness* remarked, "with somnambulistic repetition",[17] world opinion was piling up against South Africa with the same regularity. And with equal regularity South Africa had, since 1946, rejected appeals to revise her policies. She was now to do the same in respect of the request embodied in the United Nations resolution that the operation of the Group Areas Act be suspended. It was in her interests, as the *Natal Witness* wrote, for South Africa to change her attitude: "In this regard South Africa will do well to discard her argument that the Indian question is a domestic one and can be solved by apartheid and repatriation only."[18]

India took the first step towards implementing the resolution of the United Nations when she wrote to the Union Government on 3rd March, 1951, asking whether the Union Government was agreeable to a Round Table Conference being convened in accordance with the terms of the last resolution.[19] The Union Government replied promptly that it was unable to accept the General Assembly resolution as the basis for any round table talks since the terms of the resolution constituted intervention in a matter which was essentially within the Union's domestic jurisdiction. The Union Government was not prepared to accept that part of the resolution which dealt with a three-man commission. It was prepared, however, to hold a conference on the basis of the agreement arrived at during the Preliminary Talks held in Cape Town in February, 1950. It maintained that " the obstacle to the summoning of a round table conference lies therefore not with the Union".[20] The United Nations received a similar statement.

The Pakistan Government informed the South African Government that it was prepared to participate in a round table conference and suggested that the venue be Karachi or New York but the Indian Government expressed their regret at the decision of the Union Government not to accept the resolution of the United Nations as it held that that resolution was best designed to secure discussion of the dispute in an unprejudiced atmosphere; the Union Government was asked to reconsider its decision. No such reconsideration emerged. All that the South African Government did was to say at the end of its despatch: "The request of the Government of India implies that the Union Government should unilaterally abandon their standpoint on this issue, which they regret they are unable to do."[21] This decision was conveyed to the United Nations by the Indian representative who disclaimed responsibility for the failure to re-open the talks.

After this, the Pakistan Government, too, switched from its conciliatory position and informed the South African Government of its concern over the recent developments: "The Government of Pakistan note with deep regret the decision of the Government as announced in the Press to bring into force the Group Areas Act while the correspondence for holding the Round Table Conference was still in progress. This has undoubtedly made a solution of the problem of the people of Indo-Pakistan origin in South Africa even more difficult."[22]

The time-limit prescribed by the resolution of 1950 had now expired. Yet another series of exchanges between the interested parties failed to find a common ground. The rift was widening.[23] The Union Government showed how resolutely it clung to its claims that racial peace could only be assured by the policy of apartheid and that it would not brook any interference in its domestic affairs when the Minister of the Interior announced that as from 30th March, 1951, all transactions in the Cape Province, Natal and the Transvaal for the acquisition of immovable property between parties of different racial groups had been put under permit control, with the exception of mortgage bonds.[24]

Overseas comments against the Union's policy increased since the announcement that the Group Areas Act would be enforced. *Reynold's News* wrote that Dr. Malan was seeking to "thrust entire races of man into permanent and degrading inferiority because of the colour of their skin". The paper said that Dr. Malan's racial policy was "bad from every point of view, immoral and un-Christian" and one which weakened the Commonwealth. "It is a policy", wrote the journal, "which South Africa may some day pay for in blood and terror when the tensions and hatreds that Dr. Malan is building up can no longer be kept under control".

But Dr. Malan was not the only Commonwealth Prime Minister to be criticised. The Conservative London paper, the *Sunday Express* wrote that "no single man had ever caused such strain within the Commonwealth as the Indian Prime Minister, Pandit Nehru". The paper accused Mr. Nehru of antagonising the whole of White Africa.[25]

A further criticism of South Africa, though in a wider context, was expressed by President Rajendra Prasad of India when he opened the Indian Parliament. Dr. Prasad regretted South Africa's decision not to accept the General Assembly's resolution of 1950. He said that the question did not affect India only. It was vital and affected the future of the world because on a right solution of it issues of peace or conflict between great races depended. Only on the basis of equality and equal treatment of different races and peoples could there be peace in the world, said Dr. Prasad.[26]

The conflict between races and ideologies was ventilated sufficiently at the United Nations where once again by 40 votes to 1, with 12 abstentions, the item: "Treatment of people of Indian origin in the Union of South Africa" was included in the agenda of the sixth regular session and referred to the Ad Hoc Political Committee for consideration and report.[27]

Again South Africa protested against the inclusion of the item on the agenda. The Deputy Leader of the South African delegation, G. P. Jooste said: "My Government cannot but challenge such a contention and I submit there is a growing consciousness in the Organization today of the dangerous implications of continued discussion in the United Nations of the domestic affairs of member states – discussions which are exploited by some to further their own ends."[28]

But the item got onto the agenda. The Ad Hoc Political Committee considered the question at six meetings between 20th December, 1951, and 5th January, 1952. The South African delegate informed the Political Committee that South Africa was prepared to attend a round table conference outside the supervision of the United Nations. Finally, on 5th January, 1952, the Committee adopted by 41 votes to 2, with 13 abstentions, a resolution setting up a three-man commission within 60 days and calling upon the Union Government once again not to enforce the Group Areas Act.[29] On 12th January, 1952 the General Assembly adopted the draft resolution submitted by the Ad Hoc Political Committee.[30]

The latest resolution had two important aspects. The first of these was the three-man commission to assist towards a settlement; the second was the repeated appeal for the suspension of the Group Areas Act. Both these aspects had been rejected by the South African Government in their earlier declarations and there was every indication that the rejection would continue. There was need for some small concession or compromise from some quarters. The *Natal Witness* showed how the Union Government could pave the way for a settlement. It wrote that if the Union Government's contention that the treatment of Indians in South Africa was a domestic affair was correct the Government was justified in rejecting the terms of the resolution. "But", the journal counselled, "there are times when it does not pay to insist too vigorously on the letter of the law, particularly when what constitutes the law is in dispute. If the commission proposed could help to improve relations between South Africa and her accusers, it should be accepted."[31]

But the Union Government had no inclination to depart from its declared policy. It continued to regard the United Nations resolutions as incursions in the domestic affairs of a member state, as intrusions and inroads in matters which were entirely the concern of a sovereign, independent state. In the face of such a policy there was no hope of the resolutions of the United Nations making any impression at all on the Union Government.

The world could not fail to be struck by the determination of the South African Government. Nor could its own subjects fail to see the position and the policies clearly. There was no room left for doubt in any direction whatsoever. The non-European opposition was gradually mustering its strength and its resources. On 29th July, 1951, the Executive Committees of the African National Congress and the South African Indian Congress met to discuss the position as they saw it. They agreed to embark on a mass campaign for the repeal of the Pass Laws and Stock Limitation Regulations, the Group Areas Act, the Separate Representation of Voter's Act, the Suppression of Communism Act and the Bantu Authorities Act; and to establish a Joint Planning Council to co-ordinate the joint efforts of the African and Indian peoples in the proposed campaign.[32]

The line of action agreed upon was that the A.N.C. should call upon the Government to repeal the objectionable laws not later than 29th February, 1952, and that this call was to be supported by the S.A.I.C., who also undertook, in the event of the Government's non-compliance with the A.N.C. requests, to resort to mass action in defiance of the unjust laws; to hold mass demonstrations throughout the country on 6th April, 1952, to register protests against three hundred years of oppression and exploitation and as a prelude to the launching of the campaign to receive reports from provincial organs and to hold joint meetings of the executive committees of the A.N.C. and the S.A.I.C. to co-ordinate efforts for the launching of the defiance campaign against the unjust laws.[33]

The first step in this combined Indo-African campaign was taken by the African National Congress when they wrote to the Prime Minister on the 21st January, 1952. The letter made mention of the objectionable laws and stated that the "cumulative effect of this legislation is to crush the National Organizations of the oppressed people; to destroy the economic position of the people and to create a reservoir of cheap labour for the farms and the gold mines; to prevent the unity and development of the African people towards full nationhood and to humiliate them in a host of other manners". The letter called on the Prime Minister to repeal the objectionable laws by not later than the 29th February, 1952, failing which the Congress would hold protest meetings and demonstrations on 6th April, 1952, as a preparation for the defiance campaign.[34]

In a detailed reply dated 29th January, 1952, the Prime Minister's Private Secretary attempted to answer the points raised in the letter of the A.N.C. Paragraph 6 of the reply read:

> "It should be understood clearly that the Government will under no circumstances entertain the idea of giving administrative or executive or legislative powers over Europeans, or within a European community, to Bantu men and women, or to other smaller non-European groups. The Government, therefore, has no intention of repealing the long existing laws differentiating between Europeans and Bantu."

The ultimatum asking for the repeal of the laws was rejected. The A.N.C. replied on 11th February, 1952, that it had decided to proceed with the defiance campaign.[35]

This was followed by a letter from the South African Indian Congress on 20th February, 1952, in which Congress traced the position of the Indians as well as of the other non-European people in South Africa. It rejected the policy of Apartheid of the Government and asked for the repeal of the laws "which offend the dignity of man".[36]

The letter of the A.N.C. and the S.A.I.C. had both made reference to the mass protests that would take place. On the appointed day, 6th April, 1952, mass demonstrations organised jointly by the two Congresses were held throughout the major centres in the country. In Durban there was a mass rally at Nichol Square. Throughout the country the people dedicated themselves to the cause of freedom.[37]

The next step was a joint meeting of the two Congresses at Port Elizabeth on 31st May, 1952. This meeting established the National Action Committee to control, guide and conduct the campaign for the defiance of unjust laws. It appointed a National Volunteer Board and accepted Dr. Y. M. Dadoo, Mr. M. Kotane, Mr. J. B. Marks, Mr. D. W. Bopape and Mr. J. Ngwevela as the first volunteers. It was decided to launch the mass campaign on 26th June, 1952.[38]

The defiance campaign was launched on the appointed day and in about two years since that date a total of 8 557 persons were arrested for participating in the struggle.[39]

In Durban, on 30th August, 1952, twenty-one resisters marched from Nichol Square followed by about 4 000 people along Pine Street, Grey Street and West Street to the Berea Road Railway Station where the resisters were arrested for entering the European section of the railway station.[40]

These developments attracted the attention of various observers. Criticism against the Government's racial policy came from many quarters. The Indian Government regarded the demonstrations in South Africa against the apartheid laws "as a development of the highest importance from the point of view of the peace of the entire African continent and indeed of the whole world".[41] On the 13th September, 1952, the All-India Congress Committee adopted a resolution stating that "the basic principles of the United Nations Charter are being violated in South Africa and barbarous methods of suppression are being employed against a peaceful population". It appealed to the "conscience of the world" to take heed of the latest developments in South Africa.[42]

While criticisms against the Government's policy poured in from many overseas sources the Government of India announced that it would raise the issue of the defiance campaign before the United Nations. When this announcement was made it was time again for the United Nations to debate the "Treatment of people of Indian origin in the Union of South Africa". There was every indication that the 1952 Seventh Session of the United Nations would be a memorable one in view of the defiance campaign in the Union and in view of the failure of the parties concerned to implement the resolution of the UN General Assembly of 12th January, 1952, recommending the appointment of a three-man commission to assist the Governments of India, Pakistan and the Union of South Africa to resolve their differences.

The Secretary-General reported to the Assembly that the parties had failed to nominate members to the proposed commission. He held consultations with the representatives of the three governments and with those of other governments. As a result of these consultations he arrived at the conclusion that there was at that time no possible solution to the problem and that the appointment of an individual in terms of the resolution of 12th January, 1952, was not opportune.[43] What did appear opportune to the Assembly after the usual debates was the setting up of a United Nations Good Offices Commission to assist the Governments concerned in their negotiations. A number of countries, including the older members of the Commonwealth, neither supported nor opposed this step. Their abstention, however, was readily interpreted as support for South Africa.

Nor did this step put an end to the matter. The defiance campaign of the A.N.C. and the S.A.I.C. now received echoes in New York. For the first time in the history of the United Nations, South Africa was now to be arraigned specifically for her racial policies as a whole. World opinion, as reflected at the United Nations, was hardening against South Africa.

On 12th September, 1952, the permanent representatives of Afghanistan, Burma, Egypt, India, Indonesia, Iran, Iraq, Lebanon, Pakistan, Philippines, Saudi Arabia, Syria, and the Yemen, addressed a letter to the Secretary-General requesting that the item "The question of race conflict in South Africa resulting from the policies of apartheid of the Government of the Union of South Africa" be included in the Agenda. In an explanatory memorandum the petitioners recalled the racial problems in South Africa and the campaign that was being waged against the unjust laws. They stated that a continuance of the repressive measures would "aggravate race conflict throughout Africa" and endanger world peace.[44]

South Africa's consistent stand on this issue was that in terms of Article 2 (7) of the Charter the General Assembly was not competent to deal with or even discuss the matter. This contention was rejected by 45 votes to 6 with 8 abstentions. The General Assembly referred the item to the Ad Hoc Political Committee for consideration and report.[45] This Committee adopted two draft resolutions, Draft Resolution A, by 35 votes to 2, with 22 abstentions and Draft Resolution B, by 20 votes to 7 with 32 abstentions.[46]

Both these draft resolutions were submitted by the Ad Hoc Political Committee to the General Assembly with the recommendation that both be accepted. Before they could be voted upon, Mr. Jooste (South Africa) introduced a motion that the draft proposals be not accepted. He said that "if my motion is rejected, the consequence will be that the Assembly will claim to be competent not only to discuss and consider matters of essentially domestic concern, but also to adopt resolutions with regard to such domestic matters". Jooste's motion was rejected by 43 votes to 6, with 9 abstentions.[47]

Resolution A was then voted upon. The result of the voting was 35 in favour, 1 against and 23 abstentions and it was adopted, having obtained the required two-thirds majority. The result of the voting for Resolution B was 24 in favour, 1 against, and 34 abstentions. This was also adopted, having obtained the required two-thirds majority. It is important to note, however, that more states abstained than voted for the resolution.

At the end of the voting, a number of delegates explained their reasons for voting as they did. Mr. Lloyd (United Kingdom) said that his delegation had repeatedly made it clear that the placing of the item on the agenda and all discussion of the substance of it had been entirely out of order. Mrs. Pandit (India) explaining why her delegation had voted for Resolution A said that Africa and Asia were on the march and would no longer accept the indignities imposed on them in the name of a white civilisation.[48] For South Africa, Mr. Jooste said that by adopting the latest resolutions the General Assembly had created a precedent to intervene in purely domestic matters by way of discussion and the adoption of resolutions. South Africa, he said, would continue to claim the protection afforded by Article 2 (7).[49]

The Seventh Session of the General Assembly of the United Nations had, in effect, adopted three resolutions which had a bearing on the position of Indians in South Africa. The two resolutions on the subject of race conflict in South Africa resulting from the policy of apartheid of the Union Government had a very close relation to the Indian question. In fact, both the items had their origin in one fount.

The important result of the developments of 1952 both in South Africa and at the United Nations was the merger of the question of the South African Indian with the larger question of the black peoples as a whole in South Africa. It would be increasingly difficult – even impossible – in future years to separate the one from the other. Because of their interaction both these issues will have to be traced side by side for any complete picture to be drawn.

In the light of these developments and the climate at the United Nations it would be futile for South Africa to continue to argue its case – as it did with a great measure of consistency, throughout – on the legal issue of competence alone. This had been done before and had been rejected. It was bound to be rejected over and over again. The only way for the Union Government to succeed at the United Nations was by way of a change of heart at home. But this it was unwilling to do. It made its position perfectly clear. As Jooste had said it would consider the United Nations resolutions as *ultra vires* and therefore null and void. In such an attitude it was explicit that domestic policies would not change. Indeed, the declared policies were given further expression in 1953 in the form of the Public Safety Act, No. 3/1953, the Criminal Law Amendment Act, No. 8/1953 and the Immigrants Regulation Amendment Act, No. 43/1953.

While the South African Government went on with a consistency and a fixity of purpose that could not fail to arouse the admiration of their supporters who constituted a considerable part of the white electorate, the United Nations Commission on the Racial Situation in South Africa went about its work. In accordance with Resolution 616A of 1952 the following members were appointed on the 21st December, 1952, to serve on the Commission: Dr. Ralph Bunche, Dr. Jaime Torres Bodet and Mr. Hernan Santa Cruz. The first two persons were unable to accept the appointment. Dr. Bunche, who was the Director of the Trusteeship Division of the United Nations, could not be relieved of his duties by the Secretary-General, Mr. Trygve Lie.[50] It was not until 30th March, 1953, that the General Assembly, on the proposal of its President, Mr. Lester B. Pearson of Canada, appointed Mr. Dantes Bellgarde and Mr. Henri Laugier to fill the positions together with Mr. Hernan Santa Cruz.[51]

The Commission held its first meeting on the 13th May, 1953, at Geneva at the Palais des Nations; the last meeting was held at Geneva on 3rd October, 1953. In approximately five months work, the Commission held 43 formal meetings. The Commission wrote to the Union Government on the 28th May, 1953 and again on the 19th June, 1953. On 26th June the Commission received a reply to the effect that as it had consistently regarded the question of the Union's racial policy as a domestic matter, it regarded Resolution 616A (VII), which set up the Commission as unconstitutional and consequently did not recognise it.

The Commission made one further attempt to obtain the co-operation of the Union Government. The Chairman of the Commission applied to the Union Legation in Chile for a personal visa, stating that he desired to visit South Africa not with the intention of holding hearings or making any official or public inquiry but to gather direct impressions. The application was refused. The Union Government explained that his application could not be divorced from his membership of a Commission which the Union Government did not recognise.[52]

In spite of this handicap the Commission carried on with its work as best it could. It examined the declarations of South African politicians; it studied the principal legislative texts governing the lives of individuals and groups and it studied whatever memoranda were submitted to it or heard witnesses who were in a position to inform it on the problem under study. Non-governmental representations and representations from private individuals were also received. The Governments of member states of the United Nations also submitted memoranda or sent their representatives.[53]

The Commission concluded its report on 3rd October, 1953, and submitted it to the Eighth Session of the General Assembly. Notwithstanding the peculiar handicaps under which it worked it brought out a comprehensive report. The following excerpts from the Summary of the Commission's Conclusions explain the main conclusions of the Commission:

On the question of competence the Report stated that the exercise of the functions and powers conferred on the Assembly and its subsidiary organs by the Charter did not constitute an intervention prohibited by Article 2 (7) of the Charter. The Commission was convinced that its interpretation was not only legally correct but that it would serve the cause of world peace.[54]

The Commission rejected the policy of apartheid based on racial differentiation and superiority as scientifically false and dangerous to international peace and international relations. It reported that it was highly unlikely that the masses of non-whites in South Africa would ever be willing to accept the policy of apartheid; that efforts to persuade them that this policy was based on justice would never succeed; and as the policy developed it would become more explosive daily and would be a menace to internal peace as well as to the foreign relations of the Union Government; it would also increase the forces of "agitation and subversion" against the Government.

It then suggested that the competent organs of the United Nations should give their moral support to those who were persecuted in South Africa. It suggested that the United Nations should also give moral and material aid to the Union of South Africa and thus "to confirm international solidarity and co-operation by deeds". It stated that the United Nations "might suggest ways and means in which the Union might draw up a new policy".[55]

The work and the Report of the Commission have been dealt with at some length in this study as the question of racial conflict was fast superseding the more restricted problem of the treatment of Indians in South Africa and was, on the national and international fields, the focus of attention. It was increasingly apparent that no solution to the Indian question in South Africa could be isolated from a solution on the wider plane of the racial question in this country. The Indian question, from 1952 onwards, therefore, receded, in the background while the problem of racial conflict in its full and entire context, embracing the millions who constituted four-fifths of the Union's population, came more into the forefront. At international level, the Indian Government gave more attention to the problem of racial conflict in South Africa. The Indian Prime Minister, Mr. Nehru, said in London in June, 1953, that the South African Indian question, though important, had been deliberately allowed by his Government to become a secondary issue to the larger question of racial conflict.[56]

Interest in the racial conflict in South Africa was kept alive by the defiance campaign. In a report tabled in the House of Assembly by the Minister of Justice, Mr. C. R. Swart, it was stated that 8 391 persons were arrested for resistance offences in 1952 and of this number 7 544 persons had been convicted. On offences regarding registration and production of documents by Africans the total number of prosecutions for 1952 alone was 74 000.[57]

There was no improvement in the position since the last meeting of the General Assembly of the United Nations. When the General Assembly convened in September, 1953, Mrs. Vijaya Lakshmi Pandit of India was elected its President by 37 votes to 22. Of the Commonwealth countries only South Africa did not vote for Mrs. Pandit.

The South African Indian question came up for review once again. In accordance with Resolution 615 (VII) of 5th December, 1952, the General Assembly had established a United Nations Good Offices Commission, consisting of three members, to assist the Governments of the Union of South Africa, India and Pakistan to arrive at a satisfactory solution of the question of the treatment of people of Indian origin in the Union of South Africa. Cuba, Syria and Yugoslavia were nominated to serve on it.

On the 20th March, 1953, the Commission wrote to the three countries advising them of its willingness to assist in any negotiations. In reply the permanent representative of the Union to the United Nations informed the Commission that his government had consistently held that the Indian problem in South Africa was a domestic question and that it could not grant recognition to a Commission appointed in terms of a General Assembly resolution which it considered to be unconstitutional.[58] As a result of this attitude the Commission could only report its failure to the UN General Assembly.

The item was once again referred to the Ad Hoc Political Committee where, on 29th October, 1953, a draft resolution was adopted by 38 votes to 2, with 19 abstentions, recalling the history of the earlier resolutions and expressing regret that the Union Government had refused to make use of the Commission's good offices whilst continuing with the enforcement of the Group Areas Act and more recently introducing the Immigrants Regulation Amendment Bill. The resolution decided to retain the Good Offices Commission and urged South Africa to co-operate with it. Once again South Africa was called upon not to implement the provisions of the Group Areas Act. The draft resolution was adopted by the General Assembly a few weeks later.[59]

With this item disposed of for 1953, the other item, the question of race conflict, came up. The Commission on the Racial Situation in South Africa submitted its Report to the eighth session of the General Assembly on 3rd October, 1953. The Ad Hoc Political

Committee considered the question and again rejected South Africa's resolution on competence by 42 votes to 7 with 7 abstentions.[60]

The Committee adopted a draft resolution in which some of the observations of the Commission on apartheid were embodied. The resolution requested the Commission to continue its surveillance of the racial situation in South Africa and to suggest measures which would promote a peaceful settlement of the problems. Once again an appeal was directed to South Africa to co-operate.

When the resolution came before the General Assembly, Jooste (South Africa) again raised his Government's objections on the ground of competence to discuss the matter. He also pointed out that the field of work intended for the Commission included inter-ference in the internal affairs of South Africa. One example of his argument is contained in the following words: "The draft resolution authorises the commission to suggest mea-sures to bring about a change in the internal situation of my country. Is it necessary for me to point out the extremely serious implications of such a suggestion?"

The Indian delegate pointed out that the repercussions of the problems before the Assembly could be felt beyond South Africa's borders; that the whole continent of Africa was in travail and in a process of transition. He asked whether that transition which required the adjustment of relations between the indigenous people and their White masters would be effected peacefully or by "the sowing of the seeds of racial hatred and conflict".[61]

South Africa's motion was defeated and the draft resolution submitted by the Ad Hoc Political Committee was adopted with the addition of an amendment submitted by the delegations of Chile and Uruguay to the effect that if any of the members of the Com-mission were unable to continue their membership replacements should be made by the President of the General Assembly in consultation with the Secretary-General.[62]

The 1953 resolutions of the General Assembly both extended the lease of life of their respective Commissions; for the Indian question – the Good Offices Commission; for the race conflict – the Commission on the Racial Situation in South Africa. How far they would go or how effective they would be remained to be seen.

So far what had happened at the United Nations was little more than a game of chess, with moves and counter-moves or, as the *Natal Witness* aptly termed it, "a certain game of cards".[63] But it could not go on indefinitely without any positive results. The prestige of the United Nations was at stake. Up till now there was not the slightest hope that a settlement was in sight.

One factor which seemed to stand in the way of a settlement to the Indian question in South Africa – though how this was to be achieved outside the larger issue of race con-flict in South Africa was not clear – was the personal animosity between the heads of the Governments involved in the impasse, especially between Dr. Malan and Mr. Nehru. Mr. Nehru had always been outspoken on the question of racial discrimination and colonialism. In the booklet *Nehru on Africa* some of his views and public utterances are reproduced. Some extracts from his major speeches will amplify the position. In a foreign policy speech on May 21st, 1952, he said in reference to the problems of Africa that the Africans were becoming politically conscious and that their ambitions were justifiable; the Indians, he said, should co-operate with them.

Referring to the Indians in South Africa in a foreign policy debate in Parliament on December 6th, 1950, he said that India had shown great patience in regard to the South African Indian question, having taken it to the United Nations since 1946. He stated quite emphatically that whether it took a month or a year or more India would never submit "to any racialism in any part of the world".

Speaking in the House of the People on September 17th, 1953, on the international situation, he said that while racial discrimination existed in other countries there was an element of apology about it but in South Africa there was no apology. He said that there were forces in the world which would fight racial discrimination to the end.[64]

Such and similar speeches were numerous. What they aimed at was quite clear. It was also clear that they did not register well in official circles in South Africa.

Dr. Malan reacted to Mr. Nehru's utterances in a speech at a luncheon in honour of Mr. Robert Menzies, Prime Minister of Australia, at Cape Town on July 9th, 1953, when he said that the time might come when India would be "knocking on Australia's door", and when it did that Australia could "depend upon South Africa as a friend". He went on to say that the recently-heard cry of "the white man must quit Africa" was only one side of what was becoming a slogan. The other side was "and let India enter".[65]

What followed in the House of Assembly on 4th May, 1954, was more outspoken. Part of what the South African Prime Minister said on that day is given verbatim because of its importance:

> "Nehru has his eyes on Africa. He does not hide the fact. He is very clever in that regard. He wants European influence to depart from Asia, but he also wants the white man to get out of Africa, and therefore his policy is anti-colonialism – away with the white man everywhere in Africa. He even suggested that the various Native races in Africa should have conferences with each other and that they should hold them in New Delhi, when he encouraged and assisted them. I say here deliberately that Nehru is the enemy of the white man."[66]

Indian leaders in South Africa protested against the attack on Mr. Nehru. P. R. Pather said: "There is no greater enemy of the white man than Dr. Malan and his fellow Nationalists since it is the policy of their Government which is placing the security of the white man in danger and creating bitter racial hatreds and conflict."

Dr. Dönges echoed the sentiments of the Prime Minister in a speech at Worcester on 7th May, 1953, when he advised that the Prime Minister of India should eliminate the ills of his own country before he meddled in the affairs of others. He said that India was one of the nations which was always prepared to villify South Africa in the United Nations yet, he said, 90 per cent of India's population was illiterate. He said that Nehru had stated recently that he wanted to eliminate tension throughout the world, but the fact was that wherever there were Indians there was tension and unrest.[67]

Oswald Pirow, one-time Union Minister of Defence, writing in his newsletter, carried the onslaught against Nehru a step further when he referred to people with "book learning" as having "a total lack of moral responsibility". "An outstanding example of this undesirable type is the Prime Minister of India, Mr. Nehru. He knows the West, is a good speaker and a sharp debater, but immediately he opens his mouth, he makes it all too clear that he is only a coolie."[68]

In his reply, Nehru said: "The Prime Minister of South Africa and some other Ministers there have gone so utterly beyond all reasonable bounds of decency in international affairs that I find it a little difficult to deal with the matter." He said that it was totally false and misleading that he had his eyes on Africa.[69]

All these recriminations were not conducive to a settlement of the Indian question in South Africa. And while they went on the non-whites continued with their protests. A conference under the auspices of the South African Congress of Democrats, the A.N.C. and the Transvaal Indian Congress was held in Johannesburg and it pledged to answer the call of Chief Luthuli for 15 000 volunteers "to oppose undemocratic actions". Father Huddleston, who opened the conference, said: "I have said repeatedly in the last few years, and I repeat it today, that world opinion is on our side and that it is a weapon we can and must use."[70]

These developments and the growing tensions were evident when towards the end of June, 1954, the Union Department of External Affairs announced that at the request of the Union Government the Indian Government had agreed to withdraw its diplomatic representation in South Africa with effect from 1st July, 1954. When, with the passing of the Asiatic Land Tenure and Indian Representation Act in 1946, the Indian High Commissioner was withdrawn in protest against the Act, the Secretary to the High Commissioner remained; later the Assistant Secretary to the High Commissioner was the only representative of India in South Africa.

By this withdrawal the last official link between the Governments of South Africa and India was broken. It was an augury of the hard times ahead for the Indians in South Africa, though the last Assistant Secretary to the High Commissioner, J. L. Malhautra, saw a different side of the picture. At a farewell reception in his honour in Durban on 1st August, 1954, he said that in his five years' stay in South Africa he had seen a great revolution taking place among the non-European people; their whole outlook was transformed and their inferiority complex had gone; their fear was going and when such a stage was reached their rulers could never continue to subjugate them.[71]

It is true that there was a tremendous upsurge of feeling for freedom. A "Freedom Charter" was in circulation and in the hearts and minds of the black people in South Africa. At the Natal Conference of the Congress of the People 168 811 members gave their support to the Charter in Durban early in September, 1954.[72]

Events were fast moving towards a climax, though what form this would finally take no one could tell. For the moment the time had come for the Good Offices Commission and the Commission on the Racial Situation in South Africa to present their annual report for 1954 to the UN General Assembly.

The first of these Commissions reported its progress to the Secretary-General in a letter dated 13th September, 1954. The first meeting of the Commission was held on 23rd February, 1954, when the Commission decided not to make an official direct approach to the parties but to attempt a new approach through private, informal conversations between its members and officials of the countries concerned. This method, however, was not fruitful and the Commission decided to send a formal invitation, as in 1953, to the Permanent Representative of the Union of South Africa. The Deputy Permanent Representative informed the Secretary of the Commission on 2nd September, 1954 that his Government's attitude and policy towards the Commission remained unchanged. The Commission therefore reported that it was "unable to submit any proposal likely to lead to a peaceful settlement of the problem on account of the unco-operative attitude of the Government of the Union of South Africa".[73]

In 1954, as with monotonous regularity for years before, the South African Indian question was raised once again in the world body. As before, a resolution emerged when the old arguments had been flogged yet again. This time there was a slight difference.

The new resolution was a most conciliatory one and could be interpreted as a victory for the South African Government which had, in the past, withstood and ignored condemnatory resolutions which referred to its racial policy and which asked it to negotiate with India and Pakistan in the firm and restricted framework of the United Nations Principles and Purposes as enshrined in the Charter. It had even been requested to refrain from implementing the Group Areas Act. All that was dropped in the new resolution. The position seemed to have reached a new starting point with no condemnations, no Commissions, and no undue limitations. The stage was reached for the whole question to be reviewed *de novo*.[74]

At this time, too, the other item, that of racial conflict in South Africa resulting from the policies of apartheid of the Government of the Union of South Africa, came up for the attention of the United Nations. In accordance with Resolution 721 (VIII) the United Nations Commission on the Racial Situation in the Union of South Africa presented the second part of its report to the General Assembly on 26th August, 1954. On 25th September, 1954, the Assembly referred the item to the Ad Hoc Political Committee for consideration and report.[75] The upshot was that the Commission was commended for its constructive work; its life was extended for another year; it was noted with regret that the Union Government had refused to co-operate with the Commission; a further appeal was lodged asking this government to seek a peaceful settlement of the racial problems in South Africa. All this had been gone through before.[76]

There was no change in the outcome of the question of race conflict when compared with the position in 1953. The *status quo* remained. The position was the same as in 1952 when the question of race conflict in the Union resulting from the policy of apartheid had first come up at the United Nations. It was to remain the same for many years to come.

In 1955 a similar resolution was adopted, the only difference being that the United Nations Commission on the Racial Situation in South Africa was dropped after it had presented its third report. Though the draft resolution of the Ad Hoc Political Committee recommended the continuance of the Commission, the clause was rejected by the General Assembly when it failed to get the requisite two-thirds majority.[77]

The only explanation possible for the failure of the General Assembly to ratify the recommendation of one of its own committees was that South Africa now resorted to strong tactics.

Its representative, Mr. du Plessis, said that his Government regarded in a most serious light the inquiry in the internal affairs of the Union of South Africa. Such an inquiry constituted the most flagrant violation of Article 2 (7), a violation which no self-respecting sovereign state could tolerate. His Government had accordingly decided to recall the

South African delegation and its permanent representative to the United Nations from that session.[78]

South Africa's decision to withdraw from that session no doubt influenced the final voting in the General Assembly when the Assembly dropped the clauses dealing with the United Nations Commission. A serious breach in the unity of the United Nations had thus been created with the question of race conflict being only four years old in the forums of the world organisation. But a resolution was adopted asking South Africa to change her racial policy.

On 30th January, 1957, the General Assembly adopted, for the fifth time, a draft resolution on the racial question submitted by the Special Political Committee. Those who voted against the draft resolution were Australia, Belgium, France, Italy and the United Kingdom, who were allies of South Africa at the United Nations and had in the past either voted with South Africa or abstained from voting. South Africa took no part in the debate or in the voting in accordance with her decision of 1955. There was no change in the purport or tenor of the new resolution.

When the issue of race conflict came up for the sixth time, there was hardly any change in the voting or in the resolution which was adopted on 26th November, 1957. The last part of the latest resolution appealed to the Union Government to revise its policy in the light of the United Nations Charter and of world opinion.

But no response was forthcoming. So, for the seventh successive year, a resolution was adopted by the General Assembly on 30th October, 1958 "expressing its regret and concern that the Government of the Union of South Africa has not yet responded to appeals of the General Assembly that it reconsider governmental policies which impair the right of all racial groups to enjoy the same rights and fundamental freedoms."

Yet again there was no response to the appeals of the United Nations. The Union of South Africa had boycotted the debates on this question since 9th November, 1955. This item had now become a "hardy annual" and when it came up before the United Nations General Assembly for the eighth successive time a resolution was adopted on 17th November, 1959, containing the main points embodied in the earlier resolutions and ending with an appeal "to all Member States to use their best endeavours as appropriate to achieve the purposes of the present resolution".[79]

It was as if another cycle had been completed and the new starting point was the appeal to the member states "to use their best endeavours". The United Nations was dependent on its member states, on their goodwill and initiative, and, what was more, on their good offices and their co-operation to bring about a solution to this vexatious problem of race conflict in South Africa. But before the results of this new appeal could be discerned the internal racial situation in South Africa exploded with such force and ferocity that the echoes were heard in the chambers of the Security Council for the first time ever, in April 1960.

The tide of events was reaching a crescendo. But there was also another "hardy annual" that had been interrupted in this study with the adoption of Resolution 816 (IX) on the 4th November, 1954, the question of the treatment of people of Indian origin in the Union of South Africa. The last resolution was a conciliatory one and afforded all parties an honourable starting point for fresh negotiations. The 1954 resolution, like its earlier counterparts, had called upon the three governments to open negotiations.

The Union Government made the first move when the Minister of External Affairs, E. H. Louw, wrote to his counterparts in India and Pakistan on 17th December, 1954, recounting the stand of the Union Government that it regarded the question of the treatment of Indians in the Union of South Africa as one of purely domestic concern in which the United Nations was precluded from intervening by the provisions of Article 2 (7) of the Charter. This communication stated that if the two governments were prepared to discuss the South African Indian question outside the United Nations the Union Government would be available for such discussions.[80]

The Government of Pakistan replied on 14th January, 1955, stating that it had no intention of interfering in the domestic affairs of South Africa but that it could not agree that the Indian question in South Africa was of domestic concern to South Africa; the Pakistan Government expressed its interest in the matter because of certain international implications. The reply went on to state that the Pakistan Government could not ignore the purposes and principles of the Charter and the resolutions passed by the United Nations since 1946. The Government of India replied on the same day and in the same terms.

It was clear that these governments were now polarised in respect of their attitudes, principles and policies. Negotiations seemed to be not only wasteful but sometimes insincere. The slightest pretext or disagreement was pounced upon to bring negotiations to an end. On this occasion, too, the South African Government complained that certain critical speeches made by the Indian Prime Minister were aimed specifically at wrecking the negotiations.

On 21st April, 1955, it came to the expected conclusion that it had been forced to the view that the Government of India was deliberately attempting to wreck the proposed discussion initiated by South Africa since the Prime Minister's speech at New Delhi was a reply to the South African proposals of 17th December. The Union Government was therefore obliged to abandon its attempts to hold discussions with the Indian Government.

Yet another reason was found to bring the negotiations between the South African and the Indian Governments to an end. It is a moot point whether the talks would have materialised if the Prime Minister of India had not spoken as he did for, even before his speeches came to the notice of the Union Government, a point of disagreement – that of the basis for the talks – had already been reached, and acknowledged.

Though the Governments concerned had failed to find common ground to hold talks in order to settle their differences, the South African Indian question was discussed at the Afro–Asian Conference held at Bandung in Indonesia in April, 1955. The Communique issued on 24th April, 1955, expressed the warm sympathy and support of the Conference to the "victims of racial discrimination" in South Africa.[81] And at home the question received new strength and support when another conference of no less importance – the Congress of the People – was held at Kliptown, Johannesburg, on the 25th and 26th June, 1955. The Congress was attended by 2 884 delegates, of whom 360 were Indians, 320 Coloureds and 112 Europeans. The rest were Africans. The Congress of the People adopted the Freedom Charter.[82]

The Indian leaders of the Congress gave their full support to the Freedom Charter and its aims. The aims of the Freedom Charter were lofty and idealistic, certainly the goal which Black people in South Africa had striven for for many years. The realization of the Freedom Charter would obviously be resisted by the South African Government. The struggle would therefore be a long and weary one. An example of official reaction to it was the Union-wide police raids for evidence of "treason and sedition" on 26th September, 1955.[83] Four days later the United Nations General Assembly referred the Indian question in South Africa to the Ad Hoc Political Committee for consideration and report.

As already seen, the negotiations to bring about talks between the parties had failed. In terms of the directive given to him to appoint a person to assist in the negotiations after the expiry of six months, in Resolution 816 (IX) of 4th November, 1954, the Secretary-General designated that duty to Mr. Luiz de Faro, the Brazilian Ambassador. The Union Government, however, refused to recognise the United Nations agent and he reported the failure of his mission to the Secretary-General.[84]

The Ad Hoc Political Committee discussed the question as before. But as the South African delegation had withdrawn from the tenth session of the General Assembly on 9th November, 1955, the draft resolution adopted by the Committee on the Indian question did not have a dissentient vote. This resolution, like its immediate forerunner, was a simple one. It urged the parties concerned to pursue negotiations with a view to bringing about a settlement of the South African Indian question.[85]

The resolution had dropped the appointment of any agent and had now left the position solely in the hands of the three parties concerned. But one of them had walked out of the Assembly on 9th November, 1955; it was not likely, therefore, that South Africa would enter into any tripartite talks under the auspices of the United Nations. It had set out its position with a clarity that was as clear as crystal. Yet the architects of the annual resolutions persisted in their repetitive programme knowing full well that any output from that source was doomed to fail. Why, then, did they persist so zealously and so regularly in their futile task? Was it to save the face of the United Nations which had been plagued with the Indian question in South Africa from the very first moments of its foundation and had, year in and year out ever since, passed empty resolutions on the question without having gained an iota of ground or success?

The failure of the United Nations to gain any ground in the matter heartened the Union Government immensely. The way things were pointing for this Government it could, with as much facility as it was resisting the inroads into its domestic domain, very well walk out bag and baggage from the United Nations.

It had taken the first step in April, 1955, in that direction when it withdrew from UNESCO. Eric Louw, the Minister of External Affairs, complained that official UNESCO publications like *Racial Myths* by Juan Comas, Professor of Anthropology at the Mexican School of Anthropology, were disseminating information which ran counter to the Union Government's philosophy on race matters. He contended that the £30 000 which the Union subscribed towards the funds of UNESCO could be used for Government propaganda purposes overseas through his State Information Office.[86] The next step in that direction was the withdrawal of the Union delegation from the tenth session of the General Assembly as from the 9th November, 1955.

South Africa's withdrawal raised certain important issues. It meant that a member state had walked out because of the United Nations intervention in her domestic affairs. It was a pointed reminder that the time had come for the world body to define its position more clearly and to remove the contradiction which demanded compliance with the principles and purposes enshrined in the Charter whilst forbidding intervention in internal matters in terms of Article 2 (7).

The position as it existed was that South Africa was acting within her legal rights and her critics, too, had a solid foundation for their claim that what was happening in South Africa was a violation of fundamental human rights and of the dignity and worth of the human person, all of which were contrary to the United Nations International Declaration of Human Rights. In such a situation it was not to be expected that South Africa would "submit tamely to being perpetually pilloried" nor was it to be expected that India or Pakistan would remain indifferent to the treatment of people of Indo–Pakistan origin in South Africa.[87]

What was needed at this stage was a compromise which would bring about a reconciliation of these not irreconcilable factors, without holding on to the age-old traditions which had served their day and were now anachronisms, pointing towards a workable solution, even an imperfect solution yet for all that, an attempt at a solution. "Splendid isolation" held out no hope for the future, for

> ". . . Race relations are fundamental to world politics of this decade, and in no country are the human problems more acute than they are in South Africa. It is an idle dream to think that we can be left to work out our destiny untroubled by the alarums and excursions, on the international stage."[88]

In an age of growing internationalism what happened on the international scene could not be ignored by South Africa – whatever her legal rights to walk out of the United Nations. In some ways, even indirect ways, international opinion and international pressure could affect the internal affairs of South Africa and bring about the long-desired change of policy in spite of the unabated official resistance. If the change could yet come about by friendly negotiations the prospects of a peaceful settlement were not altogether gloomy. The first steps towards the resumption of negotiations were taken on 21st May, 1956, when the permanent representative of India to the United Nations wrote to his South African counterpart suggesting the re-opening of negotiations. The reply received on 5th July stated that the Union Government saw no good purpose to be served in covering the same grounds as before and trying to bring about discussions which were "wrecked by the Prime Minister of India in his speeches".[89]

The Government of Pakistan made a similar attempt on 11th June, 1956. The response of the Union Government was that though the Government of Pakistan had not been responsible for the failure of the negotiations of 1954 it could not hold discussions with Pakistan alone because no distinction was made in South Africa between Indians of the different faiths and because 80 per cent of the South African Indians were Hindus.[90]

On 30th January, 1957, after the same ground had been traversed as before, the General Assembly adopted a resolution, as before, calling upon the parties to enter into negotiations "to facilitate a settlement of the problem".[91]

The eleventh resolution on the Indian question in South Africa had been adopted and neither the end nor the solution seemed in sight. If, on the international plane, the problem had reached its eleventh year with monotonous regularity, what was now to happen on the domestic field was unique in its magnitude and revealed the determination of the Union Government to maintain the *status quo* at any cost and in defiance of the international implications and repercussions that would follow.

On 5th December, 1956, 140 persons of all races were arrested in a Union-wide police swoop. Two weeks later when the preparatory examination into allegations of treason against the State opened in Johannesburg, the number of accused persons stood at 156. The senior prosecutor, J. C. van Niekerk, said that the Government's case rested on the allegation that certain political organisations (the Congresses chiefly) were pursuing a policy designed to promote a classless society based on racial equality and that this policy involved the overthrow by violent means of the existing structure of the existing state. The Crown case would show, said the prosecutor, that the holding of the Congress of the People and the adoption of the Freedom Charter were steps in the direction of establishing a Communist state; that the accused advocated a revolutionary change, encouraged hostility between the European and non-European races, and incited people to revolt.

For the accused, Advocate Berrange said that the defence would show that they stood for racial unity and had at all times promoted racial harmony and mutual assistance and co-operation.[92]

Ninety-two persons were finally charged with high treason. The trial proper began on August 2nd, 1958. In November, 1958, charges against 61 of the 92 accused were suspended. The number of accused finally dropped to 28.[93]

Finally, on 29th March, 1961, after a four-year long legal battle, all 28 accused were found not guilty in a unanimous verdict. In his judgment, Mr. Justice Rumpff said there was no evidence of Communistic infiltration into the African National Congress and that it was not proved that the A.N.C. had become a Communist organisation. Mr. Justice Rumpff said that the evidence proved that the A.N.C. and other organisations and the present accused were working together to replace the present form of State with a radically and fundamentally different form of State based on the demands set out in the "Freedom Charter" but "it has not been proved that the form of State pictured in the Freedom Charter is a Communist State". Mr. Justice Rumpff said: "On all the evidence presented to this Court and on our findings of fact it is impossible for this Court to come to the conclusion that the A.N.C. had acquired or adopted a policy to overthrow the State by violence – that is in the sense that the masses had to be prepared or conditioned to commit direct acts of violence against the State." With the A.N.C. exonerated, the judgment said that the other organisations were also not guilty of subversive activities.[94]

The Treason Trial aroused a lot of sympathy both internally and externally for the non-white struggle in South Africa. Ghana, which received full independence on 6th March, 1957, announced that she would do everything possible to influence world opinion against the Union Government.[95] The Government of Ghana announced that persecuted Africans would be welcome in Ghana. Dr. Nkrumah said: "Ghana will not only be a centre for the liberation of Africa from foreign domination, but also the hope of the black man throughout the world." He announced plans for a pan-African Conference in Accra and said that South Africa would be invited to the Conference.[96] Mr. Strydom, the

Union Prime Minister, turned down Dr. Nkrumah's invitation to attend the Conference.[97]

In South Africa, too, a Conference was held towards the end of 1957 with the object of finding a solution to the country's racial problems. At this Multi-Racial Conference papers were read by eminent South Africans like the Most Rev. Denis E. Hurley, Mr. Alan Paton, Dr. S. Cooppan, Mr. G. H. L. le May, Dr. R. E. van der Ross, the Rev. Z. R. Mahabane and Professor Z. K. Matthews. The Conference set up a Commission on civil rights and a standing committee to publicise the pernicious effects of the denial of civil rights to all peoples and to create a united opposition to the laws which withheld such rights.[98]

While attempts were being made in South Africa to find a solution which had so far eluded the United Nations, the world organisation was itself in the throes of its twelfth session, with South Africa maintaining its "token representation".

The permanent representative of India to the United Nations wrote to the South African permanent representative on 8th July, 1957, suggesting the re-opening of negotiations with a view to talks between their Governments in order to arrive at a settlement of the question of the treatment of people of Indian origin in South Africa.[99] No reply was received from South Africa's permanent representative. The Government of Pakistan had a similar experience. This "ritual" over, the matter was once again channelled through the well-worn course and for the twelfth time the issue was raised and disposed of, with no tangible gain for the Governments of India and Pakistan. South Africa continued to score moral points, though how far the cumulative weight of these points meant real strength for South Africa was not yet tried or known.

At this time there was in circulation in New York a petition, which contained the signatures of 123 world figures from 38 different countries, protesting against racial discrimination in South Africa. Among those who signed the petition in South Africa were the Rt. Rev. Ambrose Reeves (Bishop of Johannesburg), Mr. Alan Paton (Chairman of the Liberal Party), Prof. Leo Kuper (University of Natal), Dr. E. Hellman (Social Anthropologist), Mr. Patrick Duncan (Organiser of the Liberal Party of South Africa), Dr. G. M. Naicker (President of the S.A.I.C.), and Father Trevor Huddleston (former Anglican priest in South Africa).

The petition was designed to influence world opinion against the policies of the Union Government as the United Nations had so far failed to go beyond the resolution stage. There was little to be enthusiastic about though "Politicus", writing in the *Leader*, felt that "the moral force of that verdict cannot be ignored".[100] Moral arguments are not easily translated into political realities and the years 1958 and 1959 were years of comparative calm, like the lull before the storms which were to rage in 1960. On the internal plane they were characterised by the continuation of the Treason Trial; by the mass rallies against the Group Areas Act; by the monster protest meetings on June 26th of each year and by the economic boycott of certain goods like cigarettes and potatoes.

On 26th June, 1958, an estimated crowd of 25 000 people assembled at Curries Fountain, Durban, to protest against the recent Group Areas proclamations which threatened to uproot more than 60 000 Indians from their homes.[101] The rally on the same day a year later was even greater. An estimated crowd of upwards of 40 000 Africans, Indians and a few Europeans attended the "Freedom Day" rally in Durban.[102]

The tempo of the opposition was rising towards a climax. On the 26th June, 1959, the A.N.C. announced a boycott campaign of products of Nationalist-controlled firms. One of these firms listed was the Langeberg Co-operative Ltd., one of the largest canning firms in the Union. The directors wrote to the A.N.C. denying that the firm was Nationalist-controlled and stating that no member of the Board was a Member of Parliament. On the 30th May, 1959, the boycott was extended to potatoes as a protest against the alleged ill-treatment of African workers on certain farms. This boycott was comparatively effective and for some time "stocks of potatoes piled up in the markets".[103] The potato boycott was only lifted on the 31st August, 1959, after Indians, both as traders and as consumers, had shared in the sacrifice that was being made.[104]

The protest rallies and the boycott campaigns of 1959 were part of the programme of the black leadership to keep the struggle alive in South Africa. These leaders were realising more and more that the desired change could only come about from within and as a result of internal agitation. As Dr. G. M. Naicker said in his Presidential address to the N.I.C. conference held from 9th to 11th October, 1959: "While declaring our firm belief in the ability of the South African people to find a solution themselves to the problems that face them in our country we take this opportunity of thanking all the peoples and governments who have declared their support to our just struggle for democracy."[105]

Congress had always appealed to the Government of India and later to the Pakistan Government, too, for support in its endeavours to improve the position of Indians in South Africa. A change in Congress policy which resulted in the greater confidence which the S.A.I.C. had now in its "own ability" came about from 1952 when the Congress Alliance was formed between the A.N.C. and the S.A.I.C. Indians dared not go it alone after that. The catastrophic, sanguinary riots in Durban in 1949 were a constant reminder that goodwill and mutual co-operation in the dealings between the Indians and the Africans offered the only hope for Indian survival as a political and economic entity in South Africa. The Indian had to be a brother to the African and a younger brother at that.

The racial problems in South Africa made no distinction between Indians, Africans and Coloureds. They were all one on the other side of the line, where they were joined, in increasing numbers, by Europeans of goodwill and exemplary fortitude.

The Indian and Pakistan Governments revealed in their utterances and activities at the United Nations an appreciation of the seriousness of the South African situation. In 1958 the permanent representatives of India and Pakistan wrote once again to their counterpart from the Union Government asking that negotiations be resumed. Once again their communications were not acknowledged. Consequently, the item came up again before the Special Political Committee in that year.[106]

Mr. Krishna Menon (India) presented a lengthy memorandum to the Committee in which he recalled *ab initio* the question of the treatment of people of Indian origin in the Union of South Africa. Of particular significance was his statement that the Indian Government did not ask for special treatment for the Indians in South Africa. All that his Government asked for, said Mr. Menon, was that the purposes and principles of the Charter and the Universal Declaration of Human Rights should be extended to entire populations. He called for a unanimous decision against South Africa.[107] Though he obtained this with 63 affirmative votes, there were still nine undecided or non-committed states. These were Australia, Belgium, China, Finland, France, Netherlands, Portugal, Spain and the United Kingdom.[108]

The thirteenth year saw no progress; the stalemate still existed. During this period of the lull before the storm that broke out in 1960 causing the "winds of change" to blow the racial question (the admixture of the Indian question in South Africa, and race conflict in South Africa resulting from the policy of apartheid of the Union Government) into the chambers of the Security Council of the United Nations, there remained the last of the sessions of the General Assembly to be considered – the fourteenth session in 1959. All that happened at this session was the adoption of a stereotype resolution which served to keep the embers alive and nothing else.

After fourteen attempts, the United Nations General Assembly failed to record any tangible progress in its endeavours to find a solution to the Indian question in the Union of South Africa. Up till now the South African Indian question at the United Nations had had a monotonous existence with the passing of resolution after resolution. The events of 1960 were to rule out some of this monotony.

1960 opened with a New Year message from the Prime Minister of the Union, Dr. H. F. Verwoerd, in which he appealed to all South Africans to set aside their differences of the past and to join in thanksgiving for what had been achieved in the fifty years of Union. Race relations, said Dr. Verwoerd, were only one facet of South African life and too much should not be made of it to the exclusion of the other facets.[109]

However, race relations was certainly the best yardstick with which to measure the Union Government's work. And not only that of the Union Government but of other South African bodies like the South African Foundation which was established to "sell South Africa" overseas.[110]

There was no doubt that the attention of the world would be focussed on Africa in 1960 more than it was even in the days of the partition of the Dark Continent in the days of the New Imperialism in the last quarter of the nineteenth century. As Stanley Uys commented in the *Sunday Times*: "This is Africa's year!"[111]

The Union Government took note of the position created by the emergence of independent African states. Opening the 10th annual congress of the South African Bureau of Racial Affairs in 1959, the Minister of External Affairs, E. H. Louw, spoke on "The Union and the Emergent States of Africa" and said that it was the desire of South Africa to live in harmony with them and to maintain friendly relations with them.[112]

The "harmony" and the "friendly relations" of which Eric Louw spoke would depend largely on the extent to which his Government's racial policies would be acceptable to the emergent states. There was no hope that the Government's declared racial policy would meet with official approval in the emergent African States. As Professor L. M. Thompson said in his address to the Institute of Race Relations on the subject: "A Political Review of 50 years of Union", apartheid thinking, like segregation thinking before it, was an escape from the real facts of life in South Africa – an unsuccessful attempt by whites to evade the moral responsibility which went with their political power. "Apartheid", said Prof. Thompson, "is no justification for man's daily inhumanity to man in South Africa. The non-Europeans are and will remain integral parts of a multi-racial society".[113]

Speaking at the same conference on "South Africa and the Wider Africa, 1910–1960", Professor E. H. Brookes said, *inter alia*: "We can never go back to a world where Africans and Asians are inferior. The world is their world as well as the world of the Europeans, and this new world cannot tolerate a permanent barrier against Africans or Indians in the Union."[114]

Mr. Harold Macmillan, Prime Minister of Great Britain, spoke on virtually the same theme when he addressed the members of both the Union Houses of Parliament on February 3rd, 1960. Mr. Macmillan said that note should be taken of the changes taking place in Africa – of the wind of change that was blowing throughout the continent. He said: "Whether we like it or not, this growth of national consciousness is a political fact. We must all accept it as a fact. Our national policies must take account of it."[115]

The significant development in the early months of 1960 was that there was serious stocktaking of the position. The Union of South Africa could not be excluded from this attention; in many ways she was the centre of great interest. If this stocktaking and the utterances of great men were not enough to sustain the interest and the attention of the outside world in the affairs of the Union, the internal upheavals of March, 1960, served to focus greater attention on local developments in the country. These developments were in turn to result in the United Nations taking action. And in all these matters the Indian question in the Union was interwoven into the larger context of the entire racial structure. There was no longer any question of treating this issue apart from the whole question of racial affairs in the country. The question was one and indivisible. And so it would remain.

On 18th March, 1960, Mr. R. M. Sobukwe, President of the Pan-African Congress, announced the campaign of his organisation aimed at the abolition of the pass laws. The campaign was to commence on 21st March. On that day a crowd estimated at between five and seven thousand marched to the Municipal offices at the entrance of the Sharpeville Location, Vereeniging. After being dispersed by a baton charge by the police, the crowd increased to a number between 15 000 and 20 000. The police, fearing for their safety, fired on the crowd, killing 67 Africans and wounding 186, including 40 women and 8 children.[116]

At the Cape, at Langa Location, one young African was killed and 54 Africans were injured as a result of similar police action. About 1 200 Africans had congregated at the Philippi police station and a few hundred at Nyanga.[117]

The Government appointed Mr. Justice P. J. Wessels as a one-man commission to inquire into the Sharpeville disaster. Mr. Justice Diemont was appointed to inquire into the disturbances at Langa Location.[118]

As a result of these disturbances the Union Government banned all public meetings of all races in a large number of magisterial districts on 24th March. On 28th March legislation was introduced to ban the A.N.C. and the P.A.C. On 30th March a state of emergency was proclaimed and hundreds of persons of all races were arrested before dawn on that day.[119]

These days were, as Miss Muriel Horrell's Fact Paper is entitled, *Days of Crisis in South Africa*. The internal events in the Union were proving to be as turbulent as the "wind of change" that was blowing elsewhere in Africa. These events found their echo in the chambers of the Security Council when 29 members of the Afro-Asian group of the

United Nations requested that the Council should consider "the situation arising out of the large-scale killings of unarmed and peaceful demonstrators against racial discrimination and segregation in the Union of South Africa."[120]

The Security Council met on 30th March, 1960, to discuss the complaint. It was the first time ever that the Council met to discuss the racial situation in the Union of South Africa and Brand Fourie, the head of South Africa's permanent mission to United Nations, pointed this out; he pointed out also, that by discussing the complaint the Council was creating a dangerous precedent which could affect other countries.[121]

The fact that the racial question in South Africa had now found its way to the Security Council was an indication that an explosive stage had been reached; that there was danger enough in the situation to threaten international peace and security. But as in the case of the General Assembly contradictions between the purposes and principles of the Charter and the Universal Declaration of Human Rights on the one hand and Article 2 (7) on the other, so there existed a paradox in the Security Council. As the policeman of the world, the Council has the power to impose its decisions; but as an arbitrator of disputes it could (like the Assembly) only recommend – even if its recommendations were ignored.[122] As to which role it would play in South African affairs – that of policeman or arbitrator of disputes – it was obvious that the second role was the more likely one.

The Security Council debated the issue. On 1st April, 1960, it adopted a resolution by 9 votes to nil – with Great Britain and France abstaining.[123] The resolution deplored the recent disturbances in the Union and called upon the Government to abandon its policies of apartheid and racial discrimination. The fact that South Africa's racial situation was now a subject for the attention of the Security Council was in itself sufficient indication of the gravity of this situation. There was no doubt any longer that the position had now reached such world-wide proportions that on the international scene the developments in South Africa would be followed more closely than ever in the past.

The important question now was how would South Africa react to the new resolution? Explaining the stand of his Government, Eric Louw, the Minister of External Affairs, said in the House of Assembly on 20th April, 1960, that the whole complexion of the United Nations had altered and that ten years hence there would be 37 Western White nations to 50 Afro-Asian, 12 Communist and 7 "border" nations in the world organisation. He said: "Not only South Africa but every Western nation is faced with the question of what the position will be in 1970."[124]

It is significant in considering the official stand of the Union Government of non-interference in the domestic affairs of nations, to recall what the senior Cabinet Minister in the Union Cabinet, Mr. Paul Sauer, said at Humansdorp on 19th April, 1960. Speaking at the Union Festival celebrations, he said that the "old book" of South African history had been closed at Sharpeville and, for the immediate future, South Africa would have to consider "in earnest and honesty" her whole approach to the African question. He said: "We must create a new spirit, which must restore overseas faith – both White and Non-White – in South Africa. There must be an important change in the practical application of Government policy although it will not mean a deviation from the set policy."[125]

The "Native question" was no longer a question reserved exclusively for the Africans, just as much as the Indian question was no longer a separate question. What remained of these hitherto exclusive questions was only a "non-White question" or Black question, to be seen in its entirety as one issue.

This development was evident when the Commonwealth Prime Ministers' Conference was held in London in May, 1960. The Prime Ministers of the Afro-Asian Commonwealth states discussed South Africa's policy of *apartheid* with Eric Louw. These meetings were far from pleasant and on one occasion the Malayan Prime Minister, Tunku Abdul Rahman, walked out on Mr. Louw. The comments of some of the Prime Ministers at the end of the Conference are worthy of note:

Field-Marshal Mohamed Ayub Khan, of Pakistan, said: "We have made our position very clear to South Africa. They think they are discharging a religious duty. It is not. They may be able to hold this situation for 10 or 15 years or it may be less, but history has shown they cannot go on. I think that human decency demands they should resolve this problem in a more sensible fashion."

Tunku Abdul Rahman of Malaya said: "Whatever happens in South Africa they cannot ignore the fact that the opinion of the world is against them. . . . There should be no discrimination."

Mr. Nehru of India said: "I do not think it is possible for any country to follow a racial policy like that. It just cannot be tolerated."[126]

Nowhere in the discussions or in the comments of the Prime Ministers of these Asian countries of India, Malaya and Pakistan was there any mention of the Asiatics alone in the Union of South Africa. Whereas in the Imperial Conferences of 1918 and 1921 the work of the conferences was confined, on the racial issue, to the Indian question in general in the Dominions and in particular in South Africa, the Prime Ministers' Conference of 1960 saw the question as it now was and as the future would and must see it: as the non-white question.

The future of the Union of South Africa in the Commonwealth and the Union's policy of *apartheid* were one and indivisible at the Conference. At the end of the Conference, a communique was issued. On the *apartheid* issue, which had overshadowed the whole conference, the communique said that the Commonwealth was a multi-racial association and consequently there was need to ensure good relations between all the member states and peoples of the Commonwealth.[127] It was tacit in the communique that good relations could not be maintained while the Union's policy of *apartheid* remain unchanged.

If the utterances against South Africa at the Commonwealth Prime Ministers' Conference seemed to come from a distance, they found a kindred echo when distinguished people from all parts of the world assembled in South Africa for the historic Education Conference sponsored by the University of Natal in July, 1960. What most of them had to say on the racial policy of the Union Government is adequately summed up in the words of Professor C. W. de Kiewiet, when he delivered the 16th Hoernle Memorial Lecture in Durban on 7th July, 1960: "In today's world South Africa is isolated and in danger. Destiny is marching to its borders."[128]

It was to avert this danger that the Security Council of the United Nations had instructed its Secretary-General, Dag Hammarskjold, to hold discussions with the Union Government in terms of the resolution of that Council of 1st April, 1960. Hammarskjold's first step was a meeting with Eric Louw, the Minister of External Affairs, in London. Following this meeting, it was agreed that the Secretary-General would fly to South Africa in July to continue his talks on the South African racial question in Pretoria.[129]

But events in the Congo delayed the visit till the early days of 1961. Meanwhile, on 20th July, 1960, the permanent representatives of India and Pakistan requested, in letters to the Secretary-General, that the item: "Treatment of people of Indian origin in the Union of South Africa" be included in the agenda of the fifteenth regular session of the General Assembly which was to begin on September 20th.[130] A day later thirty-nine countries requested that South Africa's *apartheid* policy be debated again during the 1960 session of the Assembly. In 1959 only twelve countries had requested that this item be debated.[131]

South Africa opposed the inclusion of these items on the agenda. Her representative asserted that many critics of South Africa did not themselves "come to court with clean hands". Replying to this charge, V. K. Krishna Menon, the Indian Defence Minister and delegation leader, said that he pleaded guilty to the existence of racial discrimination in India, and he feared that there was such discrimination in other states. But he pointed out an important difference in the following words: "We understand this to be a social crime against the laws of God and man, and we try to get away from it. But South Africa legislated discrimination as a God-given right and prescribed it for others too." On this issue, the *Natal Mercury* commented that distinctions based on class, colour, religion and the like existed in all societies and were often tacitly accepted "but heaven help the country that seeks to perpetuate them in law".[132]

South Africa's position in the United Nations was becoming more and more difficult. On his return to South Africa, Mr. Louw admitted that it was "the most difficult and frustrating session of the United Nations I have ever attended".[133]

For other parts of the continent of Africa the year 1960 was far from being "frustrating". The year saw 16 new states being granted their independence and 83 000 000 people win self-government; the year saw Africa's breakthrough into international councils: with 26 votes Africa became the largest single bloc at the United Nations. The Afro-Asian bloc was worth 46 votes out of 99 in the General Assembly.[134]

Though the General Assembly could not get to debating the Indian and *apartheid* questions at the fifteenth regular session and the issues stood adjourned till the Assembly re-convened in April, 1961, there were interesting developments in the domestic field. On 8th February, 1960, the *Natal Mercury* called for a National Convention to take stock of the changing times; the call was repeated by the *Sunday Times* on 29th May, 1960. And on 27th March, 1960, twelve ministers of the three Dutch Reformed Churches "rejected the Government's enforced apartheid policy as unethical, unbiblical and without any foundation in the Scriptures . . .".[135]

From various other sources, more especially from the traditional exponents of racism, from Church leaders, from the professors of SABRA and from the Editor of *Die Burger* came calls for a firm and enlightened stand on the colour issue. As the *Sunday Times* heralded the dawn of 1961, it wrote:

"... the forces unleashed by 1960 are on the move. Thoughts and ideas, which were encrusted and fossilised in an archaic tradition, have suddenly become liberated. This, we believe, represents one of the great turning points in our history. Men of the

Afrikaans churches have risen in protest against a racial policy which they find has no moral or Scriptural justification."[136]

The early days of 1961 were of exceptional interest to observers of the international scene and to the parties concerned in the Indian and *apartheid* questions before the United Nations. On 6th January, 1961, the Secretary-General of the United Nations, Mr. Dag Hammarsjkold, arrived in the Union for talks with the Prime Minister, Dr. Verwoerd. This was the first occasion when the Union Government permitted the entry into the country of an official of the UN in terms of a resolution of that organisation arising from a consideration of these questions.

The Secretary-General had six meetings with the Prime Minister. In Cape Town, Umtata, Johannesburg and Pretoria the Secretary-General had opportunities for unofficial contacts with members of various sections of the South African community. In his report to the Security Council the Secretary-General said that in "the discussions between the Secretary-General and the Prime Minister of the Union of South Africa so far no mutually acceptable arrangement has been found. In the view of the Secretary-General this lack of agreement is not conclusive and he wishes to give the matter further consideration."[137]

The door was kept open for this by the promise of the Prime Minister "to invite him at an appropriate time, or times, to visit the Union again in order that the present contact may be continued".[138]

How far this contact would contribute towards a final solution to the vexatious problem of racial differences in South Africa only time would tell. At the time of the negotiations in which the Secretary-General himself took part, it was hoped that a solution to the question of "Treatment of people of Indian and Indo-Pakistan origin in the Union of South Africa", an issue which has been debated in the chambers of the United Nations for fifteen years, and the question of "Race Conflict in South Africa resulting from the policies of *apartheid* of the Government of the Union of South Africa", an issue which has been with the United Nations for nine years, were getting nearer to hand. But a realistic appraisal of the antecedents of the past fifteen years revealed a gloomy picture. There was little hope that the world organisation would find any solution to these two burning problems in view of its failure to achieve any success on these issues so far and especially because of its inability to take any positive steps after the historic days of Sharpeville and Langa. If the work of the United Nations in the muddled and tragic events of the Congo in 1960–1961 was any measure of the efficacy of the organisation or of its power and prestige to solve the burning problems of the day, then the statesmen, the politicians and the people concerned had to think and plan anew and they had to transfer their faith and hope to national institutions. In this case a domestic solution rather than an international solution would have to be hoped for.

The fifteenth session of the United Nations wound up its work by adopting two resolutions on the two issues in question before it. These resolutions were little more than echoes of the past, even if Australia and the United Kingdom voted for the resolutions for the first time. On the first of these, member states were exhorted once again to use their good offices to help bring the contending parties together and the usual invitation was renewed calling upon the parties to report to the General Assembly. On the second, the earlier condemnations of the racial policies of South Africa were repeated and the Government was asked to comply with the obligations assumed under the Charter of the United Nations.

At the time when these resolutions were adopted there was some doubt about the continued existence of the United Nations. Sapa-Reuter reported at the close of the fifteenth session on April 23rd, 1961, that as a result of the events of that year many people were saying that the United Nations was almost incapable of contributing to the settlement of pressing political issues.[139] This development threw a greater responsibility on the local scene if Bismarck's pungent remarks that the important questions of the time were to be decided not by parliamentary debates and majority decisions but by "blood and iron" were to be proved wrong in South Africa.

In 1961 there was much thinking and planning on the local scene; the three-day multi-racial Natal Convention of April, 1961, which adopted a comprehensive report at the end of its deliberations, promised to be the nucleus of a South African inter-racial convention to be held at a later date. The idea of a multi-racial convention received widespread support in South Africa. Though such conventions were not new to the country and to the enlightened members of the population no such endeavour is ever barren of some positive contribution. Every multi-racial meeting is a step in the right direction.

As for the Indian people in South Africa, their problems and vicissitudes have now lasted over a hundred years. A solution to them still seems distant, though not as distant as it appeared to be twenty years ago. This is not so because of the intervention of the United Nations but because of the events in Africa north of the Limpopo and the increasing pressures being brought to bear by the Asian countries as well as through the changing attitudes among the Whites in South Africa, slow and limited as this might be.

When the Indian question was submitted to the United Nations in 1946 it was hoped that the new world body would succeed where earlier international efforts had failed. But after the item had been considered for fifteen years and after fifteen resolutions had been adopted the position in 1961 was no different to that which had obtained in 1946. Why has the United Nations failed? The answer lies in the ineffective machinery of this organisation, exemplified in its many paradoxes: what is aimed at in one respect is prohibited in another. Whilst member states are asked to bring their policies in line with the purposes and principles of the Charter and in line with the Universal Declaration of Human Rights, they are protected in any non-compliance with these requirements by Article 2 (7). It is no wonder, then, that South Africa has refused to acknowledge the right of the United Nations to intervene in her domestic affairs.

This does not mean, however, that South Africa can continue to disregard world opinion calling for a change in her racial policies. This call, which was first made at the United Nations in 1952, has been increasing in volume since. In fact its importance has so grown as to overshadow the Indian question which can no longer be dealt with in isolation.

The important lesson to be noted in this chapter on the United Nations is that the monotonous appearance of the Indian question since 1946 and the racial question since 1952 is not likely to be treated lightly by the opponents of the South African Government and by the protagonists of racial harmony in South Africa. It has now afforded these elements the right to say (and with great justification, too) that their patience has been overborne; that they have tried everything available in a diplomat's repertoire. That they have failed is not their fault. The conventional approach they can claim to have exhausted. The blame, therefore, for any unconventional developments would not be theirs.

The other significant consideration is the position in which the South African Government now finds itself. In its determination (however much a display of courage this is) to keep to the old order, ostrich-like, the Government has not only lost friends abroad but at home, too. Right-thinking people, even without resorting to the examples of the history of mankind exemplified in the fall of the old order in France, to give but one example, are thinking of the need to effect a change in the uncompromising structure of *apartheid* which is a serious anachronism in the space age and a very weak foundation for the new Republican era to be built on. In its determination to resist this appeal – as it did in the case of all the appeals of the United Nations – the South African Government has weakened its position at home and abroad. And though, with equal determination, it will continue to do so, it can never hope that by so doing it is strengthening its position at home or abroad.

The United Nations might have failed to find a solution to the Indian and racial questions of South Africa but it has succeeded in welding together world opinion against the South African Government, to such an extent that even Great Britain and Australia voted against South Africa for the first time in 1961. This opposition will never cease, as Afro-Asian leaders have taken pains to point out, until an amicable solution to South Africa's problems has been found. There is no middle course in the issues at stake. There is also no turning back.[140]

FOOTNOTES

1. P. R. Pather, *Seventy Years of Frustration and Unhappiness*, p. 12, and Alan Paton, *The People Wept . . . The Story of the Group Areas Act*, p. 9.
2. Exchange of Correspondence, India and South Africa, 1949–1950, pp. 29–30, Aide Memoire, 5th April, 1950.
3. *Ibid.,* pp. 30–1, Aide Memoire, 20th April, 1950.
4. *Ibid.*, p. 31, Telegram No. 15, April 20th, 1950.
5. *Leader*, 29th April, 1950.
6. *Ibid.*, 6th May, 1950.
7. Exchange of Correspondence, India and South Africa, 1949–1950, p. 33.
8. *Ibid.*, pp. 34–35.
9. *Ibid.*, pp. 35–6, Telegram No. 19, 8th June, 1950.
10. *Vide* Appendix *infra*, Kunzru–Donges Talks, p. 295.
11. Exchange of Correspondence, 1949–50, pp. 7–8.
12. It is not intended to give the various Sections of this Act in this study. Various criticism of the Act have given a full treatment of the subject. *Vide* Muriel Horrell (in association with Miss Mary Draper), *The Group Areas Act – Its Effects on Human Beings*; P. R. Pather, *Seventy Years of Frustration and Unhappiness*; Alan Paton, *The People Wept . . . The Story of the Group Areas Act*; Kenneth Kirkwood, *The Group Areas Act*.
13. P. R. Pather, *Seventy Years of Frustration and Unhappiness*, p. 37. The Act was consolidated as Act No. 77 of 1957.
14. United Nations, General Assembly Official Records, Fifth Session, 1950: Document A/1548, Report of the Ad Hoc Political Committee, pp. 3–7.

15. *Ibid.*, p. 7, Resolution No. 395 (v). The voting details are not repeated here for the reason that there was no significant change in the voting disposition when compared with earlier Sessions of the United Nations.

16. *Leader*, 7th October, 1950, opening the fourth annual provincial conference of the Natal Indian Congress in Durban, on the 30th September, 1950.

17. *Natal Witness*, 16th November, 1950.

18. *Natal Witness*, 9th December, 1950.

19. *Exchange of Correspondence* during March and April, 1951, between the Governments of the Union of South Africa, India and Pakistan in regard to the possibility of convening a round table conference to discuss the treatment of Indians in the Union. This is cited hereafter as *Exchange of Correspondence*, March and April, 1951. The whole correspondence is printed in the S.A.I.O., *First Conference Records*, 1951, which was referred to for purposes of this study.

20. *Ibid.*, pp. 1–3. A similar telegram was sent to the Pakistan Government.

21. *Exchange of Correspondence*, March and April, 1951, 3–8.

22. *Exchange of Correspondence* is reproduced in United Nations, General Assembly Official Records, Sixth Session, 1951–1952, pp. 3–4.

23. *Ibid.*

24. *Leader*, 6th April, 1951.

25. *Ibid.*, quotes.

26. *Ibid.*, 10th August, 1951.

27. United Nations, General Assembly Official Records, Sixth Session, 1951–2, Report of the Ad Hoc Political Committee, Document A/2046, p. 4.

28. *Leader*, 16th November, 1951.

29. United Nations, General Assembly Official Records, 1951–2, Document A/2046, p. 5.

30. *Ibid.*, p. 6, Resolution 511 (vi).

31. *Natal Witness*, 14th January, 1952.

32. South African Indian Congress, Twenty-first Conference Records, 1954, Secretarial Report, p. 7.

33. *Ibid.* A few lines on the laws singled out by the Executive Committee:

    Separate Representation of Voters Act, No. 46/1951. The Act was designed to remove the Coloured Voters from the normal electoral rolls in the Cape Province and to place them on a separate roll and to allow them to vote for four special representatives. It established a Board of Coloured Affairs under the chairmanship of a Commissioner for Coloured Affairs. It was to consist of three nominated non-European members from Natal, the Orange Free State and the Transvaal and eight elected non-European members, two from each of the four Cape Electoral Divisions established under the Act. In Harris *v*. The Minister of the Interior, the Appellate Division of the Supreme Court held the Act to be invalid as it was passed by the Union Parliament by a simple majority of each House of Parliament sitting separately. In 1952 the decision of the Appellate Court was reversed by the High Court of Parliament. *Vide* Walker, *History of Southern Africa*, pp. 817–8 and p. 835. Report of the United Nations Commission on the Racial Situation in the Union of South Africa, pp. 63–4.

    The Suppression of Communism Act, No. 44/1950, in the words of Mr. C. R. Swart, the Minister of Justice, was intended "to declare the Communist Party of South Africa to be an unlawful organization, to make provision for declaring other organizations promoting communistic activities to be unlawful and for prohibiting certain periodical or other publications; and to prohibit certain Communistic activities". The Act is not discriminatory. It applies to Whites as well as non-Whites. Read together with the Public Safety Act No. 3/1953 and the Criminal Law Amendment Act, No. 8/1953, the conclusion is reached that the position is made "much more difficult than before for non-White organisers to launch any concerted campaign against the laws; and even to prevent non-European leaders stating their opposition to a Bill introduced by the Government or criticizing it". *Vide* Report of the United Nations Commission, p. 93.

    Bantu Authorities Act, No. 68/1951. This Act created tribal councils for the Africans under the control of Government. It abolished the Native Representative Council. *Vide Ibid.*, p. 130.

Native (Abolition of Passes and Co-ordination of Documents) Act, No. 67/1952. This Act introduced a reference book for Africans to replace the various passes carried. An African required to carry a reference book who is unable or who refuses to produce it on demand is guilty of an offence and on conviction is liable to a fine or imprisonment. If not in possession of a reference book the penalty is a fine not exceeding £50 and imprisonment not exceeding six months. *Ibid.*, pp. 66–8 *Stock Limitation Regulations*. These deal with limiting the number of head of cattle so as to prevent overgrazing. An attempt to limit the cattle in the Witzieshoek Reserve in the O.F.S. in 1942 by eliminating a thousand head of cattle and another in 1946 aroused much resentment and hostility. The situation became worse in July and August, 1950, when rioting broke out. "The authorities who carried out the limitation of stock by selection were Whites; those to whom the law was applied and who had in fact been consulted in advance, were Natives. That distinction contains all the elements of serious and lasting racial tension likely to make the problem of future food supplies for the Bantu in the Reserves insoluble." *Ibid.*, p. 88.

34. Report of the United Nations Commission on the Racial Situation in the Union of South Africa, 1953, pp. 155–6. The letter was signed by Dr. J. S. Moroka, President-General and Mr. W. M. Sisulu, Secretary-General.
35. *Ibid.*, pp. 156–8. The full correspondence between the A.N.C. and the Prime Minister is a most interesting and revealing document.
36. *Ibid.*, pp. 158–160.
37. S.A.I.C., Twenty-first Conference Records, 1954, Secretarial Report, p. 8. *Vide* also *Leader*, 11th April, 1952.
38. S.A.I.C., Twenty-first Conference Records, 1954, Secretarial Report, p. 8. The first volunteers were all banned under the Suppression of Communism Act.
39. *Ibid.*, p. 9. The number of volunteers arrested in each centre was as follows: Eastern Cape: 5 719; Western Cape, Mafeking, Kimberley: 423; Transvaal: 1 911; Natal: 246; and the Free State: 258.
40. *Leader*, 5th September, 1952.
41. *Ibid.*, 12th September, 1952.
42. *Ibid.*, 19th September, 1952.
43. United Nations, General Assembly Official Records, Seventh Session Annexes, 1952–3: Report of the Ad Hoc Political Committee, Document A/2257, p. 4.
44. United Nations, General Assembly Official Records, Seventh Session Annexes: The question of race conflict in South Africa, 1952–3, pp. 1–3.
45. *Ibid.*, p. 6, Report of the Ad Hoc Political Committee, Document A/2276.
46. *Ibid.*, pp. 8–9. As these were the first resolutions on the racial question in South Africa, they are reproduced in part so as to show how the United Nations viewed this new development. The operative part of Resolution A reads as follows:
The General Assembly –
1. Establishes a commission consisting of . . . to study the racial situation in the Union of South Africa in the light of the Purposes and Principles of the Charter, with due regard to the provisions of Article 2, paragraph 7, as well as the provisions of Article 1, paragraphs 2 and 3, Article 13, paragraph 16, Article 55c and Article 56 of the Charter, and the resolutions of the United Nations on racial persecution, and to report its conclusions to the General Assembly at its eighth session;
2. Invites the Government of the Union of South Africa to extend its full co-operation to the commission;
3. Requests the Secretary-General to provide the commission with the necessary staff and facilities;
4. Decides to retain the question on the agenda of the eighth session of the General Assembly of the United Nations.
The operative part of Resolution B reads as follows:
The General Assembly –
1. Declares that in a multi-racial society harmony and respect for human rights and freedoms and the peaceful development of a unified community are best assured when patterns of legislation

and practice are directed towards ensuring equality before the law of all persons regardless of race, creed or colour, and when economic, social, cultural and political participation of all racial groups is on a basis of equality;

2. Affirms that governmental policies of Member States which are not directed towards these goals, but which are designed to perpetuate or increase discrimination, are inconsistent with the pledges of the Members under Article 56 of the Charter;

3. Solemnly calls upon the Member States to bring their policies into conformity with their obligation under the Charter to promote the observance of human rights and fundamental freedoms.

47. United Nations, General Assembly Official Records, 401st Plenary Meeting, Seventh Session, 1952, p. 332.

48. *Ibid.*, pp. 334–6.

49. *Ibid.*, p. 336. The draft resolutions were adopted by the General Assembly on the 5th December, 1952. Their references are: Resolution A: 616A (vii) and Resolution B: 616B (vii).

50. *Leader*, 24th December, 1952, and 2nd April, 1952. Dr. Bodet of Mexico had recently resigned as head of UNESCO.

51. Details in regard to the Members of the Commission.
   Chairman–Rapporteur: Mr. Hernan Santa Cruz, former permanent representative of Chile to the United Nations; former President of the United Nations ECOSOC (1950–1); former member of the Commission on Human Rights (1946–1953); member of the Sub-Commission on Prevention of Discrimination and the Protection of Minorities.
   Members: (1) Mr. Dantes Bellegarde, former Minister of Education of Haiti; former representative of Haiti to the League of Nations; former Minister of Haiti in Paris and former Ambassador of Haiti to Washington; former permanent representative of Haiti to the United Nations. (2) Mr. Henri Laugier, professor at the Sorbonne; former Assistant Secretary-General in charge of the United Nations Department of Social Affairs (1946–1951); Honorary President of the International League for the Rights of Man (New York); Member of the Executive Board of UNESCO.
   Vide Report of the United Nations Commission on the Racial Situation in the Union of South Africa, p. xi. This is cited hereafter as UNCORS.

52. UNCORS, pp. 6–7.

53. *Ibid.*, pp. 7–8. Six witnesses were heard. They were: Mr. H. S. L. Polak, former Editor of the *Indian Opinion* in South Africa from 1906–16 and Assistant Secretary of the Transvaal British Indian Association and very close friend in South Africa of Mahatma Gandhi, representing the Theosophical Society of London; the Rev. Michael Scott, representing the International League for the Rights of Men, New York; Mrs. M. Crosfield, representing Christian Action of London. The three private witnesses were Mr. E. S. Sacks, Mr. J. Hatch, Mr. T. Wardle. Written statements were received from the following organisations and private individuals: Patrick Duncan, Orange Free State; Council on African Affairs, New York; the Moderator of the African Gospel Church, Durban; H. S. Coaker, Talloires; Congress of Peoples against Imperialism, London; Anti-Slavery Society, London; South African Indian Organization, Durban; Pakistan Islamic Council for International Affairs, Karachi; the African National Congress and the South African Indian Congress, Johannesburg; the Congress of Democrats and the Springbok Legion of ex-Servicemen and Women, Johannesburg; W. v.d. Vaart, Pietersburg; Women's International League for Peace and Freedom.

54. *Ibid.*, p. 115.

55. *Ibid.*, pp. 115–9.

56. *Leader*, 19th June, 1953.

57. *Ibid.*, 17th July, 1953.

58. United Nations, General Assembly Official Records, Eighth Session, Annexes, 1953, p. 1; Report of the United Nations Good Offices Commission, Document A/2473, pp. 1–2.

59. United Nations, General Assembly Official Records, Eighth Session, Annexes, 1953, p. 7. Greece voted with South Africa against the resolution.

60. United Nations, General Assembly Official Records, Eighth Session, Annexes, 1953; Report of

the Ad Hoc Political Committee, Document A/2610. Australia, Belgium, Columbia, France, Greece and the United Kingdom voted with South Africa.

61. United Nations, General Assembly Official Records, 469th Plenary Meeting, 1953, pp. 433–435.
62. *Ibid.*, pp. 432–7. Those who sided with South Africa were France, Greece, Luxembourg, U.K., Australia, Belgium and Columbia.
63. *Natal Witness*, 9th December, 1953.
64. Current Affairs Publications, *Nehru on Africa*, pp. 3, 4 and 30–1.
65. *Natal Witness*, 10th July, 1953.
66. House of Assembly Debates, Vol. 85, 1954, pp. 4494–5.
67. *Leader*, 14th May, 1954.
68. *Ibid.*, 28th May, 1954.
69. *Ibid.*, 21st May, 1954.
70. *Ibid.*, 2nd July, 1954.
71. *Ibid.*, 6th August, 1954.
72. *Ibid.*, 10th September, 1954.
73. United Nations, General Assembly Official Records, Ninth Session, Annexes, 1954; Report of the United Nations Good Offices Commission, Document A/2723, pp. 1–2.
74. *Ibid.*, p. 5, Resolution 816 (ix).
75. United Nations, General Assembly Official Records, Ninth Session Annexes, 1954; Report of the Ad Hoc Political Committee, Document A/2857, p. 5.
76. *Ibid.*, p. 7. The main points in the Report have already been dealt with. The Summary of the Report is contained in UNCORS, pp. 114–116.
77. *Leader*, 12th October, 1956. Resolution 917 (x) 1955.
78. United Nations, General Assembly Official Records, Ad Hoc Political Committee, 12th Meeting, 9th November, 1955, pp. 45–46.
79. Resolution 1375 (xiv) United Nations, Fourteenth Session, 20th November, 1959.
80. United Nations, General Assembly Official Records, Tenth Session, Annexes, Document A/3001/ Add. 1, pp. 2–3.
81. S.A.I.C., Conference Records, 1956, Annexure D2, p. 5.
82. S.A.I.C., Twenty-first Conference Records, 1956, Annexure B1.
83. *Leader*, 30th September, 1955.
84. United Nations, General Assembly Official Records, Tenth Session Annexes, 1955; Report of the Secretary-General, Document A/3001, p. 1.
85. United Nations, General Assembly Official Records, 1955, p. 7, Resolution 919 (x).
86. *Leader*, 22nd April, 1955.
87. *Natal Witness*, 11th November, 1955.
88. *Ibid.*, 29th November, 1956.
89. United Nations, General Assembly Official Records, Eleventh Session Annexes, 1956–7, Document A/3186, p. 2.
90. *Ibid.*, pp. 3–4, Document A/3188.
91. *Ibid.*, p. 5, Resolution 1015 (xi). On the 27th November, 1956, Mr. Eric Louw had withdrawn the South African delegation partially and maintained "a token or nominal representation" only.
92. *South Africa's Treason Trial*, pp. 6–7. Among the accused were 20 Indians and 17 Europeans; the rest were Africans, and a few Coloureds. The accused included an M.P., one M.P.C., medical doctors, a university professor, a minister of religion, trade unionists and persons from nearly every walk of life.
93. *Natal Daily News*, 29th March, 1961.
94. *Ibid.* The case cost the State nearly R300 000 and the Defence till the 29th March, 1961, had spent around R326 000.
95. *Indian Opinion*, 15th March, 1957.
96. *Ibid.*, 29th March, 1957.
97. *Ibid.*, 3rd May, 1957.

98. Report on the Findings of the Commission on Civil Rights and Duties in a Multi-Racial Society.

99. United Nations, General Assembly Official Records, Twelfth Session Annexes, 1957, Document A/3643, p. 2.

100. *Leader*, 18th January, 1958.

101. *Leader*, 4th July, 1958.

102. *Ibid.*, 3rd July, 1959.

103. Muriel Horrell, *A Survey of Race Relations in South Africa*, 1958–1959, p. 12.

104. N.I.C., Twelfth Provincial Conference Records, 1959, p. 23.

105. *Ibid.*, p. 13.

106. United Nations, General Assembly Official Records, Thirteenth Session Annexes, 1958, p. 3.

107. United Nations, General Assembly Official Records, Report of the Government of India, Document A/3850, p. 18, and pp. 39–40.

108. *Ibid.*, Document A/4051, p. 3.

109. *Natal Mercury*, 4th January, 1960.

110. *Sunday Times*, 10th January, 1960. Mr. A. M. van Schoor was appointed first Director of the Foundation, whose chairman was Sir Francis de Guingand.

111. *Sunday Times*, January 10th, 1960. "Whereas in 1946 there were only four independent States in Africa, there are now 11, and before the end of this year the number will have grown to 17. This means that by the end of 1960 nearly two-thirds of the 230 000 000 inhabitants of the Continent will have attained independent self-government. Others are already on the road there." *Ibid.*, 5th February, 1960.

112. South African Information Service, *The Union and the Emergent States of Africa*, p. 7.

113. *Natal Mercury*, 14th January, 1960.

114. *Ibid.*, 15th January, 1960.

115. *Ibid.*, 4th February, 1960.

116. Muriel Horrell, *Days of Crisis in South Africa*, S.A.I.R.R., Fact Paper, No. 5/1960, pp. 9–10.

117. *Ibid.*, pp. 10–11.

118. The two reports were tabled in the House of Assembly by the Minister of Justice, Mr. F. C. Erasmus, on 23rd January, 1961. Mr. Justice Wessels reported that there was no organised attempt by the crowd to attack the police at Sharpeville. The report made no findings concerning the liability or responsibility of those who gave evidence to the commission, and offered no recommendations for any action for or against them. Mr. Justice Diemont, in his report on Langa, said that the police decision to use force to quell the disturbances must be criticised in three respects: firstly, the commanding officer should have attempted to communicate the order to disperse to the chair man of the meeting or to the organisers before using force; secondly, the three minutes warning that force would be used was an unreasonably short period of time to give 10 000 people to disperse; thirdly, the loudspeaker was ineffective because of the noise and the commanding officer should have realised this. *Vide Natal Mercury*, 24th January, 1961.

119. M. Horrell, *Days of Crisis in South Africa*, p. 15.

120. *Ibid.*, p. 66, and United Nations, Security Council Records, S/4300, p. 1.

121. M. Horrell, *Days of Crisis in South Africa*, p. 66. The Security Council, which had 11 members, was, at this time, constituted as follows: the U.K., the U.S.S.R., France, Nationalist China, the U.S.A. and Italy, the Argentine, Tunisia, Ceylon, Ecuador and Poland.

122. Nicholas, *The United Nations as a Political Institution*, p. 76.

123. United Nations, Security Council Records, S/4300, pp. 1–2.

124. *Natal Mercury*, 21st April, 1960.

125. *Ibid.*, 20th April, 1960.

126. *Ibid.*, 17th May, 1960.

127. *Ibid.*, 14th May, 1960.

128. *Ibid.*, 8th July, 1960.

129. *Ibid.*, 16th May, 1960.

130. United Nations, General Assembly Records, Documents A/4416 and A/4417, 20th July, 1960.

131. *Natal Mercury*, 22nd July, 1960.
132. *Ibid.*, 12th October, 1960.
133. *Ibid.*, 25th November, 1960.
134. *Sunday Times*, 1st January, 1961.
135. Muriel Horrell, *Days of Crisis in South Africa*, p. 52.
136. *Sunday Times*, 1st January, 1961. *Vide* also: Rene de Villiers, *Afrikanerdom's Changing Race Attitudes*; Prof. B. B. Keet, *The Ethics of Apartheid*; P. V. Pistorius, *No Further Trek*, for the changing attitudes.
137. United Nations, Security Council Records, S/4635, pp. 2–3.
138. *Ibid.*, p. 3. In a Memorandum presented to the Secretary-General, the S.A.I.C. called on the UN to appeal to its member states to apply economic sanctions against the Union Government and to outlaw it from the world organization.
139. *Natal Mercury*, 24th April, 1961.
140. Latest population figures for the Union, 1960:

White	Coloured	Asian	African	Total
3 067 638	1 488 267	477 414	10 807 809	15 841 128

Information obtained on behalf of the writer by the Librarian, South African Institute of Race Relations, 17th April, 1961.

CHAPTER NINE

THE SOUTH AFRICAN INDIAN QUESTION AS AN INTERNATIONAL ISSUE: CONCLUSION

"There are so many among the non-whites who are civilised and developed and there are so many on the same level as the whites that it does not behove us any longer to look down on them as being inferior persons who do not also have economic and political rights to enjoy in our common land."

MR. A. W. RETIEF

(Chairman of the South African Onderwysersunie, addressing a congress of the organisation on 25th June, 1962.)

With the coming into being of the Republic of South Africa as from 31st May, 1961, Indians have been in South Africa for just over a hundred years. Their history over this period has not been an easy one; instead, it has been the story of a people whose coming to South Africa has resulted in great "problems" for the country and its peoples to the extent that the label "Indian Problem" has become quite synonymous with Indian life in this country. The coming of no other people (and quite a number have come to South Africa from abroad) has left an equally powerful imprint in the general mind of "problems" being created by their coming.

That this label is without factual foundation and grossly exaggerated is not difficult to establish. The fact that there is an Indian "problem" in South Africa (if it can be called so) is due, as the late Jan H. Hofmeyr said, to the white man and to the white man alone. It was to serve the interests of the white sugar planters in Natal that the tripartite pact was arrived at, involving the Governments of Natal, India and Great Britain. The claim that the Indian question is the "domestic concern" of South Africa is without historical foundation. The importance of this in the international setting is that it gives the Indo-Pakistan Governments the right, based on treaty obligations, to maintain an interest in the affairs of the South African Indians. This interest, of course, will have to cease once the Indians in South Africa are absorbed in the body politic in South Africa. Indians in the country have always been told that it was not proper for them to appeal to India. As Smuts told them in regard to the Pegging Act: "to appeal to India adds salt to the wound". But this right to appeal, too, is not without foundation. Dr. Alan Paton touches on the pulse of the matter when he says: "Let us never forget that any people when they feel helpless and hopeless will do that. They do it because they see no help at home." When appeals have been made to India or to other countries the South African Indians have always done so as South African citizens and not as nationals of India.

Another aspect of this issue dealt with in this study concerns itself with international intervention in the affairs of the South African Indians. That there has always been inter-national as well as international intervention is sufficiently amplified in this study. It remains now to summarise the strength, the value, and the weakness of such intervention. The first power to have any important role to play was Great Britain. The record of the British in the history of the South African Indian is a dismal one of inconsistencies and evasions. Where the British did intervene, as in the case of the Transvaal, the intervention was motivated by the interests of Britain. This record, therefore, places the Britisher in many respects in a more unfavourable light than it does the Afrikaner in the over-all assessment. If the Afrikaners have tightened the reins since their accession to power, it was an evolution quite in keeping with their declared policies. There is no question here of any broken pledges. The story of the British in South Africa in relation to the Indian question since the early days of Natal is a sad indictment of a faith not kept.

The Imperial Conferences (influenced as they were by British policy) failed to bring about any improvements. The League of Nations was almost exclusively concerned with European affairs. But the United Nations has played an important part in the South African Indian question – not that it has brought about any direct improvements but (as shown in the last stages of the last chapter) its indirect influences have been considerable. The Afro-Asian countries have stood together, with India at first at the head. Indeed, at the United Nations, India has played a leading role in this matter and her influence over the Afro-Asian countries and her guidance to them might result in important and far-reaching developments in South Africa.

India, since 1905 and in particular after gaining her independence in 1947, has taken strong steps against South Africa. The termination of diplomatic relations, the imposition of economic sanctions, are but minor steps in the overall picture. India was in the early 'sixties the head of the Afro-Asian bloc in the United Nations. India's Mrs. V. Pandit was the first lady to hold the position of President of the General Assembly. India's Rajendra Dayal was the personal representative of Mr. Dag Hammarskjold in the Congo in 1960–1. It is this bloc, either at United Nations or separately, that South Africa has to contend with. This is the external influence which will affect internal events in South Africa. South Africa cannot afford to ignore this factor or to treat it with contempt. The intervention of India, therefore, has been of great value to the South African Indians in that an opposition to the Republican Government of South Africa has now been closely knit. This intervention has been of more value than British intervention.

Up till now the Government of South Africa has resisted all external intervention. It has succeeded in doing so at great cost to itself at home and abroad. In continuing to do so, as it is expected, the cost will soar higher and higher to the detriment of a peaceful adjustment without bloodshed to the needs of our age.

On the international scene of 1961 the Indian question takes second place to the issue of race conflict in South Africa resulting from the policy of apartheid of the Government. In a real sense the Indian question has merged with the general black question. This is to be seen in the Congress Alliance and in the growing unity between Indians and Africans. In this development the important question is how politically conscious is the Indian? The barely half-million Indians have two Indian political organisations, the South African Indian Congress and the South African Indian Organisation – with their provincial units. Though the first named claims greater support there are no figures available to show its strength. Except for the leaders and the immediate following, the masses are usually ignorant of what goes on – except when a call is made for mass demonstrations. By and large most Indians would care more for economic improvements than for political power. But as the all-White Parliament of South Africa has failed to render equal facilities, in most things, to the non-Whites (thus failing to show that separate development means the equal and just development it is made out to be in official circles) even the politically indifferent Indians cannot but welcome the ballot box.

That the Indian, generally, has reached the stage where he can use the ballot box wisely is exemplified in the vast educational strides taken by him. If education is a yard-stick for the proper use of political opportunities the claim of the Indian (and indeed of fellow blacks as well) must rank high in South Africa. This development has made it possible for the South African Indians to follow a western mode of life largely as a result of western patterns of life in South Africa and also because of their commitment to South Africa as home. Except for social and religious differences, which exist among most peoples, no other differences stand in the way of the South African nation of all races with a fair degree of education living together as one family as General Smuts visualised in 1919: "We have to live side by side in conciliation, and we must endeavour to under-stand each other's standpoint, so that we may live together and grow together. We are members of the one family . . . ." This is as it should be.

Much of South Africa's economic and political stability, and her future well-being, depends on the racial harmony which prevails at home. There is urgent need for the different races to emphasise and extend the lines of understanding and to eliminate the points which create distrust and disharmony. In so far as these factors affect the South African Indians, as a unit in the country, there is need to take note of the fact that the Indians are themselves too often divided on many issues and in many respects. The division is by no means always noticeable in the political organisations only. There are situations which create division and disunity among the Indians which do not always catch the public eye. These are often found to exist on communal foundations – on Hindu-Muslim lines, particularly in group activities, though the growing tendency is to eliminate such divisions in order that a measure of unity might be achieved. Nor are all differences traceable to communal sources. Among the Hindus, for example, caste feel-ings and distinctions are not altogether absent, though they are on the decrease. And on the issue of the non-white peoples in South Africa, of which the Indians form a part, it cannot be stated that all Indians are in agreement with the merging of the Indian ques-tion with the larger issue of the non-white question in South Africa. Some would still like to have the one matter dealt with separately from the other. The developments since 1949 have shown clearly that there cannot be separate ways.

For the Indians true morality and political wisdom demand that they not only resolve their own differences but that they accept the other black peoples with the same measure of frankness and friendliness which they expect to receive from others. Their moral and political claim for international intervention is much weakened unless they attain this unity. For them a great measure of charity must begin at home.

The free world today stands as one large family with different units bound together, maintaining only their geographic separateness but magnifying their human solidarity, owing common allegiance to the purposes and principles of the United Nations Charter and the Universal Declaration of Human Rights. The common aim for all is the dignity and worth of the human person. Anything less, from whatever source, or anything in defiance of this ideal, can only be promoted at one's own moral peril.

CHAPTER TEN

EPILOGUE: DEVELOPMENTS SINCE 1961

"Although it claims to be solving the minority problem, the approach of the present government to the Coloured and Indian question is symptomatic of an unwillingness to try to find a lasting solution to it. So, in effect, the responsibility is just shifted on to future generations . . . "

DR. A. L. MULLER[1] (writing in 1968).

South Africa is a country in which many minorities live. The only unusual aspect is that one of the minorities holds the reigns of government. The economic and political position of the two other minority groups (Indians and Coloureds) as well as that of the majority group (the Africans) is affected by the unwavering determination of the ruling minority to retain and to consolidate its position. This determination has characterised the whole history of white politics in South Africa since 1652. It has not changed substantially since 1961.

South Africa has now been a republic for ten years. It is no longer directly affected by pressures within the Commonwealth of which it was once a valued member. But indirect pressures continue to be generated, however unevenly, as in the case when the country's sporting fraternity was hit by the cancellation of the Springbok cricket tour of the United Kingdom in 1970 or when the Commonwealth raised a furore during 1970–1 over the issue of the sale of arms by Britain to South Africa.

These external pressures are no longer aroused only by isolated cases of discrimination against either the minorities or the majority. Isolated instances have had their day. The assault is now on a system and not on a part of it. The spotlight is not on Indians or Coloureds or Africans or Europeans. It is on a system, on a policy. *Apartheid* is no longer on trial. It stands condemned on the international scene.

It is with this background in mind that the present chapter is being developed. Like the earlier chapters it is convenient to examine both local and external developments. Locally, the most significant change or experiment concerning Indians that the South African Government has introduced since 1961 has been one of involving Indians in a limited way in local and national politics for the first time since Indians lost the parliamentary franchise in Natal in 1896 and the municipal franchise in 1924. It will be remembered that when limited participation was mooted in 1946 Indians rejected it because it was tied to the acceptance by them of separate residential and trading areas.

In the post-republican age the new arrangement is no longer based on a *quid pro quo* as in 1946 but on an intensification of the Group Areas Act which has been around since 1950 to carry out the Government's segregation policy. The Department of Indian Affairs was set up in 1961 under the wing of the Department of Interior to take charge of all matters pertaining to the South African Indians. The old half-measures which apportioned to the Provincial Councils control over their respective Indian populations were jettisoned. Indian affairs came under centralised government control in 1961.

The next step was to use the machinery of the devastating and omnibus Group Areas

275

Act to create local government bodies, called Local Affairs Committees, for Indians in their own separate urban residential areas.[2] The first of these committees was set up in 1963. The committees are to serve as Consultative and Advisory Committees to the local authority which is the only body that has statutory rights. The emphasis is on *consultation*. It is still early to say how effective this consultation is or will be. The Local Affairs Committee certainly has the trimmings of a vaunted body without the reality of power. The Indian people have generally accepted this provision. The choice open to them is extremely limited to one of non-participation and increased hardships or to participation with the hope of mitigated hardships. As always, the Indians have had to rely more upon the grace or condescension of the white councillors in the local authority bodies than upon the pressures that can be mobilised by their own largely apolitical leaders.

Elections for the few positions on the Local Affairs Committees are hotly contested. There is no lack of enthusiasm or candidates but the success of this venture – like all others of this kind – will depend upon the effectiveness of the committees to get results and results for the citizens who are affected mean good roads, good recreational facilities, good amenities including libraries, swimming baths, public health clinics, houses and employment opportunities. Since all these matters are really dictated from above, the South African Government has quite rightly sought to involve Indian participation on a higher platform as well.

This higher body is the National Indian Council which was set up in 1964. When the South African Prime Minister addressed a meeting of hand-picked Indian representatives on 26th August, 1963, at which he outlined his government's policy on this subject, he said, "The Indians should be given the opportunity of controlling their own affairs from the bottom up. One way in which this could be done was first to give them control over their own local affairs". The Prime Minister explained that the ultimate hope was that the National Indian Council would take charge of the Local Affairs Committees and become the medium of consultation and co-operation between the controlling bodies of the various racial groups.

The terms of reference and scope of the National Indian Council were explicitly defined by the Minister of Indian Affairs on 10th December, 1963, when he said that the Council had a two-fold function: firstly, to serve as a body with which the Government could consult on matters affecting the Indian community; secondly, to assist the Department of Indian Affairs "to pave the way for and develop an eventual democratically elected Council which in time will control those affairs of the Indian community in South Africa as may be delegated to it from time to time by Parliament".[3]

The limitations were stated clearly but they were accepted by the invited members of the Indian community who resolved that the Minister of Indian Affairs should appoint the first twenty-five members of the council who would hold office until elected representatives would replace them. These invited members realised that the usefulness of the council would be gauged from its success; that to be acceptable to the Indian community at large it had to prove that it was more than a council of sycophants. The invited members realised how vulnerable the hand-picked council would be and they made a special plea to the Government "to stay its hand on all adverse matters presently affecting the Indian Community".[4]

It is precisely on this issue of staying its hand on matters which adversely affect the South African Indians that the case of the Government and the value of the Council will stand or fall.

Different people see different virtues in the setting up of the South African Indian Council. A Nationalist M.P. supported the proposal in Parliament which, to read his words, pointed to a new world for Indians in South Africa with the Indian Council developing one day into "an Indian Parliament which will deal with Indian education, Indian health and so forth. Then you will have Indian local authorities, practically an Indian Parliament with an Indian Prime Minister and an Indian Cabinet . . . "[5]

A casual reading of such an utterance suggests the possibilities of an *Indianstan* but in actual fact it is not part of government policy to create such a unit for Indians. The United Party finds that the creation of an Indian Council fits in with its own plans in its race federation policy[6] though the Natal leader of the United Party (it *is* in Natal that most of the South African Indians live) has said in Parliament that when the frills are removed one cannot escape the conclusion "that except for advising the Minister there is no power vested in this new council". The same speaker referred to another aspect which is wholly relevant to the case and that is the criticism by Indians of the council, its membership, and its limitations.[7]

While there was indecent haste and an upsurge of enthusiasm to join the Indian Council bandwagon, in which both former members of the Natal Indian Organisation and the Natal Indian Congress were aspirants, the Group Areas Act was taking its relentless toll. For the aspirants the consolation was one of "times – have changed" rationalisation.[8] For the victims of the Group Areas Act there was no consolation.

One affected area was the western sector of Johannesburg from where over five hundred traders in Newclare, Sophiatown, Newlands, Martindale and Westdene had been removed since 1956. Of this number under fifty had successfully set themselves up elsewhere. The remaining traders were threatened by the direct and indirect consequences of the operation of the Community Development Act. In terms of this Act the white local authorities have power to remove a trader from expropriated property on one month's notice without a court order. An order to move is not conditional upon the availability of alternative accommodation for displaced traders. Of the 1 500 Indian traders who were still in Johannesburg in 1968 about 250 had businesses in Fordsburg and Vrededorp on properties which were recently expropriated under the Act.[9]

The Martindale Indian Association appealed to the Indian Council as early as September, 1967, for help. Its plea was desperate: "If your Council does not rally to prevent this catastrophe, the growing favourable image of the National Indian Council will be irreparably damaged and demise of the Indian traders of Martindale will for ever remain a monument to your Council's impotency."[10]

An administrative officer of the Johannesburg Indian Welfare Association summed up the effects of empty promises. "We Indians," he said, "are living on borrowed time. The Minister of Indian Affairs clearly said that no Indian will be uprooted and so deprived of his livelihood. But this is exactly what is happening to the Indian community."[11]

These are by no means isolated cases of difficulties that continue to be caused by the most devastating irritant in South Africa's economy, the Group Areas Act. Other instances are equally pathetic. There is the case of Nana Sita, the aged disciple of Mahatma Gandhi, who spent fifteen months in prison for refusing to vacate his own house in an area which was declared a white area. He had lived there for forty-four years before it was declared a white area.[12]

Nor are Indians the only affected people. The Group Areas Act knows no bounds and respects no colour. Statistically, and in terms of human tragedy, it has visited the non-white side of the colour line more frequently and more fiercely. While its visits continue there can be no hope of national happiness and stability which alone can fend off external odium and interference. In recent years a new and more startling dimension has crept into the malady of the Group Areas Act and this is the principle of *deproclamation*. The Group Areas Act confers on displaced communities the right to "Security of Tenure" in their own group areas. This assurance had been first given when thousands of Indians were to be uprooted from Cato Manor. On that occasion the responsible Minister had said: "Once proclaimed a Group Area, such Group Area will not be deproclaimed except under circumstances of the most pressing and overriding nature." Yet in July, 1966, one part of Ladysmith, Forbes Street to be exact, was deproclaimed without the existence of any special circumstances. Anyone who knows Forbes Street or has seen Forbes Street knows that this street has always been occupied mainly by Indians and that it lies in a flood area. When it was declared a group area for Indians the declaration was an affirmation of a historical development and reality. Its deproclamation in 1966 could only have come about as a result of an ideological wish to place the Indians beyond a natural boundary, the Klip River.[13]

All these internal factors play in the hands of external pressure groups. They tend to keep alive international opposition to the policy of separate development. In addition, they tend to weaken South Africa's economy. In recent investigations the *Sunday Times* has come up with statistics that show that 72 per cent of the workers in South Africa are non-white; that South Africa's economic survival is "absolutely and irrevocably dependent on non-white labour"; that the "integration of non-whites into the South African economy is so far-reaching and so deep-rooted that it can never be reversed or eliminated"; and that job reservation for whites has failed. In the first instalment of its review of the economic position in South Africa, the *Sunday Times* observed that "The one thing we dare not do is to carry on gaily as if nothing significant has happened in the past decade.

"It would not be too much to say that in the past decade we have been through a social and economic revolution of the first magnitude."[14]

We have seen that no "political revolution" has taken place in South Africa in the decade after the Republic in so far as Indians and the other black communities of South Africa are concerned. Indians have been given Local Affairs Committees and the South African Indian Council which is still nominated and enjoys a doubtful reputation as far as Indians are concerned. It has been severely criticised as a council of sycophants. It has its own Indian chairman since November, 1968 (H. E. Joosub). This chairman sees the responsibility of the Council as one of "dual responsibility to the Government and the Indian people and it will translate Government policy for the future of our people".[15]

But how can the Council carry out its "dual responsibility"? Where should its first loyalty lie? Towards the end of 1968 Mr. Blaar Coetzee, the Minister of Community

Development, told Indians to give up trading and diversify into other fields.[16] How could the Council reconcile this stipulation with its own support of the Government?

The chairman of the South African Indian Council, Mr. Joosub, did not agree. He quoted the 1960 census figures to show that only 29,7 per cent of the Indian population were in commerce and 71,3 per cent were in other occupations. It was the Government itself which was obstructing diversification. "As far as the youth is concerned," said Mr. Joosub, "they would like to diversify their occupations but many avenues are closed to them because they cannot become artisans." Mr. Joosub then made the shocking disclosure that no new trading licences have been granted to Indians in the Transvaal since 1950 and other occupations were closed because of the existence of the policy of *job reservation*.[17]

As I write these lines the policy of job reservations is breaking down. The disclosures to this effect by the *Sunday Times* on 31st January and 7th February, 1971, that job reservations were collapsing has led the Government to announce the lifting of its ban in certain occupations. This is the thin end of the wedge.

Coetzee was severely criticised for his statement and the press began to give prominence to the many trading centres all over the Transvaal where Indians were being threatened with loss of their trading premises. Coetzee changed his stance in the light of unfavourable publicity in South Africa and outside. He announced early in 1969 that a regional business complex would be constructed on the East Rand to cater for displaced traders from Germiston, Alberton, Boksburg, Benoni and Springs. In Johannesburg itself an Indian trading complex would be set up in Fordsburg and another complex would be constructed at Klerksdorp.[18]

But as the 1970s move on the reins are being tightened; opportunities are dwindling while the realities of the situation do not register in many instances. The fatalists thrive on optimism. "Our reasons are economic," said a Rustenburg trader under the threat of removal, "I am not interested in politics. My politics are ringing the 'piano' in the shop here every day. All I want to do is bring up my family and be a good neighbour."

"Look, Mr. Coetzee is an intelligent man. He is a human being and a Christian. I believe he will grant our request when he hears our side of the case."[19]

The humanity aspect and the Christian aspect have been argued before and found wanting. The South African Council of Churches[20] and the World Council of Churches have not found the human and Christian sides to be present in many of the local situations in South Africa so the optimism recorded in certain quarters is either misguided or wishful thinking.

Because the internal situation continues to deteriorate, the external forces continue to find grist for the mill. The United Nations can do little more than to keep its options open and to wait for internal developments to get more chaotic. The South African Government does not agree that the internal position is anything but laudable. It claims to be in control and to have the right policy in a troubled continent. The military coups north of the Zambesi provide fodder for the South African Government's policy. This policy has no place for special consideration for different peoples. It aims purely and simply at keeping the different communities apart. Since 1950, the Group Areas Act has been responsible for re-settling 240 000 persons classified as Indians and Coloureds. Of this number 110 000 were Indians. This has been carried out in the name of slum clearance and city renewal.[21]

So much for the local position of Indians in South Africa in the decade after 1961. How has the United Nations viewed all this in the context of the two hardy annuals, treatment of persons of Indian and Indo-Pakistan origin and racial conflict in South Africa resulting from the policy of *Apartheid*.

Up to the time of the coming into being of the Republic of South Africa in May, 1961, we have seen that the United Nations failed to make any dents in the framework of official South African policy and practice. A strong draft resolution was introduced in the September, 1961, session of the General Assembly by a number of African states (Cuba was the only non-African state) calling upon states to break off diplomatic relations with South Africa; to close their ports to South African vessels; to boycott South African ports; to boycott South African goods and to refrain from exporting goods to South Africa and to refuse landing and passage facilities to South African aircraft. The draft resolution asked the Security Council to enforce these measures under the provisions of the Charter.[22] The voting on the clause calling for the adoption of these measures clearly denotes how divided the world body is when it comes to taking active measures against South Africa. There were 40 votes in favour, 30 against and 23 abstentions. Such voting really represents a victory for South Africa. In the first United Nations session after South Africa became a republic, the *status quo* obtained on the Indian question as well as on the *Apartheid* question. In the final resolution that was adopted no strong measures were called for because the major European states had too much of an economic commitment in South Africa or were unsure of the efficacy of strong collective action.

A technical, though significant, change was introduced in 1962 when the item "Treatment of people of Indian and Indo-Pakistan origin in the Republic of South Africa" was not accorded a separate place on the agenda of General Assembly business. It had appeared (in slightly different wording) as a separate item since the first meeting of the United Nations in 1946. Now its sponsors requested that it be treated as the second part of the item "The policies of *apartheid* of the Government of the Republic of South Africa". The first part was to be "Race conflict in South Africa".

As I have shown in an earlier chapter, the time for recognising the fact that these two issues were inter-related had come ten years before.

The Indian and Pakistan governments, as interested parties, were still prepared to talk but the other interested party was not. The General Assembly braced itself to adopt in 1962 what it had not been able to do the previous year and set up a watch-dog committee to keep itself informed.[23] The President of the General Assembly nominated Algeria, Costa Rica, Federation of Malaya, Ghana, Guinea, Haiti, Hungary, Nepal, Nigeria, Philippines and Somalia to make up the Special Committee.

The new resolution calling for the strong action listed above as part of the draft resolution of 1961 received support from the Security Council which adopted its own resolution on 7 August, 1963, calling upon South Africa "to liberate all persons imprisoned, interned or subjected to other restrictions for having opposed the policy of *apartheid*".

Member states informed the Secretary-General of the steps they had taken or planned to take in line with the resolution of the General Assembly. Their reports are interesting and show the extent to which member states are appalled by the *Apartheid* policy. Even South Africa's old friends, Australia, France, the United States of America and the United Kingdom reported that they would not be supplying arms to South Africa for internal repression. The sale of arms to South Africa has since blown up into a major issue and the tenuous dividing line between external defence and internal repression has come under heavy fire in 1970–1.

The report which was compiled and presented to the General Assembly in 1963 shows that some states were prepared to go the whole way and isolate South Africa completely. Others, particularly South Africa's old trading partners, are prepared to go just that far to register their token compliance with the United Nations resolution to isolate South Africa. Some stop at the sale of arms; some at the point of honouring existing contracts but *all* the states which responded (Portugal is an understandable exception) have made it clear that they do not support South Africa's *Apartheid* policy.

The South African Government, as before, was not deflected from its course by all these developments. In 1963 and 1964 a number of persons were arrested and tried for acts of sabotage and other offences. The accused were generally charged with conspiring with the Communist Party of South Africa, the African National Congress and Umkonto we Sizwe and of furthering Poqo activities. These trials included the Rivonia trial, that of Neville Alexander and others, that of Billy Nair and others in Pietermaritzburg, and similar trials at various places in the country. The accused were members of all communities, white and non-white. In January, 1964, the South African Minister of Justice stated in Parliament that 3 355 persons were detained for security reasons in 1963. In addition to the firm measures taken, the Government warned ministers of religion not to interfere with politics. At the same time, civil rights leaders feared that the rule of law was coming to an end.

The South African Government reaction to the increasing pressures from outside and pockets of resistance from within was clearly and unequivocally enunciated by Prime Minister Verwoerd on 21st January, 1964: "I contend that . . . present-day international politics prove that the world is sick, and that it is not up to South Africa to allow herself to be dragged into that sickbed. It is white South Africa's duty to ensure her survival, even though she is accused of being isolated under such a policy. . . . The tragedy of the present time is that in this crucial stage of present-day history, the white race is not playing the role which it is called upon to play and which only the white race is competent to fulfil. If the Whites of America and of Europe and of South Africa were dissolved in the stream of the black masses, what would become of the future of the world and of the human race? What would become of its science, its knowledge, its forms of civilization, its growth, its peace?

"What we are dealing with here is the preservation of the white man and of what is his, and only in respect of what is justly his, coupled with the recognition of other people's rights . . . "[25]

The United Nations took note of this and similar statements through its Special Committee on *Apartheid*. This committee was represented at the International Conference on Economic Sanctions against South Africa organized by the Anti-Apartheid Movement in London in 1964. This Conference came up with a case for the use of economic sanctions as a weapon against *apartheid*. One of its committees concluded that the crisis in South Africa was one of a race war; that it could only be resolved by outside intervention; that the only way in which outside intervention would be effective were economic sanctions and military intervention. For the moment, it felt that total economic sanctions was the better alternative.[26]

This, in sum, is what the position is as I write these concluding remarks. The case of the South African Government is one of white survival which it sees as being synonymous with white supremacy and white civilisation. Its opponents do not see that there is any scientific or logical grounds for the retention of these labels. In the 'sixties these labels came under heavy criticism within South Africa and without. In the 'seventies, the tempo of development and the general bases for thought, word and deed, especially among the younger generation, do not have room anymore for them. They are anachronisms in a world and age which does not accord a privileged position to "the white race".

For as long as the South African Government leans on the argument of "the white race" and supports itself against the prop of *Apartheid*, so long will its opponents look to church organisations, to political organisations within and without, to conferences in South Africa and outside, to international bodies of various kinds and ultimately to the United Nations. But the United Nations can do little more than give moral support. The real instruments of change rest most powerfully in the keeping of individuals, peoples' organisations and in State organisations. In 1971 plans are being intensified to boycott firms dealing with South Africa. The success of the agitation to ban the Springbok tour of Britain in 1970 has not been lost on the agitators. For them the next step is one of enlargement of scale.

Where do the South African Indians feature in all this? Their future is now merged with the future of all the peoples of South Africa. There is no longer a South African Indian Question. There is only a South African Question. For mankind it is a human question.

FOOTNOTES

1. A. L. Muller, *Minority Interests. The Political Economy of the Coloured and Indian Communities in South Africa*, S.A.I.R.R., 1968, p. 45. Dr. Muller is Senior Lecturer in Economics, University of Port Elizabeth.
2. Local Government Extension Ordinance, No. 23/1963. The first Local Area Committee was to consist of five eligible persons, two of whom were to be nominated by the local authority, i.e. the all-White Municipal and City Council. The Administrator of the Province would make the appointment. Subsequent Local Areas Committees were to comprise two members nominated by the local authority and three persons to be elected by Indian voters who were property owners or tenants of property worth R550. Five years later it was proposed that 18-year-olds be enfranchised and the property limits be brought down from R500 to R100.
3. Minutes of the first meeting of the National Indian Council held at Cape Town on 23rd–25th March, 1964, Annexure "B".
4. *Ibid.*, Resolution adopted by members of the South African Indian Community who attended the meeting at Laudium, Pretoria, 10th–11th December, 1963. By Act 31/1968, the South African Indian Council was formally instituted. It comprises 25 members, of whom 5 shall constitute an Executive Committee. Four of these shall be elected by the Council members but the fifth (who will be Chairman of the Executive Committee) will be appointed by the Minister of Indian Affairs.

5. Mr. B. Coetzee, Nat. M.P. for Vereeniging, House of Assembly Debates, No. 16, 17th–21st May, 1965, p. 6319.
6. Mr. W. Vause Raw, U.P. Durban Point. *Ibid.*, p. 1147.
7. Mr. D. E. Mitchell, U.P., South Coast. *Ibid.*, p. 1128.
8. *Leader*, 24th May, 1968, commentary by Politicus.
9. *Rand Daily Mail*, 28th March, 1968. "The Agony of our Indians" by Tony Stirling.
10. Martindale Indian Association, "The Problems of the Indian Traders of Martindale", 25th September, 1967, also reported in *Rand Daily Mail*, 17th October, 1967.
11. *Sunday Times*, 21st May, 1967.
12. *Statement by Nana Sita at his trial under the Group Areas Act*, 7th August, 1967; also *Rand Daily Mail*, 28th December, 1967; 9th April, 1968.
13. Leonard's Township Ratepayers and Tenants Association, "Memo on Deproclamation of Forbes Street", 17th July, 1966.
14. *Sunday Times*, 31st January, 1971.
15. *Rand Daily Mail*, 25th September, 1968.
16. *Rand Daily Mail*, 9th October, 1968.
17. *The Star*, 8th October, 1968.
18. *The Sunday Times*, 26th January, 1969.
19. *Rand Daily Mail*, 11th January, 1969.
20. The South African Council of Churches, *Pseudo Gospels in Church and Society*, May, 1968.
21. *Rand Daily Mail*, 25th September, 1968.
22. United Nations General Assembly, Document A/SPC/L.71., 30th October, 1961.
23. United Nations General Assembly Document A/5166.
24. *Ibid.*, Document A/SPC/94.
25. House of Assembly Debates, *Hansard*, 17th January, 1964, col. 7 and 21st January, 1964, cols. 53–55.
26. United Nations General Assembly Document A/5692, p. 45.

APPENDIX A

Definition Clause: Transvaal Immigrants Restriction Act, 15/1907

"Any person who at the date of his entering or attempting to enter this colony be subject to the provision of any law in force at such date which might render him liable either at such date or thereafter if found therein to be removed from or to be ordered to leave this colony whether on conviction of an offence against such law or for failing to comply with its provisions or otherwise in accordance with its provisions."

(Patrick Duncan, *State*, 1909. Vol. I, p. 165.)

APPENDIX B

Summary of the Recommendations of the Indian Enquiry Commission, 1914

"Some of these recommendations will require legislation to give effect to them whilst others can be sufficiently dealt with by administrative action.

1. Section 5 (*g*) of the Immigrants Regulation Act of 1913 should be amended so as to bring the law into conformity with the practice of the Immigration Department, which is 'to admit one wife and the minor children by her of an Indian now entitled to reside in any Province or may in future be permitted to enter the Union, irrespective of the fact that his marriage to such wife may have been solemnised according to tenets that recognise polygamy, or that she is one of several wives married abroad, so long as she is his only wife in South Africa.'

2. Instruction should be given to the Immigration Officers to open registers in each Province for the registration by Indians of, say three or more years' residence in South Africa, who have at present or have had in the past more than one wife living with them in South Africa, of such wives, who are to be free to travel to and from India with their minor children so long as the husband continues to reside in this country.

3. There should be legislation on the lines of Act 16 of 1860 of the Cape Colony making provisions for the appointment of Marriage Officers from amongst Indian Priests of different denominations for the purpose of solemnising marriages in accordance with the rites of the respective religions of the parties.

4. There should be legislation for the validation by means of registration of existing *de facto* monogamous marriages, by which are understood marriages of one man with one woman under a system which recognises the right of the husband to marry one or more other wives. Directions as to the mode of registration and of the particulars to be entered in the register might be given by regulations framed under the Statute.

5. Section 6 of Act 17 of 1895 of Natal which requires certain Indians to take out year by year a pass or licence to remain in the Colony and which provides for the payment of £3 a year for such licence should be repealed.

6. The conditions under which identification certificates under the Immigrants' Regulation Act, 1913, are issued should be amended so as to provide that such certificates shall remain in force for a period of three years.

7. An interpreter should be attached to the office of the Immigration Department in Cape Town who should be a whole-time officer.

8. Application forms for permits, certificates, etc., from the Immigration Department should be filled in by a clerk in the office upon information supplied to him by the applicant, if the latter so desires.

9. The practice at present existing in the Cape Town office of this Department of taking, in certain cases, the prints of all the fingers of both hands instead of the thumbs only should be discontinued.

10. The Resident Magistrate of a district in which there is no Immigration Officer should have authority to issue temporary permits to Indians residing in his district who desire to travel from the Province in which they are living to another Province of the Union.

11. The permit fee of £1 for an identification certificate or a temporary permit should be materially reduced, and no charge should be made for an extension.

12. The present practice of the Immigration Officer of one Province of communicating by telegraph with the Immigration Officer of another Province when an application is made by an Indian for a permit to travel from one Province to the other should be discontinued.

13. Domicile certificates which have been issued to Indians in Natal by the Immigration Officers of that Province, and which bear the thumb impression of the holder of the permit, should be recognised as conclusive evidence of the right of the holder to enter the Union as soon as his identity has been established.

14. An arrangement should, if possible, be made with the Government of India for the holding of official enquiries by the Magistrate or other Government official in the case of women and children proceeding from India to join their husbands and fathers in South Africa. If, on enquiry, the official is satisfied that the women and children are the wife and children of the man in South Africa whom they claim as their husband or father, a certificate should be given by him to that effect, and such evidence should be treated by the Immigration Officers as conclusive evidence of the facts stated in it."

(Report of the Indian Inquiry Commission, U.G. 16/1914, Cape Town, 7th March, 1914, *Summary of the Recommendations.*)

_____

APPENDIX C

Asiatic Population – Censuses, 1904 to 1946

YEAR	CAPE		NATAL		TRANSVAAL		O.F.S.		UNION		TOTAL
	Male	Female	Male	Female	Male	Female	Male	Female	Male	Female	
1904	9 316	926	63 497	37 421	9 799	1 522	197	56	82 809	39 925	122 734
1911	6 581	1 083	80 477	52 943	8 990	2 022	87	20	96 135	56 068	152 203
1921	5 724	1 972	80 314	61 335	11 056	4 935	242	153	97 336	68 395	165 731
1936	6 677	3 831	97 073	86 588	15 379	10 114	22	7	119 151	100 540	219 691
1946	8 557	6 617	119 784	112 533	20 729	17 029	6	5	149 076	136 184	285 260

Birthplaces (Asiatics) – Censuses, 1936 and 1946*

BIRTHPLACE	CAPE		NATAL		TRANSVAAL		O.F.S.		UNION	
	1936	1946	1936	1946	1936	1946	1936	1946	1936	1946
Union of S.A. ..	6 077	11 389	159 918	215 336	14 547	26 136	23	7	180 565	252 868
India	3 417	2 903	23 072	13 720	9 761	9 925	4	4	36 254	26 552
China	615	611	38	32	995	1 229	—	—	1 648	1 872
Japan	24	2	109	—	11	4	2	—	146	6
Other	375	269	524	3 229	179	464	—	—	1 078	3 962
TOTAL ..	10 508	15 174	183 661	232 317	25 493	37 758	29	11	219 691	285 260

* Preliminary Figures. *Vide* Union of South Africa: *Official Year Book*, No. 24, 1948, pp. 1090–1091.

APPENDIX D

The Smuts–Gandhi Agreement

"The following correspondence between Mr. Gandhi and General Smuts, in confirmation of a series of interviews, constitutes a perfect understanding between the Government and the Indian community in regard to those administrative matters which do not come under the Indians' Relief Bill:

Department of Interior,
Cape Town, Cape of Good Hope,
30th June, 1914.

Dear Mr. Gandhi,

Adverting to the discussions you have lately had with General Smuts on the subject of the position of the Indian community in the Union, at the first of which you expressed yourself as satisfied with the provisions of the Indians' Relief Bill and accepted it as a definite settlement of the points, which required legislative action, at issue between that community and the Government; and at the second of which you submitted for the consideration of the Government a list of other matters requiring administrative action, over and above those specifically dealt with in that Bill; I am desired by General Smuts to state with reference to those matters that:

(1) He sees no difficulty in arranging that the Protector of Indian Immigrants in Natal will in future issue to every Indian, who is subject to the provisions of Natal Act 17 of 1895, on completion of his period of indenture, or re-indenture, a certificate of discharge, free of charge, similar in form to that issued under the provisions of Section 106 of Natal Law No. 25 of 1891.

(2) On the question of allowing existing plural wives and the children of such wives to join their husband (or fathers) in South Africa, no difficulty will be raised by the Government if, on enquiry, it is found, as you stated, that the number is a very limited one.

(3) In administering the provisions of Section (4) (1) (a) of the Union Immigrants' Regulation Act, No. 22 of 1913, the practice hitherto existing at the Cape will be continued in respect of South African-born Indians who seek to enter the Cape Province, so long as the movement of such persons to that Province assumes no greater dimensions than has been the case in the past; the Government, however, reserves the right, as soon as the number of such entrants sensibly increases, to apply the provisions of the Immigration Act.

(4) In the case of the 'specially exempted educated entrants into the Union' (i.e., the limited number who will be allowed by the Government to enter the Union each year for some purpose connected with the general welfare of the Indian community), the declarations to be made by such persons will not be required at Provincial borders, as the general declarations which are made in terms of Section 19 of the Immigrants' Regulation Act at the port of entry are sufficient.

(5) Those Indians who have been admitted within the last three years, either to the Cape Province or Natal, after passing the education tests imposed by the Immigration Laws which were in force therein prior to the coming into effect of Act 22

of 1913, but who, by reason of the wording of Section 30 thereof, are not yet regarded as being 'domiciled' in the sense in which that term is defined in the Section in question, shall, in the event of their . . . absenting themselves temporarily from the Province in which they are lawfully resident, be treated, on their return, as if the term 'domicile' as so defined did apply to them.

(6) He will submit to the Minister of Justice the cases of those persons who have been in the past convicted of 'bona fide passive resistance offences' (a term which is mutually understood) and that he anticipates no objection on Mr. De Wet's part to the suggestion that convictions for such offence will not be used by the Government against such persons in the future.

(7) A document will be issued to every 'specially exempted educated entrant' who is passed by the Immigration Officers under the instructions of the Minister issued under Section 25 of Act No. 22 of 1913.

(8) All the recommendations of the Indian Grievances Commission enumerated at the conclusion of their Report, which remain over and above the points dealt with in the Indians' Relief Bill will be adopted by the Government;

and subject to the stipulation contained in the last paragraph of this letter the necessary further action in regard to those matters will be issued without delay.

With regard to the administration of existing laws, the Minister desires me to say that it always has been and will continue to be the desire of the Government to see that they are administered in a just manner and with due regard to vested rights.

In conclusion, General Smuts desires me to say that it is, of course, understood, and he wishes no doubt on the subject to remain, that the placing of the Indians' Relief Bill on the Statute Book of the Union, coupled with the fulfilment of the assurances he is giving in this letter in regard to the other matters referred to herein, touched upon at the recent interviews, will constitute a complete and final settlement of the controversy which has unfortunately existed for so long, and will be unreservedly accepted as such by the Indian community.

I am, etc.,
(Sgd.) E. M. Gorges.

M. K. Gandhi Esq.,
7, Buitencingel,
CAPE TOWN.

7, Buitencingel,
Capetown,
30th June, 1914.

Dear Mr. Gorges,

I beg to acknowledge receipt of your letter of even date herewith setting forth the substance of the interview that General Smuts was pleased, notwithstanding many other pressing calls upon his time, to grant me on Saturday last. I feel deeply grateful for the patience and courtesy which the Minister showed during the discussion of the several points submitted by me.

The passing of the Indians' Relief Bill and this correspondence finally closes the Passive

Resistance struggle which commenced in the September of 1906 and which to the Indian community cost much physical suffering and pecuniary loss and to the Government much anxious thought and consideration.

As the Minister is aware, some of my countrymen have wished me to go further. They are dissatisfied that the trade licences laws of the different Provinces, the Transvaal Gold Law, the Transvaal Townships Act, the Transvaal Law 3 of 1885 have not been altered so as to give them full rights of residence, trade and ownership of land. Some of them are dissatisfied that full inter-provincial migration is not permitted, and some are dissatisfied that . . . on the marriage question the Relief Bill goes no further than it does. They have asked me that all the above matters might be included in the Passive Resistance struggle; I have been unable to comply with their wishes. Whilst, therefore, they have not been included in the programme of Passive Resistance, it will not be denied that some day or other these matters will require further and sympathetic consideration by the Government. Complete satisfaction cannot be expected until full civic rights have been conceded to the resident Indian population.

I have told my countrymen that they will have to exercise patience and by all honourable means at their disposal educate public opinion so as to enable the Government of the day to go further than the present correspondence does. I shall hope that when the Europeans of South Africa fully appreciate the fact that now, as the importation of indentured labour from India is prohibited and as the Immigrants' Regulation Act of last year has in practice all but stopped further free Indian immigration and that my countrymen do not aspire to any political ambition, they, the Europeans, will see the justice and, indeed, the necessity of my countrymen being granted the rights I have just referred to.

Meanwhile, if the generous spirit that the Government have applied to the treatment of the problem during the past few months continues to be applied, as promised in your letter, in the administration of the existing laws, I am quite certain that the Indian community throughout the Union will be able to enjoy some measure of peace and never be a source of trouble to the Government.

I am,

Yours faithfully,

(sgd.) M. K. Gandhi."

E. M. Gorges Esq.,
Department of Interior,
Capetown.
(UN Document A/68/Add 1, 14th November, 1946.)

APPENDIX E

Imperial Conference Resolution, 1921

"The Imperial Conference, while re-affirming the resolution of the Imperial War Conference of 1918 that each community of the British Commonwealth should enjoy complete control of the composition of its own population by means of restriction of immigration from any other communities, recognizes that there is incongruity between the position of India as an equal member of the British Empire and the existence of disabilities upon the British Indians lawfully domiciled in some other parts of the Empire. The Imperial Conference, accordingly, is of the opinion that in the interests of the solidarity of the British Commonwealth, it is desirable that the rights of such Indians to citizenship should be recognized.

The representatives of South Africa regret their inability to accept this resolution in view of the exceptional circumstances in a great part of the Union.

The representatives of India, while expressing their appreciation of the acceptance of the resolution recorded above, feel themselves bound to place on record their profound concern for the positions of Indians in South Africa and their hope that by negotiation between the Governments of India and South Africa some way can be found as soon as may be to reach a more satisfactory position."

(C. F. Andrews, *Documents Relating to the New Asiatic Bill and the Alleged Breach of Faith*, p. 22.)

APPENDIX F

Cape Town Agreement, 1927
(Announcement made simultaneously, in India and South Africa on
21st February 1927, of the terms of the Cape Town Agreement, 1927.)

1. "It was announced in April, 1926, that the Government of India and the Government of the Union of South Africa had agreed to hold a Round Table Conference to explore all possible methods of settling the Indian question in the Union in a manner which would safeguard the maintenance of western standards of life in South Africa by just and legitimate means. The Conference assembled at Cape Town on December 17th and its session finished on January 12th. There was, in these meetings, a full and frank exchange of views which has resulted in a truer appreciation of mutual difficulties and a united understanding to co-operate in the solution of a common problem in a spirit of friendliness and good-will.

    Both Governments re-affirm their recognition of the right of South Africa to use all just and legitimate means for the maintenance of western standards of life.

2. The Union Government recognises that Indians domiciled in the Union who are

prepared to conform to western standards of life, should be enabled to do so.

3. For those Indians in the Union who may desire to avail themselves of it, the Union Government will organise a scheme of assisted emigration to India or other countries where western standards are not required. Union domicile will be lost after 3 years' continuous absence from the Union, in agreement with the proposed revision of the law relating to domicile which will be of general application. Emigrants under the assisted emigration scheme who desire to return to the Union within the 3 years will only be allowed to do so on refund to the Union Government of the cost of the assistance received by them.

4. The Government of India recognise their obligation to look after such emigrants on their arrival in India.

5. The admission into the Union of the wives and minor children of Indians permanently domiciled in the Union will be regulated by paragraph 3 of Resolution XXI of the Imperial Conference of 1918.

6. In the expectation that the difficulties with which the Union has been confronted will be materially lessened by the agreement now happily reached between the two Governments, and in order that the agreement may come into operation under the most favourable auspices and have a fair trial, the Government of the Union of South Africa have decided not to proceed further with the Areas Reservation and Immigration and Registration (Further Provision) Bill.

7. The two Governments have agreed to watch the working of the agreement now reached and to exchange views from time to time as to any changes that experience may suggest.

8. The Government of the Union of South Africa have requested the Government of India to appoint an agent in order to secure continuous and effective co-operation between the two Governments."

Annexure containing summary of the conclusions reached by the Round Table Conference on the Indian question in South Africa, 1927.

I. "*Scheme of assisted emigration.*

1. Any Indian of 16 years or over may avail himself of the scheme. In case of a family, the decision of the father will bind the wife and minor children under 16 years.

2. Each person of 16 years of age or over will receive a bonus of £20 and each child under that age a sum of £10. No maximum shall be fixed for a family. A decrepit adult who is unable to earn his living by reason of a physical disability may, at the discretion of the Union authorities, receive a pension in lieu of or in addition to the bonus. The pension will be paid through some convenient official agency in India out of a fund provided by the Union Government to such amount as they may determine. It is expected that the amount required will not exceed £500 per annum in all.

In every case the bonus will be payable in India on arrival at destination or afterwards, through some banking institution of repute.

3. Free passage, including railway fares to port of embarkation in South Africa and from port of landing in India to destination inland, will also be provided.

4. Emigrants will travel to India via Bombay as well as via Madras. Emigrants landing at Bombay will be sent direct from the ship to their destination at the expense of the Union Government.

   Survey and certification of ships will be strictly supervised and conditions on the voyage, especially in respect of sanitary arrangements, feeding and medical attendance, improved.

5. Before a batch of emigrants leaves the Union, information will be sent to some designated authority in India at least one month in advance giving (a) a list of intending emigrants and their families, (b) their occupation in South Africa and the occupation or employment which they would require in India, and (c) the amount of cash and other resources which each possesses. On arrival in India emigrants will be (i) advised, and so far as possible, protected against squandering their cash or losing it to adventurers, and (ii) helped, as far as possible, to settle in occupations for which they are best suited by their aptitude or their resources. Any emigrant wishing to participate in emigration schemes authorised by the Government of India will be given the same facilities in India as Indian nationals.

6. An assisted emigrant wishing to return to the Union will be allowed to do so within three years from the date of departure from South Africa. As condition precedent to re-entry, an emigrant shall refund in full to some recognized authority in India the bonus and cost of passage including railway fares received on his own behalf and if he has a family, on behalf of his family. A *pro rata* reduction will, however, be made (i) in respect of a member of the family who dies in the interim or a daughter who marries in India and does not return, and (ii) in other cases of unforeseen hardship, at the discretion of the Minister.

7. After expiry of three years Union domicile will be lost in agreement with the proposed revision of the law relating to domicile which will be of general application. The period of three years will run from the date of departure from a port in the Union and expire on the last day of the third year. But to prevent the abuse of the bonus and free passage by persons who wish to pay temporary visits to India or elsewhere no person availing himself of the benefits of the scheme will be allowed to come back to the Union within less than one year from the date of his departure. For purposes of re-entry within the time limit of three years, the unity of the family group shall be recognised though in cases of unforeseen hardship the Minister of the Interior may allow one or more members of the family to stay behind. A son who goes with the family as a minor, attains majority outside the Union, marries there and has issue will be allowed to return to South Africa, but only if he comes with the rest of his father's family. In such cases he will be allowed to bring his wife and child or children with him. But a daughter who marries outside the Union will acquire the domicile of her husband and will not be admitted into the Union unless her husband is himself domiciled in the Union.

II. *Entry of wives and minor children*

To give effect to paragraph 3 of the Reciprocity Resolution of the Imperial Conference of 1918 which intended that an Indian should be enabled to live a happy family life in the country in which he is domiciled, the entry of wives and children shall be governed by the following principles:

(*a*) The Government of India should certify that each individual for whom a right of entry is claimed, is the lawful wife or child, as the case may be, of the person who makes the claim.

(*b*) Minor children should not be permitted to enter the Union unless accompanied by the mother, if alive, provided that

   (i) the mother is not already resident in the Union, and

   (ii) the Minister may, in special cases, permit the entry of such children unaccompanied by their mother.

(*c*) In the event of divorce no other wife should be permitted to enter the Union unless proof of such divorce to the satisfaction of the Minister has been submitted.

(*d*) The definition of wife and child as given in the Indian Relief Act (No. 22 of 1914) shall remain in force.

III. *Upliftment of Indian community.*

1. The Union Government firmly believe in and adhere to the principle that it is the duty of every civilised Government to devise ways and means to take all possible steps for the uplifting of every section of their permanent population to the full extent of their capacity and opportunities, and accept the view that in the provision of educational and other facilities the considerable number of Indians who remain part of the permanent population should not be allowed to lag behind other sections of the people.

2. It is difficult for the Union Government to take action, which is considerably in advance of public opinion, or to ignore difficulties arising out of the constitutional system of the Union under which the functions of Government are distributed between the Central Executive and the Provincial and minor local authorities. But the Union Government are willing:

(*a*) in view of the admittedly grave situation in respect of Indian education in Natal, to advise the provincial administration to appoint a provincial commission of inquiry and to obtain the assistance of an educational expert from the Government of India for the purpose of such inquiry;

(*b*) to consider sympathetically the question of improving facilities for higher education by providing suitable hostel accommodation at the South African Native College at Fort Hare and otherwise improving the attractiveness of the institution for Indians;

(*c*) to take special steps under the Public Health Act for an investigation into sanitary and housing conditions in and around Durban which will include the question of—

   (i) the appointment of advisory committees of representative Indians; and

   (ii) the limitation of the sale of municipal land subject to restrictive conditions.

3. The principal underlying the Industrial Conciliation Act (No. 11 of 1924) and the Wages Act (No. 27 of 1925) which enables all employees including Indians to take their places on the basis of equal pay for equal work will be adhered to.

4. When the time for the revision of the existing trade licensing laws arrives, the Union Government will give all due consideration to the suggestions made by the Government of India Delegation that the discretionary powers of local authorities might reasonably be limited in the following ways:

   (*a*) The grounds on which a licence may be refused should be laid down by statute.

   (*b*) The reasons for which a licence is refused should be recorded.

   (*c*) There should be a right of appeal in cases of first applications and transfers, as well as in cases of renewals, to the courts or to some other impartial tribunal.

IV. *Appointment of Agent.*

If the Government of the Union of South Africa make representations to the Government of India to appoint an agent in the Union in order to secure continuous and effective co-operation between the two Governments the Government of India will be willing to consider such a request."

(Government of India, *Papers Relating to the Second Round Table Conference*, 1932, Appendix I.)

APPENDIX G

Joint Communique, 1932

Statement made in the Legislative Assembly and the
Council of State, on Tuesday, 5th April, 1932.

1. "In accordance with paragraph 7 of the Cape Town Agreement of 1927 delegates of the Government of the Union of South Africa and of the Government of India met at Cape Town from January 12th to February 4th, 1932 to consider the working of the Agreement and to exchange views as to any modifications that experience might suggest. The delegates had a full and frank discussion in the Conference which was throughout marked by a spirit of cordiality and mutual goodwill.

2. Both Governments consider that the Cape Town Agreement has been a powerful influence in fostering friendly relations between them and that they should continue to co-operate in the common object of harmonising their respective interests in regard to Indians resident in the Union.

3. It was recognised that the possibilities of the Union's scheme of assisted emigration to India are now practically exhausted owing to the economic and climate conditions of India as well as to the fact that 80 per cent of the Indian population of the Union are now South African-born. As a consequence the possibilities of land settlement

outside India, as already contemplated in paragraph 3 of the Agreement, have been further considered. The Government of India will co-operate with the Government of the Union in exploring the possibilities of a colonisation scheme for settling Indians, both from India and from South Africa, in other countries. In this investigation, which should take place during the course of the present year a representative of the Indian community in South Africa will, if they so desire, be associated. As soon as the investigation has been completed the two Governments will consider the results of the inquiry.

4. No other modification of the Agreement is for the present considered necessary."

(Government of India, *Papers Relating to the Second Round Table* Conference, 1932.)

APPENDIX H

The Kunzru-Dönges Talks, 1950

"On February 8th, before the third meeting of the preliminary talks in Cape Town, the Honourable Minister of the Interior of the Union Government expressed a desire to see Pandit Kunzru in his office. In his personal discussion Dr. Dönges reiterated the arguments advanced by him in his opening speech. Pandit Kunzru emphasised India's point of view . . . Dr. Dönges, *inter alia*, said that the non-homogeneous population of South Africa created very difficult problems which India did not appear to appreciate and stated frankly that the Union Government felt that they could not give political, social and economic rights to the Indians in South Africa, for fear that the Native population would inevitably claim the same rights for themselves. He also asserted that Indians who were different by race and religion could not assimilate the European civilization in South Africa. Pandit Kunzru, in refuting a number of these issues, maintained that civilization had nothing to do with race and religion and that Indians could follow the 'Western way of life', referred to in the Cape Town Agreement of 1927 without any difficulty. Dr. Dönges, however, insisted that according to them apartheid was the only solution of the racial problem and it would place all the races on the same footing and remove the stigma of inferiority that the Asiatic Land Tenure Act placed on the Indian community. Pandit Kunzru understood from this that the Union Government probably intended removing discrimination against any community by introducing the same conditions for others. The Indian Delegation had no impression, as a result of this talk, that any legislative measure like the Group Areas Bill was intended to be introduced in South Africa before the Round Table Conference."

(Exchange of Correspondence, India and South Africa, 1949–1950, pp. 7–8.)

BIBLIOGRAPHY

The field covered in this book spans the entire period of the history of the South African Indian since the arrival of the pioneer immigrants in 1860 up till the date of the advent of the Republic of South Africa in 1961. An Epilogue up to 1971 has been written but the references have not been included here.

Difficulties Experienced

There were two notable difficulties experienced by the writer:

1. *Absence of a sense of preservation of documents on the part of the Indian generally*

Valuable documents have been lost through this weakness. Though this loss to the student of history is tremendous, Indians who have been culpable in this regard do not view this weakness in serious light for they contend that the Indians' struggle for survival against the many odds in the country have left them with little time or inclination for the thought of preserving for posterity the records of the past and present.

The place of the archives of the land as repositories for documentary and other material of historical value is not yet recognized and should be stressed and publicised as much as possible for the present generation to avoid the mistakes of the past.

2. *The widespread police raids on organisations and individuals and the consequent confiscation of documentary material*

Some day it is hoped, when the mass of material, covering handbills, posters, minutes of meetings, conference record books and the mass of material which reflect the life and work and pains and pleasures of a people whose history in this land has been a turbulent and eventful feature of the past century, is once again available, the student of the history of the South African Indians will find his task so much easier.

The Sources of Material Studied

The material accumulated and studied were obtained from government departments, from international organisations, from libraries, from the archives and from individuals. The sources may be enumerated as follows:

1. Government of India: Ministry of External Affairs, New Delhi, and the Permanent Mission of India to the United Nations, New York.
2. Government of the Republic of South Africa: State Information Office.
3. United Nations and League of Nations: Public Inquiries Unit, Visitors' Service, United Nations, New York.
4. University of Natal Library, Pietermaritzburg.
5. Natal Society Library, Pietermaritzburg.
6. South African Institute of Race Relations, Johannesburg.
7. Natal Archives, Pietermaritzburg.
8. Mrs. Muthray Pillay and Executors of the late Mr. S. Muthray Pillay: loan of books and periodicals and Congress records of the late Mr. S. M. Pillay.
9. Mr. S. R. Naidoo: Congress records, Commission reports, Press cuttings, and various publications.
10. Mr. P. R. Pather: Commission reports and various publications.
11. Mrs. Dhanee Bramdaw: *Leader* files.
12. Various friends and well-wishers who would prefer not to be mentioned.

CLASSIFICATION OF MATERIAL

1. MANUSCRIPT DOCUMENTS
   (*a*) Colonial Secretary's Office, Natal: Letters Received, Volumes 2203–2233, 1892 to 1910.
   (*b*) Natal Parliamentary Papers: Documents Presented, Volumes 200 (1903); 209 (1905); 225 (1907); 228 (1908).
   (*c*) Government House: Natal Indian Question, Volumes, 1897 to 1902.
   (*d*) Indian Immigration Department: Letters Dispatched, 1903 to 1910.

2. STATUTES
   Ordinances and Laws, Vol. I, 1843–1870.
   Natal Laws, 1890–1894.
   Natal Government Gazette, Vol. 47, 1895.
   Laws and Acts of Natal, Vol. 5, 1890–1902.
   Transvaal Government Gazette, 1906, C.S.O. Vol. 52.
   Transvaal Government Gazette, 1907, C.S.O. Vol. 53.
   Transvaal Government Gazette, 1907, C.S.O. Vol. 54.
   Transvaal Government Gazette, 1908, C.S.O. Vol. 56.
   Statutes of the Union of South Africa, 1937.

3. PRINTED DOCUMENTARY MATERIAL
   A. **Government of India: Ministry of External Affairs, New Delhi, and the Permanent Mission of India to the United Nations, New York**
   Important Correspondence Relating to the Two Passive Resistance Movements in South Africa, 1905–1914 (Government of India Press, New Delhi), 1946.
   Important Correspondence between the Government of India and the Government of the Union of South Africa on:
   (i) Class Areas Bill 1924 and Areas Reservation Bill 1925;
   (ii) Negotiations leading up to the Paddison Deputation and the Cape Town Conference, 1926–1927 (Government of India Press, New Delhi), 1946.
   Papers Relating to the Round Table Conference of 1926–1927 between the Representatives of the Government of India and of the Government of the Union of South Africa on the Indian question in the Union (Government of India Press, Simla), 1927.
   Memorandum on Indian Education in Natal, by K. P. Kichlu (*Natal Witness*, Pietermaritzburg), 1928.
   Private and Personal Correspondence leading to the Second Round Table Conference at Cape Town in 1932 (Government of India Press, New Delhi), 1932.
   Papers Relating to the Second Round Table Conference between the Representatives of the Government of India and of the Government of the Union of South Africa on the position of Indians in the Union, 1932 (Government of India Press, New Delhi), 1933.
   Annual Reports of the Agent/Agent-General/High Commissioner for India in South Africa:

Year ending	Publishers	Date
31st December, 1933	Government of India Press, New Delhi	1934
1936 and 1937	Government of India Press, New Delhi	1938
1939	Government of India Press, Simla	1940
1941	Government of India Press, Simla	1942
1942	Government of India Press, Simla	1944
1943	Government of India Press, Simla	1945
1945	Government of India Press, New Delhi	1947

Question of the Treatment of Indians in the Union of South Africa before the United Nations, Documents and Proceedings (Government of India Press, Simla), 1947.

Question of the Treatment of Indians in the Union of South Africa before the United Nations: Verbatim Record of 106th to 112th Meetings of the First Committee held in November, 1947 (Government of India Press, New Delhi), 1948.

Fallacies of South African Government Case (Government of India Information Services, Washington), n.d.

Treatment of Indians in South Africa – Recent Developments (Ministry of External Affairs and Commonwealth Relations, New Delhi), 1949.

B. Annual Natal Blue Books
N.B.B., 1900 to 1910.

C. Imperial Blue Books

Cd., 1683, 1903	Cd., 5363, 1909–1910
Cd., 3251, 1906	Cd., 5579, 1910
Cd., 3887, 1907	Cd., 6283, 1911
Cd., 4327, 1908	Cd., 6940, 1913
Cd., 4584, 1908	B.P.P. No. 79, 1903

D. Eybers
Select Constitutional Documents Illustrating South African History (G. Routledge and Sons, London), 1918.

E. Works of C. F. Andrews
Documents Relating to the Indian Question (Cape Times Ltd., Cape Town), 1914.
The New Asiatic Bill and the Alleged Breach of Faith (Cape Times Ltd., Cape Town), 1926.
"The South African Indian and World Politics", *Voorslag*, Vol. I, No. 6, 1926.
"The Indian Agreement", *Voorslag*, Vol. I, No. 11, 1927.
"Indians in South Africa", *The Indian Review*, Vol. XXXX, No. 12, 1939.

F. United Nations and League of Nations Documents
League of Nations, *Debates in the Third Assembly*, 1922. (Photostat copies.)
United Nations, *Year Book of the United Nations*, 1946–7.
United Nations, General Assembly Official Records, Annexes: *Treatment of People of Indian Origin in the Union of South Africa*. Fifth Session, 1950; Sixth Session, 1951–2; Seventh Session, 1952–3; Eighth Session, 1953; Ninth Session, 1954;

Tenth Session, 1955; Eleventh Session, 1956–7; Twelfth Session, 1957; Thirteenth Session, 1958; Fourteenth Session, 1959; Fifteenth Session, 14th April, 1961.

United Nations, General Assembly Official Records, Plenary Meetings: *Treatment of People of Indian Origin in the Union of South Africa, and The Question of Race Conflict in South Africa Resulting from the Policies of Apartheid of the Government of the Union of South Africa.* Seventh Session, 401st Plenary Meeting, 1952. *The Question of Race Conflict in South Africa.* Eighth Session, 469th Plenary Meeting, 1953; Ninth Session, 511th Plenary Meeting, 1954; Tenth Session, 551st Plenary Meeting, 1955; Eleventh Session, 648th Plenary Meeting, 1957; Twelfth Session, 723rd Plenary Meeting, 1957; Thirteenth Session, 778th Plenary Meeting, 1958.

United Nations, General Assembly Official Records, Annexes: *The Question of Race Conflict in South Africa Resulting from the Policies of Apartheid of the Government of the Union of South Africa.* Seventh Session, 1952–3; Eighth Session, 1953; Ninth Session, 1954; Tenth Session, 1955; Eleventh Session, 1956–7; Twelfth Session, 1957; Thirteenth Session, 1958; Fourteenth Session, 1959; Fifteenth Session, 14th April, 1961.

United Nations General Assembly Official Records, Ad Hoc and Special Political Committee Meeting Records: *The Question of Race Conflict in South Africa.* 31st to 43rd Meeting, 1953; 42nd to 47th Meeting, 1954; 3rd to 12th Meeting, 1955; 11th to 16th Meeting, 1957; 50th to 57th Meeting, 1957; 86th to 94th Meeting, 1958; 140th to 148th Meeting, 1959; Provisional A/PV. 838, 17th November, 1959; Provisional, 4th April, 1961.

Security Council: S/4300, 1st April, 1960; S/4305, 19th April, 1960; S/4551, 11th October, 1960; S/4635, 23rd January, 1961. *Report of the United Nations Commission on the Racial Situation in the Union of South Africa* (General Assembly Official Records, Eighth Session, Supplement No. 16 (A/2505 and A/2506/Add 1), New York, 1953.

G. South African Indian Political Organisation Records

S.A.I.C. Emergency Conference, Sixth Session, 1926.

S.A.I.C. Annual Conference, Eighth Session, 1928.

S.A.I.C. Annual Conference, Ninth Session, 1929.

S.A.I.C. The Transvaal Asiatic Bill, 1930: A Brief Survey of the Bill.

S.A.I.C. Emergency Conference, 1930.

S.A.I.C. Annual Conference, 1930.

S.A.I.C. Statement Submitted to the Government of India Delegation to the Second Round Table Conference, 1932.

S.A.I.C. Emergency Conference, 14th Session, 1933.

S.A.I.C. Statement Submitted to the Indian Colonisation Enquiry Committee, 1934.

S.A.I.C. Colonial-born and Settlers Indian Association, First Natal Provincial Conference, 1933–1934.

S.A.I.C.   Memo to Select Committee on Transvaal Asiatic Land Tenure Amend-
           ment Bill, 1936.
T.I.C.   Memo on the Asiatic Land Laws Commission, 1938.
T.I.C.   Analysis of the Asiatic Land Laws Commission, 1939.
N.I.C.   Report Submitted to the General Meeting, 1940.
N.I.A.   Natal Indian Association, Final Statement to the Indian Penetration
           Commission, 1940–1.
S.A.I.C.   Annual Conference, Sixteenth Session, 1943.
S.A.I.C.   Memorandum Submitted to Field-Marshal J. C. Smuts, 1944.
N.I.C.   Memorandum on Civic Status Submitted to the Natal Indian Judicial
           Commission, 1944.
N.I.C.   Provincial Conference, 1944.
S.A.I.C.   Report of the Deputation that waited on the Rt. Hon. Gen. J. C. Smuts
           on the 11th February, 1946.
N.I.O.   South African Indian Conference Convened by the Natal Indian Organ-
           isation, 1948.
S.A.I.O.   First Conference, 1951.
N.I.C.   Seventh Annual Provincial Conference, 1954.
S.A.I.C.   Twenty-first Conference, 1954.
N.I.C.   Eighth Annual Provincial Conference, 1955.
S.A.I.C.   Twenty-second Conference, 1956.
N.I.C.   Tenth Annual Provincial Conference, 1957.
N.I.C.   Eleventh Annual Provincial Conference, 1958.
N.I.C.   Twelfth Annual Conference (Provincial), 1959.
N.I.C.   Thirteenth Annual Provincial Conference, 1961.
S.A.I.C.   Memo presented to Mr. Dag Hammarskjold, Secretary-General U.N.O.,
           1961.

H. Commission and Select Committee Reports

Report of the Indian Immigrants' Commission (Wragg), 1887.

Report of the Indian Immigration Commission (Clayton), 1909.

Report of the Indian Enquiry Commission (Solomon), U.G. 16/1914.

Report of the Asiatic Inquiry Commission (Lange), U.G. 4/1921.

Report of the Indian Colonization Enquiry Committee (Young), U.G. 23/1934.

Report Part I and II of the Transvaal Asiatic Land Tenure Act Commission
(Feetham), U.G. 7/1934.

Report of the Asiatic Land Laws Commission (Murray), U.G. 16/1939.

Report of the Commission on Mixed Marriages in South Africa, U.G. 30/1939.

Report of the Indian Penetration Commission (Broome), U.G. 39/1941.

Report of the Second Indian Penetration (Durban) Commission (Broome), U.G.
21/1943.

Report of the Select Committee on the Occupation Control Draft Ordinance,
N.P.S.C. 9/1944.

Interim Report of Commission of Enquiry into Matters Affecting the Indian
Population of the Province of Natal (Broome), U.G. 22/1945.

Report of the Commission of Enquiry into Riots in Durban (v.d. Heever), U.G. 36/1949.

Extract from Joint Report of the Asiatic Land Tenure Laws Amendments Committee and the Land Tenure Act Amendments Committee (Van der Merwe), U.G. 49/1950.

I. Hansard

Votes and Proceedings of the Legislative Assembly of Natal, 1906.

Natal Legislative Assembly Debates, Vol. XLII, 1907.

Natal Legislative Assembly Debates, Vol. XLV, 1908.

Transvaal Legislative Council Debates, Vols. II, 1903–4; III, 1904; IV, 1905–6; V, 1906.

Transvaal Legislative Assembly Debates: First Session, First Parliament, 1907; Second and Third Sessions, First Parliament, 1907.

House of Assembly Debates, Vol. 2, 25th July to 6th September, 1924.

House of Assembly Debates, Vol. 6, 22nd January to 29th March, 1926.

House of Assembly Debates, Vol. 7, 30th March to 8th June, 1926.

House of Assembly Debates, Vol. 8, 28th January to 14th April, 1926.

House of Assembly Debates, Vol. 10, 14th October, 1927 to 3rd April, 1928.

House of Assembly Debates, Vol. 19, 5th April to 22nd May, 1932.

House of Assembly Debates, Vol. 20, 20th January to 2nd March, 1933.

House of Assembly Debates, Vol. 21, 26th May to 22nd June, 1933.

House of Assembly Debates, Vol. 5, 1936; Vol. 12, 1936; Vol. 13, 1936; Vol. 12, 1939; Vol. 13, 1939; Vol. 10, 1946; Vol. 11, 1946; Vol. 12, 1946; Vol. 13, 1946.

House of Assembly Debates, Vol. 62, 1948; Vol. 65, 1948; Vol. 83, 1953; Vol. 85, 1954.

House of Assembly Debates, No. 18, 29th May to 2nd June, 1950 (Weekly Edition – Group Areas Bill debates).

Senate Debates, Vol. 5, 1939; Vol. 6, 1939; Seventh Session, Eighth Parliament, 1943; Third Session, Ninth Parliament, 1946–7.

J. Union Government Publications

The Indian in South Africa (issued by the Union of South Africa Government Information Office, New York), n.d.; *Treatment of Indians in the Union of South Africa:* Union Government's Statement to the United Nations General Assembly, September 15th, 1947 (Information Office, New York), 1947; *Principal Documents Relating to Consideration by the United Nations General Assembly of the Representations of the Government of India on the Treatment of Indians in the Union of South Africa* (Cape Times Limited, Cape Town), 1947; *South Africa's Peoples* (State Information Office, Pretoria), n.d.

The South African Indian (State Information Office), 1956; *Asia Resurgent*, Fact Paper 4 (Hayne and Gibson, Johannesburg), 1956.

The Asian in Africa, Fact Paper 6 (Hayne and Gibson, Johannesburg), 1956.

The Implication of Separate Development Policy (Hayne and Gibson, Johannesburg), 1956.

The Treatment of Indians in the Union of South Africa: Discussions and Proceedings in the United Nations Assembly, September 1948 to May 1949 (Government Printer, Pretoria), 1950.

The Treatment of Indians in the Union of South Africa: Discussions and Proceedings in the United Nations Assembly, September to November, 1953 (Government Printer, Pretoria), 1954.

The Treatment of Indians in the Union of South Africa: Discussions and Proceedings in the United Nations Assembly, January to December, 1954 (Government Printer, Pretoria), 1955.

The Treatment of Indians in the Union of South Africa: Discussions and Proceedings in the United Nations Assembly, January to December, 1955 (Government Printer, Pretoria), 1956.

The Treatment of Indians in the Union of South Africa: Discussions and Proceedings in the United Nations Assembly, January 1956 to January 1957 (Government Printer, Pretoria), 1957.

The Treatment of Indians in the Union of South Africa: Discussions and Proceedings in the United Nations Assembly, February to November, 1957 (Government Printer, Pretoria), 1958.

The Question of Race Conflict in South Africa Resulting from the Policies of Apartheid of the Government of the Union of South Africa: Discussions and Proceedings in the United Nations Assembly, September to November, 1957 (Government Printer, Pretoria), 1958.

South African Quiz (South Africa Information Service, Pretoria), n.d.

E. H. Louw, *The Union and the Emergent States of Africa* (South African Information Service, Pretoria), 1959.

4. NEWSPAPERS

Indian Opinion
1903–1914
1917–1923
1935–1939
1950–May 31st, 1961.
The Hindi
1922–1925
The Natal Witness
1950–1960
The Natal Mercury
1855–1860
1906–1914
1960–May 31st, 1961.
Contact
1961, January to May.
The Golden City Post
1960–May 31st, 1961.

Natal Advertiser
1906–1914

The Dharma Vir
Vols. 2–4, 1918–1919.
The Leader
1940–May 31st, 1961.
The Sunday Times
1960–May 31st, 1961.
The Graphic
1960–May 31st, 1961.
Dagbreek en Sondagnuus
Translation from August 1960 to May 31st, 1961.
The New Age
1961, January to May.
The Natal Daily News
1961, January to May.

5. PERIODICALS

African Monthly
Vol. 3, 1908; Vol. 4, 1908;
Vol. 5, 1908.

The State
Vol. 1, 1909; Vol. II, 1910.
The Indian Review
1925: Nos. 2, 4, 8, 9, 10, 11, 12.
1926: Nos. 2, 3, 4, 5, 6.
1928: Nos. 3, 4, 8, 9.
1929: Nos. 1, 6, 7.
1930: Nos. 4, 11.
1931: No. 12.
1932: Nos. 3, 12.
1939: No. 12.

The Round Table
Vol. XV, 1914; No. 46, 1922; No. 50, 1923;
No. 52, 1923; No. 53, 1923; No. 54, 1924;
No. 63, 1926.
The Annual Register
Vol. 190, 1948.
Whittaker's Almanac
1948.

6. THESES

Adamson, H. M. "The Indian Question in South Africa", 1900–1914. (Unpublished M.A. thesis, University of Cape Town), 1932.

Atteridge, W. H. "The Problem of Imperial Organisation with Special Reference to the Place of the Imperial Conference". (Unpublished M.A. thesis, University of South Africa), 1925.

Corbett, J. E. "A Study of the Capetown Agreement". (Unpublished M.A. thesis, University of Cape Town), 1947.

Pachai, B. The History of the "Indian Opinion": Its Origin, Development and Contribution to South African History, 1903–1914. (Archives Year Book, 1961.)

Thompson, L.M. Indian Immigration into Natal, 1860–1872. (Archives Year Book, Vol. II, 1952.)

7. PAMPHLETS AND BOOKLETS

All-African Convention. Addresses (All-African Convention, Cape Town), 1941.

Bramdaw, Dhanee. Out of the Stable (Natal Witness, Pietermaritzburg), 1935.

Brookes, E. H. and others. South Africa Faces UNO (S.A.I.R.R., Johannesburg), 1947.

Burrows, H. R. (Ed.). Race Relations, Vol. X, No. 1: Indian Life and Labour in Natal. (S.A.I.R.R., Johannesburg), 1943.

Callaway, Godfrey. The Race Problem in South Africa and the Average Man. (S.A.I.R.R., Johannesburg), n.d.

Choudree, Ashwin and Pather, P. R. A Commentary on the Asiatic Land Tenure and Indian Representation Act and a Short Survey of the Indian Question in South Africa. (S.A.I.C., Cape Town), 1946.

Congress of the People. (The "Call" Committee, Durban), 1955.

Constitutional Development in the Commonwealth (Central Office of Information, London), 1957.

Coopan, S. The Indian Community of South Africa: Past, Present and Future. (S.A.I.R.R., Johannesburg), 1960.

Dadoo, Y. M. *The Indian People in South Africa*. (Communist Party of South Africa, Johannesburg), 1946.

Dayal, Bhawani and others. *Economic Sanctions Against South Africa: Their need and Feasibility*. (*Hindustan Times* Press, New Delhi), 1944.

De Villiers, Rene. *Afrikanerdom's Changing Race Attitudes*. (S.A.I.R.R., Durban), 1958.

Ferguson-Davie. *The Early History of Indians in Natal*. (S.A.I.R.R., Durban), n.d.

Gandhi, M. K. *Grievances of British Indians in South Africa*.

Government of India. *Group Areas Act of the Union of South Africa: What It Means*. (Government of India Press, New Delhi), 1950.

Government of India. Memorandum on Question of Treatment of Indians in the Union of South Africa – Exchange of Correspondence between the Governments of India and the Union of South Africa for holding a Round Table Conference. (Ministry of External Affairs, New Delhi), 1950.

Harhoff, T. J. *Why not be Friend? Natural Apartheid and Natural Friendliness in South Africa*. (Cape Times Ltd., Parow), n.d.

Kajee, A. I. and others. *Treatment of Indians in South Africa: A Memorandum of Facts*. (S.A.I.C., Cape Town), 1946.

Khan, Sir Shafa'at Ahmad. *The Indians in Natal*. (Pioneer Printing Works, Durban), 1943.

Horrell, M. *Days of Crisis in South Africa:* A Fact Paper, 5/1960. (S.A.I.R.R., Johannesburg), 1960.

Horrell, M. *Indians in Pretoria*. (S.A.I.R.R., Address delivered in Pretoria, 21st July, 1958.)

Joosub, E. H. *Bitterness Towards Indians*. (Anchor Printing Company, Johannesburg), 1958.

Keet, B. B. *The Ethics of Apartheid*. (S.A.I.R.R., Johannesburg), 1957.

Mellor, John. *Black and White in South Africa*. (Fellowship of Reconciliation, London), n.d.

Molteno, D. B. *Fifty Years of Union*. (S.A.I.R.R., Johannesburg), 1960.

Natal Indian Congress. Statement on the alleged question of Indian penetration to the Hon. the Minister of the Interior. (N.I.C., Durban), 1943.

Natal Indian Association. Statement to the Hon. the Minister of the Interior on Alleged Indian Penetration. (Natal Indian Association, Durban), 1943.

Nattrass, H. *A Tribute to Hajee M. L. Sultan*. (Mercantile Printing Press, Durban), 1954.

Nehru, J. *On Africa*. (Current Affairs Publications, New Delhi), n.d.

Palmer, Mabel and others. *The Indian as a South African*. (S.A.I.R.R., Johannesburg), 1956.

Palmer, Mabel. *Natal's Indian Problem*. (Society of the Friends of Africa, Johannesburg), n.d.

Pather, P. R. *Seventy Years of Frustration and Unhappiness: An Examination of Land and Trading Rights as they affect Indians in Natal and Transvaal and a criticism of the Group Areas Act, 41 of 1950*. (Mercantile Printing Press, Durban), 1950.

Passive Resistance Movement in South Africa: 1906–1914. (*Indian Opinion*, Phoenix, Natal), 1914.

Paton, Alan. *The People Wept . . . The Story of the Group Areas Act.* (Clarendon Press, Durban), n.d.

Polak, H. S. L. *The South African Indian Question.* (Le Play House Press, Ladbury, England), 1947.

Race Relations. *Patterns of Segregation,* Vol. XV, Nos. 1 and 2, 1948. (S.A.I.R.R., Johannesburg), 1948.

Sastri College Magazine. Centenary Number, 1860–1960. (Pioneer Printing Works, Durban), 1960.

Singh, George. *The Asiatic Act . . . The Asiatic Land Tenure and Indian Representation Act of South Africa: A brief survey of its background, terms and implications.* (Mercantile Printing Works, Durban), 1946.

South Africa's Treason Trial. ("Afrika!" Publications, Johannesburg), n.d.

The United Nations in the Making: Basic Documents. (World Press Foundation, Boston), 1945.

United Nations. *How to find out about the United Nations.* (United Nations, Department of Public Information, New York), 1958.

Webb, Maurice. *In Quest of South Africa.* (S.A.I.R.R., Johannesburg), 1945.

Webb, Maurice, and Kirkwood, K. *The Durban Riots and After.* (S.A.I.R.R., Johannesburg), 1949.

8. MISCELLANEOUS DOCUMENTS

Universal Declaration of Human Rights, 10th December, 1948.

Message to the Congress of the People of South Africa, Kliptown, Johannesburg, June 25–26, by Mr. A. J. Luthuli, President-General, A.N.C., 1955.

Multi-Racial Conference of South Africa, 1957:
  (i) Opening Address by Rev. Z. R. Mhabane.
  (ii) Economic Rights and Duties in a Multi-Racial Society – G. A. Mbeki.
  (iii) Educational Policies in a Multi-Racial Society – R. E. van der Ross.
  (iv) Civil Rights and Duties in a Multi-Racial Society – W. B. Ngakane.
  (v) Political Arrangements in a Multi-Racial Society – G. H. L. Le May.
  (vi) Civil Rights in a Multi-Racial Society – Alan Paton.
  (vii) Educational Policies in a Multi-Racial Society – S. Cooppan.
  (viii) The Responsibilities of Religious Communities in a Multi-Racial Society – Most Rev. Denis E. Hurley.
  (ix) Political Arrangements in a Multi-Racial Society – Prof. Z. K. Matthews.
  (x) Report on the Findings of the Commission on Civil Rights and Duties in a Multi-Racial Society.

The Franchise in South Africa – I.C. Meer, 1959

Union of South Africa, Monthly Bulletin of Statistics, Vol. XXXIX, No. 5, 1960.

Statement to His Excellency Field-Marshal the Rt. Hon. Viscount Wavell, Viceroy and Governor-General of India, by the S.A.I.C. Delegation, New Delhi, 12th March, 1946 (reprinted by the S.A.I.R.R., Johannesburg).

Memo Submitted by the Indian Delegation to British Commonwealth Relations

Conference on the South African Indian Question, 8th January, 1945 (reprinted by the S.A.I.R.R., Johannesburg).

Press Report issued by the South African Indian Congress, 14th March, 1946 (reprinted by the S.A.I.R.R., Johannesburg).

Pietermaritzburg Indian Centenary Committee, Centenary Commemoration Brochure, 1960.

9. PUBLISHED WORKS CONTAINING A HIGH PERCENTAGE OF DOCUMENTARY MATERIAL

Agrawal, P. N. *Bhawani Dayal Sanyasi*. (Indian Colonial Association, Ajitmal, India), 1939.

Aiyar, P. S. *Conflict of Races in South Africa*. (*African Chronicle*, Durban), n.d.

Aiyar, P. S. *The Indian Problem in South Africa*. (*African Chronicle*, Durban), 1925.

Benians, E. A. and others (Editors). *Cambridge History of the British Empire*, Vol. III: The Empire–Commonwealth. (Cambridge University Press, Cambridge), 1959.

Bird, J. *Annals of Natal*, 1495–1845, Vol. II. (P. Davis and Sons, Pietermaritzburg), 1888.

Bolton, G. *The Tragedy of Gandhi*. (George Allen and Unwin Ltd., London), 1934.

Bright, Jagat S. *Important Speeches of Jawaharlal Nehru*. (The Indian Printing Works, Lahore), n.d.

Bryant, J. F. *Gandhi and the Indianisation of the Empire*. (J. Hall and Son, London), 1924.

Calpin, G. H. (Ed.). *A. I. Kajee: His Work for the South African Indian Community*. (Iqbal Study Group, Durban), n.d.

Calpin, G. H. *There are no South Africans*. (Thomas Nelson and Sons, London), 1941.

Calpin, G. H. *Indians in South Africa*. (Shuter and Shooter, Pietermaritzburg), 1949.

Dayal, Bhawani and Chaturvedi, Benaresi Das. *Public Opinion on the Assisted Emigration Scheme under Indo–South African Agreement*. (Pravasi-Bhawani, Khargarh, India), 1931.

Gandhi, Mahatma. *Young India*, 1919–1922. (Tagore & Company, Madras), 1922.

Gandhi, M. K. *Satyagraha in South Africa*. (Navjivan Publishing House, Ahmedabad), 1928.

Gandhi, M. K. *An Autobiography or The Story of my Experiments with Truth*. (Navjivan Publishing House, Ahmedabad), 1927.

Hattersley, A. F. *More Annals of Natal*. (Frederick Warne and Company Limited, London), 1936.

Hattersley, A. F. *Portrait of a Colony*. (Cambridge University Press, London), 1940.

Hattersley, A. F. *The Natal Settlers*, 1849–1851. (Shuter and Shooter, Pietermaritzburg), 1949.

Hellmann, Ellen (Ed.). *Handbook on Race Relations in South Africa*. (Oxford University Press, Cape Town), 1949.

Henderson, J. T. (Ed.). *Speeches of the Late Rt. Hon. Harry Escombe*. (P. Davis and Sons, Pietermaritzburg), 1903.

Horrell, M. *The Group Areas Act . . . Its Effect on Human Beings*. (S.A.I.R.R., Johannesburg), 1956.

Horrell, M. *A Survey of Race Relations in South Africa*, 1955–6. (S.A.I.R.R., Johannesburg), 1957.

Indian Council of World Affairs. *India and the United Nations*. (Manhattan Publishing Company, New York), 1957.

Joshi, P. S. *The Tyranny of Colour*. (E.P. and Commercial Printing Company, Durban), 1942.

Joshi, P. S. *Apartheid in South Africa*. (*Diamond Fields Advertiser*, Kimberley), 1950.

Khare, N. B. *My Political Memoirs*. (J. R. Joshi, Sitabuldi, Nagpur), 1949.

Keith, A. B. *Responsible Government in the Dominions*. (Oxford University Press, London), 1928.

Khan, Ahmad Shafa'at. *The Indian in South Africa*. (Allahabad Law Journal Press, Kitabistan, Allahabad), 1946.

Kuper, Leo. *Passive Resistance in South Africa*. (Jonathan Cape, London), 1956.

Mansergh, N. *Documents and Speeches on British Commonwealth Affairs:* 1931–1952, Vol. I. (Oxford University Press, London). 1953.

Mansergh, N. *Documents and Speeches on British Commonwealth Affairs:* 1931–1952, Vol. II. (Oxford University Press, London), 1953.

Marais, J. S. *The Fall of Kruger's Republic*. (Oxford University Press, London), 1961.

Mills, F. W. *The League of Nations, Its Aims, Activities and Achievements*. (Juta and Company, Cape Town and Johannesburg), n.d.

Naidoo, S. R. and Bramdaw, D. (Editors). *Sastri Speaks*. (Natal Press, Pietermaritzburg), 1931.

Nehru, J. *Glimpses of World History*. (Lindsay Drummond, London), 1949.

Nehru, J. *The Discovery of India*. (Meridian Books, London), 1947.

Natesan, G. A. *Speeches of Gokhale*. (G. A. Natesan, Madras), 1920.

Natesan, G. A. *Mrs. Sarojini Naidu*. (G. A. Natesan, Madras), 1922.

Natesan, G. A. *Congress Presidential Addresses:* Second Series, 1911 to 1934 (G. A. Natesan, Madras), 1934.

Natesan, G. A. *Speeches and Writings of the Rt. Hon. V. S. Srinivasa Sastri*. (G. A. Natesan, Madras), n.d.

Nicholas, H. G. *The United Nations as a Political Institution*. (Oxford University Press, London), 1959.

Olivier, M. *The Colonial and Imperial Conferences*, Vol. I: Colonial Conferences. (Queen's Printer and Controller of Stationery, Ottawa), 1954.

Olivier, M. *The Colonial and Imperial Conferences*, Vol. II: Imperial Conferences, Part I. (Queen's Printer and Controller of Stationery, Ottawa), 1954.

Olivier, M. *The Colonial and Imperial Conferences*, Vol. III: Imperial Conferences, Part II. (Queen's Printer and Controller of Stationery, Ottawa), 1954.

Palmer, Mabel. *The History of Indians in Natal*. (Oxford University Press, Cape Town), 1957.

Pistorius, P. V. *No Further Trek*. (C.N.A., Johannesburg), 1957.

Polak, H. S. L. *The Indians of South Africa*. (G. A. Natesan, Madras), 1909.

Polak, H. S. L. *The Indians of South Africa*, Part II: *A Tragedy of Empire*. (G. A. Natesan, Madras), 1909.

Smith (Ed.). *The Oxford History of India*. (Oxford University Press, London), 1958.

Sullivan, J. R. *The Native Policy of Sir Theophilus Shepstone*. (Walker and Snashall, Johannesburg), 1928.

Tabata, I. B. *The Awakening of a People*. (Johannesburg Peoples' Press, Johannesburg), 1950.

Union of South Africa. Official Year Book, 1910–1918, No. 3. (The Government Printing and Stationery Office, Pretoria), 1920.

Union of South Africa. Official Year Book, 1948, No. 24. (Government Printer, Pretoria), 1950.

Walker, Eric A. *A History of Southern Africa*. (Longmans, Green and Co., London), 1957.

Walton, Sir Edgar H. *The Inner History of the National Convention of South Africa*. (Maskew Miller, Cape Town and Pretoria), 1912.

Wetherell, Violet. *The Indian Question in South Africa*. (The Unie-Volkspers Bpk., Cape Town), 1946.

William, Sir John Fischer. *Some Aspects of the Covenant of the League of Nations*. (Oxford University Press, London), 1934.

Woods, C. A. *The Indian Community of Natal:* Natal Regional Survey, Vol. 9. Their Economic Position. (Geoffrey Cumberlege, Oxford University Press, London), 1954.

INDEX

A

Abdul Rahman, Tunku, 261
Abdurrahman, Dr. A., 113
Acts:
Areas Reservation and Immigration and Registration (Further Provision) Bill, 111–16
Asiatic Land Tenure Amendment Act, 1949, 227
Asiatic (Transvaal Land and Trading) Bill, 144, (Act 28/1939), 145, 153, 165, 168
Asiatic Land Tenure and Indian Representation Bill, 187 (Act 28/1946), 189, 192–94, 198–99, 203, 207, 210–11, 216, 220, 222, 236, 249
Asiatic Law Amendment Act (Act 47/1948), 222
Cape Immigration Act, 30/1906, 61
Class Areas Bill, 106–7, 111, 120
Community Development Act, 277
Draft Occupation Control Ordinance, 176–77
Durban Land Alienation Ordinance, 14/1922, 95–6, 123–24
Group Areas Act, 188, 230, 236–40, 246, 250, 256, 274–79
Immigrants Regulation Bill, 61 (Act 22/1913), 62, 65, 67, 78, 82
Immigrants' Restriction Bill, 58–9
Immigration and Indian Relief (Further Provision) Bill (Act 37/1927), 126–27, 129, 138
India Act, 1935, 141
Indian Act XXXIII/1860, 6
Indian Councils Act, 54, 63, 67
Indian Reciprocity Act, 1943, 163–64, 171–74, 178–79
Labour Importation Ordinance, 1904, 26, 32
Liquor Bill, 1926, 116, 130
Marketing Bill, 142
Mauritius Act 15/1842, 6
Mines and Works Amendment Act, 25/1926, 116–17, 120, 124
Mixed Marriages Bill, 141
Natal Act 17/1895 (£3 tax law) 23, 47–8, 59–62, 65–6
Natal Act 8/1896, 11
Natal Act 25/1891, 8, 10, 65
Natal Boroughs Ordinance, 1924, 109–10, 124
Natal Dealers' Licences Act, 18/1897, 11–12, 48–9, 52 (Amended by Act 22/1909), 53, 68
Natal Immigration Law Amendment Act, 9
Natal Immigration Restriction Act, 1/1897, 11
Natal Laws 13/14/15 of 1859, 6, 8
Natal Law 2/1870, 8
Natal Law 12/1872, 7
Natal Housing Board Ordinance, 177, 186

Natal Local Government (Provincial Powers) Act, 1924, 110
Natal Rural Dealers Licensing Ordinance, 1922, 95–6
Natal Townships Franchise Ordinance, 1922/1924, 95–6, 107, 110
Provincial and Local Authorities Expropriation Ordinance, 177
Provincial Legislative Powers Extension Bill, 142 Residential Property Regulation Draft Ordinance, 176–77
Rowlatt Acts, 87
South Africa Act, 53
Trading and Occupation of Land (Transvaal and Natal ("Pegging" Act)), 168–77, 179–80, 182, 185, 187–89, 193–94, 272
Transvaal:
Asiatic Law Amendment Act, 2/1907, 36–47, 50, 53, 57–59, 87, 89
Asiatic Law Amendment Ordinance, 29/1906, 31, 33–35
Asiatic Land Bill, 142
Asiatic Land Tenure Amendment Bill, 1930, 132–33, 136 (became Act 35/1932), 137, 193
Asiatic Land Tenure Amendment Act, 30/1936, 140
Asiatic Registration Validation Bill (Act 36/1908), 42–43, 46, 59
Companies Act, 1909, 79, 82
Dealers (Control) Ordinance, 11/1925, 116
Immigrants Restriction Act, 15/1907, 38, 43–45, 50, 53, 57, 284
Land and Trading Amendment Act, 37/1919, 83–84, 88–9, 113, 131–2
Law 3/1885, 14–18, 24, 27–28, 30–31, 34–35, 73, 79, 82, 112, 144, 180
Law 15/1898, 31
Peace Preservation Ordinance, 1902 and 1903, 25, 32, 33, 34, 38, 41
Precious and Gold Metals Act, 47/1908, 47, 68, 73, 81–3, 112, 131–32, 138
Townships Amendment Act, 34/1908, 47, 68, 73, 81
Union Immigration Bill, 59
Acutt, F. H., 128
African labour, 50
African National Congress, 190, 223–24, 234, 241–43, 255, 257, 259, 267, 281
African Peoples' Organisation, 190
African population, 3, 8–9, 19, 118, 234, 271
Agriculture, 2

Ahmed, Osman, 122
Ahmed, Sir Sultan, 178
Aiyar, P. S., 122, 171
Alam, Mir, 41
Alexander, Morris, 170
Ali, Syed Raza, 112, 140, 142–43, 154, 173, 183, 212
Ally, H. O., 34–5
Amod Aboobaker, 7, 30–1
Ampthill, Lord, 34, 56
Amra, C. I., 181
Andrews, Rev. C. F., 65, 87, 90, 97, 122, 128, 142
Andrews, Harry, 223
Aney, M. S., 172
Anglia, M. C., 122
Anglo-Boer War, Second, 28, 32, 66
Anti-Apartheid Movement, 281–82
Anti-Asiatic League, 84
Anti-Segregation Council, 177, 185, 208
Apartheid, 220, 237, 242–45, 261–2, 265, 271–74, 280–82
"Arabs", 7–8, 10, 14, 19, 49
Arbuckle, 10
Article 2(7) of the U.N. Charter, 201–2, 214, 222, 226–7, 243, 245, 252, 254, 260, 264
Asiatics (*see* Indians, Chinese, Japanese)
Asiatic Affairs Advisory Board, Durban, 163
Asquith, British Prime Minister, 75
Atlantic Charter, 171

B

Bajpai, G. S., 112, 118, 133
Bailey, Sir Abe, 36, 84, 89, 90, 93
Ballinger, Mrs. Margaret, 170, 189
Bapu, Essop, 122
Banerjee, R. N., 191
Barmania, M. D., 190
Barns, A. L., 175
Basson, J. H., 190, 216, 229
Basner, Senator, 190
Baxter, W. D., 123
Bayat, A. M., 96, 106, 113
Baynes, Joseph, 23
Beauchamp, Lord, 56
Beckett, T. W., 13, 82
Bellgarde, Dantes, 244
Berrange, Advocate, 255
Beyers, F. W., 109, 116, 118
Bhoola, T. N., 176
Bhownagree, Sir M. M., one of two first Indian members of House of Commons, 34, 57
Bibliography, 296–308
Bills (*see* Acts)

Binns, Henry, 8–9, 48
Blackwell, Leslie, 145, 150
Bloemfontein Conference, 18
Bloemsma, B., 144
Bodet Dr. Jaime Torres, 244
Boers, 2–3, 18, 21, 29, 37
Boer Republics, 21, 24, 26
Bombay, 4, 7, 27, 51
Bopape, D. W., 242
Bose, Sarat Chandra, 191
Bose, Subhas Chandra, 141
Botha, General Louis, 36, 42, 53, 58–9, 62, 64, 74, 76, 87–8, 95
Bourke, E. F., 13
Boydell, T., 109, 118
Bramdaw, D., 73
Brande, E., 118
British:
    Annexation of Natal, 2
    East India Company, 5
    Empire, 4, 11, 21, 28, 75–9, 80, 86–8, 90, 93–5, 98, 100, 102, 104–5, 109–10, 146, 172, 179, 192
    Government, 1–7, 9–10, 14–8, 22–4, 27–9, 35–7, 39, 45–6, 49, 50–1, 53–5, 57–8, 67, 74–5, 77–8, 84, 89, 103–4, 106–9, 157, 174, 178, 180, 192
    Indians, 27–8, 33, 37, 46, 53, 56, 66, 68, 75–8
    Interests, 18
    Settlement, 2
Brockway, Fenner, 185
Brookes, Edgar H., 145, 158–59, 170, 190, 195, 238, 259
Broome, Justice, F. N., 160, 163, 175
Brown, Rupert Ellis, 152, 160
Buchanan, Douglas, 155
Buller, General, 21
Bulwer, Sir Henry, 9
Burton, H., 80–1, 88, 91, 102
Bunche, Dr. Ralph, 244

C

Cachalia, Moulvi, I. A., 224
Calpin, G. H., 186, 191
Camay, N. A., 85–6
Cape, 1–4, 6, 21, 45
Cape British Indian Council, 83, 85–6, 107
Cape Indian Congress, 216, 220
Cape Town Agreement, 119, 120, 124, 126–29, 130–35, 144–46, 154–55, 160–61, 166–69, 189, 198, 202–3, 218, 290–95
Cape Town British India League, 41
Cartwright, Albert, editor of *Transvaal Leader*, 39, 40

Cassoojee, S. S., 86
Cattle farmers, 2
Ceylon, 21
Chagla, U.N. delegate for India, 202, 203
Chamberlain, Joseph, Colonial Secretary, 10, 15, 17–18, 24, 26, 32
Chamney, Registrar of Asiatics in the Transvaal, 40
Chandavakar, V. N., 152
Chari, R. T., 229
Chetty, R. B., 122
Chinese, 4, 13, 14, 19, 41, 86, 129, 230
Choudree, Ashwin, 171, 188, 193, 195, 199, 200
Christopher, Albert, 73, 86, 106, 122, 137, 148, 171, 181, 187, 200, 206
Churchill, Winston, 37, 94, 96, 184
Clarkson, C. F., 127–28, 175
Clarkson, Senator, 216
Coal, 2
Coetzee, Blaar, 278, 279
Collins, M. W., Agent for Natal, 6
Colonial Born and Settlers Indian Association, 138, 151
Colonial-born Indians (see South African Indians)
Colonial Conference, 75
Coloured people, 17, 18
Commissions:
   Asiatic Inquiry Commission, 1921, 91–3, 106
   Commission appointed to look into Law 3/1885, 17
   Commission of Enquiry into Matters affecting the Indian population of Natal (Third Broome Commission), 175–79, 186–87, 192
   Indian Colonisation Inquiry Committee, 136–38, 149
   Indian Immigrants' Commission, 7
   Indian Immigration Commission (Clayton), 47, 52
   Indian Penetration Commission, 1940 (Broome), 159, 160–66, 181–82
   Indian Inquiry Commission, 1914, 64–7, 284–85
   Lands Commission, 1900–2, 12
   Land and Emigration Commission, 4, 6
   Lawrence Committee, 153, 158–59, 163, 175, 177, 180
   Mixed Marriages Commission, 144
   Natal Commission on Indian Education, 128
   Transvaal Asiatic Land Laws Commission, 1938, 143–44, 150
   Transvaal Land Tenure Act Commission (Feetham), 137, 139, 145, 167
   Wragg Commission, 8, 10

Committee (see Commission)
Commonwealth Conference, 1, 35, 75, 78, 185, 261
Congress of the People, 252
Coolies (see Indian labourers)
Corbett, Miss, J. E., 117, 120, 124
Corbett, Sir Geoffrey, L., 118, 133, 135, 202
Cotton, Sir Henry, President of Indian National Congress, 28
Courland, s.s., 11
Cresswell, Colonel, 109
Cresswell, F. H. P., 118
Crewe, Lord, Secretary of State for Colonies, 53, 57, 75, 76
Cripps, Sir Stafford, 156
Crops, 2, 3, 12
Cruz, Hernan Santa, 244

D

Dadoo, Dr. Y. M., 145, 151, 181, 187, 195, 207–8, 211–13, 216, 220, 221, 242
Dalmia, Seth, 173
Das, Seth Govind, 143
Dayal, Pandit Bhawani, 113, 130, 145, 151, 154
De Gersigny, C. B., 22–3
Department of Indian Affairs, 274
Deportations, 43, 46, 56–7, 228
Derbyshire, 142
Desai, Bhulubhai, 173
Desai, M. A., 187
Desmukh, Ramrao, 180, 183, 186–87, 198
De Villiers, Charles, 144
De Villiers, Melius, Chief Justice of the Orange Free State Republic, 16, 18
De Wet, N. J., Minister of Justice, South Africa, 102
Dhlomo, H. I. E., 190
Dharma Vir, 83, 86
Diemont, Justice, 259, 270
Docrat, A. K. M., 171
Dönges, Dr. T. E., 224–25, 229, 236–38, 248, 265, 295
Duncan, Patrick, 38, 53, 93, 106–7, 133, 135, 284
Durban, 4, 11–12, 56, 74–5, 86–7, 92–3, 106, 109, 112, 116, 129, 137, 143, 152–53, 161, 164, 166–67, 171, 176–77, 186, 190, 220
Durban racial riots, 223–24
Durrant, R. B., 215
Dutch:
   Government, 1
   East India Company, 2
   Settlers, 2
Dyson, J., 128

E

Eaton, 142
Ebrahim, M., 122, 176
Elgin, Lord, Secretary of State for Colonies, 30–1, 33–6
Emmamally, S., 86
Erasmus, F. C., 211
Escombe, Harry, Attorney-General of Natal, 9–10 Prime Minister, 11–12
Esselen, Edward, 64
Europeans: 2, 8–9, 11, 17, 26, 30, 36, 40, 47, 53, 58–9, 60, 67, 73, 77–9, 85, 90–2, 103, 105, 107, 114–15, 117, 120, 127, 129, 131, 135, 138, 153, 162–64, 169, 172, 176, 179, 185, 206, 222
  Population, 3, 8, 19, 35, 39, 67, 77–8, 84, 100–101, 149, 167, 175, 234, 271
Evatt, Dr., 222

F

Feetham, Mr. Justice, 137, 144
Fell, F. W., 128
Fish River, 2
Fordham, A. C., 116
Forsyth, D. D., 229
Fourie, Brand, 260
Francis, J. N., 122, 199
Fraser, Secretary to the British Agent in Pretoria, 17, 18
Freedom Charter, 249, 252–53

G

Gabru, A. I., 96
Gallwey, Michael, Attorney-General of Natal, 7
Gandhi, Manilal, 137
Gandhi, Mohandas Karamchand, 11, 20–5, 32–5, 37, 39, 40–6, 53–4, 56, 58–9, 60–3, 65–8, 70–1, 73–4, 80–1, 83, 87, 89, 91, 105, 107, 112, 117, 127, 141, 145–6, 151–2, 156, 175, 181, 191, 198–9, 278, 287–9
Germans 2
Germiston, 39
Gilbert, Walter, Mayor of Durban, 86
Gladstone, Lord, first Governor-General of South Africa, 64
Godfrey, Advocate J. W., 112–13, 181
Gokhale, G. K., 54–7, 59–60, 62, 65, 67, 72, 78–9, 89–90, 107
Gordon, Miss C., 128
Gordon, R. S., 128
Gorges, E. M., 61–2, 68

Government of India (*see* Indian Government)
Goonam, Dr., 191
Great Britain, 4, 74, 84, 89, 96, 115, 170, 180, 193, 211, 272–74
Grey, Sir George, Governor of Cape Colony and High Commissioner for Natal, 4–5, 8
Griffin, Sir Lepel, 34
Grobler, J. H., 141, 157
Grobler, Piet, 109
Gromyko, 215
Gundevia, Y. D., 229

H

Habib, Hajee, 53–4, 67
Hall, J. Lockwood, 128
Hammarskjold, Dag, 184, 261, 263, 273
Hardinge, Lord, Viceroy of India, 63–4, 78
Hartshorne, J. R., 116
Havenga, N. G., 109, 218
Hertzog, General, J. B. M., 108–9, 115, 118–19, 130, 133–4, 137
Het Volk Party, 36
Hofmeyr, H. J., 123
Hofmeyr, J. H., 137, 139, 140–43, 145–46, 150, 163, 165, 169–70, 185, 189, 194, 272
Hollander, F. C., 128
Hosken, William, member of Transvaal Legislative Assembly, 38
Housing, 116, 124, 128–9
Huguenots, 2
Hulett, G. H., Member of Natal Provincial Council, 96
Hult, Mine Manager, 64
Huq, Sir Azizul, 178
Hussain, Akhtar, 229
Hussain, Dr. Mahomed, 229
Hussain, Sajjad, 229
Hussein, Sir Fazli, 133–35

I

Ifafa, 12
Imperial Conference, 36, 75–81, 85, 87, 89, 91–5, 97, 99–102, 104–6, 108, 110, 115, 132, 146, 202, 219, 229, 273, 290
Imperial Citizenship Association, 90, 145, 173, 191
Imperial Government (*see* British Government)
Indentured labour (*see* Indian labourers and Indians)
Innes, Chief Justice of the Transvaal, 46
India, 4–5, 7–8, 21–4, 28, 33, 37, 39, 46, 48, 51–2, 55, 60, 63–4, 66–7, 74–8, 80, 87, 89–92, 96, 100,

103–6, 110–17, 130–34, 136–37, 139, 141, 143,
145, 151–52, 163–64, 169, 171–72, 174, 177, 179–
80, 184–86, 189, 203, 206, 212, 214–15, 218, 228,
254
Indian:
Government, 1, 5–8, 21–5, 30, 38–9, 45, 48–9,
51–2, 54–8, 60, 64–7, 74, 77, 79, 86, 88–9,
91–2, 95–6, 103–4, 108, 110, 113, 115, 117,
126, 129, 130–31, 133–37, 139–40, 142–43,
164–66, 168, 170, 172–73, 176, 178–79, 185–
88, 192, 198, 202, 208–10, 212–13, 216–20,
224–28, 230, 236–39, 242, 246, 256–57, 272
Labourers, 4–9, 12, 14, 21–4, 47–8, 51–3, 55, 57,
62–3, 67–8, 71–2, 90, 92, 102
Immigration, 5–6, 12, 47, 51–2, 54–7, 67, 69, 71,
77, 95, 218
Population, 8, 11, 13, 19, 21, 47, 53, 55–6, 58,
60, 68, 73, 76, 78, 90, 94, 100–1, 111, 118, 134,
138–40, 149, 161, 167, 175, 184, 193, 229–30,
234, 271, 279, 286
Ambulance Corps, South Africa, 21, 32
Immigration Trust Board, 22
National Congress, 22, 28–9, 34, 54, 60, 63, 68,
75, 108, 114, 140, 141, 143, 145, 191, 212, 242
South Africa League, 54
Teachers imported from India, 147
Indians, 1, 5, 8–10, 12–13, 15–19, 22–9, 32–4, 36–7,
39, 41–7, 50–1, 56, 58–61, 64–5, 73, 75–9, 81–2,
85–6, 91–2, 94, 101–3, 107, 109, 115–16, 118,
120, 127, 129, 130, 153, 161–3, 166, 169, 170–1,
176, 185–6, 188, 194, 197–8, 213–20, 225, 237,
245, 262, 274–6, 278–9, 280
"Free", 7, 9–12, 22, 47–8, 55–7
Indian Opinion, 23, 29, 39, 45, 55–6, 75, 77, 80, 89,
94
Indianstan, 277
Ismail, A., Secretary, Cape British Indian Council,
83, 86, 171, 218, 221
Ismail, Mohomed and Company, 15
Ismail, Sheik, Chairman, Cape British Indian
Council, 83
International Court of Justice, 202, 204–6, 214, 225

J

Jameson Raid, 21
James, Sir Frederick, 173
Jansen, E. G., 133
Japanese, 29, 77, 86
Jayakar, Dr. M. R., 172–3
Jhaveri, Hajee Omar Amod, 86
Jinnah, M. A., 145, 173
Johannesburg, 17–18, 25, 33, 40–1, 54, 59, 82, 85,

127, 132, 136–7, 140, 156, 161, 171, 263, 277,
279
Joosub, H. E., 278, 279
Jooste, G. P., 240, 243–4, 247
Joint Passive Resistance Council, 200, 206, 208,
211–12, 216, 233

K

Kajee, A. I., 96, 142, 151, 153, 170–71, 175–77,
181, 186–87, 195, 199, 200, 206, 208–9, 213, 215,
217, 232
Kajee, A. S. M., 191, 195, 208, 217, 224
Kale, V. G., 173
Kallenbach, H., 54, 65
Keith, A. B., 29, 36–7, 104
Kemp, General, 109
Khan, Aga, 191
Khan Bahadur, G. A. Dossani, 172
Khan, Bahadur, Sir Muhammad Habibullah Sahib,
118–19, 130
Khan, Field Marshal Mahomed Ayub, 261
Khan, Liaquat Ali, 174, 236
Khan, Sir Muhammed Zafrullah, 185, 213–14
Khan, Sir Shafa'at Ahmad, 155–57, 159, 164, 168,
175, 183, 195
Khan, Tayob Hadji Mohomed, 17, 27
Khare, Dr. N. B., 172–74, 178–80, 185–86, 191–92
Kher, B. J., 141
Khoikhoi (Hottentots), 1–2
Kichlu, K. P., 128
Kincaid, P. F., 137
Kirkwood, Kenneth, 224
Knox, Major J. H. B., 156
Knutsford, Lord, Secretary of State for Colonies, 9
Kotane, M., 242
Kruger, President of the South African Republic
(Transvaal), 15, 18, 26, 29
Kulsum Bibi, 61
Kumararataja, 173
Kunzru, Pandit, 173, 229, 237, 265, 295

L

Ladysmith Gazette, 49
Ladysmith, Natal, 21, 156, 278
Lalla, G. D., 122
Laloo, 44
Landdrost, 14
Landsdowne, Lord, 18
Land Tenure Advisory Board, 188, 190, 207–9, 216
Langa, 259, 263, 270
Lange, J. H., 123

Laugier, Henri, 244
Lawley, Sir Arthur, Lieut.-Governor of Transvaal, 27–8
Lawrence Committee (*see* Commission)
Lawrence, H. G., 153, 159, 163–64, 168–69, 175, 213–17
Lawrence, V., 106
League of Nations, 1, 86–7, 91, 97–100, 102–3, 110, 123, 146, 184, 273
Leyds, W. J., State Attorney of the South African Republic, 15
Lidgett, J. A., 128
Lie, Trygve, 198, 244
Lindsay, Sir D'Arcy, 118, 133
Linlithgow, Lord, 152, 172–73
Lloyd-George, 75, 94
Local Affairs Committees, 276, 278, 282
Lockhat, Hajee A. M. M., 181
London Convention, 1884, 13–15, 17
Lourenço Marques, 13, 46
Louw, Eric, 221–23, 225–27, 253, 258, 260–62, 269
Lowen, Dr., 223–24
Lucas Trustees, 30–1
Lyttleton, Secretary of State, 28

M

Macmillan, Harold, 259
Madagascar, 17
Madanjit, V., Editor of *Indian Opinion*, 29
Madras, 6, 51, 63–4
Magrajh, B. A., 106
Maharaj, M. Beethasee, 106, 122
Maharaja of Patiala, 78
Maize, 2
Malan, C. W., 109
Malan, Dr. D. F., 109, 111–13, 118–20, 129–31, 133–34, 136–37, 169, 189, 194, 211, 216, 218–19, 222, 229, 239–40, 247, 248
Malan, M. L., 116
Malays, 14, 19
Malhautra, J. L., 249
Mall, E. M., 148
Marks, J. B., 242
Martindale Indian Association, 277
Marwick, J. S., 93, 116
Mason, L. H., Protector of Indian Immigrants, 8–9, 48
Masson, Ryle, 223
Mauritius, 4–7
Meer, A. I., 187, 212, 221
Meer, Fathima, 191
Menon, Krishna, 257, 262

Merriman, John X., elder statesman of Cape Colony, 53, 83
Menzies, Robert, 248
Mia, Essop Ismail, Chairman of the British Indian Association, 41–42
Middelburg, 16
Milner, Alfred, Governor of the Cape and British High Commissioner in South Africa, 15, 18, 24–9, 30–1, 37, 66
Minto, Lord, Viceroy of India, 23–4, 54, 59, 63, 67
Minty, A. I., 218, 221
Mirza, A. A., 113, 187, 191, 195
Mitchell, D. G., 176
Montagu, E. S., Secretary of State for India, 88, 89
Montagu-Chelmsford reforms, 78
Moody, Homi, P., 191
Moola, A. M., 187, 218, 220, 224
Moosa, A. B., 176
Morewood, Edward, 3
Morley, John, Secretary of State for India, 23, 45, 53–4, 57, 59, 63, 67
Motan, Habib, 27
Mozambique (*see* Lourenço Marques)
Mudaliar, Sir A., Ramaswami, 152, 178, 197–98
Muir, J., 157
Multi-Racial Conference, 256
Murray, Professor Gilbert, 98–99
Musgrave, Lieut.-Governor of Natal, 7
Muslim, 7, 14, 40–1, 61, 65, 194, 274
Muslim League, 152, 173–74

N

Naderi, s.s., 11
Naicker, Dr. G. M., 177, 187, 190, 207–8, 211–13, 216, 220–21, 256–57
Naidoo, G. K. T., 62
Naidoo, H. A., 181, 200, 211, 231
Naidoo, M. D., 187, 224
Naidoo, P. K., 85–6, 96
Naidoo, R. K., 171, 181
Naidoo, S. R., 86, 137, 148, 160, 171, 175–76, 187, 191, 195, 200, 206, 218, 220
Naidoo, Thambi, 40
Naidu, Mrs. Sarojini, 106–8, 112, 114, 133, 136, 145, 191, 212
Ngwevela, J., 242
Nkrumah, Dr. K., 255–6
Nana, S. M., 160
Naoraji, Dadabhai, one of two first Indian members of House of Commons, 34
Natal:
   Charter of 1856, 2, 9

Climatic conditions, 4
Colonial Born Association, 124
First bank, 3
Government, 1, 5–11, 21–3, 46, 49, 54–5, 97,
    193, 272
Immigrant labourers, 4–7
Indians (*see* Indians)
Indian Congress, 22–3, 41, 53, 71, 83, 85–6, 93,
    96, 106–7, 109–10, 123, 130, 151, 154, 158–60,
    165–68, 170, 174–75, 176–77, 185–87, 190, 200,
    206–8, 215–16, 218–21, 236, 257, 266, 277
Indian Association, 151, 153, 160, 168, 170–71,
    174, 213, 216
Indian Organisation, 208–9, 212, 215, 217–19,
    220–21, 224, 233, 277
North Coast, 63
Northern Natal, 63–64
Parliament, 9, 49–50
Republic of Natalia, 2
South Coast, 63–64
Wages, 5
Natal Advertiser, 55, 86, 95, 108
Natal Convention, 264
Natal Daily News, 171
Natal Mercury, 51, 55, 62, 85, 92, 100, 262
Natal Witness, 100, 171, 174, 207, 221, 238, 240, 247
"National Convention", 1904, 13, 26–27
National Convention, 1908–9, 26, 53
National Indian Association, 88
Neame, L. E., 27
Nehru, Pandit Jawaharlal, 141, 145, 192, 199–200,
    206, 209–12, 214, 229, 236–37, 246–49, 261
Newcastle, 11
Nicholls, G. H., 133, 137, 200, 203, 205

O

Orange Free State, 59, 61
Orange River Colony, 25, 30–2
Ordinance (*see* Acts)

P

Paddison, G. F., 112, 118
Pakistan Government, 214, 216–17, 219–20, 224–
    27, 230, 236–37, 239, 242, 246, 252, 256–57
Palmer, Dr. Mabel, 1, 4, 124, 191
Palsania, C., 200
Pan-African Congress, 259
Pandit, Mrs. Vijaya Lakshmi, 197, 200–2, 204, 206,
    213–14, 238, 243, 246, 273
Pant, G. B., 141

Parak, S. M., 176, 220
Parekh, M. R., 220
Passive Resistance Association (*see* Passive Resis-
    tance)
Passive Resistance, 37, 39, 41, 43–44, 47, 53–54, 56,
    58–9, 62–3, 65–6, 68, 70, 85, 87, 90, 145, 190–91,
    198–99, 206, 208, 217, 219, 232
Patel, E. I., 85
Patel, M. C., 96
Patel, Sardar Vallabhai, 141
Pathans (*see* Muslim)
Pather, P. R., 137, 171, 175–77, 181, 187–88, 193,
    199–200, 206, 208–9, 213, 217–18, 220–21, 224,
    237, 248
Pather, S. C., 122
Pather, V. S. C., 86, 113
Paton, Dr. A., 272
Pearson, Indian Civil Service, 65, 90
Pearson, Lester, B., 244
Peck, C. A. B., 128
Peel, Viscount, Secretary of State for India, 102
Philips, L. J., attorney, Krugersdorp, 84
Phoenix Settlement, 23, 62, 71, 75
Pienaar, General J. C., 141
Pietermaritzburg, 11–12, 101, 109, 157, 218
Pillay, K. S., 181
Pillay, V. A., 86
Pirow, Oswald, 133, 249
Polak, H. S. L., 25, 35, 37, 45–6, 49, 53–5, 65, 67,
    70, 75, 93, 97, 268
Portuguese, 1
Power, W. M., 175
Prasad, Sir Jagadish, 173
Prasad, Rajendra, 141, 240
Pretoria, 17, 26–7, 36, 40, 60, 62, 80, 82, 84, 108,
    117, 161, 176, 186, 189, 208, 214, 228, 262, 263
Pretoria Agreement, 175–77, 180, 187
Pretoria Convention, 1881, 13
Pretoria News, 65, 74
Pretorius, A. L., 128
Premji, M. H. Hasham, 191
Price-Lloyd, Lieut.-Colonel, ex-officer, Indian
    Army, 7
Prime Ministers Conference, 75
Pring, H., 118
Protector of Indian Immigrants, 7, 23, 29, 48, 50

Q

Quinn, Leuing, 40

R

Race Conflict in South Africa, 1, 2
Radhakrishnan, Sir Sarvapillai, 143, 151
Railway, 2
Rajagopalachari, C., 141
Rau, Sir Rama, 154–55, 162–63, 183
Reading, Lord, Viceroy of India, 95–6
Reddi, Sir Kurma, 128, 131–32, 137, 149, 183
    (*also spelt* Reddy)
Reitz, Colonel Denys, 142
Repatriation (of South African Indians), 73, 91,
    100, 110–11, 118–19, 126, 130, 131, 134–36, 138,
    147, 149, 201
Reyburn, G., 116
Reynolds *v.* Oosthuizen, 82
Reynolds, C. P., Natal sugar planter, 12
Richardson, Sir Henry, 173–74
Ricketts, C. S., 112
Ripon, Lord, Secretary of State for Colonies, 23
Ritch, L. W., 34, 82
Robertson, Sir Benjamin, 65–7, 89, 91–2
Robinson, Sir Hercules, British High Commis-
    sioner in South Africa, 14
Romulo, General, 226
Rood, W. H., 116
Rooknoodeen, M., 122
Roosevelt, President Franklin Delano, 184
Rose-Innes, Sir James, 65
Roos, Tielman, 109
Round Table Conference, 108, 112, 115–20, 126–28,
    132, 134, 136, 138–39, 189, 198, 213–14, 216–18,
    225, 228–29, 236–39
Rowlatt Acts, 87 (*see* Acts)
Royeppen, Joseph, 86
Rumpff, Justice, 255
Ruskin, 37
Russell, Lord John, 5
Rustenberg Grondwet, 1858, 12, 27
Rustomjee, Sorabjee, 86, 113, 160, 163, 171, 181,
    186–87, 191, 195, 199–200, 206, 213, 231

S

Sader, Dr. A. H., 221
Salisbury, Lord, Secretary of State for India, 7
San (Bushmen), 1–2
Sarvadhikary, Sir Deva Prasad, 112
Sapru, Sir Tej Bahadur, 102–5
Sastri, Srinivasa, S., 93–4, 96, 101–2, 105, 118,
    126–30, 133, 135, 140, 154, 173, 183
Satyagraha (*see* Passive Resistance)
Sauer, Paul, 260

Savarkar, V. D., 173
Schmidt, C. F., 118
Schultz, W., 223
Schreiner, W. P., 65
Searle, Chief Justice, 61–2
Seedat, D. A., 181
Seeley, Colonel, 57
Sethna, Sir Phiroza, C., 118
Selborne, Lord, British High Commissioner in
    South Africa, 29–31, 33–6, 53, 67
Setalvad, Chimanlal, 172, 225–26
Servants of India Society, 54–5, 173
Shafi, Sir Muhammad, 133
Shapurji, Sorabji, 43
Sharpeville, 259–60, 263, 270
Shepstone, H. C., 22, 23
Shepstone, D. G., 175, 190, 216
Shepstone, Sir Theophilus, 3
Sigamoney, B. L. E., 122, 187, 195
Singh, George, 221
Singh, J. N., 218, 221
Singh, P. B., 181
Singh, Sir Kunwar Maharaj, 137, 139, 173, 183, 185
Singh, S. L., 124
Singh, Tara, 173
Sinha, Sir Satyendra, 76, 78–9, 80, 88, 92–3, 110,
    121
Sita, Nana, 278
Slaves, 2
Smith, L. A., 190
Smuts, General (Field-Marshal) Jan Christiaan,
    17–18, 35–6, 38–9, 40–5, 53, 58–9, 60, 62, 65–6,
    68, 70, 73, 77–8, 81, 86–9, 91–2, 94, 97, 99,
    100–6, 108, 112, 117, 123–24, 127, 133, 137, 146,
    151, 154–55, 157, 164, 169–70, 172–76, 180,
    184–86, 189, 191–92, 194, 199, 200, 201–4, 206–
    12, 214, 216–19, 222, 274, 287–89
Sobukwe, R. M., 259
Solomon, Chief Justice, 124
Solomon, Sir Richard, 36
Solomon, Sir William, 44, 64
Sorrenson, Reginald, 211
South Africa, 2, 21, 24–5, 32–3, 37, 52, 56–7, 59–61,
    65–7, 74–9, 80–1, 83–4, 87–9, 95–6, 99–100,
    102–6, 109–10, 113–14, 117–18, 127, 130–32,
    134–37, 141, 143, 151, 155, 163, 168, 170, 172,
    174, 177, 184–85, 189, 192, 194, 206, 209–11,
    214–17, 228, 245, 254, 275, 281–82
South Africa British Indian Committee, 34, 54, 56,
    57, 82
South African Congress of Democrats, 249
South African Government, 22, 58–9, 60, 63–4,

66–7, 74, 83, 88, 91–3, 95–6, 105–7, 111–13, 115, 117, 120, 126, 130–31, 135–37, 143, 154, 163, 166, 168, 170, 172, 174, 180, 186–88, 190–91, 193, 198, 201–4, 208–9, 212–14, 216–17, 219, 221, 225–28, 230, 236, 237–39, 241–42, 244–46, 250, 253–54, 256–57, 259, 263–65, 273, 276, 279, 281–82

South African Indians, 1–2, 37, 63–4, 66–7, 73–4, 77–8, 80, 84, 86–7, 89, 91, 101–3, 106, 111, 113–15, 130, 134, 136, 138–39, 142–43, 146, 151, 153–56, 163, 169, 170–71, 178, 180, 184, 189, 192, 198–202, 204–5, 207, 211–12, 216, 220, 222, 224, 238, 244, 246, 250, 252, 254, 272–74, 277, 282

South African Indian Congress, 85–6, 108, 110, 112–13, 120, 126–27, 129–30, 132, 134–39, 142, 144, 146, 148, 171, 174–75, 186–87, 189, 191, 199–200, 208, 210–11, 216–17, 220, 221, 223–24, 228, 234, 241–43, 267, 271, 273

South African Indian Council, 276–79, 282

African Indian Federation, 129

South African Indian Organisation, 86, 220–21, 224–25, 233–34, 266, 273

South African League, 84, 89, 90, 93

South African National Indian Emergency Conference, 84–85

South African Party, 62, 100, 101, 108, 133

South African Republic, 16–8, 24, 28, 31

Spilhaus, Mrs., 144

Stallard, Col., C. F., 189

Stalin, Marshal J. V., 184

Stanley, Lord, 19

Stead, Major, 155

Stent, Vere, editor of *Pretoria News*, 65, 74

Steyn, Dr. L. C., 229

Strydom, J. G., 255

Sugar industry, 3, 47

Suleiman, Ismail and Company, 16–17, 27

Sultan, M. L., 122

Sunder, Pandit Ram, 38

Sundaram, Dr. Lanka, 218

Swart, C. R., 246, 266

T

Table Bay, 1, 2

Tata, Sir Ratanji, 54

Tatham, Ralph, 36

Thomas, J. H., Secretary of State for the Colonies, 109–10, 112

Thompson, Leonard, M., 3, 5, 258

Thoreau, 37

Thornton, E. N., 128

Times of Natal, 49

Tolstoy, Leo, 37

Traders:
British, 9, 16
European, 15, 27, 48, 70, 149
Indians, 2, 8, 13–15, 17–18, 26–7, 42–4, 46, 48–51, 70, 73–4, 76–7, 79, 81–4, 106, 114, 116, 122, 131–2, 135, 138–39, 141, 144, 148–49, 161, 168, 228, 277, 279, 283

Transvaal: 10, 12–13, 15–18, 24, 33–5, 39, 41–2, 50–1, 53–4, 56–8, 62–3, 66–7, 80–2, 84–5, 89, 92, 95
British Indian Association, 25, 33–4, 37, 41, 46, 71, 82–3, 85–6, 106–7, 127, 129
Colony, 25, 29, 30, 32, 38
Governments, 16–18, 28, 31, 35–6, 38–9, 41, 45–6, 56, 79
Indian Congress, 13, 127, 131, 140, 143–44, 160, 168, 170, 186, 200, 208, 216–17, 219, 211
Indian Organisation, 220
Indian Policy, 29, 37, 41–2, 45–7, 53, 56–7, 70, 81–3
Legislative Council, 1, 28

Transvaal Leader, 36, 39

Treaty of Versailles, 86

Truro, s.s., 6

Tyson, J. D., 131–32

U

Uitlander, 10, 15–16

Umkonto we Sizwe, 281

Union Government (*see* South African Government)

Union of South Africa (*see* South Africa)

United Nations, 1, 172, 184, 189, 192–95, 197–200, 202–17, 219–22, 225–30, 232–33, 236, 238–54, 256, 258, 260, 262–66, 269, 271, 273–74, 279–82

United Party, 141, 194

Umzinto, 12

V

Van der Heever, Justice F., 223

Van der Merwe, B. C., 223

Van der Merwe, J. H. N., 229

Van der Merwe, Dr. N. J., 141

Van Riebeeck, Jan, 1

Vereeniging, Peace treaty of, 35, 37

Versailles (*see also* Treaty of), 86–88

Verulam, 12, 63

Verwoerd, Dr. H. F., 258, 263, 281

Victoria, Queen, 5, 9

Volksrust, 36, 45, 62, 63, 216
Volksraad, 13–17
Voortrekkers, 2

W

Walker, Eric, 60
Walters, Dr., 98
Ward, Mr. Justice, 82
Watt, Sir Thomas, Minister of Interior, South
  Africa, 82
Wavell, Lord, 172–74, 176–78, 180, 186, 191–92
Webb, Maurice, 194
Wedgwood, Colonel, 96
West Indies, 4, 5

Wessels, Justice P. J., 259, 270
Wilson, President Woodrow, 86, 98
Wragg, Mr. Justice, 7
Wragg Commission, 8
Wylie, Lieut.-Col. J. S., 64, 123

Y

Young, James, 137

Z

Zulus, 2, 3
Zululand, 2
Zulu Rebellion, 1906, 32